BECOMING BETTY

BECOMING BETTY

E. Betty Levin

Full Court Press
Englewood Cliffs, New Jersey

Published in the United States of America
by Full Court Press, 601 Palisade Avenue,
Englewood Cliffs, NJ 07632
fullcourtpressnj.com

ISBN 978-1-938812-76-7
Library of Congress Catalog No. 2016938825

*Book design by Barry Sheinkopf for Bookshapers
(www.bookshapers.com)*

Cover art, "Betty (Sis), Age 3," courtesy of the author

Colophon by Liz Sedlack

DEDICATION

To my family—Janet, Dr. Martin Rudolph, and children Stephanie, Samantha, and Spencer; Wendy Levin-Ackerman and David Ackerman; Aunt Judith Ackerman; the Whites—Ina, Loretta (Cayellin Halley), Susan White-Haag, and Mark Haag; the Essex Ethical Culture Society Family; and all families everywhere.

"Tell me, Grandma, what was it like growing up in those days?"

—*Stephanie, age 6*

ACKNOWLEDGEMENTS

Katinka Neuhof, my writing coach, brought renewed impetus to bring out the book in me. Her patience and skill were like that of a caring friend. I couldn't have done it without her. Since I overrode some of her advice, I alone am responsible for the final product.

In the early years, Gus Lindquist, a soulful personality and special friend at the Ethical Culture Society, most consistently encouraged my memoir writing. He recommended the Montclair Public Library Write Groups, where volunteer leaders Carl Selinger and Evelyne Speedie provided conscientious guidance that shaped my awkward expositions. The comprehensive workshops led by Lorraine Ash contributed significantly to the breadth of my work.

I cut my very first writing teeth with Sylvia Kramer, dear friend and long-time member of the Ethical Culture Society. Her guidance and written words, whether professionally published or in a sensitive personal note, never failed to penetrate my sensibilities. Other member authors have contributed to my progress. Meredith Sue Willis, Mira Stillman, Barbara Lipton, Elaine Durbach-Norstein, Birgit Matzerath, and Jill Farrar, as well as Aunt Judith Ackerman. My gratitude to cousin Paul in California, who launched my computer world, and his companion, Pam Ehrlich, who dropped everything to calm my computer panics, even at midnight hours; also to my New Jersey computer gurus, Tara Grey and Bill Mark, who tamed my misbehaving computer in crucial times during local time zones. Thanks to Zella Geltman's creative writing class at the Jewish MetroWest Community Center, where my earliest efforts were honored. Susan Galatz, Coordinator of Volunteer Services there, and her staff, were helpful in a myriad of ways. Many thanks also to the teenagers of Millburn High School volunteer Tech Team and to the able young women of the Staples (Vaux Hall) Copy Center, who always responded conscientiously to my time crises.

Writing my memoir became a form of self-therapy. I gained much benefit from the process of understanding my life at a deeper level.

—*E. Betty Levin*

INTRODUCTION

At an Association for Humanistic Psychology conference, I enrolled in a workshop entitled "Experiencing the End of our Lives." Though many attendees regarded this topic with distaste, I was curious about what I could learn.

The workshop leader posed a challenge: You are being sent to a deserted island, never to return, and are allowed to take only two items with you. What would you choose? Why?

I was tempted to bring photo albums of my loved ones. I then realized they would eventually deteriorate and perish.

Instead I chose paper and pen, to record my valued past and whatever future remained. Though the paper would not survive either, I would nevertheless achieve a crucial benefit: The very process of remembering and recording would enrich me. Contemplation of my past could plumb old stories to discover new meanings and fresh truths. All through writing.

TABLE OF CONTENTS

IN THE BEGINNING

As I RE-HUNG TREASURED FAMILY PHOTOS, replaced each friendly book from the dank basement to its rightful shelf, and chose the proper light for a newly purchased plant, I marveled that I had truly survived the past year, both brain surgery and myasthenia gravis—that I was home again after a six-month absence. I had escaped the hysteria of selling my home, my cherished Eden.

I was eighty-three years old in 2009 and had just returned from rehabilitation to continue living in my Sagamore Road home in Millburn, New Jersey. During my illness, following my instructions to sell my home, it had been dismantled, wallpaper stripped, and the interior painted. I felt relieved it had never sold.

Settling in anew, I contentedly started to rebuild my life and psychotherapy practice. I planned to attend a professional workshop addressing end-of-life issues, sponsored by the Hospice Foundation. I drove to the Kessler Institute for Rehabilitation and found myself in the parking lot just below its day-room. I looked up at the day-room and remembered time spent there while healing. Back then, I would stare down at that very same parking lot, watching people strolling to their cars and thinking to myself: Would I ever walk to my car again? Drive my car again? Return to a life resembling normalcy?

I roused myself from this reverie, regained my bearings, and remembered the workshop was at St. Barnabas, not Kessler.

As I rushed to St. Barnabas, I questioned why I had driven to this wrong location, which provoked such memories. As a psychoanalyst, I felt I should put myself on the couch, so to speak, and try to understand this misstep at a more profound level. Freud said some errors and accidents can suggest meanings buried in the unconscious. Then again, sometimes a cigar is just a cigar. I couldn't let go of the experience, however, and later shared it with close friends, several who had visited me in that very same dayroom. I wondered what significance it might suggest.

What is my deeper story?

In 1926 in Chicago, Mother was jubilant at my birth. I was her second daughter, following the death of her first daughter six years earlier.

She instructed that I be called "Sister," a name connected to her piercing loss, by all family members, including my brothers, Leonard and Lester. I was treasured by her, but she lived only a short time to enjoy our relationship. My birth mother died from an infection following gall bladder surgery when I was seventeen months old. I heard she had requested bringing me to the hospital when she underwent surgery and bedded in a crib in her room. The request had been denied.

After her death, there was confusion about my name. The family called me "Sister," as my mother had directed. When I started elementary school, it was thought my name was "Betty." In later years, the name "Enid" was found to be my legal first name. Betty was my middle name. My bone fide legal name was Enid Betty, but all family members called me "Sister." Friends, very few, called me "Betty." Even the common practice of naming a newborn had become filled with deathly overtones and added ambiguity to my start in life.

I often wondered about my uncommon first name, its source and meaning, but no one ever explained and I was too distracted to inquire. I finally asked my cousin, Shirley Morris (née Rosenstein), family historian and last remaining niece of my birth mother. We were both in our eighties by then.

"Shirley, what's the significance of my first name, Enid?"

"Sis," she replied, "I didn't even know your first name was Enid. " I later found out that 'Enid' means "soul, life."

In 1927, when Mother died, my father, an uneducated, hard-working tailor, needed a nurturing home to raise a motherless child just emerging from infancy. He chose my mother's eldest sister, Tante (Aunt) Surrel to care for me. I joined a household with six adult children while my two brothers remained at home with father and a housekeeper.

I lived with Surrel and her family in the Jewish ghetto of Westside Chicago. Her husband, Moishe, earned a living renting horses to peddlers who sold thread, thimbles, and other sundries door to door from their battered suitcases. They trudged Chicago's back alleys, barely eking out a living. Like the peddlers, Surrel and Moishe were poor, uneducated, and spoke little English, but they labored with dignity.

Tante Surrel's endearing qualities provided constancy. Her sheitel (wig) framed a buttery soft, wrinkled face, and her ample body reflected a well-being beyond the comforts that money can provide. Every Friday at sunset, she lit the Sabbath candles, murmuring her prayers with gesturing hands, a comforting shawl covering her broad shoulders. Earlier that day, she usually baked the traditional challah bread.

Resting later in the sun parlor, her warm eyes shone with pleasure as she surveyed the family scene. Pudgy, the dog, sat protectively at Tante Surrel's feet. Looking back, the setting, surrounded by lush plants, resembled a mini-Rousseau, a replica of "Peaceable Kingdom." I noticed Tante Surrel's kindness and compassion, most revealed in her relations with peddlers who came to the kitchen back door. As a favorite one arrived, welcomed into the stark apartment with the friendly *Sholom Aleichem* (peace be with you), he opened his well-worn suitcase and motioned them in Surrel's direction. She looked briefly, already familiar with his mediocre goods, and then turned away, having little money for these trifles. He, too, would turn away. Having second thoughts, Surrel shifted her heavy body to take another look. The peddler turned back too, responding to her new apparent interest. They shifted in repetition in a dance of offering, but not quite withdrawing. Surrel found it difficult to turn him away. Finding a few pennies, maybe a solitary nickel, the dance ended in a purchase. It was a ballet of poverty and compassion.

Barely two years old, I witnessed this scene repeated with hardly a word spoken. It indelibly marked my experience of compassion. Tante Surrel gifted me in ways of which she was unaware.

Another gift was her two oldest daughters, Dorothy and Betty. I was closer to Dorothy, the eldest, a petite young woman of high intelligence and an endless hunger for learning. She had been forced to drop out of high school and work as an office clerk to augment the family's meager income. Feeling deprived and bitter, Dorothy became a searcher, zealously pursuing her interest in learning. She consistently attended night school in Chicago, and later in southern California at a community college, until her death at almost ninety years of age.

I inherited her love of books, like family DNA. My small hands slowly caressed what seemed magical—the Encyclopedia Britannica, an entire world's knowledge in twenty volumes. I was awestruck that someday I might know something of what was within those heavy red bindings.

One day, Dorothy brought home a gift from the office. "Sister, I have something special for you," she said. "It's Grimm's Fairy Tales, which I think you'll enjoy someday when you're old enough to read. In the meantime, I'll read to you when we cuddle together." Added later were Little Women and much later, Step-by-Step in Sex Education.

As a three-year-old, I asked Dorothy and Betty, about a prominent photo on Tante Surrel's dresser, "Who's that pretty lady in the picture?" The question prompted whisperings behind my back, like the sudden whirring of birds disturbed from a comfortable perch. Dorothy wept and spoke haltingly as her face turned pale. Barely audible, she muttered something about an aunt she had adored.

I wondered, What happened to her? Where did she go? Thus began a life-long struggle to penetrate the fog of my complicated beginning. Though loving influences cushioned my start in life, information withheld about my birth mother brought confusion about who my family really was.

Dorothy and Betty enjoyed movies and often took me to the elegant Paradise Theatre on Roosevelt Road. It resembled a palace with a broad, winding staircase, brocaded walls, and elaborate furniture. Before they watched the film, they left me at the theater's well-furnished playroom. It was run by a commanding woman whose grayish hair was arranged in a bun, similar to Tante Surrel's wig. The similarity stopped there. Surrel's gentle ways contrasted dramatically with that of the cold, stern matron. As a three-year-old, I climbed the playroom slide, sometimes tripping on one step or another. "Betty! Be more careful how you're climbing!" she cautioned. "Do you want to fall?"

Other young children played there, but I kept apart, mourning my cousins' departure. I felt abandoned and had no heart for playmates. Tears welled in my eyes, which I restrained with determination, squeezing my cheeks, too proud to cry openly. Painful thoughts accompanied my loneliness. Why did my cousins leave me here? Why didn't they choose a movie I could enjoy, or trust I could sit quietly next to them in the theater, feeling their presence? After the movie, the ice cream soda helped soothe me, at least for awhile, but left a hunger that was never quite satisfied.

Even in the midst of their care, I sensed something was amiss. I often awakened in panic by shrieking middle-of-the night engines from the firehouse across the street, frantically summoned to a blaze. Their thunderous clanging echoed the pounding of my heart.

Despite these occasional upsets, life in Surrel's family was safe and loving. They often brought me gifts after a shopping trip, a pretty doll, or lace-trimmed panties. Dorothy and Betty's doting attention was also accompanied by indulgences from their brothers, Irving, Ben, and Nate. As they gazed at me with adoration, I felt cherished.

A JARRING CONTRAST WAS A LARGE GRUFF MAN who visited Surrel's apartment many times. The stranger walked heavily. He looked sloppy and unsettled. His tie was crooked, and his wrinkled shirt barely made it into his pants. After he arrived, with barely a passing look in my direction, he gobbled a large supper Surrel had prepared. She made her usual sumptuous meal—chicken soup with plump, fragrant *knaidlach* (dumplings), roast chicken swimming in gravy, and crisp noodle pudding with black raisins.

When I heard Dorothy scold him one day— "Why didn't you at least bring her a Hershey bar?"— I suspected he was somehow important to my life. Why *was he coming to Tante Surrel's apartment again and again?* I was upset to later discover this indifferent man was my father.

When I was about four years old, this stranger called "father" unexpectedly took me to a park. A woman, another stranger, sat on the bench next to us. Surprised, I looked at her quizzically. After a few moments, my father said, "This lady will be your new mother."

The confusion felt nightmarish, like being caught in a tangle of rope from which I couldn't escape. She seemed nervous as she carefully placed me on her lap. My body tensed as if I were a jungle animal detecting danger. Strongly resisting her, I wondered what this unexpected meeting was about. She smiled pleasantly, murmuring, "I understand you're called 'Sister.' My name is Evelyn." The strained conversation made me more upset, particularly after my father married Evelyn. He abruptly tore me from Tante Surrel, and I joined a new family.

I was bewildered having several families. "Why do I have three while others have only two?" I asked. All the families avoided explanations; nobody wanted to talk about it.

I wasn't exactly sure how Surrel's family was related to me, but our connection had clasped close. Tante Surrel, Dorothy, and Betty had been like three mothers who nurtured and educated me, creating a warm, tight bond.

Many months passed after the separation from Surrel before I visited her. I was told I said to her, "What kind of mother are you—*giving me away like that?*" I have absolutely no memory of that accusation. Merciful amnesia.

At age six, I saw in the newspaper that two-year-old Jessica De Boer, who was taken from the only parents she had ever known, to be claimed by her birth parents. The photograph of her anguished face at that moment of separation was more than I could bear. Haunted, I was again stung by the reminder of having been severed from my many mothers.

IN EARLIER YEARS, I HAD A FANTASY while hearing Christian women of varied denominations argue harshly about which faith was the true one. I had heard that religion made you a good person. Upset by their sharp disagreements, I then imagined people of all backgrounds could come together amiably, find common ground and peaceful understanding. These ideas entered my life again, powerfully in later years, and have continued as a moving force to shape my life profoundly.

In my new home with stepmother Evelyn, her overly conscientious behavior caused me great anguish. I rarely spoke and never smiled. Father was mostly absent. When he returned home from his shop, usually tired and angry, he ignored me. When my brothers behaved mischievously, he would strike at them repeatedly with his strap. I was fearful I would be next.

Nightmares were frequent companions during which the room seemed to move violently in waves. My ever-present anxiety brought nausea. I ate little, and Evelyn's constantly pushing food at me aggravated everything. Many times she followed me with my unfinished glass of milk around the house, begging. I didn't learn to enjoy milk until my first pregnancy, some twenty years later. As a result, I was very small for my age, spindly, and wan, with a bloated belly, hunched over. I looked how I felt.

Evelyn closely monitored all my bodily functions, including chronic constipation. The enema bag horrified me, and Ex-Lax was hugely distasteful. My bottom knew no peace.

Her expression of love was so overprotective that I felt her greatest pleasure would be to wrap me in padding and, like delicate china, isolate me in a safe corner.

My secret wish was to be a person, whatever that was. My earliest childhood triumph was operating the self-service elevator at the apartment building around the corner. *Now, this was living*, I thought. My success, though, was private; there was no one with whom to share my accomplishment. I had become a lonely, bereft child.

Living with my new family—a cloying new mother and an ill-tempered, halfhearted father—my fragmented foundation started to crumble. I felt like Humpty Dumpty after the fall. *How many men will it take to put me back together again?*

MY MANY MOTHERS

MY BIRTH MOTHER'S NAME WAS REBECCA—or was it Beatrice? What was her real name? Who was she? Nobody said. Now, in 1930, as a four-year-old, I wondered, *Who's this Evelyn, the new mother now raising me?*

No one told me I had a mother before Evelyn, neither Father nor Tante Surrel. Many years passed before I discovered I was born of another woman who wanted me, named me, and loved me before she died. With a vague emptiness haunting me, I later wrote this poem:

Searching For Mother

She left
one tragic hospital night.
Pointed whispers
found me in diapers,
abandoned.
Who was that pretty lady picture
on Tante Surrel's dresser?
No one said.
My heavy sweater
held no heat,

sandwich no meat,
people no laughter,
no one said why.
I searched —
meadow, farmhouse, silo—
empty, silence.
Fields quiet.
Muted murmurs,
silence.

After father married Evelyn, the tearing away from Tante Surrel upset me deeply. Its abruptness made me despondent. I was usually constipated, which Evelyn confronted with zealous remedies. Her intense mothering expressed a peculiar devotion I had trouble understanding. Onlookers who viewed Evelyn's exaggerated concerns questioned that she was "only a stepmother."

With nightmares torturing my sleep, I awakened with searing sore throats. My whimpering always brought Evelyn to my bedside. "Mommy, my throat hurts so much. I need some orange juice." In my desperation, I had finally acknowledged her as 'mother'. She comforted me by squeezing oranges by hand in the middle of the night.

I sensed mother was a loving person, but her essence escaped me. Her endearing qualities were hidden by her invasive style. It took many years before I became aware of mother's noble character and depth of caring.

As I adjusted to living with my new family, I returned to enjoy weekend reunions with Tante Surrel, and cousins Dorothy and Betty, at their Chicago's Westside apartment. My father helped with this transition by driving me to Surrel's many Friday nights. Their household contrasted dramatically with mother's. It was calm and interesting as Dorothy involved me in compelling activities. Dorothy introduced me to books, which became a valuable legacy. In contrast, mother focused mostly on my bodily functions, as a scientist might scrutinize a laboratory rat.

I was confused about inner conflicts with my mother. My resentment invariably made me pull away. Yet the anguish of needing her was ever-present. I was an unappreciative spoiled brat while she was unfailingly loyal. Our different needs kept us apart and prevented a loving mother-daughter relationship. Ultimately, we were both cheated.

WHEN I WAS ABOUT SEVEN YEARS OLD, my elementary school teacher scheduled a musical recital. "Mommy, I want a new dress for the concert" was my usual expectation. Invariably, mother dropped her chores, took me to Marshall Field's Sewing Department in downtown Chicago, and searched their pattern books. We bonded, but only momentarily, choosing a pretty style she'd create to please me.

For the fabric, we usually traveled south down State Street to Goldblatt's bargain basement. Money was always a concern. We never spent a dime without careful thought. Sometimes I overheard snide remarks like, "only 'kikey' Jews who lack taste would shop at that cheap Goldblatt's." Nevertheless, Mom and I always found suitable fabric to make an attractive dress. I never appreciated her beautifully-constructed 'home-mades,' however, as much as a store-bought. I dismissed Mother's hard labors as just another way to save money.

About this time, I became preoccupied with a search for beauty, perhaps to sooth my ongoing distress. When entering the Carson, Pirie Scott & Company department store, I would pause, as crowds pushed past me, riveted by the front door's intricate sculpted metal design. Later, I discovered it had been created by the famous architect Louis Sullivan. A lifelong appetite was born.

I liked to pop into Woolworth's Five-and-Dime on Granville Avenue, always looking for a desirable trinket. I was usually left discontented by the poorly constructed merchandise. My need to discover a captivating item sent me up and down the aisles, to be certain I hadn't missed something worthy. With a lone dime in my sweater pocket, I settled on a book of paper dolls with their colorfully designed clothing. My favorite was those of the Dionne quintuplets, but the Shirley Temple collection was a close second. It was a tough decision.

I loved traveling by bus to downtown Chicago with Mom, seeing the impressively designed buildings as the bus carried us across the Chicago River at Michigan Avenue. Beautiful structures lined the street—the shiny white Wrigley Building, and the squat, historic Water Tower built many years earlier with seemingly ancient stones. When we attended the Friday evening Grant Park Chicago Symphony concerts, I noticed the Palmolive building, its shiny beacon glistening at night. I eagerly looked forward to its evening light, stretching my neck far up for the view. These sites were my introduction to architecture, a prelude to the thrill of later living in the first Mies van der Rohe apartment building built during my early married years on the south side slums of Michigan Avenue.

At about that time, Mom began helping Dad make a living in the cleaning/tailor shop. Her long hours of 'waiting on trade,' mending the torn linings of men's suits and replacing missing buttons, attracted customers willing to pay higher dry-cleaning bills for this special attention.

Mother's conscientious efforts contributed to my father competing successfully with the chain store across the street. In a skewed encounter, my father's business survived despite the competition of a savvy rival who advertised sharply lower prices on his storefront window signs.

Mother's long work hours required that she have help. Aurelia, a gaunt African-American woman, became housekeeper and companion, regaling me with vivid stories of life on Chicago's south side slums and her stormy, childless marriage. As I nestled close, I felt a warm attachment listening to her troubles. I knew Aurelia had become a true member of our family when Dad used his free time to create a fine custom suit for her in a style and fabric she personally selected. I recall his squatting alongside her as he pinned the hem, "Aurelia, is this the length you prefer?" I loved her belonging to our *moshpucha* (family.) Our warm relationship felt natural as she took me by my hand, riding the "L" downtown, to buy a Halloween costume when Mom was too busy.

THOUGH DOROTHY AND BETTY CONTRIBUTED special qualities in raising me —Dorothy her inquiring mind, and Betty her lighter mood—both sisters were somewhat shy about sex. As a nine-year-old, I asked Dorothy about a girl's developing breasts. She responded, "They're a woman's hidden charm." Even after Betty had married and had a son, the meaning of the then-ongoing expression "in like Flynn" escaped her. References to the sexual adventures of popular movie star Errol Flynn simply passed her by.

As I continued to mature, Dad no longer needed to drive me for those weekends with Dorothy and Betty. I traveled alone, trusted to meet Betty at Chicago's Merchandise Mart waiting room. I boarded the clamoring Granville Avenue "L," bursting with passengers standing shoulder to shoulder, arms hanging from ceiling straps, chatting, or with their faces buried in wrinkled newspapers. With new confidence, I got out at the busy stop and comfortably wove through the crowds to the waiting room. Though only a squeak of a child, I was familiar with the routine. As I sat on the bank of seats, I soon recognized Betty's beaming face from among the swarming strangers, confirming my growing independence.

Whenever I told Mother, "I'm spending another weekend with Dorothy and Betty," she would suddenly grow silent and tense, biting her lips. I sensed she felt some resentment over the ongoing attachment to my first family. She never openly objected to these visits. This was wise, since our relationship was already shaky.

Dorothy and Betty introduced me to the larger world. I remember when they took me to my first theater performance, *Hot Mikado*, a jazz version of the operetta, with an all-Negro cast. Their younger sister, Charlotte, accompanied us. I noticed they treated her indifferently and wondered about this more reserved part of their make-up. Charlotte laughed hilariously over the production's shenanigans, which pleased me.

I doubted she had few opportunities for life's joys, as Charlotte was responsible for all the family household chores. Yet with her lively face and bleached-blond hair, I sensed she enjoyed fun, especially telling the sexy joke: "Why does a woman wear a hostess gown? You just zip it down and you *hostas!* (You have it!). Eventually, Charlotte married in California and birthed a son, living an uneventful life.

When my cousins took me to a park conservatory, I hated it. All those plants—it seemed a jumbled jungle, similar to the lack of harmony in my life. Today, I conscientiously arrange plants as a complement to sculpture. I feel this joining has intrinsic beauty. Even vagrant greenery with its implied energy captures my imagination.

When I was about nine years old, my birth mother's family organized the Rosenstein Family Club, bringing together many aunts, uncles, and cousins. They rented a hall on Westside Chicago for the monthly reunion. The delicious warm corned beef sandwiches on seeded Jewish rye bread, with sour pickles and cole slaw, were the best I had ever tasted. Granville Avenue never had food like that, available only in Jewish neighborhoods.

The family all performed the *kozatski* folk dancing together, with great *fraulich* (joy), holding hands, shoulder-to-shoulder, managing the intricate steps. Uncle Willie, in a balanced half stoop, vigorously flung his legs out alternately in succession, accompanied by music on the Victrola record player. We all clapped our hands in unison, spurring him on to greater feats. I had never seen these steps danced as well until I attended the Russian Folk Ballet in my adult years.

How was Uncle Willie Rosenstein my uncle? And Uncle Mitchell, too, another favorite of mine? I'm not certain. My birth mother's family was so huge and loving that I never sorted out the various connections. I adored the family gatherings, but their relationships always confused me. I didn't ask many questions—I was just glad I belonged.

When my new family joined with my birth family for these reunions, a cohesion was created, unique and incomparably satisfying. I watched with pleasure as Mother fit in, accepted as the stepmother/outsider. Her style of raising me was often questioned, regarded with suspected flaws. I would overhear people murmur, slowly shaking their heads, "How come Sister's different—so sad and small for her age?"

The Rosensteins expressed their caring by appointing me 'sergeant-at-arms' each year when electing officers. After a time, this nod in my direction raised questions for me. A turning point arrived when I concluded this position was a 'handout,' meant to indulge an 'orphan.' My decision: *I'm not going to participate in this gift of pity any longer.* I prepared for the next election of officers and asked my brother Lester the proper language.

When the customary sergeant-at-arms appointment was announced, I stood up to my full four-foot height, raised my voice strongly, and asserted, "I *decline*." Though still a wisp of a kid, I had achieved a new level of pride.

OVERRIDING FAMILY TRADITION, DOROTHY SEARCHED the larger world and joined a humanistic religion, the Chicago Ethical Culture Society. She took me to my first meeting at Orchestra Hall when I was eleven years old— *an epiphany.* My fantasy at age five was confirmed! A 'large religious tent bringing together people of all backgrounds'—the mixed population attending affirmed my ideal. The Society was led by Leader (minister) Dr. A. Eustace Haydon, an emeritus professor of Comparative Religion from the University of Chicago. He possessed a crown of white hair and an energetic body that lunged with his dynamic words. "It's a wonder he doesn't fall off the stage," chuckled Ida, Dorothy's good friend. I later heard that Ida had sponsored her niece for a national teenage summer program, "Encampment for Citizenship," that teaches about social justice and nurtures self-esteem. Eleanor Roosevelt later supported this effort by hosting workshops in her Hyde Park home. *Lucky girl*, I thought. *I hope I can attend something like that someday.*

Dr. Haydon discussed big ideas I'm not sure I understood, but they sounded hopeful. I thought, *Maybe they could bring true understanding someday.* My visit to the New York Ethical Society in later years fortified these ideals with its spiritual message mounted prominently over the podium—"Where Men Meet to Seek the Highest Is Holy Ground."

This Movement has become revelatory for me—that honoring our unique humanity can bring common ground and important change. The Ethical Movement has continued to define my humanist identity, central to my life-long religious and spiritual journey. Dorothy had opened a unique path to a meaningful life as an inspiring surrogate mother and role model.

FOR MY THIRTEENTH BIRTHDAY, Dorothy and Betty took me to the fancy French restaurant Chez Antoine for a celebratory lunch. In preparation, I had diligently practiced my high school language skills so that I could order authentically—le poulet et les haricots verts.

I was thrilled when they presented me with a corsage of gardenias. Its sweet fragrance remained in my memory, long after the soft, white petals had turned brown. The waiter asked permission to zip down my high-neck dress, to place his fingers inside for pinning the corsage to my shoulder. I blushed and nodded approval. My cousins giggled. I wondered about their prudishness, noticing they were getting on in years with no sign of dating men.

It wasn't until my adulthood that the story of my birth mother and early years became more clear. Earlier, a few words dropped here and there, supposedly beyond my earshot, suggested fragments. I pieced them together to bring some understanding by many visits to Dorothy and Betty after they moved to California.

It required thirty years of questioning to gather small pockets of information. I learned they called my birth mother "Aunt Bea," though her real name was "Rebecca." The name on my later-discovered birth certificate was listed as "Beatrice"; on Lester's birth certificate, her name was listed as "Berkie." When I gently pressed Dorothy and Betty for more details, they dissolved in tears, still unable to speak freely of the decades-old tragedy. I believe their extended grief muted the quality of their lives and in some ways, mine as well. They did drop a few hints: *My birth mother was fun-loving, warm and caring. She was also a gracious hostess at social gatherings.*

Other significant information emerged later. I heard my father's marriage to Evelyn had achieved his goal of reconstituting the family, with all three children living together with a mother for his children. His reclaiming me from Surrel's home had met with her strong resistance. She had agreed only when my father threatened a lawsuit. I wasn't too surprised by his aggressiveness, considering his intent to unify the family.

WHEN I WAS ABOUT THIRTEEN YEARS OLD, Mother asked me, in a rare forthright tone, *When did you know I was not your real mother?* Her new, honest question made our entire past life together feel like one huge deceit.

I froze, speechless, choked with a myriad of emotions. I wish I'd been able to express feelings of gratitude to my stepmother for her devotion and admit that I loved other mothers more than her. I was afraid I'd lose my stepmother's love if she knew of my conflicted feelings about her. I was flooded with anger that I had not been trusted to know the truth of my birth mother earlier and starved to know details of her life.

I then imagined a healing experience with my stepmother. Her honest question had finally broken the dam, allowing the release of many years of misunderstandings about unexpressed love:

She would take me in her arms, confiding her difficulties in replacing the mothering roles of Surrel's family and my birth mother. Patting me lovingly, she would ask, "How did you feel about all these complications in your life?"

I would finally melt and admit, "I've so appreciated your conscientious efforts in raising me." Feeling shame, I'd add, *"I'm sorry I didn't express it more often,"* and, *"Oh my,"* shaking my head, *"what problems*

I brought you!"

These admissions would open a new bond of closeness as we acknowledged genuine love for one another. After gazing at one another with affection and some sighs, we would hug and kiss as never before, smiling warmly with great relief for finally surmounting past barriers. Evelyn would wipe away my tears of joy with the hem of her apron as I did similarly for her, offering belated comfort.

Unfortunately, this healing experience never took place—it was only a fantasy. Mother and I were too insecure to allow such honesty. We continued maintaining our usual distance, never admitting our deepest feelings. She went to her grave with both of us not knowing my love for her. My mother was unjustly deprived of that precious of all emotions. I am left with that emptiness by which both of us were marked—cheated of that vital bonding experience. An open wound remains.

In the following years, I remained close with Dorothy and Betty, but they continued to withhold information about my birth mother. Betty moved to California, where she married Al, owner of a haberdashery shop, and lived a comfortable, middle-class life. Dorothy remained single in Chicago, continuing her work life as a clerk for the book publisher Ginn and Company and attending night school. Eventually, she also moved to Los Angeles with Surrel, taking responsibility for her aging mother while clerking at a high school guidance office.

As I matured into my late fifties, I visited Dorothy many times at her rear apartment in the Newcastle Avenue complex in Encino. Bored-looking seniors lounged around the outdoor swimming pool, viewing me enviously as I strolled the long walk of the courtyard. Some recognized me as the repeated visitor to that lucky resident in the rear apartment.

In my California travels, I somehow never managed to visit Surrel. This omission was a dramatic departure for me. I'm deeply regretful and remain shocked at my callous indifference. I surmise the trauma of Surrel 'giving me away' totally blocked my formerly loving feelings. Perhaps, if a mature family member had reopened that past hurt with me, bringing

understanding and forgiveness, I would have reconnected with Tante Surrel's final years. That time could have become rich and loving, not remaining a huge void in our lives.

I had been inspired by the spiritual nuances of the book *Freud and
Man's Soul*, by Bruno Bettleheim, and gave Dorothy a copy. The author
had reinterpreted Freud's works, revealing profound subtleties accessible
through his unique knowledge of the native German language in which
it had been originally written. I found Dorothy's copy of the book well-
thumbed when I reclaimed it after she died.

Betty moved to a senior facility after becoming widowed and tried convincing her sister to join her there. Dorothy wouldn't relinquish her independence and continued her adventurous life, traveling extensively. Her
travels took her repeatedly to the Soviet Union, exploring our Russian heritage. Souvenirs from that culture provide rich memories of our commonly
shared origins: I converted a samovar into a lamp that currently rests on
my dining room chest. Covering the tables of my psychotherapy office are
antiquated, intricately embroidered cloths, lace-trimmed and inscribed *P.
1929*, stitched with Russian lettering, birds and flowers

Dorothy even undertook an excursion to Egypt, as a solo traveler,
without a group tour. I marveled, *What guts to take such a trip alone.*
In her eighties, she may have extended herself too far. Though she spoke
of the pyramids, she mentioned little else of the experience.

Until almost ninety years of age, Dorothy attended night school regularly at various institution,s including Pierce Community College in Los
Angeles. She had never learned to drive and traveled by bus from her Encino apartment, walking up the steep campus incline. I encouraged her to
apply for an associate college equivalency degree (forgetting she was a
high-school dropout) and volunteered to do the necessary paperwork.

"Dorothy dear, you've accumulated so many credits and knowledge
these many years. Wouldn't it be satisfying to have the actual credential
for all your efforts?"

"No, Sister, it doesn't matter. I've had the satisfaction of the learning experiences. I don't need more than that."

During one of my late California visits to Dorothy's apartment, she gave me the oversized engagement photo of Surrel and Moishe, set in an antique, decorated frame, which hung over her bed. It had become a great treasure—*a couple beginning their lives together, my devoted, loving family, simple folks, with an unwavering ethic of toil.*

After I had a small photocopy made for myself, I passed it along to the next generation, my cousin Paul Young, son of their first-born Irving. As Surrel's grandson, he had close ties to his Aunt Dorothy. It was through his visits with Dorothy that Paul and I met, over a dozen years later, when I was in my late seventies. He will inherit all of Dorothy's gifts except for the samovar. I plan to bequeath this memento to my daughter Janet, who I hope will maintain the continuity of our family.

Much later, Dorothy became frightened of the cholesterol scare and started eating sparingly. She became thin and frail. I was surprised she neglected the good nutrition about which she was usually knowledgeable. I recall her advice to me in my childhood: "Always eat the pulp of oranges for its healthy benefits."

She kept her declining condition private, not revealing it even to cousin Shirley, with whom she was close. Shirley suggested she may have had a small stroke. With no other intimate companion to intercede, she declined quietly and alone.

I AM LEFT WITH A RICH HERITAGE FROM COUSIN DOROTHY, my surrogate mother. She bequeathed me many treasures by becoming a role model for living vitally: retain curiosity with an adventurous spirit, remain open to learning and a passion for what life has to offer, even into the elder years. Her introducing me to the Ethical Culture Movement has shaped the humanistic person I have become.

When Evelyn became my mother, she brought a unique family into my life. Auntie Annie, her widowed half-sister, and daughter, Mathilda, became beloved additions. Annie carried her large body proudly, her gray hair drawn back neatly in a bun. One day, when visiting Mother, she brought a bouquet of fresh flowers. I had never seen such extravagance except in the movies. That was class.

Mathilda was the eldest of Annie's three children; she expressed compassion for others as second nature. They lived in Wilmette, a Chicago suburb, in rooms behind Annie's candy store. Auntie Annie earned a living by selling popular candies—licorice, Tootie Fruities, and Tootsie Rolls. When Mathilda set the table for supper each night, she was told by her mother, "Be sure to set an extra place at the table in case a stranger appears at the door." This spirit of giving to the less fortunate shaped Mathilda as would a gifted sculptor's tool.

In later years, they moved to Chicago, living in a luxurious Lake Shore Drive apartment. I don't know what brought that sudden improvement. Mathilda married during that time, which may have accounted for the fortuitous change. During my teenage years, on many Saturdays, I traveled by bus to Mathilda's apartment. I would overhear her on the telephone, *schnorring* (polite begging), pursuing her altruistic goals with determination: "I know you gave last month, but they're hungry again this month."

Auntie Annie eventually became seriously ill with a rare disease, myasthenia gravis (MG), an autoimmune disease inflicting severe muscular weakness, to which she succumbed. Mathilda, observing her mother's suffering, vowed, "I'm going to find a cure for this terrible disease in my lifetime."

Mathilda's husband also died at about this time, and she moved to Long Beach, California. She purchased land on which oil was later discovered, and Mathilda became wealthy.

Mathilda kept her promise and organized the Myasthenia Gravis (MG) Foundation, for which she became a major fund raiser, supporting research for a cure. The highlight of her MG fund-raising was the annual posh Honoring Dinner Dance. As I planned my California trips, Mathilda phoned me regularly about the date for the annual March event, always as her guest.

At the Dinner Dance, Mathilda sat at the front reception desk with her broad smile, welcoming us as I arrived with my brother and sister-law, Les and Ruth. Later, she came to our table to greet us more personally. There wasn't much time for socializing, as adoring fans usually clustered around her all evening, but I understood.

Mathilda made a grand entrance onto the dance floor, among many cheers, on the arm of special friend Richard, twenty-five years her junior. They then gracefully launched the opening dance, Mathilda swirling in her elegant gown, this glamorous, beneficent grand dame. As always, she wore her favorite hand-painted brooch depicting her mother as a child and inscribed with the mantra: *God couldn't be everywhere so He made mothers.* I usually contributed a tribute to Mathilda in the souvenir program, signed 'Sister.' This name, designated by my birth mother, often caused confusion about my relationship with Mathilda.

Though Mathilda and I didn't enjoy a daily intimate relationship, separated by two thousand miles, we exchanged many phone calls and holiday cards. These communications kept us connected like good friends living down the block from one another.

Our bond always surmounted the long absences between the annual MG affairs. Visiting together, Mathilda and I would sometimes spend time looking into one another's eyes, an unspoken link that drew us again and again. Perhaps I had become that child she had never birthed. Mathilda had become a sterling force in my life, family I had the good fortune to inherit from my stepmother Evelyn.

Mathilda wasn't everyone's favorite person. Her determination contained aggression and brittleness, but these characteristics never diminished her in my eyes. I was impressed by her humanistic convictions and generosity, as she often achieved her fine goals.

Our conversations centered on her latest project. Mathilda always listened to the special events of my life, but they paled compared to her inventive ideas. I inhaled her stories and digested them, which inspired mine. Her energy infused me. Mathilda's bountiful heart didn't stop with MG. While volunteering at Long Beach Hospital, she witnessed the AIDS baby scourge. These infants were discharged from the hospital in ragged clothing, and her outrage translated into practical measures. She telephoned Saks Fifth Avenue and other high-end stores, requesting they contribute new baby clothing for the inaugural Children's Closet. Newborns were thus sent home in dignity, later accompanied with teddy bears Mathilda solicited for their added pleasure.

IN 2003 AT AGE ONE HUNDRED, Mathilda started a write-in campaign for Governor of California. In a press interview, she asserted, "I'm not some senile coot or self-promoting kook." She explained her goal: "If I can make a half-dozen people think about the plight of children in this country, of how to feed and clothe and take care of them medically. . .I will be a success." Her beauty treatments were nothing more than Vaseline and living well. Mathilda added, "My doctor said I'm too cheap for a face-lift. And it's true. It's why I'd be a good governor."

She continued her altruism into her advanced years, despite serious illnesses—cancer, heart attacks, strokes and seriously impaired eyesight bordering on blindness. Mathilda wouldn't take a time out for treatment, explaining, "I've rejected the doctor's suggestion of a cornea transplant. At my age, I can't afford the six-months inactivity required for recuperation." A high-powered magnifying glass was always at the ready on her apartment reading table, piled-high with paperwork.

When I visited her Long Beach apartment, she usually offered some goodies from her kitchen drawer full of inexpensive candy bars—Hershey chocolates, Baby Ruth, Butterfingers—perhaps a reminder of those childhood candy land days in Wilmette.

FOR MATHILDA'S HUNDREDTH BIRTHDAY celebration, I wrote the following poem:

A Life Force
energizing
friends and family alike.
A comet
propelled by a loving mother.

Her religion?
"Caring."

MG patients, Aids babies,
all in her orbit.
What's she do about it?
A wound opens,
she salves it,
chuckling,
"big deal."

Yes, Mathilda, you are a
Big Deal,

leaving a legacy
few can exceed.

By some incredible synchronicity, I developed MG at age eighty-three in 2009, following my successful brain tumor surgery. The medication Mestinon brought rapid recovery, developed, in part, through the successful research funded partially by Mathilda's efforts. When Auntie Annie contracted the disease, the death rate was ninety-three percent. With my onset, the rate had decreased to nine percent.

Immediately after my MG recovery, when Mathilda was 104 years old, I visited her in Long Beach, along with my brother Lester and his wife, to express my love and gratitude for all she had given me. As I sat on the sofa next to her, holding her hand, murmuring quiet expressions of thanks, Mathilda just smiled serenely.

During our final visit, she appeared content to be surrounded with kisses and appreciative gazes from those who loved her. She suggested that marking her end should include a celebratory party rather than a memorial service. I did not attend, as I felt I had already bade my farewell. The *MG News* announced, ". . .the passing of Mathilda Karel Spak, An Era Has Ended, 1906–2010." My loss has been replaced with respect and resolve to emulate her goodness as best I can.

LIFE WITH FATHER

MOMSER! (BASTARD)—HOW COULD YOU PLAY THAT CARD?" my father shrieked at a perceived misplay at the pinochle table. This usual Sunday afternoon gathering was arranged for relaxation and a family reunion. Nevertheless, Father's anger was so ready and relentless that my mother often had to be called from the next room to calm him.

"*Bahna, Bahna*," she would murmur softly, stroking his shoulders, as if comforting a colicky infant. As she tried to soothe the outrage at the card table, I watched with mixed feelings, greatly admiring my Mother's compassion but embarrassed by my Father's unruly behavior.

Barnett, my father, always had a difficult life. He came to America at age nineteen, at the turn of the century, an immigrant from Russia without formal education, and he spoke no English. He had been apprenticed in the old country to learn the skills of a tailor. He surmounted this humble background with hard work and determination. My father established his own tailoring/cleaning shop in the U.S. His modest success enabled him to support a wife and three children.

Barney (for short) was a large man with a balding head, intense eyes, a wide nose, and thick lips, often carelessly dressed. His attire was that of a working man, just a shirt and pants, rarely complemented with tie and jacket.

Grieving and desperate after the death of my birth mother, he sent me to live with Tante Surrel, my mother's oldest sister. When he married Evelyn, he tried to achieve his ultimate goal of bringing all three children together into one household with a nurturing mother. I'm not entirely clear about my age when I eventually joined my father's family, but his effort to reclaim me from Surrel met opposition and required the threat of a lawsuit. By that time, I was about four years old, the same age as first daughter, Dorothy, when she died. It suggests Dad's timing for the reunited family was meant to fulfill her unfinished life.

My father knew only hard work and rarely engaged in anything light-hearted. The only exception was a game of pinochle on Sunday after-noons, during family gatherings. Even in those relaxed times, my father's explosive temper interfered with his pleasure.

My father's anger could also explode at my brothers' mischievous ways. He would pull his strap from his pants, or grab the shaving strap from back of the bathroom door, and strike at them.

I was scared of my father. If he could beat my brothers, who were lovable guys, I felt vulnerable, possibly deserving a similar fate. My com-pulsive obedience and agreeableness didn't guarantee I would escape his wrath.

At the same time, I longed for my father's love. This intense need was satisfied only in my imagination. I would hang on the slightly ajar bathroom door as he shaved. I hoped his grimaced facial contortions, trying to maneuver the mustache area, were a smile *meant just for me*.

The only physical contact I had with my father was my dutiful peck on his cheek for his birthday. I don't recall his offering a kiss for mine or affectionately holding my hand. I did plant a final kiss on my father's cheek as he lay in his coffin. An early photograph of him holding my older brother, Leonard, as a toddler, surprised me for evidence of his ever having had gentle direct contact with anyone.

A special delight was when he allowed himself the rare pleasure of joining us children at Chicago's Granville Avenue beach for a swim. Fa-ther occasionally permitted me to ride his broad back through the heavy waves. I was joyful for those passing moments and giggled with delight.

I never discovered why anger and emotional distance were very much part of my father. The reasons may have lain in his losses of both a daughter and his first wife.

Another possibility was his highly emotional older sister, Rose, the only close living relative from the old country. She had arrived here first and took their mother's maiden name, "Goodman," as her last name instead of the paternal "Mitchell." My father followed her to America and assumed the same misconstrued last name.

Rose visited him regularly, verbally attacking him with screaming outbursts. We children dreaded her visits, awaiting the inevitable storm.

"Oh, watch out, Aunt Rose is coming here again today. . . ." As we all gathered in my father's tailor shop, hearing her taunts and continuing fury, he sat in stoic silence. Embarrassed, my older brother Leonard would shut off the lights and lock the front door, to give the appearance of the store being closed for the day.

MEANWHILE, I WAS MISERABLE, BEING SEPARATED from my first family, Tante Surrel and her daughters. I credit my father for helping me maintain contact with them. On many Fridays, he drove me for a weekend reunion. This laborious trip required tedious hours through busy traffic, car horns blasting, stop-and-go lights every couple of blocks, creeping across almost the full width of Chicago, from east to west. My father expended this effort after a full day's work in his tailor shop. On Sunday, his one free day, he returned for me, with that tedious drive back again.

He rarely spoke to me on these trips. I longed for some direct contact with him. His most prominent sign of life was the repeated, abrupt movement of his right hand on the stick, causing a screeching of the automobile's innards as the car shifted into motion. He maintained an otherwise somber silence, except for occasionally cursing a reckless driver with his usual, *That momzer.*

I realize only now my father endured four challenging car trips in one weekend. My new insight raises this question, *Did Dad have time to eat supper before he undertook those demanding Friday evening trips? Did that weekend ordeal contribute to his later developing ulcers?*

In our daily life together, my father was very tight with money. He spent with such reluctance that, when he reached for the wallet in his hip pocket, we could see the instant pained look on his face simultaneous with thrusting his hand. We thought twice before ever spending any money.

My father did spend some at times, but only at mother's insistence. He would succumb to her demands for my personal benefit—elocution and piano lessons, and later, braces for my teeth. He also made me a coat with a genuine lynx collar when I was eleven years old, probably responding to Mom's pleas.

My father's only initiative for expenditures was insisting I attend after-school Yiddish lessons at the neighborhood Workman's Circle School. The classes were boring, but I continued, wanting to please him. No one explained the purpose of after-school instruction. The best part was my admiration of my dignified teacher.

It wasn't until my adult years that my psychotherapist interpreted its significance for me, that Workman's Circle is a socialist organization seeking social and economic justice. A large fog had been suddenly lifted and for the first time; I took pride in my father's values, with a glimmer of respect emerging. His consistent proclamation that 'only the unions would help the working people' took on new meaning. I realized the Workman Circle's mission complements the humanist concepts of the Ethical Culture Movement. I think my father would have approved of my membership in the Movement with its inclusiveness of my Jewish roots. Throughout my life, I continue to find ways to honor my heritage.

Most important was his financing my college education and housing at downstate University of Illinois. I overheard Dad's friends criticizing him for 'wasting money' on my college education, trivial in their eyes. "She'll only get married and have children." Nevertheless, Dad supported my goals, most likely influenced by mother.

My attending the University of Illinois was complicated by the difficult 1946 post-war housing situation. Veterans were returning to campus, reclaiming the abandoned housing that we had occupied in their absence. Since I rejected a college sorority affiliation, which I considered divisive and snobbish, I faced a housing crisis as did other independent Jewish women students.

Hillel, the Jewish campus organization, called a meeting of fathers to explore a housing solution. They founded an exemplary plan, acquiring a house they named *Indeco,* meaning "independent" and "cooperative." The group purchased a stately Tudor-styled house, including furnishings, for $60,000, with sixty fathers each purchasing a $1,000 share, extravagant back then. The plan was simultaneously unique and questionable— fathers hoped their share could be sold to a succeeding family when their daughters graduated from college. Since I was now a senior, my father, recouping his investment in just one year, made the deal even riskier.

I can only imagine the scene as my father met with the other men to discuss this speculative plan. My somewhat slovenly dressed father listened to the proposal, mingling with successful doctors, attorneys, and businessmen attired in their well-tailored suits, possibly complemented with a designer tie.

My struggling immigrant father made the courageous decision to invest in this plan, which enabled me to earn my undergraduate degree. Perhaps he envisioned his participation would elevate him to a loftier status in American culture.

No matter, I was grateful he took this risk. Over the chipped wooden counter in his tailor shop, he often listened intently to stock market tips from a favorite customer. I was astounded he invested $1,000 in the housing plan. I hadn't known he ever had that much money.

On the day of my university graduation, he brought a bouquet of flowers but, most important, broke into a huge grin at the stellar event. As matters developed, I was the only cousin in the large Rosenstein family who became a college graduate. I believe I brought a sense of accomplishment to my father's life.

The only other occasion I recall his expansive smile was when he first saw his infant granddaughter, Janet. That photo is mounted on my kitchen wall, accompanied with similarly happy pictures of my father's engagement and marriage to my birth mother. My eyes become misty as I gaze at those photos of his early, innocent days, a young man full of hope and promise.

He eventually recouped his investment, and I've heard that, today, *Indeco* is a solid investment with a waiting list to purchase a share. I've flourished too, having graduated with degrees in Psychology and Sociology, later earning a graduate degree in Counseling plus advanced training in Psychotherapy and Psychoanalysis. I have continued to pursue other educational opportunities as well, all flowing from my father's willingness to take that initial chance on my future.

When I was engaged to be married and had purchased our first kitchen housewares, I told my father with distress, "It cost thirty-five dollars for just those pots and pans!" He responded with a rare display of caring that overrode his close ways with money. Dad whipped out his wallet and with a swish of his hand and instantly gave me the cash. I excitedly embraced him, my arms thrown around his broad body.

I believe my achievements brought hidden pride to my father, special pleasure for having raised a previously abandoned infant to some success. My accomplishments established him as a capable father. Today, as I steam the broccoli in my copper-bottomed Revere pot, I'm very grateful that my father struggled for my benefit.

THOUGH MY FATHER'S EFFORTS WERE WELCOME, they didn't compensate for his lack of ongoing tenderly expressed love between us. As these early-life connections lay a foundation for a daughter becoming capable of mature love for a mate in her adult years, this omission has left a void. Until recently, I was still trying to fill this absence.

As a young woman, my longing for a man's devotion became apparent when I went to the movie *The Constant Nymph,* starring Joan Fontaine and Charles Boyer. It depicted the raw pain of a young woman hopelessly in love with a father figure not responsive to her. The movie featured the Sibelius *Fifth Symphony* as background music.

At the end of the movie, I cried hysterically in the lobby for almost an hour, grieving the woman's frustration. I now know it was my own deprivation that brought this outpouring. Today, hearing this symphony still evokes the tenderness of a sensitive scar, the hurt of unrequited love.

My father let me down in another way, too. Rightfully, he was the person to tell me about my birth mother. That was impossible. We were like strangers to one another. Mostly, I avoided him, fearful of his angry eyes and explosive temper.

My father was also in pain, losing his first child, first wife, and his second as well. Immediately after marrying him, Evelyn was preoccupied with raising the children, especially me. I was a wan, somber child, still on a nursing bottle. Evelyn, bereaved by the loss of an infant son during the Bolshevik revolution, had found in me a replacement for her mothering deprivation. Her indulgences and overprotection probably marred their marital relationship. I often felt the prickly tension between them and, in agony, wondered if they really loved one another.

I've come to understand my father's anger and frustrations. Now I'm able to love him in a way I wasn't capable in my earlier years. My late-life gratitude to my father, never directly expressed, sadly comes too late for his happiness. As a tribute to him, I expressed my new understanding in a poem.

To My Father

Baldish head, stern-angry eyes.
A pained look that hid deep cries.
A massive body that bode no ill

though burdened by labors and fears unstilled.

A famine of joy, an impoverished love.
A fabric of life stretched taut and rough.
Losses too huge for most men to endure.
Why then should I expect a love so pure?
His caring defined by eager needle and thread
and back-breaking hours after I'm a-bed.
A giving dripping from his sweated brow.
Sometimes a worn smile escaped from his frown.

If our marred love I still mourn and heave,
My tears belong to him the more bereaved.

My belated awakening has inspired me to feel love for men. I now have a deep desire to develop a significant relationship with a male partner. I wonder if I possess the capacity to overcome past impediments, to respond in devoted and mature ways. I accept the challenge and hope it isn't too late.

MY OLDER BROTHER LEONARD

MY FATHER REWARDED ME WHEN HE BROUGHT two important males into my life, my brothers, Leonard and Lester. By marrying Evelyn in 1929, my father accomplished his long-held dream—a mother for his three children, reunited into one family.

Leonard, the eldest and serious brother, was eleven years old, and I was four, when we all came together. He was initially my favorite brother, the first genuinely cherished man in my life. We never became close.

Surprisingly, Leonard knew of my existence before we were reunited. He and Lester had apparently visited me on occasional weekends of which I have no memory. Leonard mentioned this experience in an astonishing handwritten, undated letter. It was discovered just five years ago by his daughter, Robin, seven years after his death. Part of it is quoted here:

SISTER

She brought Joy and Love as an infant to two households.

Les and I were content to exult in the thought that we had a sister, knowing that she was in a household full of love, devotion, and tradition.

When the day came following our father's marriage that our sister was to join us as a re-united family—Les and I were filled with eager anticipation. Now we would really have someone to fight with—or fight over.

I think that this changing our weekend sibling to a full-time sister contributed greatly to the retention of the name 'Siste'r. We would cling to it warmly. . . . [See Appendix for complete letter]

I wept oceanic tears by this letter, mourning my deep sense of loss. In a discussion with Robin, she suggested his motive for writing it. "He was probably feeling regrets in his older years of his not being closer to you. He was reminiscing, especially at the time of his failing health."

Len's reference to my being named "Sister" means a great deal to me, a legacy of my birth mother's expression of her love—extended to him as well. I'm crushed that he never spoke of his loving feelings for me while he was still alive.

I don't know why he kept his feelings and letter secret. Unexpressed love, and other important feelings, were a pattern of our family life. Len and I failed abysmally in our relationship, adhering to this neglectful pattern for the almost seventy-five years we knew each other as brother and sister.

I never felt Len's excitement of my being his full-time sister, as expressed in his letter. Though we shared occasional cherished moments, impediments consistently interfered.

When Len and I first reunited, we were each still suffering from painful losses, though for entirely different reasons. Of us three children orphaned by our birth mother's death, Len, at age seven, probably felt her loss most intensely. The cause of my suffering was being torn from Tante Surrel's home.

In living with Len, he would bark when he spoke to me, adding to the tension of an insecure child in a new setting. Len avoided me whenever I approached him in our large, three-bedroom apartment. We seemed to stake out separate territory, like members of competing gangs. Len's loving intent was somehow derailed. He rarely initiated conversation with me, though he enjoyed an enthusiastic friendship with our younger brother. Leonard's aloofness made me feel like a nuisance.

Despite his rejecting me, I deeply respected his kindness and loyalty toward our gentle stepmother. As the responsible brother, Len's attentiveness to her always demonstrated his love. His consistent devotion impressed me, but I was too immature to admit it. He often helped her around the house. With my abject unhappiness about joining the family, I resented my new mother. This placed Len and me in opposite camps.

My entrée into the family commanded Mom's exaggerated attention, which may have caused Len feel replaced as the favored child. On my part, perhaps I was afraid of a close emotional tie to him since his temper was like that of our father. Nevertheless, I know he cared about me. I noticed on several occasions he gave Mom an approving smile, with a gesture in my direction, when I made a knowledgeable comment or brought home a school paper with a high grade. Whenever Mom hired new household help, Len assured the family, "Just talk to Sis. She'll know all about her—she always asks the good questions."

Len was handsome, with thick black hair ending in a gentle wave at his temple. With his shiny white teeth, he resembled Clark Gable as he matured. Len achieved a good physique, lifting weights with barbells bought with his own money.

He developed fervor for life. His jaunty personality filled our home with charming American folk songs. I vividly recall Len's hearty renditions of "Home on the Range," "Shenandoah," and "Red River Valley," interspersed with interludes on his harmonica. Saxophone lessons launched his formal musical education. Len's favorite, "Twinkle, Twinkle, Little Star," was a familiar refrain, but he never seemed to progress beyond that selection. In his elder years, he reconnected with his love of music and pursued piano lessons, but, strangely, only when away from his marital home, while vacationing in Florida.

The remainder of Len's earlier letter describes another affectionate view of me he felt during our childhood years:

> [I was]warmed by Betty's unselfish interest and support in everything that any member of the family undertook—be it Dad, Mom, Les, or Myself.
>
> Her enthusiasm and back-up has never waned—always a sister—a name deeply imbedded—so much [so] that at her first day in school, when asked her name, she answered, "Sister Goodman". It has had a lot of significance and always will.

I felt occasional warm feelings toward Len but was afraid of his anger that could suddenly explode, just like Dad's. I respected his taking responsibility for our absent mother even as I resented his becoming the boss at home. His deeds were particularly helpful to Mom as she started working longer hours in Dad's shop.

His dictatorial ways brought a crisis one day. When I returned from school, I casually tossed my coat on a chair. Len ordered, "Sis, hang up your coat." I ignored his command. He wouldn't be easily dismissed and repeated, "Now!" Not accustomed to being ordered about, I ignored him. Len then became more aggressive. "If you don't hang up your coat, I'm going to throw it out!"

I was furious with his demanding manner. *Who does he think he is, ordering me around, he's just a brother. I'll do as I please.*

This confrontation came to a head with his grabbing my coat and throwing it out, but only as far as the rear outdoor porch. I was enraged but meekly retrieved my coat and hung it up. As a rebellious colt, I had finally been saddled.

My anger with my older brother started to subside. Quietly, I started appreciating his role as a resolute parent in Mom's place. I knew I had been indulged and coddled, pitied as the abandoned orphan. I was finally being challenged by my big brother to behave more responsibly. Deep down, I knew his conscientious support of our mother was appropriate, worthy of my admiration.

LEN ALSO RESPONDED SENSITIVELY TO OUR FATHER'S BURDENS. He inaugurated a bookkeeping system for dad's shop, putting me in charge. I 'copied the books,' as our family called it, recording into a master book a description of customer's clothes to be cleaned. Accurate details of whether a man's suit included a vest, or a woman's dress was two-piece with a matching belt, were crucial. In case of loss or misunderstanding, it could cost Dad a lot of money. Aware of these concerns, Len introduced protective practices and became an unofficial family partner. He had assigned me a central role also, and I felt important.

We all contributed to the family business. Leonard designated Lester as the delivery boy. He rode his bicycle swiftly down the streets of east Rogers Park, steering the bike with one hand, the other clasping the cleaned garments thrown over his shoulder. One day, a pedestrian rushed into my father's shop. "Hey, did you hear about your delivery boy? He crashed into Walgreen's store window. There's shattered glass all over the sidewalk. I hope he's okay—and the clothes, too."

Our relief was substantial when we realized that Lester was not the delivery boy that day, replaced by a substitute who had suffered the accident. It didn't necessarily lighten our anguish—we couldn't relax until we knew the delivery boy was safe, and the clothing as well.

Len handled this family turmoil smoothly, including the insurance claim for the shattered glass. My anxiety made me nauseous, and I wondered, *How do adults accept life's mishaps, these bum raps, and still continue with hope and love?* It all felt overwhelming. Len was clearly the steadying force in our struggling family.

Len developed an idiosyncratic congested throat which he cleared periodically with a noisy, gurgling sound. We never discussed his condition or its cause. A family acquaintance identified it as a nervous condition.

One day, Len demonstrated another admirable quality. A serious crash occurred on the "L" at the Granville Avenue station. From our kitchen window, I saw a passenger on the platform shriek in alarm, fist clenched to her face. She had witnessed the crushing impact of the steel trains. Len became a first responder and dashed upstairs to help the injured passengers. I proudly shared his photo, and the account of his gallant deed, published in the *Chicago Daily News*.

In a serious incident at home, Mom threatened to take her own life. Her burdens catapulted in a desperate frustrating moment. Screeching, she threw open the dining room window of our third-floor apartment, which led to a cement courtyard below. She seemed ready to jump, but Len grabbed and pinned her arms at her waist, holding her firmly. I watched with alarm, not fully comprehending the possible calamitous event. This confirmed, however, what I already knew—my brother Leonard was a hero!

In high school, Len joined the chorus and participated in the school production of *The Mikado*. At home, dressed in his colorful costume, he teasingly bolted from our hallway and scared me. I giggled—I loved the costume, I loved the surprise, I loved the excitement, *I loved Leonard*. I suddenly became more fully aware of my brother's extraordinary qualities. They plumbed my heart. Up to then, I hadn't been ready to admit the growing love I felt for my oldest brother.

In Len's late teenage years, his thick hair started to thin considerably. A barber advised that shaving his head would return his hair to its fullness. This recommendation brought Len to another major decision.

He ran away from home to avoid the shame of looking like a convict, he explained of his abrupt departure. I suspected he was also escaping too many family responsibilities for a twenty-year old. His ultimate destination was the 1939 New York World's Fair.

Len hitchhiked across the country with very little money, planning to stay at farms, laboring for meals, and bunking in barns. His first meal was an extravagant lunch provided by Mom who was unaware of his adventurous plans. "Pack me a big one, Mom. I'm going on a very long all-day hike," he explained. Afterward, Evelyn found his note:

I'm going to visit the N.Y. Fair for a few weeks. Don't worry, I'll write and be okay.

His trip taught me that courageous challenges can bring broad adventures and unexpected friendships.

Instead of an "all's going well" letter came a startling piece of mail. An ominous package arrived one day—Len's wallet with no message, sent by a conscientious stranger. Our upset was volcanic. As usual, I became nauseous, contemplating what had happened to Len, not daring to imagine the misfortunes of his impetuous travels.

When he finally returned home safely, he confirmed his risky day-to-day existence. "I often snatched some sleep in an unlocked car, parked on any New York City street." He explained further, "My wallet had fallen from my pocket as I jumped out of the car when the owner suddenly returned."

We heard more of Len's adventures from personal contacts with an Ohio farm family he had befriended, working there for room and board. The Lindquists invited Mom to visit, wanting to meet the woman who had raised such a remarkable young man. Mom took me along, too.

The Lindquists told us that they had been surprised an itinerant hitchhiker could possess such fine character. They reported further, "At first we were fearful when seeing his shaved head after your son removed his protective beanie. We thought we may have innocently housed an escaped convict."

They revealed also that Len had landed in jail for vagrancy after riding the rails with hobos. Len reported to the Lindquists, "When I asked for my toothbrush, the prison guard replied sarcastically, 'What do you think this is, a hotel?'"

Returning home, Len stopped in Ohio again, to reunite with the family with whom he had earned sustenance, friendship, and mutual respect. For me, his experiences confirmed, *There's excitement in that big world out there.*

WHEN *LIFE* MAGAZINE WAS INTRODUCED IN 1939, I sensed it was a special event. The ten cents it cost presented a challenge but I was determined to buy the first edition. To gather the funds, I approached my two brothers, first the one more relaxed about money. "Les, have you heard about the new magazine coming out on the newsstands? If you and me each chip in three cents, maybe we can convince Len to pay the larger four-cent share."

After Les readily agreed, I hesitated approaching Len, who had adopted Dad's frugal money habits. I introduced the subject carefully. Adopting my 'cheer-leader' manner, breathing hard, I said,

"Len, the magazine's going to be exciting, something brand new, and we shouldn't miss it!" Next came my diplomatic approach, smiling broadly: "As our responsible oldest brother, would you mind chipping in the larger four-cent portion?" I anxiously awaited his answer.

Leonard deliberated quite a while, face tilted toward the ceiling, his hand resting on his jaw, lost in thought. *Is he going to be a tightwad with money, like Dad?* I silently wondered. His good heart came through, and we three enjoyed this shared introduction into a new era of magazine publication.

His adventurous spirit continued as he learned to drive and explored interesting Chicago sites. He visited picturesque restaurants whose descriptions enchanted me. Len vividly spelled out their unique qualities during supper table conversations—the Ivanhoe Restaurant, with its mysterious medieval basement catacombs; and the Prow, with a majestic over-sized carved hull extending fully across the sidewalk to the street. These unusual attractions whetted my appetite to explore other unknowns out there.

Len's love of music also supported my own as he attended the Chicago Symphony Orchestra concerts at Orchestra Hall for fifty cents in the balcony. He described a concert he particularly enjoyed:

"After the third encore, the conductor dismissed the crowd. 'Now you can all go out to the nightclubs.'" Len charmed us as he mimicked the conductor's heavy German accent.

His stories spurred my imagination. My insecurity about the larger world sometimes made these activities feel unattainable, as if I might be learning about them from some impersonal movie newsreel. Yet Len was like an ideal father, sparking my interest in what life had to offer. He gave me hope that similar adventures could come my way someday.

I left for the University of Illinois in 1947 at age twenty-one, after completing two years at Wright Junior College. Len was twenty-eight as he drove me to Champaign-Urbana in the family car. We were alone for the five-hour drive, both of us remaining totally silent. Even easygoing small talk was beyond us. Our tension seemed to harbor an unspoken fear, a dam of feelings not safely broached. Neither of us could initiate conversation.

There was a lot to say, but I could say nothing. My heart was full, but my voice was disconnected. I sat in suspense with Len, drawing a blank, enacting a familiar family pattern of maintaining the unsaid. I felt frozen.

During that lengthy drive, I wished we had the ability to discuss our mutual feelings, both past and present. *What had been wrong with our relationship? Was there secret admiration we couldn't admit to one another? Would past antagonisms continue, or perhaps be resolved? What were our hopes for our lives as brother and sister?*

I felt helpless, squelched. Threads were left untouched, tangled, unwoven and dangling. An opportunity was lost, never to be recovered.

I LATER OBSERVED WITH HEAVY HEART the sad voyage Len navigated in his marriage to Florence. They first met at work—he an accountant, she a secretary. On their first date, he took her to the opera *Samson and Delilah*. She was impressed with his fine taste. After several months of dating, Leonard became aware of the intense attachment between Florence and her father. He was terminally ill with cancer, and as he lay dying, he evoked a vow from Leonard.

"Promise me you'll always take care of Florence." As loyalty was Len's second nature, he readily agreed.

When they became engaged, Len discovered Florence was a conspicuous consumer. In shopping for the ring, Florence rejected his financial guidelines. With a sigh of resolve, Len reported her disconten: "That diamond is much smaller than what I had in mind." He went along, as only the first episode in a long series of capitulating to her. Len compulsively attempted to please Florence, no matter what the demand. I noticed with heavy heart that my brother was moving toward becoming henpecked, but I said nothing.

This pattern became cemented in a tragic admission the night before their marriage. Len and I were alone in our family apartment, and as if a condemned man, he muttered with resignation, "Well, I'm going through with it."

I was speechless, immobilized, unable to suggest he reconsider his decision. Our unshared, unspoken years blocked my ability to offer help. *The silence in the room resembled the lull after a gigantic explosion, the debris settling in place.*

During their marriage, Len and Flo adopted a son Jay, and two daughters, Robin and Diane. Jay suffered a serious injury and had to be institutionalized at an early age. Both daughters' needs were sacrificed to those of his wife. Len remained constant to Flo as their daughters suffered. I believe his loyalty blinded him to the pain he was inflicting on his children. Len's treatment of them, an otherwise kind man, was deeply tragic.

I OFTEN QUESTIONED HOW LEN REMAINED SO LOYAL to Florence, enduring until almost his eighty-fourth birthday. As a CPA with his own successful business, Len had become a workaholic, minimizing time with his wife. Robin suggested, "He was so beloved by friends and associates that it enabled him to tolerate his shallow marriage." Len was greatly admired for his generosity, good spirits, and kindness by everyone who knew him.

Len and I had never discussed his flawed marriage, but I always felt he deserved far better. His daughters clearly did as well.

We continued on our parallel paths during our marriages, never emotionally touching one another. They resembled railroad tracks stretching far into the future but never meeting. Our early checkered years sealed our fate. We had limited contact, as my husband and I lived in distant cities. Our visits to Chicago never included any socializing; Flo seemed unable to work out a convenient schedule. Though I always sent Len and Flo cards for their birthdays and anniversary, Len and I never managed a cozy get together as adults.

Florence had difficulty accepting the lovingness that Leonard and the children felt for our mother. Len encouraged his daughters' connection to Grandma Evelyn, whom they adored. He secretly took them to her apartment for Sunday breakfast on the pretext of their accompanying him to his CPA office. When the couple vacationed, Evelyn always served as babysitter. Diane described welcoming her parents' absences, eager for Grandma's devoted care. It was during vacationing in Florida that Len had the freedom to arrange for his piano lessons.

LEONARD WAS ENCOURAGED BY LESTER to attend my Honoring Dinner at the Ethical Society. Len was a stranger to this fundamental part of my life. During the tributes, he took his turn at the podium, his voice stammering with emotion:

"After hearing all the glowing accolades for my sister, I-I-I-I love her even more." I was deeply moved by Len's comments but never acknowledged his impassioned admission. I deeply regret I never ventured across that gulf to express our hidden love. We behaved as mere acquaintances.

We three siblings arranged annual family reunions that Len attended, usually without Florence. In a significant incident between Len and me during the gathering at Diane's marital home, I casually raised a question with family members: "Was it really a good idea for my father to have taken me from Tante Surrel's home? Maybe it would have been better staying with her family."

Overhearing my remarks, Len rushed across the wide backyard to our picnic table. He asserted, short of pounding the table, "Dad *always* emphasized that, someday, we three kids would be reunited in the same home. Our growing up together wasn't a chance arrangement but happened because of his determined goal!"

Len's impassioned outpouring demonstrated his appreciation for whatever family togetherness we achieved. His late-life letter showed he anticipated the pleasure of my becoming his full-time sister.

I no longer question my father's decision. It was sound and wise, granting me two fine brothers. Despite our problem relationship, Leonard provided me with significant experiences for living and learning. Ultimately, though, we were both responsible for our problematic relationship.

After Len's eighty-third birthday, I wrote a long poem, paying tribute to his stellar qualities, which he never acknowledged. Len didn't live to celebrate his eighty-fourth birthday. After his death, with belated tenderness, I wrote a shorter poem, highlighting our shared memories which reflected my lingering remorse (see appendix). He never acknowledged the longer poem, which I read at his memorial service to assembled family and friends.

Len expressed devotion to me in a final monetary bequest. I was moved by his generosity, a delayed recognition of his feelings for me. His modest contribution to my daughters, Janet and Wendy, with whom he had minimal contact, perhaps represented a further acknowledgment.

Throughout their family life, Len's daughters have both labored mightily, through many hardships, to overcome the effects of their father supporting his wife's demands over their needs. Robin's strengths have brought a fine marriage, a sound family life, and further enrichment through her considerable musical talents. Diane sadly died prematurely of natural causes in 2015 in her Wilmington, Illinois, home.

Diane's death has left me with sadness but sweet cherished memories of our cooking together. During my last visit to her Wilmington home, we celebrated our love of Evelyn as we prepared her succulent cabbage borscht.

I visited with her son Aaron and daughter, Sandye, who kindly drove us to the memorable 6166 North Winthrop Avenue in Chicago, where I had spent my childhood years of growing up with my two fine brothers, Leonard and Lester.

MY LIFE WITH YOUNGER BROTHER LESTER

LES WAS SEVEN YEARS OLD, AND I WAS FOUR, when I joined the re-united family. My upset was enormous, but Les' fun-loving nature made a big difference. He smoothed my painful change.

Visitors to my new family would ask, "Doesn't she ever speak or smile?"

My depression lifted as Les, resembling an elf, with a slender body topped with blond silky hair, became my roguish companion. As we rolled together on the floor under the dining room table, Les poked and tickled me gently in the ribs. I giggled with pleasure— "I got you, Sis!" he laughed, reaching my midriff.

During mealtime, he shot rubber bands at me. Mother, scolded, but not too seriously, "C'mon, Les, that's not proper dinner table behavior." We rascals would smirk, ignoring the grown-up. My sheer pleasure dulled the sting of the rubber bands.

Lester was a natural athlete but an indifferent student. His mischie-vousness in school required many mother–teacher conferences. Low grades resulted from his inattention to studies—A's and P's (Average and Poor). I thought, *My younger brother just isn't smart*. Even our kindly mother joked, "He owns the A & P supermarket." I later discovered Les was very intelligent, but that it was overshadowed by his acting up. He earned the reputation of being a "Peck's Bad Boy."

Of us three, Les had the most difficulty growing up. Our brother Len was bringing home above-average grades. Lester's dilemma: How do you carve out a niche for yourself, a slightly-built boy, compared to a hefty older brother earning top grades, who does almost everything right? I excelled in school too, as my love of learning replaced several lost mothers.

Despite his lightheartedness, Les had frequent temper tantrums. He pounded his feet on the wooden floor, bellowing his distress. The shouting stopped when Mom took off his shoes, making it painful to beat the floor with only stocking feet. I regret I never asked Les the reason for his anger—now it's much too late, for a person with fading memory.

No one ever asked why he was angry. The family never looked for answers to troubling behavior. I suspect part of his distress was a delayed reaction to the death of our birth mother.

LESTER'S EARLIEST ATHLETIC INTERESTS centered on organizing relay races for the neighborhood kids. My taking part was questionable, as I was small and slow. When choosing sides, Les singled out a top runner and said, "Freddy, please pick my sister for your team. Your great speed will more than make up for her handicap." I loved that he understood my need to fit in with the group.

At Christmas when I was six years old, he bought me a present, paid for with chore money. I saw Les sneak a package into the apartment, giving me sidelong glances as he hid it in the bedroom. I was impatient and tore open the gift when he was away, a soft nightgown. Les knew I enjoyed marking the holiday despite our being a Jewish family.

He introduced baseball and touch football to the family, excelling in both. Leonard tried following Les' lead but lacked his brother's athletic abilities. The most Len could do was fastidiously oil his new baseball glove, but he didn't use it much.

BECOMING BETTY

I REMEMBER WHEN LESTER GOT HIS FIRST SPECIAL-OCCASION JACKET, perhaps for his bar mitzvah. My father had given up Sunday, his only day of rest, to take Les to Chicago's Maxwell Street to shop. This neighborhood offered bargains that could be negotiated with street peddlers and shopkeepers possessing sharp eyes and crafty ways.

We were all excited when they arrived home with a handsome beige jacket, square cut as was the style back then. I noticed the fabric was somewhat coarse, not like the fine woolens and gabardines available in department stores. I beamed with joy as Les stood in front of the mirror in my father's shop, admiring his purchase. The square cut rounded out his slender physique, and he looked handsome indeed. As Les turned this way and that in front of the mirror, he noticed the label still sewed onto the back of the jacket. He reached his hand around and gave it a sharp tug. *Off came the tag, with a large piece of the fabric still attached to it.*

The room exploded with anguish, shrieks, and cries. My father's voice boomed to the ceiling and out the door, barely drowned out by the roaring of the passing elevated trains on the tracks above. Les, stunned by what he had done, could only stomp his feet and hit his forehead repeatedly with the heel of his hand.

I stood mute, nauseous with despair for Les and his damaged jacket. How could my father be so angry at Les in his great distress? I hated my father at that moment and bolted from the shop.

I ran to our apartment around the corner, threw myself on the bed, and cried hysterically for several hours. So many years of pain and anger flooded out. Hardly anyone really understood Lester—or me either. His pain was glossed over. No one ever spoke to me seriously about my ideas or feelings—or told me I had a mother who had died. I knew this only from piecing together scraps of information and whispers from corners.

Lester and I both recovered from that mishap. Dad used his tailoring skills to repair the damaged jacket, and Les went on to many accomplishments. I came to later understand my father's goodness despite his frightening temper. In those Depression days, his ability to provide adequate food, shelter and clothing was a major achievement for a parent with no education who wanted a better life for his children.

We all went to college, a privilege that few of our cousins enjoyed. The neglect and self-pity I felt were made up, in part, by my father's generous deeds. He taught us, by example, the dignity of work, not to fear the efforts required to achieve a worthwhile goal.

IN HIGH SCHOOL, WHEN LESTER PURSUED his athletic interests, he wanted to join the football team. Mom refused permission. "Les, your build is too slight for that rough sport." He ran track instead, and I admired Lester's resilience as he thrived with an alternate path. After injuring his leg on the track team, Les was promoted to Track Team Manager, which he continued in successfully all through high school, exhibiting new confidence. Our family experienced many challenges and setbacks but rarely acknowledged individual accomplishments. Affirming one another's best qualities was as foreign as the countries from which our parents emigrated. I'm certain this neglect contributed to my later becoming a psychotherapist, where I guide clients to become aware of their attributes.

When it came to musical education, Les learned classical music mostly on his own after quitting lessons midstream. There were saxophone lessons for Leonard and piano for me, but Les was far more talented than either of us. As I listened to him playing the piano, I thought, *Les' music flows naturally, while Len and I plod along.* With support, Mom asked, "Les, play 'Für Elyse' once more. It rolls off your fingers so beautifully." Hearing that selection today still affects me. I felt a loss when he stopped playing the apartment keyboard in later years at his senior facility.

IN THE 1950s, WHEN LES WAS IN HIS THIRTIES, he became a devoted jogger. He ran on local streets for many years before it became popular.

Neighbors would ridicule him. "Who's that crazy guy in shorts running down the street?" These comments irritated me, but I had faith that Les was on to something important. He enjoyed a good physique until age ninety-one, though he became hunched over when he started using a walker. Les' daily gym workouts became his new passion, replacing his jogging. Both activities apparently contributed to a delay of his deterioration.

Lester was drafted during World War II. Mom and I were dismayed. Another family member would be leaving for the war, Leonard having preceded him into service. Les survived the war with sheer guts and quite a gamble. He was initially assigned to a machine gun battalion but later requested a transfer to the infantry. He explained, "My top sergeant was so stupid. I felt I would never survive this war in one piece if I didn't get out from under his command." He was granted his request just before going overseas into combat. I was astonished at Lester's guts, shifting to a military branch even more dangerous than artillery.

Mom suffered much anguish about his army service. One quiet evening at home together, she dozed off and had a nightmare. She woke up with a start, threw up her arms and shouted, "Les! *Jump!*"

A few weeks after the infamous Battle of the Bulge, Lester injured his leg. While recuperating, he requested the Red Cross transfer him to the Army hospital in Liege, Belgium, where Len was serving as a clerk. Mom *kvelled* (marveled), "Sis, isn't it great that Len and Les will be together." *My two brothers were miraculously reunited on foreign soil in the midst of massive wartime action.* We rejoiced at their reunion and relieved they were both free from combat.

Leonard was excited with Lester's arrival at his Army hospital. To welcome him, he asked the cook to bake a chocolate cake. Thirty years later, Les still chuckled as he described the scene:

I was so happy arriving at Len's hospital, to find a bed with clean, crisp sheets, a great relief from sleeping for months in muddy foxholes. Just as I was ready to nestle in for a nap, Len shows up, triumphant, pre-

senting the cake held high on a platter. I was exhausted and waved him away with a sweep of my hand, exclaiming 'tomorrow.' By now, that expression in the popular song from the Broadway musical *Annie* had become well-known, adding more verve to Les' story.

I treasured the photo of their reunion, since lost but still imprinted in my memory—Les with a wan face, and wide-grinning Leonard. The photo had been featured in our local *Chicago Sun-Times.*

Later in the war, when our country dropped the atomic bombs on Hiroshima and Nagasaki, I was outraged by these horrific weapons. I fired off a protest V-mail (compact wartime airmail) to Lester. My angry letter had arrived prematurely, before my earlier folksy one. Lester was furious and scolded me, "How can you send wartime opinions when I miss hearing news from home?"

My ideals of non-violence had overlooked my brother's feelings. He was still facing combat hazards. I didn't realize that dropping these bombs would end World War II sooner, sparing countless American and Japanese lives. Even though I accepted war to protect our democracy, my deeper sense had responded to the catastrophe of atomic bombs. I was already incubating my ideas of peace.

On the day Lester returned home from the Army, I was jubilant and phoned from my office job. "Les, welcome home! Please do me a favor. Keep your army uniform on until I get home. I'd like to have one last look in your dress khakis."

Lester had other ideas. By the time I returned home, he was wearing his 'civvies,' the uniform packed away, never to be seen again. I kept my disappointment to myself; it was time he put his ordeal to rest.

Les rebuilt his civilian life by attending college on the GI Bill at Northwestern University, commuting from home. It was wonderful having him with us again, but now he was more serious. Wartime service had knocked something out of him. We rarely shared humor or fun activities anymore.

After Les completed his BA degree in Journalism, he got a coveted editor's job at *Esquire* magazine in Chicago. Using his creative talents, he enjoyed great success in his first job out of military service.

Our post-war family composition changed dramatically. Leonard and I each married and left home. Lester was the only sibling still living with our parents. He suddenly quit *Esquire* for a move to California. I asked, "Les, why are you leaving such a good job?"

He explained, "I started remembering the beauty of southern California when I was stationed there during my wartime basic training. It just drew me."

I believe there were other reasons, but our family always avoided discussing serious matters. We didn't express curiosity or trust someone could contribute good ideas.

My contacts with Les initially dwindled when he moved to California, though the bond between my two brothers remained close. They often phoned each other about their shared interest in sports, reviewing players' successes and scores of their favorite teams.

In California, Les unfortunately had many employment disappointments. His appliance store ownership failed, as did several real estate jobs. At the synagogue, though, Les met a terrific woman, Ruth, with whom he quickly became serious. His sports activities continued to be very important. After they set the date for their marriage, the playoffs of his winning bowling team conflicted with their wedding day, requiring postponing their nuptials. Ruth was a good sport about the delay, as were our parents, who had traveled from Chicago for the occasion.

Ruth shared a wedding night incident. "Lester was ever the jokester. Standing at the head of the bed, he enacted a phantom hand threatening him by grabbing his neck. His look of mock terror broke me up in laughter."

Ruth had reawakened Les' humor, which became an important part of their lives. They both contributed frivolity to the amateur shows at their Mission Viejo community. In my occasional visits, I recall the witty jingles Ruth had written. At one of their programs, I was highly amused when Les performed as a ballerina, outfitted in a flaring tutu, bold-colored stockings, and one of Ruth's curly blond wigs.

THEIR FIRST CHILD, SUSAN, WAS BORN WITH DOWN SYNDROME. I was disturbed by Les' phone call. "Our beautiful blond infant has some kind of handicap." Doctors advised them to have another child soon, and Roy was born two years later.

With their deeply loving nature, Ruth and Les lavished Susan with devotion and enriched activities. Lester's warmth surrounded her with his typical capricious good-natured teasing and tickling. This was similar to his fun ways with me when I entered the family as a forlorn child many years earlier. His gentle humor with Susan, combined with Ruth's ideas of enrichment, contributed to her becoming independent.

Susan played the piano, participated in a bowling league, and earned money working at a special-needs workshop. She developed wit as well. In a phone conversation with Lester, when he asked, "Who's this on the phone?" she responded,

"Anonymous!"

With all this focus on Susan, I noticed Roy's needs were sometimes downplayed. Her condition seemed to capture their almost undivided attention.

Susan died at age fifty after she developed Alzheimer's disease. Lester suffered a stroke the very next day, grief-stricken over her death. His lively spirit, playfulness and memory diminished significantly after she died.

Lester had achieved outstanding recognition in his career before Susan's death. He had become a real estate icon, triumphing in the booming Southern California market.

As an executive, his innovations established home real estate marketing as a profession, with courses offered at several California universities. Eventually, Lester was inducted into the California Homebuilders Association Hall of Fame in recognition of his novel ideas and accomplishments. They included his arranging for Boy Scouts to direct heavy traffic on popular Open House weekends. His success put him in demand, often making it difficult to reach him on the phone. By this time, we had tried to remain in regular contact.

"Les, I've called you three times this week without success. Where the heck are you all the time?"

As a polished raconteur, Les lectured often, in places as distant as Australia. He became well-known for his success which had eluded him in his early California years. Now he enjoyed financial comfort and many professional friends. For his sevetieth birthday, his colleagues arranged a surprise luncheon to celebrate his achievements.

I kvell *that our parents—simple immigrants with only devotion, unflinching goals, and an undiminished work ethic—could nurture their sons to impressive accomplishments.* Leonard was also successful, earning a master's degree in accounting and establishing his own CPA business.

Lester traveled to New Jersey many times to celebrate highlights in my life. In 1983, he joined me in giving away the bride when Janet, my oldest daughter, married her fiancé Marty. Howard, her father, was in deteriorating health, which required a wheelchair, and didn't want to come down the aisle for the ceremony. As an alternative, I suggested Lester, who was very pleased to fill that role.

Before the ceremony, there had been an interlude of face-painting and other frivolities arranged by Janet's father. Lester took charge at the reception as master of ceremonies and announced, "That's enough play. Now for family," as he introduced the bride's uncle, Sid. "He will offer the *broucha* (blessing) and cut the *challah* for all of us to enjoy." Roy, my nephew, had unexpectedly returned from his European travels and joined us for the wedding festivities. We were all immensely pleased.

Three years later, when I was sixty years old, Les traveled east again to attend my Honoring Dinner at the Ethical Culture Society, which had become my spiritual home. Les convinced our older brother, Leonard, to attend, a rare occurrence.

After tributes by both brothers, Les presented one of his perform-ances. He introduced an audience-participation ditty consisting of a sim-ple melody. "You push the damper in. . ." sung by the audience with accompanying pantomime motions and hilarity. Les often provided com-edy relief, bringing laughter wherever he went.

Les celebrated Ruth's seventieth birthday with a *This Is Your Life* surprise party. Among the features was the attendance of her Bronx girl-friend from their earlier years whom Les had located. Les also designed a handsome tee shirt for Ruth, *This Is What 70 Looks Like*, that she wore the next day at the brunch for out-of-towners.

For my seventieth birthday, Les celebrated with me in New Jersey. Ted, my boyfriend, and I, had arranged a Saturday evening celebration for the occasion. Unknown to me, Les planned a surprise appearance and would fly from California the day before the festivities.

I was en route to Newark Airport on late Friday afternoon, to meet my daughter, Wendy, from Albany, who also planned to attend, when an unexpected violent snowstorm swept in. Blinded by the snow, inching along, I was relieved when I noticed a driveway that offered an escape from the storm. I found myself at a Marriott Courtyard Motel. Wendy had somehow managed to get there also and we both stayed overnight.

When I walked into the dining room for breakfast the next morning, I was shocked. Lester was standing there—staying at the same motel! His unexpected appearance brought momentary outrage; short of fixing my hands stridently on my hips, I exclaimed, "You came all the way to New Jersey and didn't even call me!"

Les could manage only a sharp heel-of-the-hand slap to his forehead with a disgusted grimace. We both recovered, threw our arms around each other in a warm embrace, with awkward explanations and many kisses.

For the past eighteen years, we have continued to celebrate my birth-day in annual reunions. I have traveled to Les' Mission Viejo home and later to his various senior facilities.

BECOMING BETTY

WHEN I ARRIVED IN 2013 AT HIS FREEDOM VILLAGE retirement community, I found Les waiting impatiently for me, standing outside the building's front door. We exchanged hugs and kisses, a year's accumulation of unexpressed affection. At lunchtime, we went off together like carefree playmates. We enjoyed corned beef sandwiches at our favorite delicatessen, Kosher Bite, though he got lost driving there. We smiled often at one another, recapturing the cloak of endearment.

On New Year's Day, 2014, Ruth, now ninety-four years old, phoned to report good news about the holiday. "I want to share how we spent our delightful New Year's Eve. You've called so many times with cheerful messages. Now I want to reciprocate." She continued, "Our facility had arranged a special celebration with better food than usual, even including lobster." Her description sparkled. "An entertainer brought his keyboard and played dance music. Nothing much was happening on the dance floor. Then there was Les and me. He was his former self, full of rhythm, dancing to the music, making his amusing faces as he kept up the beat." Ruth's tone changed. "He was a bit annoyed with me. I nixed his throwing me out with our usual flair. I couldn't risk a fall since it's only a year that I'm out of the wheelchair. We sure had fun, though, dancing to 'Mack the Knife' and some rumba tunes."

I responded, "You've been outstanding dance partners all your married lives. How delicious you enjoyed last night so much."

I was gratified that Les' love of dancing had helped him relive his old self, if only briefly. He had overcome memory problems by tapping into his musical passions.

Les and Ruth have been married for over sixty-two years. At ninety-five, she has cared for him with loyalty and devotion, even as his memory continues to fade.

For Ruth's most recent birthday, I decided to mark it somewhat differently. I had heard that the White House traditionally sends birthday greetings to citizens who have become a hundred years old. This custom sparked an idea: I created a cardboard plaque, citing Ruth's birthday in flowery language, with personal congratulations and a photo of President Obama: His message: *It's not necessary that you wait a hundred years to receive the congratulations you deserve.*

In the lower left corner, lacking an official medallion, I placed an elaborate paper bow to make it appear authentic. Ruth seemed genuinely delighted with her ninety-fifth birthday memento. I was equally pleased to create her congratulatory message.

October 2014 brought a serious new development. Roy phoned from California that his father had developed an aggressive cancer with no treatment practical at his ninety-one years of age. His son had made repeated visits from his Tucson home to participate in medical decisions for his father and support his mother.

The good news was that Les was free of any pain, the cancer showing only in clinical reports. He was able to continue enjoying his Saturday evening bridge group, with his caregiver, Luz, accompanying him. Roy recommended, "I think you should plan a visit with my Dad much sooner than your February birthday. An earlier visit could offer some quality before the cancer takes over."

I made plans for an early December visit and felt connected to Les by recalling our sweet memories for this memoir. I phoned Ruth about my plans, including recalling my childhood playing Honeymoon Bridge, which had filled my loneliness. When I suggested I'd teach it to Les, she became enthusiastic and said she'd like to learn, too. Shifting to a more serious mood, I asked Ruth how she was dealing with his illness.

"The alarming clinical reports concern me a lot. I wonder what the future holds for both of us."

My heart plummeted. "Is there *anything* I can do to lessen your burden?"

"Just that you're coming and involving him in activities will help a lot."

I accelerated my plans again and arranged to visit Les in early November. I arrived in California ten days before Thanksgiving, to check the state of his illness and share what could possibly become my final visit with him. As I packed, along with clothing suitable for a funeral, I tossed in a swimsuit.

Upon arrival at Les' apartment, I was jolted by his deterioration. He was slouched in his recliner chair, head leaning on his chest, eyes half closed, attention only on the TV. That is, until I made a grand entrance and greeted him with triumphant, "Les, I came to California to see you. And I want a big hug and kiss!"

He perked up immediately, laboriously stood up from the recliner, and placed his arms about me to kiss my cheek. He managed a meek smile, but his glistening eyes were more embracing. Les' halting speech could manage only a muted, "Hi."

Luz alerted me to Les' interest in the Mills Brothers' recordings that Roy had selected from their music collection. We played the songs repeatedly, including "I've Got a Paper Doll to Call My Own."

Les became more responsive when I suggested, "Les, let's dance together. We three, you, me, and your walker." And so we did, after a fashion. The momentary physical closeness matching the rhythm made it feel like old times. We continued, clapping our hands and wiggling our fannies.

I reviewed with Les some of our past light moments, reminding him of the fun ditty he had introduced at parties, "I put the damper in. . . ." He corrected me when I cut short one line. I was pleased he remembered so well. Yes, past musical joys can truly overcome memory problems. Another personal touch—I fastened one of my Peace Alliance pins to his shirt and gave Ruth a matching one.

Luz told me of the Wednesday afternoon socials, featuring spirited music, which she felt both Lester and I would enjoy. As Les didn't feel able to attend, I went alone and found Luz was right. The music *was* uplifting, with many couples doing their thing on the dance floor. When the line dancing started, I leapt from my seat. A table companion questioned, "You know the steps?"

"Not really, but I can wing it." This was especially true when the popular "New York, New York" blasted out. The two glasses of wine I had guzzled assured my lively participation. I hope I didn't look too foolish. In his better days, I think Les would have approved.

My three days focused on our sharing intermittent musical pleasures, even as Les ate little and dozed much. The hospice nurse confirmed that this rapid decline was to be expected with his advanced cancer.

Recalling Kubler-Ross' wise words for difficult circumstances, "Grow in the experience that is yours," unleashed an idea. I sensed, in the past, Les may have felt stuck in his older brother's shadow. I grabbed the opportunity to compare the quality of their marriages. I gently murmured, "Remember the carefree dancing with Ruth all during your marriage? Another constant delight for you both has been sharing a life of humor— well beyond anything that Len had the pleasure of experiencing." Les grinned slightly as he nodded, apparently acknowledging the contrast.

When it became evident I couldn't add any more, I said my final goodbyes, kissing Lester's cheeks and wrists, holding back my tears. I left distraught but in control.

Within a day of my return to New Jersey, Roy phoned me that Les was failing fast. For the planned funeral, Roy advised, "Plan to return to California immediately after Thanksgiving."

Three days before my planned return, Lester died. This became the ultimate truth, which I had to accept.

Several years earlier, when I imagined Les possibly dying before I did, leaving me the only surviving sibling, again an orphan, I was terrified. Now I feel secure—anchored, confident and resilient, able to face the future. Losing Lester has brought deep sadness and tears as I recall what a beautiful person he had become and the cherished times we shared.

Roy then came up with a comforting idea. He suggested we host a celebration of Lester's life for family and friends, planned for the weekend of the Martin Luther King holiday. His plan lifted my spirits immensely.

Then, a new development—Ruth became ill with bronchitis, which made the funeral date uncertain. I decided to bypass the funeral, particularly when Roy assured me, "We'll visit Lester's burial site together when you return for his life celebration."

My sadness lifted as I looked forward to Les' celebration. There I could openly and proudly share treasured memories of why I love my brother Lester so much.

Roy's compassionate idea, to celebrate Lester's life, gave me great solace. I'm very proud of my nephew Roy's new role as the patriarch of our family, competently replacing his father—generous, noble, valiant. This swells my heart. I believe his strength represents forgiveness, overcoming any shortcomings of childhood years.

I FEEL DEEP GRATITUDE TO RUTH despite our different perspectives. She has always been there for Les, her lifelong mate, bringing him the understanding and good humor he has needed and deserved.

I appreciate my good fortune to have shared many loving years with my brother Lester. My gratitude is huge that Les and I openly expressed our caring for one another throughout our lives, very differently from the guarded relationship I had with my older brother. How fortuitous that this "Peck's Bad Boy" of childhood years overcame many obstacles to enjoy success in both his marriage and profession.

After Lester died, I discussed, with the hospice nurse, his last day. "After you left, his decline became abrupt." She then added, "I believe your visit helped him let go and brought the closure he needed." Our final visit together apparently brought him a measure of peace. For myself, as well.

After Roy, his wife Susie, and I visited Les' burial site near Laguna Beach to bid a final goodbye, we meandered to the town waterfront. We waded and frolicked in the water, similar to the play Les and I had enjoyed as children at the Granville Avenue beach. I think Les would have liked knowing that.

GRADE SCHOOL AND GROWING UP

I DREADED LEAVING MY MOTHER for school each day, a long separation, fearful of losing another mother. Each morning, my churning stomach erupted violently, vomiting the residue of my meager breakfast. Evelyn held my forehead tightly as the mess exploded into the toilet. Sometimes it splattered onto the pretty dress she had sewed with her *goldene* hands. Evelyn sponge-bathed my body, but nothing could sanitize my shame for these upheavals.

I clutched Mom's hand as we walked to Hayt Elementary School, a cement-and brick-building with separate entrances for girls and boys. We arrived at the classroom outrageously tardy. The children were sitting neatly in rows, like birds on a utility wire, busy with their tasks.

Almost as one, they shifted their heads, eyes wide with disapproval at my impudence for arriving late. As mother whispered explanations to the teacher, I quickly tried to meld into the classroom. This awkward situation identified me as the odd kid out.

In today's climate, this repeated situation would have probably brought a referral to a Child Study Team. In 1932, children with problems didn't seem to be identified for professional consultations. Back then, the usual recourse was a mother–teacher conference. I don't believe that ever happened in my situation.

Eventually, I settled into the routine at school. Teachers became a comfort, not fussing over me. I eagerly learned what teachers offered and appreciated that they never seemed concerned about my finishing my milk at recess time. I loved them all. They opened a new view of the world for me.

Reading became my passport to pleasure and growth. Books served as medication that soothed my digestive system. They also stretched my imagination to wide shores. Teachers let me just *be*. I found my own way, creating notebooks and drawing colorful illustrations of the countries we were studying.

As my stomach settled down, I started walking to school alone. One day, I noticed Elaine, a schoolmate who used the same daily route. I caught up with her. "Can I walk with you? She may have said, "Yes" but I didn't wait for the acceptance I needed. I pulled up alongside her, imagining we were good friends. I trekked the distance to Hayt with her. I looked for Elaine every day to share our walk and decided we were buddies, though we had minimal conversation.

One day I found Elaine with a group of playmates, discussing an after-school party she was planning. As I joined the group, I overheard her embarrassed regrets: "I just can't invite everyone. Mom is limiting me because of money and living room space."

I wanted to comfort her and said, with a glimmer of insight, "Those not invited will just have to understand. Gatherings can't always include everyone."

Within several days, I realized I was one of those excluded and felt the sting of rejection. I finally accepted that Elaine wasn't a good friend and comforted myself that someday I would have a real best friend just like other girls.

My isolation continued through elementary school and I thought, *Someday I'd like to become a counselor for kids*, a role I had heard helped grown-ups. It seemed the smelly girl who arrived at school daily reeking of stale urine, which kept us at a distance, could also profit from this idea. I felt dismay that other children ridiculed her, in a sing-song voice, "*Miss Suzie, way over the ocean, stay oceans away, away, away from me.*"

I hung back from this deprecating behavior, which only added to my being different. I was relieved that her mother was called into school one day, but surprised by her being fashionably dressed, with makeup beautifully applied. I wondered, *How could such a difference happen between a mother and daughter?* I was cheered that maybe this girl would finally get some help.

In the summer, Mother knew my two brothers and I loved swimming at Chicago's Lake Michigan beaches. She lugged a large jug of hand-squeezed lemonade, a huge brown bag of sandwiches, fresh fruit, a beach blanket, towels, and an umbrella. She then gently herded three sweaty children onto a street car, transferring to a bus, which ultimately transported us to the Lake Shore Drive beach. My usually helpful older brother may have also toted the paraphernalia, but I'm not certain. We usually depended on Mother to carry the load. I don't believe we were aware how her determination provided us a supportive childhood.

Beautiful fun-filled beach days could turn miserable when my unpredictable bowels misbehaved. There were no public toilets back then. I felt humiliated as mother knocked on strangers' doors, asking permission to use their bathroom. Encountering this forthright mother with a runt of a child in a damp bathing suit, wiggling in discomfort, often brought their cooperation. My lazy bowels needed to take advantage of this opportunity. The pressure was immense, adding to my discomfort.

Summer Grant Park concerts were a great joy.

"Mom, I saw the Friday night symphony concert listed in the *Sun-Times*. It's a beaut, a Tchaikovsky piece among the other ones. Can you convince Dad to go?" He usually came around to Mom's requests.

On some steamy nights we persuaded dad to drive past the western city limits, to find an ice cream stand for a treat. For Fourth of July fireworks, Mom had to cajole Dad to drive to these outskirts. When Dad was startled by the high prices for firecrackers and Roman candles, he limited us kids to just sparklers.

Good Humor trucks often traveled our local streets. It was clear I was the favorite child when Mom rejoiced that I was *the one* who ended with the "free," imprinted at the end of the stick. This advantage made up for my having to sit in the uncomfortable, steamy middle seat in the back of the car. When the entire family, including all three kids, rode together, there was always tumult about who got stuck there.

Air conditioning, if available at all, was only for the wealthy. Sleeping in our top floor apartment on oppressive nights became almost impossible. Many times, we grabbed blankets and pillows and curled up as a family at a nearby park for the night. These were safe practices in those days.

FIFTH GRADE MARKED A SEISMIC EVENT—I fell in love! Benjamin Blackman played the violin beautifully. His "Flight of the Bumblebee" performance made my heart take flight as well. I'm not certain he noticed me, but I hung on every rhapsodic note that he played.

Ben appeared on a famous young person's radio music show. In the interview he mentioned "Hayt" as his school. The announcer exploited the title by concluding that Benjamin hated school. Ben awkwardly corrected the misinterpretation. I was angered that the announcer had contrived the remark for a cheap chuckle at my dear Benjamin's expense.

His performances were in demand, and my imagination did a loop-de-loop. I fantasized that he loved me also and would achieve great success. The scenario romped on to our marrying some day and on how, with much success and riches, I would be challenged to spend our wealth wisely. I dreamed up the following plan:

I noticed that when immigrants became U.S. citizens, bone fide compatriots of usnatives, their momentous achievement brought only modest celebrations. In contrast, we Americans enjoyed extravagant hoopla when our native baseball teams won the pennant or World Series, which included a ticker-tape parade down Wall Street, Canyon of Heroes. Similarly, welcoming in the New Year in Times Square had become almost a national celebration. I felt newly minted citizens of these United States deserved a triumphant experience as well.

I imagined I would use my Benjamin's wealth to rectify this neglect. I would arrange family celebrations marked with flowers and flags, decorating large amphitheaters to rejoice in their achieving United States citizenship. I mentally chose settings like Chicago's Civic Theater or New York's Madison Square Garden for the special occasion.

Reality departed sharply from this fantasy. Benjamin continued his musical success without even a tip of his bow in my direction. When we graduated from Hayt, the class celebrated with a barbecue at the Granville Avenue beach. I recall Ben making and tending the bonfire where I took a snapshot of him, crouched low, his thick hair flowing in the lake breezes. I cherished that photo for many years, gazing at it regularly. My teenage contact with him ended there.

As a young adult attending a dance some years later, my heart fluttered when I noticed Ben playing violin in the band. I sought him out during intermission.

"Hi, Ben, do you remember me from Hayt Grade School? I'm Betty Goodman." He looked embarrassed, clearly not recalling me. We were both uncomfortable with the awkward encounter. Ben remained silent. My feet, sporting shiny new black pumps, wiggled awkwardly. "I see you're still playing the violin," I ventured.

Ben eventually regained his composure and explained solemnly, "I don't solo anymore but play in dance bands to earn money for college tuition. I want to attend medical school and become a doctor."

I wanted to talk some more. Instead, I thought it better to relieve his discomfort, ending the conversation quickly. I extended my hand with a warm smile. "Good-bye and good luck." He touched my hand lightly and left.

I WAS ELEVEN YEARS OLD WHEN WE MOVED to 6166 North Winthrop Avenue, a third- floor apartment. This change created a new awakening;

for the first time, I had a bedroom of my own! The window faced east, welcoming the sun each morning. To my childish eyes, it was comparable to a window on the world.

I finally got a grown-up bed, placed under the window. First thing each morning, I would raise the shade to say hello to my new-found friend, the morning sun.

In the previous apartment, I had been sleeping on a studio couch in a dark corner of the dining room. In our new location, when the studio couch became infested with bed bugs, the red bumps all over my body had prompted Mom to act fast. She grabbed me. "C'mon, Sis, we're going to Nelson's Furniture Store to get you a new bed." I had noticed Nelson's before and always wondered how simple folks like us could ever afford to buy new furniture. Bless those bed bugs, they brought me a gift.

A great advantage of my bedroom was the adjoining open-air balcony with cement urns on its two corners, perfect for planting flowers. Every spring I bought seeds at the Granville Avenue Woolworth's with a rare dime in my small hand.

I planned a glorious blooming season, but my efforts brought only spindly stalks. Buds never appeared. I laboriously repeated the planting every season with the same disappointing results.

I asked, *What is it don't I know?* I vowed with gritted teeth, *Someday I'm going to find out the secret of growth.* The need for fresh soil and fertilizer had entirely eluded me. This failure opened a new path to more understanding. I became determined to learn the elements of successful nurturing.

IN SIXTH GRADE, I WAS FLATTERED to be singled out by our part-time teacher, Miss Foster, to help create glass slides of nature. In tracing a bird with India ink onto the slide, I had dipped the pen too generously into the ink well, causing a sloppy smear on the glass. Infuriated, Miss Foster grabbed the slide and spit out, "You'll never be creative!"

Inside, I protested vehemently. *I'm more creative than she realizes.*

How much does she know? She's basically a gym teacher, only filling in for art classes. My reassuring thoughts brought me a new sense of confidence. Rejecting a flawed adult required much fortitude.

During the summer lull after sixth grade, we neighborhood kids who loved to read organized a plan for getting to our public library. It was located almost two miles away, just off Devon Avenue. Since none of our mothers could drive a car, six of us agreed, "We could hike the distance. Hey, let's make it a fun time together!"

We played "Follow the Leader," tramping single file through backyards, alleyways, and whatever paths lured us. As we toppled garbage cans that clanged in the quiet of a Saturday morning, spewing pungent debris over tidy walkways, we all laughed at our mischievousness. We were free to create our own recreation.

Gathering every Thursday and Saturday mornings on the street corner at ten a.m., we all clutched the maximum five library books to be exchanged for another five. I read ten books weekly that summer, none of which I remember.

I remained without a best friend all through grade school. I never found a real pal until my freshman year at Senn High School.

In eighth grade, my final year of grade school, I recall May Day, 1940. We were celebrating the occasion in the school yard with the band trumpeting Sousa's "Stars and Stripes Forever." As the over-sized flag rose up the pole in bright sunshine, my heart surged. I knew what love of country truly meant.

Florence Reed, my favorite teacher, was standing next to me in her usual stately manner. In our classroom, her style was quietly challenging. As the flag went up the pole, she leaned toward me, commenting, "This glorious patriotic display helps you understand why men would be willing *to lay down their lives for their country.*"

She spurred my thinking: *I love my country and feel genuine pride as an American.* Yet her remark triggered uncertainties that troubled me. I realized, men *do*volunteer to die for their country as a patriotic act, thinking further, *Is this the only form of patriotism that expresses love of country and honors its glory?*

That May Day in 1940 began my journey to becoming a life-long Peace Educator.

THE FINAL YEAR AT HAYT ALSO BROUGHT a classroom challenge called algebra, concepts I had difficulty understanding. As an otherwise outstanding student with top grades, this deficiency was a major setback. It felt like being in a foreign country without the language, passport, or friends to smooth my difficult passage.

I struggled all year, grateful for the summer break. I knew this bewildering subject would come up again in high school and hoped I would grasp the ideas the next time around.

KNOWING MY NAME

Mother named me, born after
an older girl-child died—
"Call her 'Sister.'"

After mother died, my new mother
        told the teacher as I started school,
"Call her 'Betty'"

not knowing I was birth-certified
with a third and different name —
'Enid.'

Through many labored seasons of
tending my garden,
I've come to know

the toiler who hybrids the plant
can best do the naming.

—E. Betty Levin

ENTERING THE SENN
HIGH SCHOOL CULTURE

THE SENN STUDENT BODY CAME FROM TWO contrasting neighborhoods, the Gold Coast and the Slum. The former featured sturdy tall buildings enhanced by lush trees lining Lake Shore Drive, with gentle Lake Michigan breezes from the east. Further west was poverty *en masse*—shacks, boarded-up houses, and decay.

I felt privileged to become part of this diverse population. My awareness of the financial circumstances of the two groups never hit me. We were too busy growing up.

I later discovered some of the great strengths of the curriculum. Freshman English class involved an entire year of research on a topic of one's choice and learning to use advanced literary references. The International Relations course, taught by skilled Henrietta Haiphmann, resulted in her profile featured in *Life* magazine. The history teacher, David Muzzey, so greatly admired by my brother Leonard, turned out to be one of the foremost thinkers of the Ethical Culture Movement.

The Sociology course originally piqued my curiosity. I asked my brother Lester, "What's that subject about?"

His simple response misled me. "It's about society." I dismissed the offering. Who wants to study people from the newspaper society pages with their fancy balls and charity galas?

As it turned out, though I initially bypassed the subject, I later became aware of its broader ideas and served as a settlement house volunteer in my teenage years. Sociology eventually became a special interest, which I selected as my minor while studying at the University of Illinois. I was elected president of their Sociology Club—even after first rejecting that subject. This newly discovered perspective influenced my later great interest in social work.

THE CANDY STORE ACROSS THE STREET jarred memories of earlier problems with money. I felt jealous and deprived when I saw kids plunk down a nickel for a candy bar. I simply didn't have the loose change for those *noshes* (goodies). At lunchtime, watching them buy a hot dog, with mustard, piccalilli, and soda pop—I bet it cost as much as thirty-five cents. I shrank, feeling I would never be relaxed spending money.

Even if I had the change, Mom frowned at my indulging in that *chazzarai* (junk food) as she continued to monitor my eating habits.

"You know, Sister, they always make you constipated." To this day, even the odor of hot dogs cooking whets my appetite. I rejoice, *Hebrew National, you're my buddy*. And I've been known to indulge in wieners whose lineage is unknown.

I had no way to foresee my frustrated relationship with Senn High students Bianca and Gus, whom I came to admire. How fortunate they escaped the Holocaust. Such impressive intellect; I didn't believe I could ever measure up. I wanted to be friends with Bianca but never approached her. I rejected myself before she could. I was also envious of her relationship with an attractive guy whom I admired from afar. Here again, I stalled at the starting gate. And handsome Gus, what guy would cozy-up with a skinny, awkward girl with small breasts?

The later health class introduced a unique experience. Our teacher said with a sigh, "Our students produce only two babies a year." I sensed some girls had a questionable upbringing but never knew girls *like that*. My friends had restrained ideas about sex. Upon further consideration, *even an honorable girl can err when the situation is ripe*.

Yes, I eagerly anticipated my starting high school at Senn.

FINALLY MAKING FRIENDS

IN SEPTEMBER 1939, ON MY FIRST DAY and class at Senn High School, I was confronted with algebra, that dreaded subject from eighth-grade elementary school. I was hoping a different teacher with a new approach would make it easier.

The change came unexpectedly with my first friend, Dorothy Cooney. She was warm, smart, and open. She knew math, Latin, and other sophisticated subjects, which she had learned in Catholic school. Raised in an Irish home, her mother asserted, "Enough of parochial school. Now be educated in public school."

Dorothy stood tall and lanky, with dusty blond hair cut short. When I admitted to her that I was "dense in algebra," she offered, "I'll be glad to explain how it works. We can meet after school if you like."

What an accomplishment—someone other than my mother, willing to put herself out for me. So maybe I'm okay after all, I told myself, deserving real friendship.

Dorothy sat with me patiently, explaining how the formulas worked. Soon I was in control of my academic work again and had a real friend to boot!

Her Catholic smarts really helped, especially when we lingered too long strolling home on a frigid Chicago day, winds howling, cold gripping like a vise. I felt desperate for relief. Dorothy assured me that help was nearby, just a slight detour. We warmed our frozen hands, relaxed in the pews of her St. Gertrude's Church. I wasn't comfortable kneeling in a full genuflect, as Dorothy did. Not wanting to appear disrespectful, I bent my knees gently as a compromise.

I was grateful her Catholic sanctuary brought solace to this little Jewish girl. I had entered her different world— one of belief, commitment, and loyalty. This puzzled me, but I liked that we shared faith in our friendship. The challenge of understanding different religions troubled me. I hoped I could find answers some day.

My pal and I met frequently. I discovered that you don't have to be Jewish to be a good person. Dorothy often came to my home after school, where we talked and nibbled on snacks. On weekends, she biked to my place, avoiding her family's apartment. Her father worked nights as a railroad employee and needed a quiet daytime home for sleeping.

I was flattered Dorothy undertook the lengthy distance to my home. I was also a bit jealous of her biking ability, which I had never learned. Mom often promised, "We'll get you a bicycle on Tuesday." It wasn't until Wednesday that I remembered shopping for a bike never happened. I wondered, *Was she short of money or afraid of me falling and getting hurt?*

Dorothy and I exchanged Christmas gifts but couldn't wait for December 25. "Let's do it *right now*," we enthused.

Her long legs biked the few miles to my home for an early exchange. I don't remember the actual gifts, but the memory of tearing open the gaily-wrapped packages still brings a glow to my heart. Joy to the world!

Mother didn't object to my befriending a *goy* (non-Jew). I believe her accepting my breaking the boundaries of Jewish customs related to having two older brothers. They would carry on the mandatory traditions for which girls didn't qualify. Back then, only sons were considered valued members of "the tribe," able to qualify for a *minyan* (religious gathering of ten). My brothers had already celebrated their bar mitzvahs while girls choosing their bas mitzvahs remained in the future. My mother's liberal attitude may also have resulted from her feeling pity for past losses of my birth mother and Tante Surrel's home.

I later befriended an across-the street neighbor, Danielle. An Episcopalian and only child of divorced parents, she shared her loneliness following the broken marriage. I had been lonely also but for entirely different reasons.

I felt liberated, even privileged, having girlfriends of the Christian faith beyond my Jewish roots.

I somehow lost contact with both Dorothy and Danielle. I don't know why. I'm not a disloyal person who just drops people from her life. As I recall, I hadn't rejected them, nor had either friend ever tried contacting me. The reality is that I have no memory of any contacts with them after I met Gloria Hochsinger.

Gloria became something of a sister from the time we met, sharing our chatting in the hallway of our building. She and her family had moved into 6166 North Winthrop, first floor, to the right, and we were almost inseparable. Her parents, Eva and Rudy, and her mother's siblings, childless Aunt Julie and Uncle Dave, became close family. I'm not certain if her aunt and uncle lived with them, but they were almost always present when I visited. I saw little of Rudy, who worked long hours as a waiter.

Gloria became so central to my life that I'm devoting a separate chapter to our relationship.

GLORIA, MY VERY BEST FRIEND

MY MOST IMPORTANT TEENAGE FRIEND was Gloria Hochsinger. We met in 1939 when I was thirteen years old and she was twelve. We enjoyed our friendship into young adulthood and a new generation now maintains its continuity.

As an only child, she had moved into our Winthrop Avenue building with her parents and a devoted extended family, Aunt Ethel and Uncle Paul. They all doted on her, the only young person among them.

Though she had severe eczema and hay fever attacks, Gloria was a bright, vibrant, joyful personality with jet black hair and dancing dark eyes. She was short and a bit plump, with a warm, lovable personality. Gloria made a striking first impression, and we hit it off immediately. We spent engrossing hours chatting, either on the darkened hallway stairs or the outdoor front stoop.

A few years after we met, Gloria appeared in a stage performance where she was cast as a young child. Her very short dress and long white stockings made her appear small and cuddly. As she made her entrance onto the stage, the audience gasped in unison, murmurs sweeping the auditorium, "Oh, how darling!"

Gloria and I pondered the questions of life both large and small. Our attraction to the opposite sex initially dominated our discussions. She admitted, screwing up her chin in embarrassment, "I have quite a crush on your brother Leonard." I congratulated her on her good taste but didn't further comment, not wanting to disappoint her. He had expressed no interest in her. We talked about attraction to other boys and hopes for future dates.

She later became attracted to a tall, good-looking boy, a *goy*. When she mentioned this to her mother, she felt crushed as her usually accepting parent disapproved. "He's probably not even been circumcised."

Gloria confided her hurt to me, carrying his photo in her notebook for a considerable time. I tried consoling her, "Mothers tend to have set ideas."

"Monthlies" also occupied our interest. We both pondered, *How do girls insert those tampons?* We agreed that we were "more comfortable with a sanitary napkin and belt."\

Gloria's wide interests also included music, particularly the emerging talented pianist Leonard Bernstein. Enchanted with his abilities, she often volunteered as an usher whenever he performed. She frequently practiced piano in the family living room, isolating herself there, with windows closed and shades drawn, trying to subdue her hay fever attacks.

Her mother, Eva, took me aside one day. "Gloria is so impressed by the extraordinary care given by your mother that she has trouble believing Evelyn is not your birth mother. She wonders whether my devoted care could also be that of a stepmother." Eva finally came to the point. "Gloria insisted I show her the family baby book, proving I'm her real birth mother."

Yes, I understand. I often heard people comment when they noticed Evelyn's unusual attention to my care; she doesn't seem anything like a stepmother.

The most serious discussions between Gloria and me pondered the ultimate cosmic questions—*Why are we here? What is our purpose? What does it all mean?* We reluctantly concluded, *If there were no world, there would be nothingness, nothing, noth. . . . We wouldn't even exist.* Again and again, we questioned, not finding any answers to these life dilemmas.

Together, we found the answer to that possible "nothingness." We had each other, our valued friendship, our caring for one another. Those moments often ended with a warm hug and squeeze. After an affectionate look, the final parting invariably included a small hand wave. "See you tomorrow. . . ."

We rarely missed a day.

Gloria offered me comfort at the time of my high school prom. Without extra money to buy a special dress, Mom claimed a discard from an older relative and cut it down for my slight body. Despite her efforts, I felt like a klutz. In a feigned glamorous moment of swirling and showing off the gown, I felt reassured as Gloria offered a favorite quote from the Bette Davis epic film *Now, Voyager*. "Your finery may be borrowed, but it suits you beautifully." She always knew what to say.

Everything changed when Gloria's father got a job in Los Angeles, which required the family to move. Gloria and I sat on the front stoop, lamenting, "How could this happen? How will we manage without one another?" Eventually, we had to accept the inevitable. We vowed we would write often and share *everything*.

We arranged an elaborate farewell—a Sunday brunch at Chez Antoine and an exchange of presents.

My gift was ordinary compared to hers. I gave her attractive stationery; she gave me a collector's edition of Walt Whitman's *Leaves of Grass*. I had heard of this famous poet but was not yet aware of his profound influence on American intellectual thought.

And so we parted.

HIGH SCHOOL ENGLISH

TS BASIC FIRST YEAR HIGH SCHOOL COURSE was extended into a full year of both autumn and spring semesters with each student expected to complete a comprehensive research project. On that first day, the teacher announced, "We expect everyone to become accomplished researchers, learning this task properly, including footnotes like *ibid* and *op. cit.*"

This assignment grabbed me. I hung on every word, serious about succeeding in this challenging new world. She explained, "Choose your topic carefully, since you'll spend both semesters on the project, with your English grade covering the whole year." *A daunting project*, I thought.

During lunch hour, in the enormous cafeteria with high-vaulted ceilings, chattering students sat in groups munching their food. I felt minuscule and lost. I selected an isolated corner table and sat alone. A burly-looking older student approached me. It seemed unlikely that I would attract such a guy. Boldly leaning close, he asked me as if I were on trial, "Have you heard about the freshman English research project?" I wondered what this was about. He jutted out his jaw. "Well, this project is a tremendous amount of work. For just a few dollars, I can save you hours of labor." He took a wad of papers out of his hip pocket. "Here are all the research notes, filed systematically on three-by-five index cards, ready to go."

I recoiled in my seat. Was he actually selling his research? He noted my reluctance and became more aggressive. "Look, I just couldn't use the material. I changed my mind. It's really a good deal."

This deal reeked. It was not only dishonest but would cheat me of an opportunity that promised a solid learning experience. He had picked the wrong frosh. My big brother, Leonard, had warned me about suspicious proposals that would appear in life. "Beware!" he had cautioned.

I became more confident and shook my head. "*No!* I'm not interested." I wanted the excitement of choosing my topic, researching and presenting it well.

My passion for music, even surpassing my love of baseball, came to mind. My favorite composer was Tchaikovsky (Brahms, Dvorak, Sibelius, Ravel, Samuel Barber, and Philip Glass came much later.) Somehow I was drawn to Tchaikovsky's *Sixth*, his final symphony, the *Pathetique*. Perhaps this selection reflected my depressed childhood.

I planned to do my research in the downtown branch of the Chicago Public Library. Since every Saturday became a research day, I extended my school schedule to six days. I caught the bus at the corner of Granville Avenue at Sheridan Road and traveled a familiar route. Sheridan melded into Lake Shore Drive, followed by Michigan Boulevard with the unfolding of the impressive architectural structures. These sites became fresh, always viewed as if for the first time.

When I arrived at the Chicago Public Library, I was disappointed, finding only limited Tchaikovsky resource materials. The librarian noted my frustration and suggested, "Why don't you try the Newberry, the private library just across the street?" In my past experience, "private" had often meant "restricted," not intended for Jews. *Oh, that problem I've heard about.*

"Would I be allowed there?"

"Sure, everyone is welcome."

I had never heard of the Newberry. The librarian was correct—it was clearly inclusive. I not only found the vast hall welcoming but was pleased to be served by an efficient young boy of color. I was impressed that a Negro had this job, in a prestigious institution at that.

Library policies were clearly liberal toward both Jews and blacks. He located the books I referenced from the wooden file boxes and personally brought them to my table where I recorded notes. I was surprised to be waited on, as if a lady of leisure were being served her afternoon tea.

In reading the history of Tchaikovsky's life, I discovered he had visited New York City in 1891 to honor the opening of Carnegie Hall.

Tchaikovsky was nevertheless earning meager funds. He maintained himself only through the generosity of a wealthy patroness, Nadejda Von Meck. While composing the *Sixth*, there was a very serious cholera epidemic in St. Petersburg. Everyone was strongly advised to boil water before drinking it.

A compelling moment in the literature that stood out for me: Tchaikovsky's brother, Modeste, found him drinking *unboiled* water and exclaimed, "Petrov, what are you doing? Drinking unboiled water! How can you?"

Much controversy prevailed about whether Tchaikovsky had taken his own life. It's true he was depressed—his patroness had discontinued financial support. There's much sadness in his final symphony, and he may have deliberately drunk the dangerous water.

I make no judgment, but the facts are suggestive. Tchaikovsky conducted the premier of his *Sixth Symphony* in October 1893 and died seven days later. Since I had overcome my childhood depression, I became aware of how tragically it can end for others.

Our teacher suggested, "In writing the opening of your paper, try connecting your topic to an inviting idea that will hook the reader to continue reading."

This idea clicked. I had been listening regularly to a popular radio program whose theme opened with one from the *Sixth Symphony*. A literary description of the music, describing its rapturous flow, became the opening paragraph of my research paper. Gloria, my best friend, typed the manuscript.

The teacher explained her procedure for reviewing the papers. "I'm going to spend my spring vacation reading and grading them. I plan to sit on the floor, keeping those that seem most promising close to me. The others I'll fling across the floor to read later."

I believe mine was one she probably kept near her, since I received an A+ for my work. The project hadn't felt anything like work, had been enormously satisfying. Richness and complexity had been revealed to me about a famous piece of music.

So this is what learning is about. I appreciated I had insisted on taking the initiative to explore a compelling interest of mine.

A NOTABLE CONCERT

A FAMOUS VIOLINIST, JASCHA HEIFETZ, was coming to Senn High School to present a concert. This special event excited me but brought considerable family upset through an innocent decision I made.

The concert was scheduled during the homeroom period, and only seniors would be allowed to attend due to limited auditorium space. My freshman status excluded me. Since I was passionate about music, this denial outraged me. Contributing to my fury, the event was free, no small matter in our penny-pinching family.

I developed a plan—just skip homeroom and attend the concert. So what, I told myself, if my freshman status violates the rules? I realize I'm always compulsively obedient, but this is different, a time to push the boundaries. Anyhow, homeroom is mostly a waste of time—just the roll call and trivial announcements. I became determined—this was a "go" for me, seeing a real live professional violinist perform.

What I didn't know was that the school had a new policy regarding truancy. Students not showing up for homeroom would be reported with a phone call home. This brought dramatic consequences for mom and me.

I can only imagine the crushing effect on her when the call came into my father's tailor shop, where she worked with him daily. "Mrs. Goodman, this is the Senn High School office calling to inform you that your daughter, Betty, didn't show up for school today."

Back at school at 11:45 PM, I was in Clothing Class sewing a pair of pajamas when the phone rang. *Would Betty Goodman please come to the office.* No urgency was communicated, just a routine business-like message. My teacher said,   "Since it's practically lunchtime and you probably won't be back before then, please put your sewing materials away before reporting to the office."

Why were they making this request? I casually wondered. I methodically gathered fabric scraps, thread, pins, and the unfinished pajamas in a leisurely way and replaced them all in my assigned cubbyhole. I nonchalantly strolled to the high school office.

There, I was confronted with high drama. My mother was draped over a large chair, only half conscious, with a white-uniformed nurse holding smelling salts under her nose. My father's dark, angry eyes stared daggers at me. I imagined his accusations: *I could kill you! How could you treat your mother like this, after all she has done for you?*

I believed only the presence of the school personnel prevented him from pulling his strap from his pants and "letting me have it," as I had often seen him punish my brothers.

My brother Lester was there, too. Apparently, with my delay in arriving at the office, they had called him from class to reassure my mother that at least her second youngest was okay.

He looked puzzled, probably thinking, *How could his goody-goody little sister, so obedient and harmless, have done anything thoughtless to hurt mother?*

I was ashamed—I practically never assert myself—and this rare opportunity had brought terrible anguish to my mother. Helplessly, I thought, *I only wanted to hear a concert.*

Through the growing-up years, tumult and anger had always unnerved me, inducing nausea. In our family, we never discussed experiences of high emotion.

Upon reflection, I realized that my immigrant families' past had often brought cruel, incomprehensible, even death experiences. Their formula for survival was to forget about it and move on.

In this upsetting school incident, where discussion could have brought understanding of my mother's fears and father's rage, there was no follow-up. I never apologized for my misdeed, and we missed enjoying the relief, even chuckling over the jarring event that had caused no lasting harm.

The family had never discovered my deep feelings for music, at least redeeming the hard-earned *shekels* (monies) my father had reluctantly spent for those many years of piano lessons.

This pattern presented a challenge for me. At the time, I accepted I had an oversensitive mother and a usually angry father. I realized that I would have to learn elsewhere how emotional reactions flow from past life experiences.

This motivated me to pursue a path of learning, committing myself to lengthy studies and personal therapy. Ultimately, I became a psychotherapist, psychoanalyst, and eventually, a Peace Educator.

FRANK SINATRA AND BROTHERHOOD

A HIGHPOINT OF MY HIGH SCHOOL YEARS was when Frank Sinatra came to visit. In those days, Bobby-Soxers squealed and swooned over Mr. Blue Eyes, especially when he crooned his soulful tunes. But I was different—just not impressed.

My teenage heart pounded for the Chicago Cubs baseball players, especially Stan Hack, Billy Jurges and Gabby Hartnett. These were the men who made my blood course recklessly through my veins. To see the shortstop scoop a liner out of the dirt and hurl it swiftly to first base to beat the batter for an out—now, that's something to scream about!

Surprisingly, Sinatra was not coming to sing. He planned to participate in a special assembly sponsored by the National Conference of Christian and Jews. This piqued my interest. Since Frankie wasn't going to sing, I would be spared the spectacle of girls making fools of themselves.

On the day of the assembly, a priest, a rabbi, and Frank Sinatra shared a panel discussion on brotherhood. I don't remember everything they said, but just seeing men of the cloth from different religions sharing the stage shoulder to shoulder, listening to each other, held my rapt attention. I didn't know priests and rabbis spoke to one another, much less shared similar ideas. And Frank Sinatra himself voiced ideals: to respect people of different beliefs and the importance of tolerance.

The democratic, progressive ideals expressed by these religious leaders were not entirely new to my experience. I had already encountered them in the past, largely from cousin Dorothy with her inquiring mind, my father's convictions about working people, and concepts of the Ethical Culture religion. It was gratifying to hear them affirmed by others, especially religious leaders and a national celebrity.

From early childhood, I wondered why people of different religions set themselves apart. Religion was supposed to make you a better person. But if it kept people separated, even distrustful, and sometimes angry at each other, where was the good? And if each group claimed to have the real truth, how could that be? Was it possible there was more than one truth? Here was a mystery that confused my childish mind, and I longed to figure it out someday. The high school discussion demonstrated that people from different religions and perspectives could find common ground.

At the conclusion of the assembly, the three men held hands and rose to their feet as one. They raised their clasped hands over their heads, triumphantly, like boxers claiming their prize. This was a profound moment for me, a vision burned into my consciousness as hope of what could be someday.

When people hear this story about Frank Sinatra, they're surprised to learn he had a social conscience. I recalled hearing an early recording of Sinatra singing "The House I Live In," reflecting democratic ideals and this high school experience. The refrain he vocalizes repeatedly, "This is America for me," celebrates our American society of hometown values, diversity and respect (see appendix for the lyrics).

The school assembly spurred me on my religious journey toward ethical and spiritual growth. The applause of the students as they shouted their approval of the common quest of priest, rabbi, and Frank Sinatra still echoes for me today.

GETTING AND LOSING MY FIRST JOB

FOR MY FIRST JOB, I WAS HIRED as a bookkeeper at a neighborhood gas station. I felt grown-up entering the world of work, three days a week after school, a convenient walking distance from my home. The pay was huge—seven dollars a week. Gloria and I shared my good fortune. Sitting on the front stoop of our apartment building, we listed the ways I could spend this generous sum: milkshakes instead of Cokes at the corner drug store, a sweater set, a movie in downtown Chicago, even a more expensive one at the Oriental Theater, which featured stage shows.

Frank and Ed, the lanky brothers who owned the gas station, were coarse, loud, and rude. As I was intimidated by my bosses and naturally shy, I avoided them whenever possible. Conscientiously, I did my work, asking instructions only when necessary.

When I first arrived at the job, I noticed a sketch on the wall of the only bathroom. t faced the toilet— a crude pencil drawing labeled *cunt*. Not long after I arrived at my job, *Betty's* was added just above the drawing. This disgusted me, but I didn't expect much from these crass men, though I noticed with surprise they knew something about punctuation. I was passive, as usual, accepting the insult; simply, a paying job trumped degradation.

One day after I finished my work and was half a block down the street, walking home, I saw Frank come running after me. Barely catching up, he shouted, "We don't need you anymore. You don't have to come back again."

I was stunned. I, practically a straight-A student, was getting fired, unceremoniously, on the sidewalk, with the street cars clanging and cars belching their exhausts. I felt hurt and confused.

An image came to me— of my Dad sitting with friends around the kitchen table in our Winthrop Avenue apartment. He often screeched his rage.

"Working people are not treated fairly!"

He would punctuate his indignation with his powerful clenched fists, pounding the table, almost making the walls shake. His words rang through our apartment, "Only labor unions will protect the rights of working people!"

The working people. This was a phrase I heard often in my home. When not shouted to the heavens, it was dignified by hushed tones worthy of an incantation in a house of worship.

My father employed several people in his tailor shop where he was both a boss and a worker. His sympathies were mostly with the working people.

I particularly remember one employee, Roscoe, a gentle man, sweat constantly pouring down his shiny black face as he expertly steamed men's suits with the large hand presser. One day, tears joined the sweat after his beloved wife died of cancer. Even as he wept his mourning, his work continued unabated. His efficient hands smoothed fine suits through the machine, crisp and ready for an executive's most important meeting.

This memory of the dignity of working people fortified me. Slowly, I regained my composure as I stood with my boss on the street. Ideals fueled my confidence. I stretched my slight frame, pointed my chin at Frank and looked directly into his eyes, proclaiming, "You're supposed to give two weeks' notice!"

Frank staggered in surprise. Throwing his arm up in resignation, he muttered as he shuffled back to the gas station, "I guess you can have one week." I completed my last week's work, a lost job but a moral victory.

OTHER INTERESTS AND ACADEMICS: MY SWEET SIXTEEN PARTY

Y OU'RE NOT INVITING BOYS?" questioned my brother Lester after I told him of plans for my sweet sixteen party. I had explained, "I'm having a few girlfriends in for gabbing and eats."

He became a bit annoyed with me. "You can't pass up this opportunity—you don't want that mark on you, do you—sweet sixteen, and never been kissed?" he said, scolding me gently.

Les' perspective became something to consider. Yeah, it could be fun to have a boy–girl party, Spin the Bottle and all it could bring. "Les, you're right. I'm following your advice." Some girls thought it a bit brazen, but what the heck, you have to take some risks in life. . . .

It was a frolic, not only Spin the Bottle with the usual smooching but also a groping adventure with the lights out. I chuckled when some kids, while creeping in the dark, tripped on my childhood doll carriage in the corner. You have to give up stuff as the price of growing up.

After everyone had gone home, there was a knock at the door. It was handsome, blond-haired Gus at the door, the German high school student who had escaped from the Nazis. He explained he had forgotten something. "You know, sweet sixteen and never been kissed," he stammered, blushing, "and I didn't get to kiss you. . . ."

I tilted my chin forward, offering my lips. He planted a quick kiss and rushed away, goal achieved. It was so innocent and delicious.

For the party that launched my teen years, I was pleased. My brother Les has special wisdom. *Bless him.*

E. BETTY LEVIN

JOINING A SORORITY

FELT I HAD ARRIVED WHEN POPULAR JUNE HEYMAN invited me to join the high school sorority, a sign of social approval that I fit in. The sorority was unusual—no name, no mission. Another unique quality was that members attended different high schools in the area, not just Senn High, a diversity of sorts.

Our common denominator was our members were all Jewish, middle-class teens. We met for support as we advanced in our adolescence with many questions confronting us.

The girls had various goals after graduation. A few, including me, aimed for college. Most others planned to work in office jobs, contribute to family finances, and await a proper mate for marriage. I believe June was in this latter category.

I was surprised that my cash-strapped family never expected me to forgo advanced education in favor of early employment to help out the family income. My mother was determined I have a college education. Whenever she and Father differed, her will usually prevailed.

Sorority membership brought richness to my life; I attended business meetings and varied social gatherings including an annual Mother's Day luncheon. This latter event became a ritual—an elaborate celebration including the spirited discussion of whether our treasury could afford corsages for so many mothers. Teenage compassion prevailed and the majority agreed, "Look, our mothers have always given us so much. We must express appreciation in return."

I vividly recall Mom beaming with joy, wearing those beautiful flowers on her left shoulder. I finally had found a group event for honoring my devoted Evelyn.

Our sorority's fun activities included an annual pajama party, overnight at a local modest hotel. Sharing anecdotes, silly games, and extravagant food was our idea of a good time.

DURING ONE OF OUR GET-TOGETHERS, we loyally responded to a member in crisis. Her urgent phone call: "I did something dreadful last night and must discuss it with all of you." Helen hysterically confessed a shameful experience with her steady boyfriend. "Tim and I had a hot session last night." In anguished tones, she revealed, "I allowed him to fondle my breasts!" Helen wept hysterically, dropping her head into her hands.

Though inexperienced, I regarded her admission as inconsequential. I knew that couples experimented with their emerging sexual urges and "even went all the way."

I remained silent as my other companions reassured her, trying to free Helen of her guilt. One friend offered, "You and Tim have cared for one another for such a long time. It's natural you would allow him to explore your body a bit."

I quietly considered, *I so envy Helen's pretty face, magnificent fully developed breasts, and an ongoing relationship with a fine man. I'm so flat-chested, gawky, and unattractive—no sign of any male interested in me. I don't know what it means to even date a guy. Helen has everything, and yet she is miserable. How do you achieve ultimate happiness in life?*

There was still so much for me to figure out.

ALICE WAS ANOTHER MEMBER OF THE SORORITY of whom I was fond. She told me of traumatic experiences with an older sister who suffered epileptic fits, how her sister sometimes fell on the exposed heated radiator. With mother not home, Alice and another sister pulled their unfortunate sibling from the heater, which sometimes claimed the hideously damaged flesh.

I was not surprised when Alice left home abruptly for marriage after graduation, settling somewhere in the West. We corresponded occasionally, her letters expressing unrest in her new life until I received word of her untimely death.

Another friend developed polio in her early twenties and also suffered an early death. The demise of young people opened questions for me about the mysterious paths of life and new respect for the unexpected and unknown.

A MORE OPTIMISTIC FUTURE INVOLVED ELAINE. I heard my sorority sister completed college, married, and settled in a progressive community—ecumenical and humanistic. I believe it had qualities characteristic of a Quaker, Unitarian, or Folk Society. These liberal concepts excited me, especially as far-reaching ideas were beginning to enter my consciousness.

Elaine and I seemed to share similar values, which I wanted to explore with her. I became distracted by daily challenges that postponed these interests until more mature years. By the time they had become more compelling, I had long since lost contact with my sorority sister. I regret I missed being part of Elaine's life and hope she has developed a meaningful one.

ABOUT JUNE HEYMAN, SHE WAS MY MOST FAVORITE FRIEND in the sorority. I found her easygoing assurance and kindness very appealing, buttressed by leadership qualities. She served as president with wisdom, gently shaping the direction of our sorority. I privately singled her out to be my sister-in-law, as wife to my older brother, Leonard. I 'fixed them up,' and they dated quite seriously for an extended time. When World War II intruded and Len was drafted, June poignantly shared with me, "I would have waited for him if only he had asked. But Len seemed to feel it unjust to burden me."

Though I wished otherwise, I was not surprised. Len unselfishly re-garded other people's feelings a prime virtue, overriding his own. I felt deep regrets for them both. They seemed so well suited for one another, each appreciative and deserving of their respective sterling qualities.

Wartime separation brought this common dilemma for many loving couples. Eventually, June married another accountant; I was invited to their wedding and witnessed their private passionate kiss after the nup-tials. Sadness gripped my heart but who gets all their dreams fulfilled?

I encountered June Heyman again, only by chance, when I returned to Chicago in 1998 for Senn High's Fiftieth class reunion. I was thrilled to see her again. We met briefly, exchanging phone numbers to hopefully reunite again for a more time together. When I returned to Chicago about ten years later for a family visit, June and I met again. By then she was a widow, in poor health, breathing with a mobile respirator. Her good spirits were still apparent, but I sensed her discomfort. My heart was saddened to realize what misfortunes had befallen her. The cruel in-justices inflicted on talented, caring people remain a dark mystery for me.

Unfortunately, I have since misplaced her phone number and lost touch. At the Chicago Senntennial reunion in October 2013, I had hoped to reunite with June or, at least, discover news of her. Neither happened. Sadly, June is gone from my life forever.

EARNING MY SCHOOL LETTER

NEVER CONSIDERED MYSELF AN ATHLETE. Very small for my age, I lacked the muscular strength to compete effectively in the popular sports—baseball and basketball. My brothers' enthusiasm affected me—their recounting baseball scores and discussing games at supper time. How could I ever function without my passion for the Cubs?

Participating in the school teams didn't seem to be for me. I wondered if there were other ways to be involved. Volunteering as a referee for the Girls Athletic Association (GAA) could earn points and a minor letter. As an achiever, I thought, *Well, if a minor letter is good, a major letter could be even better.*

Wouldn't it be great to earn that coveted "S" to wear on a Senn High sweater that I saw the bigger kids, juniors and seniors, wear so proudly? How could I get enough points? Refereeing after-school games was a cinch, but the significant numbers came from playing on the varsity teams. I figured there was no way that could happen.

A strategy then came to mind, one counter to my physical strength, that I had often seen at the Cubs baseball games. At bat, I could bunt, tapping the ball in front of the plate, catching the competing team by surprise. By running fast to first base before they could field the ball, I could earn a single. I did this repeatedly before the opposing teams noticed my pattern. Even when the infield played me in close, I could often beat them to first base. I was a fast runner, thanks to Lester and those

Winthrop Avenue races he organized. This success eventually earned me a place on the varsity baseball team!

Then came basketball, and I came up with another plan. My short stature made throwing baskets impossible. Since I was scrawny and fast, I functioned well as a guard in a defense position. These abilities could prevent an ace player from shooting a basket, or even passing it to another strategically placed one. I became known as a good blocker.

To my delight, my skills were recognized and I made both teams, earning that coveted letter. I also made money to buy the expensive sweater and sewed on the "S" myself.

The aftermath was a downer, though. On the day I proudly wore my new sweater with the coveted "S" to school, health class was scheduled. This particular session featured a special guest, a cosmetics company representative who demonstrated how to apply makeup expertly—the whole works: mascara, eye shadow, eyeliner, lipstick, and rouge.

I volunteered to be the subject. After her skilled application, I looked in the mirror and was surprised at the unfamiliar attractive face.

That same day, I had an orthodontia appointment in downtown Chicago. Riding the "L," I wondered why the riders were staring at me. I then realized—my collision of styles must have looked startling, even clownish. My facial makeup, as for a glamorous chorus girl, clashed with my gym clothes.

Feeling foolish, I thought, I'll use better judgment in the future. Really, though, how important was it? I vowed that flawed decisions were not going to seriously interfere with my living an interesting life.

THE PROM, GRADUATION, AND SELECTING A COLLEGE

NOW THAT I WAS APPROACHING my high school graduation, it was time to consider a choice of college. But first was the joy of the prom. I needed a date, but, unfortunately, boys were not usually attracted to me—I had a crush on Dick Brinkman, one of Lester's handsome friends. I invited him to be my escort. I can't recall many details except the makeshift dress Mom made over for me from a relative's discard. I do vividly remember the pleasure of necking with Dick on the beach, the custom for post-prom evenings.

UPON GRADUATION FROM SENN, my grade average was substantial. I ranked eighth in a graduating class of 538 students. Reaching high for college, I focused on the prestigious University of Chicago. My guidance counselor gently and diplomatically suggested I look elsewhere. "Betty, you're clearly a high-achieving student, but you may not quite measure up to the caliber of others attending such an elite university." I felt dumbed-down but timidly accepted her opinion.

I decided to apply to Northwestern University in Evanston, just a few elevated train stops from the one at Granville Avenue. I was concerned the costly tuition would present difficulties for Father, but Mom always found the money when it was important.

BECOMING BETTY

I was astounded to be rejected by Northwestern. I don't recall the reason they cited. There was hearsay that anti-Semitism was prevalent there at the time. I spoke to a Senn High School alumnus in 1993, and she confirmed a similar experience there, but with one major difference: She had confronted them directly about their possible prejudices and gotten admitted. I had accepted their decision and looked elsewhere.

I remember little of graduation day at Senn High. The most striking one was having difficulty steadying the cap with my incompatiby thick upsweep hairdo. All through the ceremonies, I kept mediating the struggle between those two elements until a fellow student muttered, "Cut it out, Betty. You're not in a beauty parlor."

MEANWHILE, I HAD BEEN MISSING GLORIA INTENSELY. I finally decided to visit her in California, made possible by my father's unexpectedly generous gift for my high school graduation. He had pushed his hand deep into his back wallet pocket, taken out a hundred-dollar bill, and grimly thrust it toward me as a congratulatory gesture. "Here, this is for you."

I'd been overwhelmed. He had finally acknowledged my educational accomplishments. A simple message, "well done," never passed his lips. Spending money was his primary expression of love. I had thrown my arms around him in a rare display of affection and effused, "Thanks so much, Dad!"

He hadn't cracked a smile. His tense body and grim face camouflaging the deeper, loving feelings that I so urgently needed. For now, this gift would have to do.

I traveled to California by train in overnight coach and awakened while crossing the western mountains. As a Midwestern girl, I had never seen a mountain. The glistening moon revealed this geographical wonder. I gasped, staring at the luminous sight, but was frustrated that I couldn't see the very top.

I lowered myself to the floor of the train and stretched my neck. Impossible, but its mystical enormity gripped me. Mountains have since became a symbol of life challenges—no matter how formidable the obstacle, to make every effort to achieve my goal.

In my Los Angeles reunion with Gloria, she acquainted me with her new locale, including the usual tourist attractions of sight-seeing, restaurants, and theater.

After the visit, Gloria and I wrote voluminous letters to one another. We joked that saving these weighty communications threatened the very foundations of our homes.

WHILE EXPLORING COLLEGES FURTHER, I did receive a hundred-dollar scholarship from the then newly organized Roosevelt College. It was planning to locate in downtown Chicago's Orchestra Hall, where I had attended many concerts in the past. I rejected their offer as I regarded a novice, newly emerging college to be of questionable value. It became a substantial institution; many years later, both my brother Leonard and his daughter, Robin, simultaneously earned their degrees there, his an M.A. in Accounting and hers, a B.A. in Music.

I frankly felt more comfortable maintaining the family tradition of attending the institution both my brothers had chosen—Wright Junior College. It turned out to be near-perfect, considering the six-dollar-per semester tuition, living at home, and reasonable commuting distance on just two buses.

Most vital was the curriculum. The Chicago Junior College System had adopted that of the University of Chicago. This program included survey courses in all the basic fundamentals of knowledge—the physical sciences, biological sciences, social sciences, and the humanities. This approach supports the fundamental idea that a truly educated person understands the tenets of all basic knowledge, undergirding their eventual professional pursuits.

At the University of Chicago, the survey courses were a two-year program—at Wright, only one year. I was surprised that large categories of human knowledge could be organized into four survey courses. An additional satisfaction was that my attending Wright Junior College would parallel that of my original choice, the University of Chicago.

At age seventeen, in the autumn of 1943, I was off, launching my college life at Wright Junior College.

ENTERING WRIGHT JUNIOR COLLEGE

S TARTLING NEWS CAME MY WAY about starting Wright Junior College: the college was moving to a high school! I was shocked and puzzled, then downhearted. Launching my college career had been an eagerly awaited event, now disappointing even before my first class began.

This was 1943, wartime, and the Department of Navy needed a radio school to train their inductees. They chose Wright for this facility, and our displaced campus was relocated in a wing of Amundsen High School. The disillusionment was intensified by the physical condition of the setting—only a couple of dark corridors with rusty lockers. It lacked the modernity and comfort expected for advanced education and suggested a poor relative's squalor.

Another setback—the student body of young men had shrunk significantly, recruited into wartime service. Our spirits were dragging with these twin blows until a top administrator organized a committee for bolstering morale. I felt the effort was probably futile, doubting it could make a difference. An alternate thought—I'll join, what have I got to lose? The unexpected is sometimes interesting.

The committee decided to organize a War Bond drive, and, to spark some excitement, they added an incentive. The students selling the highest dollar value would be crowned King and Queen of the Spring Ball.

First, the academics. In addition to the mandatory survey courses were opportunities for electives. My fantasies suggested becoming a physician. One part of me dismissed this as a romantic notion, influenced by novels where doctors accomplished healing heroics. Another part reasoned, You'll never know until you try.

I became a pre-med student, enrolling in Chemistry, Comparative Anatomy, and incidentally, an elective, Psychology 101. The anatomy course involved dissecting a frog as an initial lab experience and then advancing to the cadaver of a cat.

I was awed by the physiological structure of these animals, particularly a cat's brain. As I held the soft walnut-sized structure in my hand, I was struck with wonder at its capacity to function with intelligence and cunning.

FOR CHRISTMAS BREAK, I HAD BEEN HIRED for a holiday job sorting mail at the downtown Chicago Post Office. I arrived with my homework to study during the two-week vacation, including the partially dissected cat and some text books. I had wrapped the carcass carefully in oil cloth and placed it in a large sack. Stretched out in dissection position, the massive bundle stretched to almost four feet.

The security guard halted my entry. "Hey, young lady, what've you got there? You know, you can't bring packages into the post office."

I replied meekly, "I'm a college student on Christmas break. This is part of my homework."

He challenged me, "What kind of an over-size notebook is that? I wanna take a look."

I warned him, with a sarcastic, "Oh boy, you won't like what you'll see. . . ."

After I had unwrapped my package for the guard's inspection, he glared at the animal's partially eviscerated body, guts hanging out. Shocked, his mouth contorted as he exclaimed, "What a gory sight! I had no idea. . . ." Changing his tone, becoming supportive. "This is important stuff. I'll hold it here for safe-keeping until your shift ends."

ALONG WITH MY PRE-MED COURSES was my psychology course, scheduled as an eight a.m. class meeting three mornings weekly. I decided immediately, "This is one subject I'm going to cut regularly. Heck, taking two buses for commuting, I'd have to be out of bed by six a.m. to get there on time."

I had underestimated the intrigue of psychology and teaching skills of the instructor, Mr. Resnick. Even an elementary psychology course opened the deeper human understanding I had been seeking for so many years. It didn't take long to decide that psychology, not medicine, was my new professional goal. Later after becoming a psychotherapist, I realized I had really wanted to become a healer, on a similar spectrum as medicine, but with a different emphasis.

AS FOR THE WAR EFFORT, I RESPONDED TO WORLD WAR II patriotism, especially with both my brothers in the armed forces. I started working after school in a war factory, serving on an assembly line in an oversized storefront building on Chicago's Broadway Avenue, only two blocks from our Winthrop Avenue apartment. I was one of the cogs on the line, making resistors for large naval guns. A proud event was when the company received a citation from the Department of Navy's high brass. We were congratulated on meeting a crucial deadline for a significant impending battle.

Besides collecting tin foil and discarded metal materials for the war effort, I volunteered at the USO Servicemen's Center on Saturday nights, socializing with lonely soldiers—dancing, gabbing, and drinking Coca-Cola from green bottles. Joe and I hit it off well. I listened with compassion at his lament of missing home and family. Joe searched me out each week.

AT COLLEGE, I ADDED THE WAR BOND CONTEST to my patriotic efforts. Armed with multitudinous nickels to make phone calls, I worked the phones almost every free minute. With three families to solicit—my father, stepmother Evelyn, and those of my birth mother—they all responded generously. I became enthusiastic. A special favorite relative was Evelyn's youngest brother, Uncle Abe, who owned a candy store. He responded eagerly as I explained, "I've entered a War Bond Queen contest. Could you direct your monthly Bond purchases my way?"

"Sure, Sister. It would please me to help make you a Queen."

Though my dollar numbers grew, this fantasy didn't seem real, a wimp of a girl in the running. In the competition, a more typical glamor queen, gorgeous, sexy Angie nagged at me. Ask any classmate—I bet they'd agree she should be the one crowned a Queen. Anyhow, I was rarely a winner in any of life's contests.

As the deadline for the contest approached, excitement mounted. The college newspaper featured an article with a photograph of the women contestants, highlighting their dollar amounts raised thus far. My numbers were good, but who knew?

The final day of the contest was about to arrive. The last evening before its conclusion, at home, I added up my totals and organized the paperwork. The next morning, hopeful, I left for college, boarding the Sheridan Avenue bus and making the Addison Street connection.

Upon arrival, I opened my purse with a grand flourish to present my final sheets— and found no papers there! I panicked. *What's going on here? Could I have somehow left them at home?* Checking my watch, I had a little more than two hours until the noon deadline. With a fifty-minute commute each way, could I make it? I dashed out the door to start my frantic round trip home.

The bus ride seemed interminable. Exiting at Sheridan and Granville, I ran the two short blocks to the Winthrop Avenue apartment kitchen, where I had last assembled the paperwork. There was no sign of it on the table.

Crestfallen, but on a hunch, I grabbed the garbage can, and *there they were*, neatly paper clipped, totaled and assembled, but crushed into a ball. Overworked Mom hadn't time to empty the trash, thank goodness. I quickly smoothed them, weeping tears of relief. I jammed the papers into my purse and bolted out the door to grab the two buses for the return trip. Bless the Timetable Gods; they were with me that day. I breathed heavily, and in my mind, pushed the buses to move faster along the crowded route. I arrived back at the college just in time for the contest deadline.

My grand total, $7,000, was a grand success! Most deliciously, I had beaten Angie with the big tits. There were tears in her eyes when she congratulated me. I hope I said something appropriate to console her. I accepted her kind words but felt unworthy. This gawky, awkward freshman was to be Queen of the Ball!

Despite this triumph, I criticized myself for carelessly discarding the papers at home. *Did I sabotage myself, feeling I didn't deserve the title of Queen? Did I somehow 'throw away' my chance?*

Now I needed a date. There wasn't much of a pool of men to choose from. I secretly hoped that good-looking Jerry, the guy who won the King title, would ask me to be his date. Again, I was disappointed in the men department. My friend Joe, from the Servicemen's Center, agreed to escort me with Dad's car used for transportation.

At the Ball, as I was crowned War Bond Queen, I wore only the suggestion of a smile. I didn't really know how to enjoy becoming a winner.

MY FINAL YEAR AT WRIGHT

WITH THE WAR BOND QUEEN EPISODE behind me, my studies progressed nicely during the final year at Wright Junior College, 1944. There was free time to explore other interests.

I was drawn to the agreeable cacophony of sounds from the music room. An attractive student hanging out there, a soprano, was rehearsing an aria. I sat next to her, listening to the vibratos floating from her throat and mouth. My heart beat faster, as I had never before been exposed to opera music. Her vocal effects, created with a serene, beautiful facial expression, were magical. I later searched diligently to identify her selection—an aria from the opera *Gianni Schicci*. Hearing it today brings back memories of opera opening for me at Wright College.

Only gradually did I find operas that interested me, but they never matched my passionate love of symphonies and concertos. I first sampled the popular operas, *Carmen, Aida, La Boheme,* and *Turandot,* moving later to the more somber *Billy Budd.*

Today, WQXR/FM, the New York/New Jersey classical music station, is the way station for my love of classical music. Often, I stop in my tracks, listening to a selection that grabs my full attention. Most recently, Karl Jensen's "Peace Benediction" became my new favorite. I have compiled a list of favorites to be shared at a memorial concert after my passing. The list numbers over two dozen—impossible for one concert. My family can choose the selections that brings them comfort.

Also beckoning me at Wright were three fellows jamming classical music after classes with clarinet, oboe, and piano. I became absorbed in the sound and up-close technique of these talented musicians. They met three times weekly, and I became an audience of one.

My favorite was Edmund, the clarinet player—good looking, with thick black hair and shiny white teeth, I liked him instantly. His two friends were congenial, one a plump guy on the oboe; the other played the piano while smiling frequently. As Edmund and I paired off, I learned more about him—his family was Catholic, and his older sister was also musically talented. She was already enjoying recognition as an accomplished French horn player.

As the enchantment between Edmund and me grew, we lingered alone after his friends left. Chatting together, we sipped Cokes from the tall drug store soda fountain glasses, chewing the melting ice at the bottom. Between flirtatious kisses and giggles, we munched Baby Ruth candy bars, completing an especially agreeable afternoon. I never invited him to meet the family at our Winthrop Avenue apartment.

Our love of music and growing sexual attraction fed our infatuation. But our heated-up relationship was interrupted by World War II. Edmund enlisted in the navy to avoid the draft. We corresponded frequently during his boot camp training. Erotic fantasies punctuated my dreams, anticipating his first leave home.

When he finally returned, he was dashingly handsome in his dress whites. I was overcome, confident, thinking, *Edmund, you're my guy!* My eighteen-year-old hormones were racing.

We reunited in the living room of the Winthrop Avenue apartment. Edmund shared details of boot camp, describing the "short-arm inspection." All the men lined up with their penises exposed that would reveal any signs of venereal disease. I imagined the scene, which aroused me even more. As a proper, timid middle-class girl— instructed to never shame the family— the no-no's with the opposite sex were a familiar rule. A capricious part of myself was taking over, though, plunging headlong wherever it might settle.

We began on the sofa, kissing and hugging passionately. With my body throbbing and panties already wet with desire, I lay down on the floor carpet. I beckoned Edmund to mount me as I tore off my underpants and flung them aside. I was ready, my legs parted wide, offering my virginity to my adored sailor. He straddled me, fumbling with the buttons of his bulging crotch, almost bursting the fabric. We were ready to go. . . all. . .the. . .way—

At that precise moment, the phone interrupted our passionate coupling. Startled, I whispered, "Edmund, I'll get the call, but I'll be right back!"

His mother was on the phone. "Is my son there?" She asked. "I wanna speak to him."

"Yes," I replied meekly. "Just a minute. I'll get him." I have no idea how she found me or my phone number, but I was obedient as always.

I dutifully delivered his mother's request. In about ten minutes, Edmund returned, ashen, saying, "My mother wants us both to come to the apartment right now."

Our passion crushed, we obeyed quietly, saying nothing to one another. Arriving at his mother's home, we were ushered into the dining room. His mother, older sister, and others were standing tensely around the table, staring at me like a despicable oddity. The scene resembled a royal court, preparing for a hearing.

His mother started aggressively demeaning me, but only addressing her accusations to Edmund. "How dare you —taking up with a Jewish girl! We, devoted Catholics— all we have given you, what were you thinking?" I felt myself getting convinced she was one of those prejudiced ignoramuses, a know-nothing. Not much you can do with one of those. . . .

Her vituperations continued, reciting all the privileges he had been granted. She droned on, further attacking Edmund's judgment. I glanced at him. He looked ill, pained, as if he was going to vomit, but he remained silent.

My anger increased to fury, especially when I realized Edmund was not going to respond. Gathering my strength, I decided, *I must be the one to take charge and stop this harangue.*

I interrupted, head held high, speaking deliberately. "I'm not going to stand here and listen to these insults. I'm leaving." Outraged, I left quickly. I don't remember how I got home.

I wasn't going to accept her egregious behavior without a fight. I gathered a pile of nickels for our coin-operated phone and called his home repeatedly, trying to contact Edmund. I got no answer. Eventually, my persistent calls met with busy signals when they probably took the phone off the hook.

My determination to challenge that dreadful behavior was futile. Edmund wasn't going to join me in protest, apparently defeated by his mother's prejudices.

I never heard from him again. I was terribly distraught, more for hearing the venomous attack than for losing Edmund. My past exposure to anti-Semitism had mostly been hearsay, and becoming a direct victim of such an onslaught unnerved me. I never shared this humiliation with my family but wrote voluminous, hysterical letters to dear Gloria in California.

Eventually, I accepted the reality of the situation—losing Edmund, the stupidity of almost forfeiting my virginity to such a weakling, and, more broadly, realizing that religious intolerance could be virulent. Back then, perhaps I was ahead of the curve, naively assuming an inter-faith relationship could work out okay.

I COMPLETED MY TWO YEARS AT WRIGHT feeling I had acquired a good start in my academic learning, even outstanding. I reaped other benefits as well that were starting to shape a new maturity—but to be continued.

PREPARING FOR AND ENTERING THE UNIVERSITY OF ILLINOIS

After graduating from Wright Junior College, I set my sights on enrolling at the University of Illinois in Champaign-Urbana. Attending a downstate college would temporarily sever my connection from home, demonstrating my increased independence. I resented Mom's overprotection, but I knew the costs were formidable. State college tuition was sixty dollars a semester, with room and board increasing expenses appreciably. In my own self-serving way, I was confident I could depend on her to come through with the money.

During the summer before entering the University of Illinois, , I found a good job as a secretary/typist working for the American Bandage Corporation in downtown Chicago. Many young women back then settled for a secretarial job until marriage. I wanted to earn money to continue my college education.

Unexpectedly, the job filled my need for an understanding, affectionate father. Irving Stone, the president, hired me and supervised my work in the small office. Slightly built, with short gray hair and a twinkle in his eyes, he reminded me of an aging Huckleberry Finn. Mr. Stone often chuckled, no matter the business difficulties.

His modest company was struggling, not unlike my father's. I had landed in familiar territory, but with a major difference. Mr. Stone was warm, attentive, and forgiving when I goofed up an important letter.

"Oh, c'mon, Betty, get it right this time," he admonished me. I had a surrogate father of my dreams, nothing rough about him. He accepted my shortcomings.

As I struggled one day trying to accurately type a crucial letter, his consistent patience calmed me. Memories of my stern, gruff father gripped me as I retyped the letter for the third time. Mom, Dad and I had left the apartment early one day for an errand, eating breakfast out. "Sis, why aren't you eating breakfast today?" my Dad had demanded to know, glaring at me, when I ordered nothing.

In a meek voice, eyes downcast, I'd responded, "Well, Dad, the chocolate milkshake Mom ordered for me has filled me up. You know, I can't stand the taste of regular milk, and they didn't have chocolate milk in this diner. A chocolate shake was the only drink that could cover up my disgust with the regular stuff." I couldn't bear to look at his angry, disapproving eyes. He rarely acknowledged me, and I had been earning his sharp displeasure in that diner. Memories of his often hitting my brothers with his strap haunted me. Would I trigger his violent wrath? My fear of him was constant.

"Well, that's not good enough. You'll *never* grow up to be big and strong if you don't *eat*," he'd shot back gruffly. By this time, my stomach had been churning, and I'd felt ready to vomit. I'd had no response and accepted I would never become "big and strong."

Mr. Stone accepted my faults as I typed the letter repeatedly. He also paid me well.

I was shocked, though, when I realized my boss possessed prejudiced opinions, referring to Negroes as "savages from Africa." I felt stung, as if he had insulted my own family. My uneducated father would never have spoken so deprecatingly of blacks. I wanted to protest Mr. Stone's ignorance and prejudice, but my position as his employee prevented me from speaking out.

His widower son, a successful businessman and father of a toddler daughter, depended on his parents to assist in her care. I had walked into a family situation whose circumstances struck a tender note. I felt part of the family as Mr. Stone shared babysitting experiences with me about his cherished granddaughter. "My wife scolded me when I allowed my granddaughter to climb on a wall with her newly polished white shoes," he told me with his charming, mischievous smile. These were experiences totally missing from my background—my father never took me for outings or shared engaging incidents—and I almost inhaled Mr. Stone's tales. Here was a family that loses a mother, I thought, and the grandparents respond lovingly to the crisis.

In one unusual moment in the rear stock room, Mr. Stone suddenly grabbed me with an affectionate hug and squeeze. As a twenty-year-old, I was shocked but quietly pleased that this business executive would be so inclined. I exclaimed, "Oh, Mr. Stone!" as I squirmed out of his grasp. I don't think he was thinking of anything sexual, but my fantasies were working overtime. On several occasions, Mr. Stone had told me, "I wish you were my daughter-in-law."

In late August, time to finalize college plans, I felt reluctant to separate from Mr. Stone, his company, and his family. With a job enjoying a unique relationship with my supervisor and a good salary, most of which I had saved, I decided to stay at my job and postpone entry into the University of Illinois until the spring semester. Some lost time was already made up by meaningful psychology courses I was taking at Northwestern University night school (a few even explored interpersonal relations). Vague thoughts of perhaps later doing a summer session could also compensate for my extended academic time-out.

As spring approached and I got ready for my university departure, I broke the news to Mr. Stone. I was pleased he didn't get angry; perhaps he sensed I had larger ambitions.

Before leaving for the university, my cousin Joan telephoned me with a challenging question. "Are you going there to meet an eligible suitor?"

She added, "Many women don't consider their college time successful unless they return engaged to be married."

"It would be great to meet an attractive guy," I said, "but that's not why I'm going."

THAT FIRST MORNING IN CHAMPAIGN, IN 1947, I recall joyously skipping down the street. Ebullient, it was like living in the country! The fresh air, vast lawns, abundant trees with twittering birds, shrubs with swollen buds about to burst in the spring— they all expanded my sense of well being. So this is what they call suburbia—what a contrast from the city. How I love living close to nature. I thought, *This is the kind of environment I'd like for a permanent location some day, education and nature in one package.*

I discovered the main campus with the mall called the Quad, many classroom buildings along its lengthy path. The stately Student Union building rose elegantly at the apex. Built in the upscale American colonial style, to my naive eyes it looked like Thomas Jefferson's Monticello. I felt I had become a privileged visitor to a wealthy estate. As a daughter of an immigrant tailor, how had I become so fortunate?

My joy changed to despair when I registered for my classes. I was closed out of a unique course I had been determined to pursue, Child Development. I had hoped this course might reveal some insight into my past. I desperately wanted to understand how my personality had been affected by my complicated childhood and persistent insecurities. The course included observing nursery school children through a one-way mirror, which enabled students to observe children's interactions and adapt studied approaches to guide them. The innovative mirror was unique at that time, the university having one of the first.

The quirks of the registration schedule closed me out of this class in each of the four semesters I attended the university. In my final semester there, I appealed to the Education Department Chair for entry. Painfully disappointed, I wept unashamedly in her office. Only then did I realize this privileged course was for students majoring in education, not psychology. I silently criticized myself for not exploring those related majors more thoroughly.

I discovered later that my psychology studies would indeed become the route for the understanding I so deeply desired. It required many years of unease before I acquired the ultimate education that resulted in the good life, "big and strong," as some might say.

In many courses, I found myself lost in huge lecture halls of almost two hundred students. We sat there uptight and silent, which prevented our spontaneously examining fresh ideas that came up. A good educational blueprint was demonstrated in one my my electives, Logic and Reasoning. We met in a small classroom that encouraged spirited discussions between professors and students. This experience was similar to those at Wright College, where we achieved learning milestones, meeting in just one high school wing at six dollars a semester. I discovered that expansive, more costly experiences are not inherently superior.

Our University housing, Indeco, was a special privilege. Devoted fathers, including mine, had invested generously to create this first independent/cooperative housing for their daughters. They had appointed a Governing Committee that provided many advantages: a resident graduate student to serve as a student proctor, and a trained former Pullman chef to create the most sumptuous meals. We were also supplied with a vast musical library of 78 RPM phonograph records with appropriate, top-scale electronic equipment. When a student noticed I could identify many selections after hearing only a few measures, she responded, "Wow Betty, you ought to sign up for Music Appreciation; that'll be an easy 'A'!"

I felt disgust at her focus only on grades. Her comment ignored our reason for attending a university—to acquire more *in-depth* knowledge. I said nothing.

A particular interest of many Indeco students was playing bridge in spare time, and I was invited to join the group. As a lonely child, I had frequently played "honeymoon bridge," two-handed, manipulating the cards for my phantom partner. The opportunity to play the game with other people and master some of its skills tempted me. Here was a chance for companionship in an old pleasure of mine. I declined the invitation, though, for fear I would become addicted to the card game and neglect my studies. My determination to become educated trumped the friendship of peers.

I vowed to myself that, in future years when leisure time hung heavy with no stimulating activities to excite me, I would learn the skills of bridge. Now, at ninety, and in my "third lifetime," these uninspiring interludes have yet to happen.

The Governing Committee hired a housemother, Miss Gregory, to supervise any potential misbehavior, a custom back then. For me, she was one of best attributes of Indeco. She was a warm, stately woman in her late sixties who seemed to understand young women's feelings. She wore her graying hair in an old-fashioned bun, and her style exercised authority with gentleness, her regime basically "no nonsense." Miss Gregory would chastise our messiness with a firm but kind "that won't do." And she did achieve her goals.

Many times I sought out Miss Gregory for a chat, to understand how she felt working at Indeco. I wanted to know her as a person, not just an employee. These feelings mirrored my early childhood experiences of wanting to know our housemaid Aurelia and Dad's presser, Roscoe, more intimately. I inquired, "How does it feel living here part time, separating yourself from your own home and family?"

Miss Gregory responded pensively, "I'm a childless widow, not much family locally. So it's satisfying to have you young ladies at Indeco with whom to be involved." She heaved a sigh as she added, "It fills my life in a special way." And then she quickly went on, "Would you like to visit my home one day for a cup of tea?"

I was pleased to be invited into the personal life of an older woman I admired. As I sat in her living room sipping tea from a fine china cup,

I discovered her home to be comfortable and unpretentious, reflecting care and quiet taste. I leaned my arms on her overstuffed chair, covered with crocheted lace covers, and listened attentively to her story. Miss Gregory offered as a confidence, "You're the only student I would invite to see my home. Not many young people would appreciate its simplicity and homeliness." This poignant interlude felt flattering, offering recognition of me as a person who appreciated the uniqueness of individuals and aspects of their character.

BEYOND THE ACADEMICS, CULTURE AND QUALITY CLASSICAL MUSIC were readily available. Star Course was unique, included in our general fees, which provided many evening cultural events for the student body. I still remember the thrilling cello performance of musician Gregor Piatigorsky, identified by another stellar artist as the "greatest string player of all time."

The Student Union offered daily recorded music almost continuously in the main lobby. Since volunteers were needed to announce the selections, I said to myself, "O.K., Betty, go for it. This is right up your alley."

I became frustrated. Inhibited speech had marked my childhood; I wasn't lucid and failed to accurately pronounce composers' names. Though I didn't achieve my goal as a hostess, I spent many quiet afternoons there filling my soul with Tchaikovsky, Dvorak, and Beethoven.

Being an independent student at the University of Illinois thrust me into a larger milieu. I was particularly pleased to become identified with a singular group called the Independent Women's Organization. We sponsored our own activities, proud of our plans to invite Paul Robeson to present a special concert. To obtain such a notable personality in 1947 was an unusual accomplishment.

"Robeson himself has agreed to appear!" I excitedly exclaimed to fellow students. As an African American world citizen and fervent advocate for civil rights, peace, and justice, he unfortunately also evoked controversy and accusations of being a communist. I was proud to become publicity chair for the event and was gratified his concert attracted a large audience, considering the largely White university population. Robeson's deep baritone voice gripped the audience, singing in five languages depicting various cultures. After the concert, he asked me, "Would you like to be part of our group photo?" I felt honored and still recall my handsome photograph with this luminary. My admiration for him was evoked by his extraordinary talents and concern for the disenfranchised. Sadly, I lost the historic photo when my University of Illinois souvenir album disappeared.

Buddy Young, the outstanding Black quarterback for the university's football team, possessed star qualities that offered possibilities that he might participate in the newly inaugurated Pasadena, California, Big Ten Rose Bowl event. This adulation led me to another human rights issue.

My excitement about Buddy Young was so complete that I didn't think about the school's mascot, "Chief Illiniwek," characterized as a Native American, whose colorful dancing and strutting evoked cheers and screams of loyal fans. I'm ashamed to admit I was one of those mob-excited students, responding to the fervor, joyfully acclaiming our university's symbol of spirit and pride.

I finally experienced an awakening in later years later when a Native-American student enrolled at the university boldly objected to the caricature of her people used as a mascot. Belatedly, I understood how degrading it was to exploit a noble people, victims of genocide, in order to excite support of the university's athletic teams.

Her objections were largely dismissed; a subsequent survey of students and alumni approved retaining the mascot. I was deeply disappointed and, in protest, resigned my membership in the alumni association. Though the practice was discontinued in 2007, I have lacked the incentive to rejoin the association.

AT THE CONCLUSION OF THAT FIRST SEMESTER, I decided to remain for a summer session to make up for my delayed start at the university. Still mourning our separation, Gloria visited me during this summer school session. We shared bunking together in the dorms, swimming at the Urbana Town pool, and noshing at a favorite hamburger digs. Always a camera enthusiast, I took many photographs of our second reunion, lovingly mounted in my University of Illinois album, along with those of Paul Robeson. The photos suffered a similar fate when the album was lost.

When Gloria and I parted after this precious time together, we affectionately repeated our vows: "Promise you'll write often—everything."

Neither of us realized we would never see one another again.

THE FOLLOWING YEAR, 1948, was my final one at the University of Illinois. Graduation Day offered another great pleasure—witnessing my father's delight as I completed my undergraduate degree. He joyously arrived at campus; I can't ever remember him so happy, as a sphinx suddenly breaks out with jubilance.

As usual, we spoke few words together, but I can imagine his deep thoughts: *I never pursued formal education, either in Russia or my home in America, but my persistent needle and thread have brought accomplishment for my youngest child beyond anything I could have hoped. Too bad Becky [his first wife and my birth mother] isn't here to celebrate with me.*

WHILE AT THE UNIVERSITY OF ILLINOIS, I had never developed a significant relationship with a man. This disappointment set the stage for the excitement of meeting Howard, an energetic, highly ambitious suitor who entered my life eighteen months after I graduated.

HOWARD AND ME:
MEETING AND GETTING MARRIED

EVEN THOUGH WE WERE LIVING IN DIFFERENT STATES, I met a man on a blind date in 1948 whom I subsequently married. This is our story.

After college, I became employed as a City of Chicago welfare worker, a job I loved. Little else engaged me in my humdrum existence. I lived at home with Evelyn, who infantilized me, unwilling to accept any room-and-board payments, and a mostly uninvolved father. I was almost twenty-three years old, dating very little, and none of my past romantic relationships had ever fulfilled their promise.

Settled into a routine pattern, I sometimes panicked. *What if I never marry—could I ever find the courage to leave my mother and live on my own? Worse, if I became an old maid, still at home, how could I live out my years with Evelyn?*

Both possibilities so terrified me that I never allowed my imagination to complete the scenario, like a motion picture projector suddenly broken—*impossible to continue, unthinkable to contemplate, a plagued ending to my life.*

Cynde, a friend from college days, called me one day with a tempting offer. "A woman I've met has a very bright nephew she wants to fix up with a promising girl. He's a mathematician. Are you interested?" I became excited —here was an opportunity.

"Yeah, sure. How soon can it be arranged?" I found courage to grab a blind date.

Cynde hesitated, stammering, "Well, it's a bit complicated. He doesn't live nearby—he's in Baltimore and works for the Glenn L. Martin Company in the missile industry." She added, "But he's willing to drive to Chicago to meet an interesting girl."

Unusual, but with possibilities, I thought. "Let's go for it."

When I first saw Howard Levin, I was disappointed. He was a slightly built man with a pale face and thin hair scattered on his scalp. His smile, though bright, revealed baby teeth still prominent among the permanent ones.

He swept into the room, as might Superman, exclaiming, "Hi, Betty!"

His unimpressive physical appearance evaporated as he quickly grabbed my hand, "Let's have a fine dinner together. I know a charming restaurant in the country. Would you like to go there?"

"Country" jumped out at me. It spoke to me about the beauty of nature, an idyllic romp that could improve my vanilla-flavored life. I mused a bit: *What a difference— compared to my dull weekends at home with Mom—meandering to a Saturday evening so-so movie at the neighborhood Devon Theater, walking-distance, convenient since neither of us could drive, ho-hum ice cream at the corner shop, returning home to Dad snoring in the bedroom. Sundays were even worse—marked only with Dad's early-morning walk down Granville Avenue, buying his weekly* Jewish Forwards *with the brown rotogravure picture section and bland Kaiser rolls from Davidson's Bakery.*

Awakening from my thoughts, I replied, "Of course! I'd love it!"

He added, "But it's a bit of a drive – actually it's in Wisconsin. Do you mind?" He aroused adventurous feelings in me.

"Just what I'd enjoy!"

He concentrated on the seventy-minute drive, somewhat subdued by the task at hand. I commented on the lovely landscape of woods. "My, this is beautiful country this time of year. I sure love nature."

Howard agreed. "I like nature, too." Despite our cordial exchanges, I was apprehensive, but curious to know more about this man beyond our routine chit-chat.

After the chef-special chicken dinner, now relaxed, his lively conversation revealed an engaging personality, highly intelligent, with lofty ambitions, chattering about his ideas and the math book he was writing. A very fascinating man had entered my life. I was engrossed with his vitality, my mood heightened by the dynamic companionship of a possible suitor. It was only much later that I realized, overwhelmed by his aliveness, I wasn't aware he had never asked about my interests.

When the dinner check arrived, somehow Howard didn't have enough money to pay. I wondered, *Who is this guy, really?*

Surprised, I agreeably paid the bill, having money from my salary check cashed that day. I rationalized, *It's all really trivial. A man who would drive fourteen hundred miles in one weekend to date a woman lives a bit recklessly. Anyhow, it's flattering. . . .*

My fantasies took hold.

He could become my prince on a white horse, rescuing me from Mom.

I didn't encourage Howard's weekend trips from Baltimore to date me. His capriciousness raised questions whether he was the man for me. But he was determined and continued the commute several times.

Howard then resigned his Baltimore missile job and returned to Chicago. He explained, "I could afford to give up the missile job, since several new offers have come my way. I also want to finish writing my math book with my co-author who lives here in Chicago. Most important of all, I want to see you more regularly."

As we continued dating, I found Howard's interests deeply appealing, especially in music and art. They matched, even exceeded, mine. He owned an impressive collection of 78 RPM long-playing records and those of folk music artists— Harry Belafonte, Miriam Makeeba, and Pete Seeger.

When I noticed Howard had liberal inclinations, I shared my Ethical Culture religious ideals of creating a more humane world. I described the movement as particularly valuing people of all backgrounds.

"In one Society, even a modest milkman became an active member, showing great interest in humanist ideals. In another, a man of color has already taken on a lay leadership role."

I'm not certain Howard absorbed these concepts. He possessed a oneness of purpose, mostly absorbed with his own ideas. For the moment, I only wanted to notice Howard's attributes, which were more compelling than my doubts. Since he seemed so footloose and fancy-free, I did wonder about his sense of responsibility. *Stay calm, Betty. He's clearly ambitious, and he has good work habits, a quality your parents have always valued.*

Someday, I had hoped to be married with an Ethical Culture Leader officiating, but that was premature for now.

As I came to know Howard better and invited to his parents' Addison Avenue apartment for casual suppers, I made several discoveries. Sara, his mother, was an excellent cook, her food wholesome, simple American, and delicious. She sautéed fresh Great Lakes white fish, tasty as I had never before experienced, perhaps caught that very day. Accompanied with soft, fluffy mashed potatoes and green beans done to perfection, it was my favorite meal at their home.

In contrast, my mother's meals were not usually palatable. Everything was slapped together quickly, the food usually overdone, preparation squeezed into a rushed schedule between work hours in Dad's store. She did make superb, succulent cabbage borscht, cooked slowly with flanken meat and marrow bones. It could safely simmer on the stove while she labored at her other chores. Using the back staircase, she would dash from the back-alley tailor shop, up to the third floor of our Winthrop Avenue apartment, to check its progress. I covet this dish today, its recipe written in her struggling handwriting.

I still enjoy one of her other favorite dishes, pickled herring. She picked up the fish at the local shop on Granville Avenue and pickled it herself, another dish that didn't require much attention.

Howard and I clearly had very different parents. Though our families shared Jewish roots featuring strong women, they came from contrasting backgrounds. My parents were uneducated Russian immigrants compared to Howard's, who were American-born with traditional schooling.

These differences sometimes clashed, particularly in the eyes of Howard's mother. Mom reported a phone conversation where Sara emphasized, in a derogatory tone,

"We're a different kind of Jew." The idea of dignity totally escaped Sara's understanding and I was offended that she had acted superior to my mother.

Harry's white-collar job as a bookkeeper in a well-furnished office was dramatically different from my father's sweaty work setting in a tailor shop off an alley way, with a steamy, pressing machine constantly emitting hot blasts into the back room.

Empathy was also a quality the Levins seemed to lack. In the evenings after supper, they revealed a narrow view of people, spending interminable hours pointing out the shortcomings of others. They rarely discussed current events or social concerns. Aunt Ruth, Sara's devoted younger sister, commented one day, "Shopping in the malls— that's people at their best." I strongly differed but remained silent, not wanting to appear disagreeable.

My parents were fundamentally accepting and compassionate. Mom responded readily to a neighbor experiencing hard times, asking for money at the back door. She dug into her shabby purse for some loose change.

The Levins belonged to fashionable Temple Sholom, a synagogue on Chicago's north side. My parents couldn't afford temple membership but found means to bar mitzvah their sons. Their observation of the High Holy Days was marked by simply closing the tailor shop.

My family emphasized hard work as the key to a promising future and always supported our interests. When Howard discussed his professional prospects with his family and declared he wanted to become a mathematician, they had criticized his choice. "What would you do as a mathematician?" they'd asked stridently.

He replied with confidence, "I'll teach it to others."

He fulfilled this goal as an instructor at the University of Illinois, Navy Pier, after earning his B.A. at the University of Chicago. He subsequently became inspired to write, a talent in which he excelled. After completing his math co-editorship, he later became author of *Office Work and Automation,* an innovative computer/business book that was translated into several languages. Howard had become a rebel in his family, only partially resolving conflicts with his mother in later years. As an only child in a matriarchal family comprising of Aunt Ruth and a grandmother, I was told he had behaved like a tyrant as a child, always demanding his way.

I watched aghast as he ridiculed his mother's obesity and loud voice. He routinely called her a "battle ax," and the family passively accepted his rude habits. Howard manipulated them with exaggerated charm and lightheartedness. The family often chuckled, I believe, more to cover embarrassment than as a response to genuine humor.

I tried not noticing his peculiarities, regarding them as unimportant. Howard clearly represented an opportunity for a new life. I was something of a rebel myself, resenting Evelyn's overprotection, and I kept my distance from her.

Within several months of dating, Howard and I became engaged to be married with Aunt Ruth donating her engagement ring. I didn't experience the same sense of excitement as cousin Joan Kramer (*née* Karel), who had become engaged at the same time. She had a modest but joyous engagement party to mark the occasion.

There was no celebration for me. I knew Howard fell short of my parents' choice of a husband for their overprotected daughter. When I arrived home wearing my engagement ring, I was hesitant about sharing my momentous news. I walked apprehensively into the living room, where my parents were chatting. My mother noticed the diamond on my finger and asked, "Why aren't you saying anything about that ring on your finger ?"

I merely thrust my hand forward for her scrutiny, smiling meekly but remaining silent.

My parents were disappointed. Howard had never offered them respect or kindness, or acknowledged them in any minimal way. They might as well have been the floor carpet. Neither Mom nor Dad ever uttered a word of disapproval, then or anytime thereafter. Only their pained faces revealed their truth.

"Yes, Mom, Howard and I are engaged to be married," I said solemnly. I didn't include my dad in the conversation, keeping the usual silence between us. Evelyn was always the spokesperson, interceding between us.

Our family never rejoiced, and wedding plans were undertaken as just another task. With my parents' histories of angst, I suspect they felt this was an additional ordeal they'd have to bear.

Howard was clearly different from my brothers and other men of our *yiddishe* (Jewish) culture. He lacked warmth and *hamishe* (homelike) qualities. Though he hadn't endeared himself to my parents, I thought little of this neglect, since I also wasn't too appreciative of them.

I never sat down with Mom for a cozy chat to discuss our deeper feelings about our relationship or life itself. I accepted Evelyn's kindness toward me as an entitlement with only minimal expressions of gratitude. I dismissed my father, fearing and avoiding him whenever possible.

Though I felt guilty for wounding Evelyn in my choice of Howard as my husband, I needed to grab this opportunity. I'm not certain I truly loved Howard. What I knew for sure was that I loved the life he was offering.

We set December 5 as our wedding date, and it was time for the mothers to finally meet. Neither offered a home to the other for that momentous occasion.

They selected the dress department of Marshall Field's as a place to rendezvous, Howard and I joining them. Back then, the prominent department store represented the ultimate symbol of successful merchandising. Sara wore her usual dark, well-tailored dress, in good taste, somewhat stretched at the seams, covering her generous body. Her appropriate pumps held her broad feet snugly, looking cramped. I often wondered how she managed to walk so well. Evelyn was dressed in an unremarkable economy frock. Evelyn tried bravely to smile. Sara's her lips parted only barely, so as to not reveal her broken front teeth. Their tentative embrace brought a few tears to the eyes of each mother. I can only imagine what they were thinking:

Sara: *I'm giving you my only begotten child, my cherished son.*

Evelyn: *I'm giving you my adored daughter, this orphaned child who replaced the infant son I lost over twenty-two years ago in the old country. I have poured all my devotion and energy into rearing her.*

Both determined mothers were merely relinquishing their offspring, not celebrating a welcome addition to the family.

The recession of 1948 then followed, which caused all of Howard's new job proposals to be withdrawn. Though he was now unemployed with limited savings, he did manage to purchase a Kaiser automobile, an innovation in the auto industry. The car was a lemon, but he prided himself on being on the forefront of new developments. His response to advancing business innovations was exquisitely prescient, as was his later role in the computer industry.

Howard's unemployment didn't deter our marriage. I made $174.00 monthly, and with three solid meals weekly, from our two mothers and Aunt Ruth, I was confident we would make out okay.

IN CALIFORNIA, AS GLORIA GRADUATED from college, dated, and married Martin Dubowsky, her letters, and mine also, became less frequent. Unfortunately, I didn't attend her wedding, as I was busy planning my own, scheduled just two months after her October nuptials. The married couple purchased a two-family home with her parents on Rimpau Boulevard, and eventually, Gloria gave birth to Corrie. Her letters were lucid, if not voluminous, describing in turn, her courtship—"Marty expressed desperation, like a drowning man, if our relationship ever ended"— her father walking her down the aisle—"he held his head so proudly"—their wedding night—"my heart pounded heavily"—and being captivated by mothering her infant daughter—"I can't get my work done. I'm always peeking into her room while she's napping"—and mother–daughter relations—"my mother always wants to come upstairs to dust my furniture. We gently quibble about it."

Letters diminished significantly. She made vague references to "recurring headaches." A letter from friend Beverly Plotkin explained that Gloria had been hospitalized with brain surgery—"some memory has been removed—she recognized me, shaking her arms with excitement, but she couldn't remember my name. . . ."

Rebecca, my birth mother, with her fiancé, my dad, during playful days of being engaged.

Rebecca's grave site at Workman's Circle Cemetery, Chicago, alongside that
of a previously deceased first-born daughter, little Dorothy, with peace dove ornament.

Evelyn upon arrival in the United States, age 23, 1926.

Betty (Sister), age 3, with surrogate mothers Dorothy and Betty.

Three-year-old Betty (Sister) with Tante Surrel, c. 1929.

Betty (Sister), about 9 years old, and brothers reunited as one family with new mother, Evelyn. Older brother Leonard is on left, and Lester on right, of our parents (the Goodmans).

Older brother Leonard during World War II.

Best friend Gloria as a young mother, with baby Corrie and husband Martin Dubowsky.

Betty and husband, Howard S. Levin, with Hubert Humphrey during the glamorous marital days, marking a political event; four years later, I filed for divorce.

"Mankind Is Her Family's Name," announced in a Star-Ledger *headline after an interview with Betty as Founder and Director of the ECS Educational Center.*

*"Autumn Dancers," linoleum print created by Wendy Levin
in ECS Creative Arts workshop.*

*Janet, age 23, in front of Brooklyn Ethical Culture Society
after her presentation, "Nature, Mythology, and Ethical Culture."*

Janet, young woman in love, just prior to becoming engaged to Dr. Martin Rudolph

Big sister Stephanie feeds her younger sister, Samantha, about 3 ½.

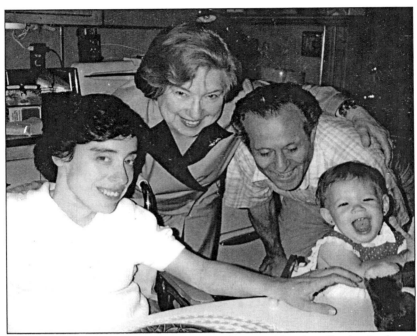

The Solomon White family visits Betty when her granddaughter Stephanie also visits
—Ina, Gert, Sol, and Stephanie.

Family gathering at Grandma's, including Tom and the Rosows (Raye and Jerry).

Samantha and Stephanie doing a weekend at Grandma's, playing on her bed with the Mexican gate headboard in the background.

Leonard playing with great-niece Stephanie as Janet looks on.

The Rudolphs visit Grandma.

Spencer brings Grandma joy by playing his violin at her Millburn home. Filmus's "Old Jewish Man" in background.

Re-dedication of Peace Site, Essex Ethical Culture Society. Betty with keynote speaker Lynn Elling, Founder, World Citizen.

Celebrating Re-dedication of the Ethical Culture Peace site at dinner—Anya Moen, President; Myron Kronisch, Vice-Chair, Board of Directors, Center for War/Peace Studies; Betty; and Lynn Elling, Founder, World Citizens, keynote speaker at the Re-dedication.

Betty and dear friend Helen Tepper share New York City time together.

Evening reception before wedding of Wendy and David, including Spencer, July 6, 2007, Albany, New York. Marty is also in attendance.

Marnie Valdivia, Drew University Religious Study student, before departing for Egypt's Arab Spring, Sunday Service speaker, Ethical Culture Society. Left to right: Zia Durani, Vice-President; Margaret and Gabriel Valvidia, flanking their daughter.

Tom emerging from the lake at Chanterwood, South Lee, Massachusetts.

Family celebrates Samantha's graduation from Pomona College in 2008 with major in Religious Studies. Left to right: Spencer, proud father; Marty; "Sammie" (later off to medical school); Stephanie (presently at Stanford Law School); proud mother Janet; Uncle Lester; Betty; Wendy; nephew Roy (in rear).

Betty (Sis) and Lester at his California senior citizen facility. Betty's triple-goddess necklace was a gift from her daughter Janet; the circular pendant is the ECS humanist symbol.

Mathilda Karel Spak, spunky cousin from Long Beach, California.
Her brooch is a photo of her mother.

Betty (Sister) and Shirley Morris renew their affection during one of Betty's California trips.

*"Big Brother" Paul and Betty visit the Rotary Peace Garden
where Betty's name is inscribed, Cambria, California.*

*Betty conducting an "Imagine Peace" workshop for
high school students, Cambria, California.*

Betty makes still another visit to "Big Brother" Paul in Cambria, California.

Betty, recuperating from brain surgery at Winchester Gardens, Maplewood, New Jersey, welcomes her family for a hearty meal. Left to right, front, Wendy and Janet; rear, Betty and Spencer.

Barbara (Boe) Meyerson, Leader Emerita, Essex Ethical Culture Society

"Big Brother" polishing the metal marker of his father's grave site,
Hillside Cemetery, Los Angeles, California, 2014

Samantha, Stephanie, and Spencer send holiday greetings

After Sunday Service. Left to right, Betty; Martha Gallahue, Clergy-Leader; Diane Beeny, Board member; Meredith Sue Willis, Chair, Social Action Committee; husband, Dr. Andrew Weinberg; Terri Suess, President.

James White, Leader Emeritus, Essex Ethical Culture Society, and Betty visit together at the American Ethical Union 100th Annual Conference in Stamford, Connecticut, at which Betty was awarded the Anna Garland Spencer Leadership Award

Paul Young and companion Pam Ehrlich in Cambria, California.

Robin Fossum, niece, Leonard's daughter, with her violin;
highly talented, she performs with three professional orchestras.

Mothers ("machatunem," Yiddish for the mothers-in-law relationship) rejoice over
the wedding of their children, Michele and Jonathon. Left, Barbara Levin, mother
of the bride; right, Corinne Barsook, mother of the groom.

Family gathering at "Celebration of Lester Goodman's Life," Martin Luther King weekend, 2015. Rear, left to right, Shirley Morris; twin granddaughters Avery and Alezandra; Jeffrey, father of twins; Susie and Roy Goodman, Les' daughter-in-law and son. Front, left to right, Betty and sister-in-law Ruth, Les' widow.

Aunt Judith Ackerman came from New York City on Betty's official birth date, February 24, to celebrate her ninetieth birthday with lunch at one of her favorite restaurants, Khum Thai, in Short Hills, New Jersey.

"Raging Grannies" singing group, gathered in front of the New York Society for Ethical Culture on West 64th Street in New York City, raise their voices during the 2015 Climate Control Demonstration weekend.

Celebrating Betty's forty years in private practice as a psychotherapist in her azalea-laden backyard. Left to right, Janet, Wendy, Stephanie, and Betty. Janet is retrieving watercress plants she planted forty years before.

Granddaughter Stephanie and Wendy at a March celebration of Betty's ninetieth birthday

Betty meets with her guru environmental friends, Beth and David Harrison, of Short Hills, New Jersey, during her Ethical Culture Ninetieth Birthday celebration, March 2016.

Dr. Edward Tick, Founder and Director of "Soldier's Heart," with guests at the Ethical Society —Bob Madara, and officer veteran of the Viet Nam War, and his wife Liz.

CLASS OF

2014

Announcing the Graduation of
Alison Marie Brunschwiler
Coast Union High School
June 12, 2014
1:30 P.M.

*Alison Brunschiler, Peace Emissary, Cambria, California,
now at the University of California, Davis.*

Lester, relaxed, at senior citizen home.

Wendy, enjoying a visit at Mom's home, back patio.

A great trilogy—Sis, Roy, and Les.

Matthew Besdine, Betty's psychoanalyst, Clinical Professor of Psychology, Adelphi University

Three generations of Ethical Culturists at the Essex Society honor Stephanie Rudolph and her presentation at the Sunday Service. Left to right, mother Janet Rudolph, graduate of Essex Sunday School; grandmother Betty Levin; and guest speaker, Stephanie, Sunday School Graduate, Garden City, Long Island, Ethical Society, March 2016

THE WEDDING
AND EARLY MARITAL YEARS

MY WEDDING ARRANGEMENTS BECAME STRAINED, especially regarding costs. With dad having great difficulty spending money, big news arrived one day that brought some relief to his wallet. Max Karel, Mother's stepbrother and a successful printer, had called to say, "I'll provide the wedding invitations as my gift to the newlyweds." I was disappointed, having hoped for cash to jump-start our new household.

I lacked fashion know-how. Since a traditional bridal gown would be costly, I decided a street-length dress and complementary hat would do nicely. After I bought a tailored beige crepe dress and an extravagantly flowered hat, I called cousin Mildred Rosenstein (Shirley Morris' older sister) to *kvell* (gloat with pleasure) about my choices. After I described my "over-the-top" hat, she tactfully volunteered to shop further with me. "Sis, let's see what other choices are out there—maybe one more complimentary to your tailored dress."

I welcomed her guidance. We chose a more appropriate beige pillbox beret, topped with a simple burgundy velvet bow. We added matching suede pumps to complete the ensemble.

Wedding plans continued but with a troubling hitch. I planned to invite Charles Campbell, my educated friend, a warm, brilliant, articulate Negro whom I admired, similar in demeanor to President Obama. He had middle-class values, and was active in the AFL–CIO union and a special companion of my cousin Naomi Cherner, who would be my maid of honor. At that time, I was unaware they were secretly married.

After meeting Charles, our relationship flourished, and we often invited him for dinner when his work schedule brought him to Chicago. The colleague I planned to have sing at my wedding was also Negro.

When Sara heard there would be Negroes at our wedding, she protested vehemently, "If there's going to be Blacks at the wedding, I'm not attending!"

Evelyn then said, "If the in-laws aren't coming, there won't be any wedding."

I was disgusted with both mothers' attitudes. Since Evelyn always accepted Blacks warmly, I suspected her response partly reflected her disappointment with my choice of husband. Howard suggested we rise above the behavior and just elope. I admired his practical take-charge approach, but I was too enthralled with the romantic idea of a wedding to relinquish my dream.

I compromised my principles and didn't invite my Negro friends. I caved in, even feeling virtuous about discarding my convictions for the larger goal of harmony with my in-laws. I swallowed hard, another problem of marrying into a family with different priorities. The bald truth was, I had shamefully abandoned my values, not able to take a stand and honor my beliefs. I also gave up my long-held dream of being married by an Ethical Culture Leader and conceded to Sara's desire for her synagogue's rabbi to conduct the service. I did arrange for a distant relative to sing my choice of music, "Ah, Sweet Mystery of Life." Little did I know how this mystery would unfold.

Howard and I agreed on two traditions of Jewish wedding ceremonies—including a prayer for my deceased mother and the elimination of the commitment, traditional back then, of newlyweds agreeing to eventually establish a home in Israel. When the rabbi ignored both these instructions, Howard was so furious he wanted to stop payment on the wedding check. I comforted him and counseled forgiveness—"After all, we're finally married, and that's now behind us."

I discovered later that Howard often hankered for battles and responded aggressively to even mildly challenging situations.

A disagreement between Howard and me involved Mildred Rosenstein's parents, beloved Aunt Ida and Uncle Frank, my uncle, a brother to my deceased mother. They were invited to the wedding, and out of respect to this family, which observed a strictly kosher home, I felt butter shouldn't be included with the wedding's turkey dinner.

Howard strongly protested, "You can't serve rolls without butter!" Another compromise followed, as I reluctantly accepted his assertion.

I trusted the Rosensteins would overlook this religious transgression—the entire clan were such forgiving people. My heart was heavy that their sacred observance was being ignored. My aunt and uncle never mentioned my misdeed. They probably didn't eat any of the non-kosher meal but had attended the wedding of a special niece who had grown up after having been a motherless child.

We chose a modest honeymoon at Starved Rock State Park, lodging in a charming but simple cabin. I was content and loved the natural setting. I did suffer a bit of embarrassment, however, sporting my new black Persian lamb fur coat with a white ermine collar. My father, an accomplished furrier, had made this handsome coat to honor my marriage. Traveling in coach on the train, I felt uncomfortable with my luxurious coat, glaringly ostentatious to the other modestly dressed passengers.

Harry, my father-in-law, had offered Howard money to upgrade us to a first-class ticket, but he had refused. I was proud of his decision and accepted Howard's limited means. Full of ideals, I felt confident a happy marriage would not depend on my husband's financial circumstances.

We had a serious fight on our wedding night about birth control. This era preceded the use of the popular pill. In preparation for making love, I couldn't find the rod to insert the birth control pouch. Howard became furious. He accused Evelyn of deliberately hiding the instrument.

My thoughts: *How could he attack my mother, so contrived and distorted? Perhaps I'm not truly aware of my husband's downside personality. Well, this is only the beginning of our life together, and I need to be a supportive wife no matter what.*

Though hurt and confused, I tried soothing my husband. "Howie, maybe you have some condoms we can use." To myself, I said, *I'll have to be patient.*

OUR FIRST YEAR PRESENTED ANOTHER PROBLEM, this one about housing. After the honeymoon, the severe post-war shortage resulted in our settling into a modest but very expensive downtown day-rate hotel. After three days, a furnished, shoddy apartment became available with a Murphy bed (pulled-down from the wall) for sleeping, but in a disreputable neighborhood. Though in dreadful condition, we gratefully accepted this more affordable housing. To counter the wretched neighborhood, when I walked down the street, I held my head high, carefully clutching my social work casebook to my chest, proud of my welfare job.

Howard, still without employment, vehemently refused to look for temporary work, even as a shoe salesman, something my brothers often accepted during hard times. I realized Howard was a different kind of man and considered such a job beneath his stature. I was a hopeless innocent comparing him to my brothers.

We had our first major argument about television. This exciting new medium was just emerging in 1948. It was very expensive, about seven hundred dollars, and few families could afford one. The only major programs were *Milton Berle's Comedy Hour* and *Flash Gordon*. There was little incentive for people to own one, with most channels showing only test patterns. Sara had good friends who owned a TV and they occasionally invited us on Tuesday nights to enjoy Milton Berle. Other nights we nursed a cheap beer at a local bar to view Uncle Miltie. I felt pleased that, despite our limited means, we could enjoy the comforts of life, usually granted only to the privileged.

One day, an enterprising business offered a TV for rent at one dollar a day with a future purchase plan as an option. Howard, always a visionary, leaped at this opportunity. I protested strongly that taking advantage of this offer was unethical if not downright dishonest. With Howard unemployed and only my meager salary to sustain us, and us living in a shabby apartment with someone else's decrepit furniture, we could never afford such a luxury. Howard insisted, "The company knows not every family who rents will eventually make a purchase. It's the way business operates—to create desire. Why shouldn't we take advantage of it?"

His wishes prevailed. On occasions of conflict, when I voiced my opinion, Howard invariably tried to destroy my arguments with insults. I felt it useless to challenge him. Why did I even bother? I had little confidence he would pay attention to my ideas. Howard seemed to always need to be correct. Expressing my views to him only invited defeat.

I later leaned toward Howard's understanding of how business operates. It eventually contributed to his becoming enormously successful. I have to admit I enjoyed the new piece of furniture brightening our dismal living room.

HOWARD EVENTUALLY GOT A MATHEMATICS FELLOWSHIP at IIT (Illinois Institute of Technology), named Armour Institute back then. His appointment included faculty housing, our first decent marital home.

It was beyond anything we could have imagined, a brand-new apartment furnished with clean, modern furniture designed by Mies van der Rohe, the acclaimed architect. Again, we had no conventional bedroom but two attractive, contemporary daybeds that converted for sleeping in the large living room. The stately apartment building, with unembellished architectural lines, rose nobly, almost like a mirage, above the leveled ruins of a burned-out slum on Chicago's south Thirty-Fourth Street.

On first viewing, this stark building was isolated from the warzone-like neighborhood. When Florence, my sister-in-law first saw it, she muttered, "How depressing."

No matter, we were thrilled with our good fortune, a large studio about twenty-eight feet long with an up-to-date kitchen and bath. There are now about six similar buildings in the complex.

We needed drapes to cover the expansive picture windows, provide privacy, and block the intense summer sun. With her *goldene* (gifted) hands, Evelyn sewed attractive, colorful drapes to cover the windows. Howard immediately found fault that the design pattern at the seams didn't match. His criticism of my mother was blatantly insulting. "What a terrible job! But then, she's only a peasant—what do you expect?"

He continued with other deprecating language, often pointing out his view of my family's shortcomings. I was mostly silent, but thinking, *There he goes again, with his usual prejudices against my parents.*

I swallowed his venom and failed to point out her generous intentions. And the money she saved us—such a department store purchase would have cost hundreds of dollars. But whenever we had a disagreement and I attempted a tactful approach, Howard would muzzle me with his sarcastic, "Oh, little miss social worker." I would be reduced to tears, feeling disparaged in my coveted profession.

Our different values were starting to erode our relationship, but I was unaware of just how destructive it was becoming. I kept hoping the ideals I sensed about Howard in those early days would override his hostilities.

At IIT, Howard met Karl Menger, an internationally renowned mathematician, who was developing innovative theories. He admired Menger and tried convincing him to publish his work. The professor initially declined, explaining that he didn't want to be diverted from his research. Howard reassured him, in his charismatic way, "We can publish it easily. My wife's a good typist and has plenty of time after work to prepare the manuscript."

My pride in Howard's ambitions took front and center, and I welcomed cooperating in this exciting venture. I accepted his assumption that I would step right in to support his goals. Typing the intricate formulae became mere detail. In the process, Howard had never demonstrated respect by asking me directly if I were willing to do the work.

Howard also explained the manuscript could be published at an IBM reproducing facility. He offered, "I'll be quite willing to do the editing."

A substantial lifestyle pattern had been established in our academic life. My ultimate life goal was indirectly flowing from Howard's abilities: *We met interesting people, explored intellectual ideas, and attended lectures at a seat of learning.* Howard may not have consciously bequeathed me this gift, but it was flowing incidentally as a byproduct of his ambitions. I was nevertheless grateful to him for fulfilling my ideals. In my life today, these components continue to be paramount, descriptive of the Ethical Culture Society (ECS) community in which I am deeply involved.

Our usual custom was to join each Friday night with my brother Leonard and Florence, also newlyweds, at my parents' apartment for a traditional family dinner. After one evening gathering, Howard issued an edict, his lip curling slightly: "We're not going to your mother's Friday night dinners any more." It never seemed to have occurred to him to first discuss his decision with me.

"Why?" I asked.

"Because it's dull. I just don't want to go anymore."

Part of me understood. Compared to the excitement of academic life and the likes of Karl Menger, an evening with family could be boring. But family is different—*it's a connection that hardly knows words and transcends ordinary social life.* How could I be expected to give up those precious hours with my beloved brother and the little contact I still had with my parents?

We argued interminably. I felt like a sword had sliced me in half, an impossible choice for a bride married just over a year. I cried hysterically for hours, alone in the bathroom, feeling lacerated by Howard's decision.

Attending family dinners without Howard never occurred to me.

Cowed as always, I went along with him. I lamented: I'm full of fear, lost in a dark pathless cave, one entrance, no exit. A separation was beyond thought. *How could I survive? I would be an orphan again.*

OUR NEW JOBS

HOWARD FINALLY FOUND A FULL-TIME JOB as a mathematician, working for Department of Air Force in 1949—a civil service position in Washington, D.C. When we moved to D.C., I looked for a social work job but was disappointed to discover those jobs are under the auspices of civil service. I would have to list on a roster, awaiting my turn, which could take many months.

I chose the next best avenue for earning an easy, quick salary. We needed money to purchase furniture for our first unfurnished apartment and a down-payment on a car. My typing skills enabled me to get a clerk-typist job, which were in such demand that employment booths were set up on the Mall. It required no ingenuity to get a modest GS-3 position, about $3,000.00 yearly. Sheer luck placed me in a very high echelon, the Department of Army Procedures and Regulations. I typed the rules for the entire army worldwide.

Though Howard had been offered a comfortable rate of pay, a GS-9, about $9,000.00 annually, his parents had objected to this job: "Civil service is a dead-end job, filled only with incompetent people unable to get decent employment elsewhere."

Howard and I strongly disagreed. We had no funds to move to D.C., though, and his parents had generously purchased a new car to drive ourselves there. Jumbling along on the floor of the car were all our worldly possessions: a card table, an ironing board and iron, our phonograph player, many phonograph records, and two art prints.

Howard and I had spent almost all our wedding gift money on newly introduced 33 1/3 long playing phonograph and records. He discarded his vast 78 RPM collection, to which I strongly objected. I abhorred this waste—how I had longed for such a record collection in my growing-up years. Howard had reassured me, though, that music reproductions with greatly improved fidelity were the wave of the future. and of course, he was right.

We had also purchased two art prints, one dollar each, but $40.00 to frame both. I was stunned at this latter cost, *ex-trav-a-gant!* I introduced Howard to the new world of collecting art, for people in modest circumstances. We started by purchasing graphics, the inexpensive multi-produced art form. I still enjoy the Picasso print we acquired then, now hanging in my psychotherapy office.

En route to Washington, we were all smiles, anticipating our rosy future. Regretfully, I'd had to resign my social welfare job but that was inconsequential compared to promoting Howard's career.

I had loved my job immensely. My supervisor, Helen Pyne, had recognized my special aptitude for working with people. She allowed me to do professional casework with promising welfare clients.

I'LL NEVER FORGET HOWARD'S RETURN HOME after his first day of work. You'd think he'd just been to Mars, his eyes aglow like stars. He exclaimed, "You can't imagine what the air force is doing. They own *a computer,* doing wartime planning and operations research!"

I wasn't sure what he was talking about, but his enthusiasm was infectious. I was pleased to see Howard so happy. Later, we discovered the U. S. Air Force owned the second computer *in the world*, the first acquired by the U. S. Weather Bureau. Brilliant mathematicians numbered among Howard's colleagues, such as Dr. George Dantzig, who eventually became a high-powered math consultant to Fortune 500 companies.

Howard's introduction to this new computer field was like a rebirth. Amazingly, though he had never worked in the business world, his incisive imagination anticipated the powerful potential of this technology. He grasped its ability to sort the voluminous data into useful form, conveniently accessible to business enterprises. In his brilliance, he intuited this was the true destiny of computers.

Despite Howard's insight, computers were so primitive back then, they relied on punched cards for their input and printouts. I remember a holiday party in which exhibiting the printed *Merry Christmas–Happy New Year* message required all four walls of the twenty-five-by-fourteen-foot room. Employees also celebrated the holiday by programming the computer to play *The Eyes of Texas are Upon You.*

AT MY CLERICAL JOB, BONNIE, my amiable senior procedures supervisor, mentioned that, occasionally, advanced training programs were offered even to lowly clerks possessing special talents. She regaled me with stories of employees, who had been identified as possessing just such abilities, elevated to the lofty echelons of civil service, even breaking those ceilings. I regarded these stories as mere chatter, considering my modest skills in a limited job, and still harboring social work aspirations.

Howard's first full-time job enabled us to look for an unfurnished one-bedroom apartment. Then we could sleep together in a conventional bed, the first time in our marriage. How refreshing to finally purchase our own furniture and share an intimate sleeping arrangement.

We found an ideal garden development, Culmore, on a seemingly rural road. It was down from Bailey's Crossroads, with a Falls Church, Virginia, address, marked with a sign that read *Horses at Stud.*

We both worked in the Pentagon, and Howard drove there each day through a forested area. He literally forded, without any difficulty, a gentle creek of trickling water. Heaven couldn't have been more pleasurable.

We had ordered a bed and dresser immediately upon arrival in D.C. but delivery would take several weeks. Sara came to the department store credit interview with me, answering the financial questions before I could even open my mouth. Until the bed arrived, Howard and I slept on the floor of our apartment.

At the Pentagon, one great delight was discovering that Jerry Rosow was working down the hall from my office. Jerry and his wife, Raye, were old friends from my Chicago childhood days. Jerry, a graduate in economics from the University of Chicago, was a high school fraternity buddy of my oldest brother Leonard. Back then, he was already marked as the fraternity brother brightest and most likely to succeed.

Jerry and Raye were childhood sweethearts, visiting our family apartment often on Winthrop Avenue for social events. As they were kind, friendly, and easy-going, they became my favorite of Len's friends. Their *hamishe* manner, intelligence, and practical qualities endeared me even further, and here they were in the D.C. area, living in Maryland.

When Raye and Jerry heard we were sleeping on the floor, they drove down from Maryland, bringing their summer army cots for us to use until the new bed arrived. We had been eating our meals on the card table with makeshift dishes, quite content.

We enjoyed a warm social life with Raye and Jerry throughout our D.C. stay that continued for many years after we both moved to the New York Metropolitan Area. They had become family. Our friendship felt like the coziness of a cherished family. At one of my birthday gatherings in New Jersey, Jerry exclaimed, "Betty, we've known you longer than anyone else here!"

Our move to Washington also brought Howard memories of its past unusual outdoor live music. He often spoke of the concerts he had enjoyed at a barge anchored on the Potomac River, a setting called "Watergate."

Howard had attended these concerts while on furlough from Fort Belvoir, Virginia, where he had been stationed during World War II. Later in the war, he had been hand-picked for the top-secret Manhattan project in Oak Ridge, Tennessee, where the atomic bomb was developed.

With our mutual love of music, we eagerly looked forward to the concerts at Watergate, but were disappointed that the barge was long abandoned and forgotten. A luxury facility, the Watergate Hotel, now occupied the landmark musical site; it later became the infamous locale of the Democratic Party headquarters burglaries and subsequent downfall of the Nixon presidency.

DURING MY TYPING LULLS AT WORK, I indulged two keen interests of mine: designing the ideal layout of a dream home that I hoped we could afford one day, and also an optimum hi-fi music system—a turntable, radio, amplifier, and speakers that complemented one another. These activities spelled out my optimism about our future together, occupying many hours beyond work assignments.

Howard encouraged me to pursue statistics and sampling courses at American University. My professor was head of the Bureau of Labor Statistics, and these intellectual pursuits pleased me considerably, my entry into the hard sciences.

The Washington Ethical Culture Society also greatly interested me, overseen by Leader (Clergyperson) George Beacham. The programs strengthened my humanistic vision of people, expressing their unique qualities and ideals. Howard, though only mildly interested, attended meetings with me.

AS BONNIE HAD MENTIONED EARLIER, the Department of the Army offered an opportunity for ordinary employees to advance themselves—an Executive Training Program. It was open to individuals who could qualify by examination and interview. Those accepted would be promoted to a GS-5, and completion of the three-month Training Program would bring advancement to a GS-7, equal to about $13,000–18,000 per annum and much more in the future. These employees would be on a fast track, identified as people of exceptional merit.

When I told Howard I was applying to this unique program, he merely nodded in assent without comment. Despite his indifference, I was certain I wanted to give the program a shot. If he had raised significant objections, I might have easily ignored the opportunity.

I was proud to be accepted into the Training Program, on the cutting edge of employee advancement, one of two women in a total of thirteen trainees. My training was full of self-doubts: *Am I really that capable?* It felt unreal. Bonnie congratulated me enthusiastically, but I sensed Howard's reservations.

Simultaneously, my civil service social work job came through. I was thrust between two compelling choices. The Training Program would bring me many promotions with substantial salary increases. Most important, I would finally be affirmed as a person of worth and ability, with a so-called government stamp of approval. I desperately needed recognition, both in the self-worth and marriage departments. I often felt diminished and alone.

I was hesitant about the social work job. I thought, Why go that route again? If I considered this professional path seriously, I would have to pursue a masters degree in Social Work. For the moment, I didn't have an appetite for returning to academic studies—the timing was totally askew. The Executive Training Program presented an invaluable opportunity, and I accepted it.

BEFORE ITS OFFICIAL START, Howard and I agreed to a mini-vacation. He wanted to reunite with a former army buddy, Robbie, in Binghamton, New York.

On Route 17 in New Jersey (then a two-lane road) on the way there, with Howard driving, he started to have sharp pains in his abdomen. We stopped at a roadside medical facility, and the doctor gave him some pills to alleviate his discomfort.

He became drowsy and suggested I get in the driver's seat and drive a short distance while he rested. Since I'd never had driving lessons, Howard offered a few instructions. "It's easy. All you have to do is hold the wheel steady, the same with your foot on the accelerator—and, oh, this is the brake in case you need it." Dutifully, I accepted this responsibility without concern for any possible danger. If Howard believed I could do it, I could.

In a few minutes, he was sound asleep in the passenger's seat. Fortunately, traffic was light, and the more I drove, the more I felt capable. The smooth road conditions relaxed me, and I rarely needed using that thing called the brake.

What really sustained me was a car I noticed staying behind me for many miles, like a steadying force. Though other cars whooshed past me repeatedly, this guy, whoever he was, maintained pace with me. Maybe he was a beginner, too. I counted eighty miles, about two hours, that he followed me, never passing, though he had many opportunities.

Howard awakened as we arrived at the outskirts of Binghamton, and I pulled into a filling station, using the brake.

"Howie, are you feeling better?" After a reassuring reply, I continued, "Please call Robbie for driving directions to his house—and also tell him to meet us in the front to park the car. I haven't the vaguest idea of how to do *that*."

When I pulled off the highway, the other driver waved a friendly "goodbye" to me. I continued driving to Robbie's home on local streets, with help from the brake. Howard was too woozy to take over.

When I got out of the car at Robbie's home, I couldn't quite accept that I had driven all that distance, unschooled and unlicensed. Robbie took Howard to his family doctor, who immediately hospitalized him. They discovered a kidney stone had caused his acute pain, and Howard stayed in the hospital for several days until the stone passed.

I couldn't believe what I had done and felt I never wanted to drive a car again. We spent another day visiting with Robbie, and I recall falling asleep curled up on the floor, traumatized. Howard drove back to D.C.

I STARTED THE EXECUTIVE TRAINING PROGRAM and was dismayed about one special requirement. Participants would be required to do a six-week stint in an out-of-state army facility to experience the broader cultural context of the Department of the Army regulations.

Uneasy, I heard they had an important installation in San Francisco—what if they assigned me there, and me afraid to fly? How would I handle such a lengthy trip and an extended separation from Howard?

They designated the Deep South, however, for this Yankee—Atlanta, Georgia. I regarded the location as challenging, having heard about the racial discrimination and political backwardness there.

During my stay, an army employee, at an otherwise friendly lunch, casually commented that her Negro nanny was currently breastfeeding her infant son, and then asserted in a threatening tone, "If that nanny ever tries to sit down to eat with us White folks, she would be one dead nanny."

This homicidal statement ate deeply into me. I was horrified by her declaration, eager to end my Atlanta stay.

A DEEPER JOLT SUBSEQUENTLY STRUCK, much closer to home. My relationship with Howard had deteriorated, as he resented the six-week separation. His demands included that I return to Washington almost every weekend. "I've checked the schedules. You can handle it nicely on the bus. It's cheaper than taking the train," Howard informed me matter-of-factly.

I agreed, of course—I did everything but salute. I was determined to make the Training Program work, doing almost anything Howard asked. Overnight bus commuting each weekend seemed a trivial price to pay.

I boarded a bus in Atlanta immediately after work on Fridays, sleeping overnight on the bus to D.C. I reversed the commute on Sunday evenings, returning to Atlanta on Monday, still in my sleepover clothing. Cooperative and sensible, I chose clothing that resisted wrinkling. What eased my successive overnights on the bus was my ability to sleep well under most conditions. I overheard two army servicemen discussing their difficulty getting proper rest on the long-distance bus. "This woman at the window next to me—boy, can she sleep! I don't know how she does it."

One Sunday afternoon, I was alone in my Atlanta lodgings, an exception that weekend to my dutiful trip home. I phoned Howard, troubled about the tension between us. In a tender voice, I murmured, "Howie, dear, I'm calling to talk about our relationship. I know we can be good partners to one another in a caring marriage despite this Program's intrusion. I'll *always* be your loyal wife."

He was surprisingly comforting, responding, in a way I had always wanted, "If this Program is important to you, it's good you're pursuing it, and I'll accept it."

There were other supportive words that seemed to express love. I was overjoyed. He was becoming the compassionate husband I had hoped for.

Immediately after the call, I wrote Howard a passionate love letter, telling him how much I loved him, and even expressed self-criticism for doubting his devotion.

No sooner had I sealed and stamped the envelope, Howard returned the phone call, reverting to the more familiar person I knew. "Don't misunderstand that earlier call. I still can't stand that goddamn Training Program, and I wish to hell you'd get home where you belong."

He continued with more angry words. And so my fantasy that he was becoming a different person was just that—a fantasy. I later discovered a friend had been visiting at the time of that first call when he showed some understanding. With a friend overhearing the conversation, he had contrived his words to sound caring.

Denying the obvious truth, I took a step that sealed my self-deception in the marriage. *I clung to the insecure, deluded love, the misled wife, of that first phone call.* I walked down the street slowly, somewhat dazed, mailing the love letter in which I desperately wanted to believe.

Howard never mentioned receiving the letter or any effect it might have had on him. As usual, my feelings were discounted. It was so customary that I didn't expect a response. I pushed away the hurt. Howard seemed unaware of the gross injuries he dished out.

At the conclusion of my Atlanta assignment, I was asked to complete an evaluation. I boldly criticized Southern racial practices that violated human dignity. My Atlanta supervisor remained gentlemanly but aloof. In response, he suggested I read the book, *Divided We Stand*. I respectfully noted his recommendation, but have never pursued it.

AFTER I RETURNED TO WASHINGTON, the Executive Training Program completed its schedule within a few weeks. Soon a new Department of the Army Chief Officer was appointed, didn't approve of the program, and abruptly canceled it. He granted all participants three months to find another job or be terminated. "Typical of the army's waste," several friends commented. I was greatly disappointed but pulled myself together to search for a new job.

Meanwhile, during Howard's air force employment, as his brilliant mind intuited the huge potential of computers in the business world, he foresaw entering private industry in a significant role. Howard suggested we place weekly ads in the *Sunday New York Times*, offering his skills as a master systems programmer. I initially debated this large expenditure; spending these sums always aroused great anxiety in me. Eventually, I agreed.

HOWARD HAD A MARKED SENSE OF ADVENTURE AND FUN. When I settled back in D.C. after my Georgia stint, he urged our dashing off to Philadelphia for viewing try-outs of Broadway plays, a theatrical custom back then.

We attended the world premier of *Guys and Dolls,* which left us on a high. With Howard's expansive capacity for pleasure, he insisted we return to Philadelphia two more times to see the production. By later attending this musical romp on Broadway, we had viewed the production four times.

In a similarly indulgent Washington birthday weekend, motoring to New York for a theater orgy, we viewed four plays, standing room only, to defer expenses: *Ondine,* with Audrey Hepburn; *Tea and Sympathy,* with Debra Kerr; *Teahouse of the August Moon*, with David Wayne; and a fourth production I can't recall. We went to more quality theater in one weekend than most people attend in a lifetime. In some ways, Howard's appetite was larger than life.

Along with Howard, I was becoming greedy about theatergoing. In retrospect, I now realize this shared passion had become a primary glue to keep our marriage intact.

OUR THEATER INTERESTS COULD CAMOUFLAGE disturbing personal events. In the summer of 1952, before departing for the theater, I received an enormous shock, a phone call from my brother Lester in California: *"Sis, Gloria has died. Marty has asked me to be a pallbearer at her funeral."*

My fury at this immense, unexpected loss exploded in an accusation. "Why didn't you write me how seriously ill she was?"

He tried to console me. "I didn't know either until I received the phone call." Commenting on his wartime army experiences, Les offered, "I saw the good guys get it, and the sons of bitches just go on."

If I hadn't been so distraught, I would have countered, "But, Les, you're one of the good guys who made it."

My deep grief and sense of futility over the loss resulted in an obsession. I mourned—why had Gloria left all those who loved her so much? I became haunted with an unreasonable idea: *The fate that tore her from us must mean she would be spared some unspeakable misery, yet to be inflicted on those who survive her.*

Her untimely end in the prime of her life made little sense to me, as she lovingly anticipated raising a daughter into a full life.

It struck a memory—several young friends of mine had died shortly after high school graduation. The uncertainty of life, the fate that unexpectedly befalls us, especially the young with long futures to explore—these thoughts brought back the very questions Gloria and I had pondered together as teenagers.

Despite my upset, I managed to go to the theater with Howard, a summer theater production of *Carousel* at the Bucks County Play-houseTheater in New Hope, Pennsylvania. I didn't want to disappoint Howard, though he expressed no particular concern for my loss.

My tears of mourning continued during the play. Howard took no note of my weeping, perhaps thinking my crying stemmed from the play's tragic events. Again, I pushed away the pain.

His capacity for understanding the feelings of others always remained minimal. As with other emotionally charged experiences, I often felt alone in my marriage. Howard simply short-circuited his connection to others.

AFTER MY DEPARTMENT OF THE ARMY JOB ENDED, I eventually found another with the Department of the Navy. I coded Naval Reserve Officers' "jackets," identifying their military job assignments in the event of warfare. After about nine months, the navy decided to have its own Executive Training Program, to which I applied and was accepted, with the same rosy future predicted. I felt genuinely affirmed by this second selection. My having been chosen for the army program had been no fluke.

The authorities made an unusual decision. "Since you completed the army program, you can forgo the navy's formal training and write your own." I was ecstatic.

By then, I was more aware of the importance of identifying employee talents and utilizing them more effectively. I was in the process of incorporating this concept into my newly designed navy training program, but it came to naught. We had to leave D.C. when Howard's career took another leap.

MY TROUBLED HUSBAND

OWARD'S EXPENSIVE ADS in the *New York Times* were not directly productive, but a Chesapeake and Ohio (C&O) Railroad advertisement was. They sought an advanced computer programmer for their complex revenue-sharing procedures, Howard responded, and he immediately received a generous job offer. He quickly accepted, but the new job meant moving to Cleveland.

I regretted forfeiting my new training program, but Howard's career was clearly more important. I was always invested in his talents and downplayed my own. Receiving recognition by the Department of the Navy made it easier for me to move on.

We left for Cleveland in 1952, where Howard hoped to fulfill his business computer dreams. I was thrilled that he had advanced to private industry for this innovative work. Unfortunately, Howard soon developed difficulties there. His C&O job started well, but before long he was in conflict with his supervisor.

I soon found a new job in Cleveland, though only a clerical position, with the Industrial Publishing Company. It was located just across the Square in downtown Cleveland, convenient to Howard's office. They hired me for a marketing clerk position, and I met Ingrid there, a new special friend. Originally from France, she had avoided a concentration camp and moved to England. Ingrid had eventually settled in the United Stated with her parents and married an American. I felt honored when she asked me to be her witness when she became a U. S. citizen in 1953.

FOR A TIME, HOWARD AND I SETTLED into a comfortable routine where we met for lunch almost daily. We joined a budding Cleveland Ethical Culture group, not yet a full Society but peopled by similar humanistic, intelligent individuals I had met at the Washington Society. The group rented public school meeting space for our Sunday services. As a new-comer, I was especially pleased when a participant invited us for a sump-tuous roast brisket dinner at his home.

Howard encouraged me to enroll in an Operations Research course at Case Western Reserve University, taught by the eminent Wes Church-man. I found the coursework stimulating, a relief from the boredom of my clerical job, where I didn't feel appreciated.

In one of our happier moments, we made the second art purchase of our marriage at Higbee's Department Store on the Square. We were en-chanted by a modest sculpture of two native African figures molded from plaster-of-Paris and sprayed in a brown hue that looked like carved wood. One figure depicts a woman tenderly holding an infant to her bosom. A complementary, separate figure positions a man kneeling at-tentively at her side. The grouping, as well as the price, attracted us. Sold separately, they cost three dollars and fifty cents each, seven dollars for the pair. We pondered, *Should we buy both figures? Should they re-ally be separated?* We could afford the expense and bought the pair. This art work foreshadowed our later acquiring *The Family*, a bronze by Henry Moore costing many thousands of dollarsm as well as other im-portant additions to our art collection. These acquisitions later figured prominently in deciding my future.

I couldn't have been more pleased with our African family sculpture than if we had acquired our own *David*. Over six decades later, though chipped and repaired, I still appreciate the figures today, prominently dis-played in my living room. I gaze at them longingly as an example of the togetherness I have yet to achieve.

HOWARD AND I DEVELOPED A FINE FRIENDSHIP with another young cou-ple. Emily was highly intelligent, vivacious, and insightful. Her husband,

Patrick, complemented her nicely and hit it off well with Howard. We exchanged visits frequently at our respective apartments.

One day, Emily called to arrange a private meeting. "I have something important to tell you, but only when Howard's not around." Later she explained, "We can't continue our relationship with you and Howard any longer. . . . Betty, we're fond of you but can't take him anymore. His idiosyncrasies are intolerable."

I was stunned, regretful at losing their friendship. I dismissed Emily's decision as partly her problem. She went on to explain: "He dominates the conversation—he has to always be the center of attention. It's so annoying. I tried pointing it out to him several times, but he would just revert to his usual ways."

With Howard traveling a discordant path, he never questioned our friends severing the relationship, nor did he seem to miss them. I didn't mention the conversation with Emily, protecting him as we continued a false demeanor. Howard's ambition and work life overshadowed everything. I tried making our flawed marriage work and rationalized, We had the valued friendship with the Perrys, the husband a co-worker of Howard's at C&O. One of our neighbors, Paul, though knowing us only superficially, admired Howard's charming manner: "Howard uses the word 'splendid' so elegantly." Paul was among the neighbors who attended Howard's surprise thirtieth birthday party, which I arranged in 1954. At the last moment, Howard contracted chicken pox, but was a good sport despite his unattractive facial splotches.

ANOTHER TROUBLING EXPERIENCE: When leaving for a business trip one day, Howard stopped at my office to confirm some last minute arrangements. My boss stopped him, since visitors were not permitted during work hours. Not accustomed to being thwarted, Howard ignored the boss's objection and continued into the office. The boss, tall and lean, then tried to physically stop him, and Howard lunged at him. The boss then attempted to bodily throw Howard out of the office. Hearing this tumult, I entered the front office to find Howard lying on the floor, humiliated, his topcoat ripped.

Concerned, I immediately joined him in leaving the office and returned only to quit my job. Ingrid called me the next day to find out about Howard's ejection and what my quitting had been about. I sobbed, "Howard was treated so shabbily—ejecting him for just trying to deliver a message."

More deeply, I knew how inappropriately aggressive he could be. I chose loyalty to my husband when I quit my job. I naively applied for unemployment benefits, which were justifiably denied.

AFTER QUITTING MY INDUSTRIAL PUBLISHING COMPANY JOB, it took a considerable time to find another. An excellent position opened as a marketing clerk for the Cleveland Electric Illuminating Company, with decent pay, good people, and interesting assignments.

I was always fortunate in finding new jobs. My ability to move ahead, despite setbacks, has consistently enhanced my way throughout life.

An important assignment at my new job, from the president himself, felt more like play than work. He asked that I comb important newspapers for articles related to finance and culture. Paying me to read the *New York Times* and *Wall Street Journal*—I loved it!

With new confidence, I decided it was time to learn how to drive. Despite these optimistic feelings, I was apprehensive about my past Binghamton experience. Merely thinking about picking up the phone to call a driving school brought an anxiety attack. I finally took hold of myself, made the call, and hired an instructor. I avoided asking Howard to teach me, believing his willfulness could interfere with my learning.

My teacher was tall, slightly built, and not very verbal. His unimpressive manner didn't settle my nerves. I wondered, *Could he be the one getting me over my hang-ups?* I made an interesting discovery. An unlikely looking person could be an effective teacher. After I shared my harrowing Binghampton driving experience, he took charge and asked me directly, "What's your biggest fear now about driving?"

"Oncoming traffic terrifies me when I'm driving in the outer lane."

After I learned to handle that situation with confidence, my teacher guided me in mastering parallel parking. Soon I became ready for my driving test. I passed nicely. . .until parallel parking became an issue.

I had practiced conscientiously near parked cars on the streets of my apartment complex. I carefully selected older vehicles for the experience. Even then, neighbors often pleaded, calling from their windows, "Please use someone else's car."

I was proud I efficiently parked my car during the test.

The official nevertheless declared, "You flunked!"

I was puzzled, dismayed. He explained that I had failed to turn my head to look out the back window when backing up, relying only on the rear view mirror. "You could hit a child dashing into the street. Your mirror wouldn't help. I know you're angry with me, but you'll always remember."

I was furious, since I had reserved Saturday, my one free day, for the test. Working full time, I relied on this day to complete all my chores. Back then, supermarkets offered no evening hours, and they even closed entirely on Thursdays. Now I would have to sacrifice another Saturday to repeat the test; but the official was correct. To this day, I always remember to turn my head before backing up the car.

ON BUSY SATURDAYS, I COOKED ENOUGH FOOD for an army. Our favorite supper included spaghetti with meat sauce. Saturdays were when I prepared many pints of meat sauce and other pre-cooked meals to stock in the freezer.

The freezer—another subject for disagreement. With Howard's vision, he had decided we need one. As usual, I protested this large expenditure.

My resistance to Howard's decisions was related mostly to his style— dominating and controlling, bordering on the tyrannical. There was no room for discussion, which he corrupted, never including give-and-take with respectful listening. My input was always discounted.

In some ways, I was partially responsible. My reluctance to spend money could discourage anyone from even opening the topic. Perhaps it would have been helpful if I had assured Howard I'd withhold any objections until hearing the pros and cons, keeping an open mind.

In fairness, his spending habits were often reasonable, even desirable, ahead of their time, and brought benefits. It was his style that caused the problems. We bought the freezer despite my protest, and as usual, I enjoyed my new convenience. Would I ever learn?

AT MY NEW JOB, THE UTILITY'S MARKETING DEPARTMENT conducted monthly surveys of customer services as an ongoing practice. In my discussions with Howard, he questioned whether data from non-respondents would have supported the results gathered from only the original sample. Would the non-respondents' opinions significantly alter the results? Again, Howard's inventive mind opened an original question. I passed his idea on to my supervisor.

With Howard's coaching, I proposed that the marketing department undertake a supplementary survey of the non-respondents to determine whether the new data would demonstrate a significant change from the original result. To my surprise, they agreed, and I started designing the new survey. The idea also involved a special strategy for contacting customers usually not at home or having had other reasons for not responding in the original survey.

As was often true, Howard's stunning intuition about new ideas proved valid. In the survey of non-respondents, their opinions were indeed significantly different from those in the original survey!

NEVERTHELESS, HOWARD CONTINUED his troubling behavior, both in our married life and at his job. He consistently pursued other employment possibilities and eventually was hired as a consultant with Ebasco Services in New York City. We would move again.

NEW YORK, PHOENIX, AND THOUGHTS OF MOTHERHOOD

HOWARD'S NEW JOB WITH EBASCO SERVICES made him feel triumphant. He proclaimed with a touch of arrogance, "If you don't live in the New York Metropolitan area, you're just camping out!"

I needed another month to complete the marketing survey at my Cleveland job. We agreed to separate temporarily; Howard left for New York by train, and I stayed behind to finish my work.

I experienced unexpected relief being separated from Howard's controlling ways. Since I had just learned to drive, I welcomed the freedom to hone my own style without his oversight. Each day I drove to work very competently on the shoreline superhighway and felt the exhilaration of both confident driving and liberation from Howard.

My idiosyncratic driving experiences continued when I later joined Howard in New York City. On my way through the Lincoln Tunnel, I wondered why the trucks were making horrendous noises, grinding their gears. Numerous attendants were flailing their arms, waving me on. *What's the matter here?* I wondered.

Only later did I discover I had been slowing traffic to a snail's pace, doing about fifteen miles an hour, not realizing my speedometer was broken. What a frustration for motorists creeping through that heavily trafficked entry into the city.

"Oh, that bumpkin with the Ohio plates."

Welcome to the Big Apple!

I started apartment hunting, armed with ads scattered throughout the New York Metropolitan Area. Naive about its vastness and still a novice driver, I soon became exhausted in my search. I explored varied rental apartments on traffic-jammed roads in the tri-state area, driving about eighty miles daily. One day in the Bronx, limp with fatigue behind the wheel, I abandoned the car at a gas station and took the subway back to the St. Georges Hotel in Brooklyn Heights, our temporary quarters. It was several days before I overcame my embarrassment and reclaimed the car.

I eventually found a lovely garden apartment at 121 North Broadway in White Plains, and we settled in—but for only three weeks. Ebasco assigned Howard a consulting job in Phoenix, Arizona.

The apartment's generous outdoor grounds, secluded from traffic by its inner court, captured my imagination. It was totally safe, perfect for child-rearing. I was making future family plans in my mind; what a desirable place to start raising a child.

At the same time, Howard was working on his book *Office Work and Automation*, with my doing research on some portions. He was so far ahead of the curve that, if his book was finished expeditiously, it would be the first of its kind in the business world. As it turned out, it was published in 1956 as the *second* computer book contributing to the emerging industry.

En route to Phoenix, with Howard behind the wheel, he started not feeling well as we entered the outskirts of Cleveland. He gently suggested, "Why don't you take over for a while as I rest a bit?"

By then, I was an experienced driver, prepared to try more extensive highway challenges. I felt confident enough to remain behind the wheel almost all the way to Phoenix. I recall the vast emptiness of the highways in the western United States, hardly noticing I was speeding at eighty miles an hour.

As we approached Phoenix, Howard consulted the AAA trip ticket map and said, "Their way seems too long. I see a short cut. Just turn here—we're only about twenty minutes away."

"Sounds good," I replied. "It's only three in the afternoon. We'll be there for an early leisurely dinner."

My dark driving fortunes then struck again. Within a few miles, we were on an uneven gravel road, with only occasional construction signs warning us, nothing substantial for guidance, and no shoulders for safety. I decreased my speed to almost a crawl. Vast mountains and deep gullies started to appear. With no way to turn around, we continued this way for many hours and untold miles.

Soon, night was upon us, with no end in sight and no highway illumination to guide us. It was pitch black. I noticed headlights of other cars very high above us, and also many below, way below. We must have been climbing on some mountain road with no place to go but forward. It was difficult to see the road or get our bearings, just more gravel and dirt. I gripped the steering wheel so tight that my white knuckles protruded. My nose was practically on the windshield straining to see the road. Howard's nose matched mine; both of us were terrified. Not a word was said as we swallowed our gasps.

The unspoken—could we skid down an unseen cliff into the darkness? We continued this way for several more hours.

Finally, some distant lights appeared far ahead. Was this some relief? I started to breathe more fully again. We eventually joined an illuminated, paved road. Our ordeal had finally ended. A few more miles, and we were in the outskirts of Phoenix.

Upon arriving, we got out of the car but could barely stand—-shaken and exhausted, with no appetite for food. We fell into the first decent motel and plopped down for a welcome rest.

The next day, the sun shone brightly, blocking out the nightmare of the previous one. We found a charming bungalow colony with an in-ground swimming pool, perfect for my swimming passion. This could be quite nice, I thought.

Later, when residents heard of my driving ordeal, they exclaimed, "You must have traveled through Oak Creek Canyon. That's challenging even in daytime—and you did it at night, under construction!"

They looked at me wild-eyed. I just shrugged, and explained my usual life pattern: "When I'm trapped in a bad situation, I just put one foot in front of the other and carry on."

When the construction was complete and we again traveled the canyon, I marveled at its beauty and at what I had traversed.

Our sightseeing explored notable national landmarks in this picturesque part of our country—Grand Canyon, Hoover Dam, and some lovely desert country. I was saddened by the border town of Nogales, Mexico, struck by its poverty and stark environs. The contrast was vivid—different from the many economic advantages of our country and lush expanse of the Western states.

Howard insisted we include Las Vegas on our itinerary, which we visited as poor tourists, not as we did in later years, when he became wealthy and an important property owner, comped at all the hotels, night clubs, and gambling casinos, where we became experts at playing blackjack.

Living in Phoenix in 1954, even with good weather and a convenient pool, I was discontented.

My upset stemmed from the city's dreadful treatment of Hispanics and Native Americans. If they were able-bodied, though destitute and unemployed, their situation was essentially ignored, making them ineligible for welfare. These deprivations were dismissed as "tough luck." With neither food banks, food stamps, or homeless shelters then available, this policy felt inhuman.

I also considered it disgraceful that cars had preference over pedestrians at all intersections, however dangerous. Equally upsetting, citizens were allowed to carry guns openly, not only on Dress Western days. To me, some Phoenix customs seemed uncivilized.

At that time, Phoenix offered only few cultural events—little theater and no classical music radio station. On a rare occasion, when a major symphony orchestra visited Phoenix, the best town fathers could manage was setting up a band shell in a baseball field. The rich sound wafted away into the desert.

I admired one particular Phoenix rule. In school zones, vehicles must travel fifteen miles per hour at all times, even when school was not in session. There had not been a child fatality in a school zone in over twenty-five years.

While working on Howard's book, I looked for a social work job but was unsuccessful. In researching some data for the book, I phoned the librarian at the local college. We both lamented the lack of resource materials available. She said, "The computer age will dramatically improve data accessibility." I chuckled; this was the very innovative issue Howard was addressing in his book.

Since Phoenix was close to Los Angeles, I SUGGESTED TO HOWARD THAT WE VISIT there to finally see little Corrie, Gloria's daughter. She was now five years old, it had been three years since her mother's death, and I could reunite with Eva.

As I approached the two-family Rimpau Boulevard home, I trembled as markedly as a prospective adoptive mother visits the child for the first time. Eva welcomed me at the front door, where we greeted each other warmly. I hugged her only briefly, as I was impatient to see the precious cherub. Eva said, "Go in the kitchen. Little Corrie is there."

She had been teaching her granddaughter how to tie her shoes. I observed a sandy-haired, slightly plump child sitting on a stool next to Eva's, their heads nestled close. Their focus on shoe lace intricacies, a scene of grandma and granddaughter togetherness, befitted a Norman Rockwell illustration. My heart surged with many emotions, viewing this family scene—*the gift Corrie was receiving, and the exquisite parent–child richness of which Gloria had been cheated.* My consciousness also opened a new appreciation of Tante Surrel's devotion when she agreed to raise me.

Eva took me upstairs afterwards to show me Gloria's marital home. It felt eerie intruding into their past intimate life. A note, in Gloria's handwriting, was taped on the bedroom sliding closet door: *Dear Marty, please close the door when finished.*

A CHILD IS BORN

That woman phoned me three times yesterday—she's so anxious to get the adoption process moving faster," Maidie said about her social work job. "Their waiting for a baby to adopt becomes so intense, it sometimes moves them to unusual measures."

These captivating stories whetted my appetite to finally become a mother. I had held my motherhood desires in abeyance while waiting for Howard to stabilize his work life.

Maidie was the wife of Howard's Ebasco colleague in Phoenix. Though the assignment was a temporary one, Howard appeared settled in his professional choice.

It was 1954, I was twenty-six years old, and we had now been now married almost seven years. It seemed time to discuss having a baby. We had never talked about this possibility before our marriage; parenthood was not on our minds. I tentatively opened the subject. "Howie, dear, you know I believe we should start a family. What do you think?"

He looked at me with a gentle smile, and his eyes twinkled. As he nodded in agreement, we went right to bed. I suspect he was more excited by the thought of sex without birth control than with the idea of becoming a father.

It was Thanksgiving time. In that season of celebrating family and gratitude, I was blessed by becoming pregnant almost immediately. I felt inspired, launching this life-changing event, taking personal responsibility of a magnitude I could barely imagine. The profundity of motherhood struck me, fulfilling being a woman, perpetuating family and life itself.

The difficulty of choosing an obstetrician in a new city challenged me. The Phoenix Medical Society supplied a list of obstetricians but no distinctive qualities. One day, however, the front page of the local newspaper reported that the Phoenix Symphony Orchestra roster included a doctor, the first violinist—and he was an obstetrician on my list. I had found my OB!

Yet I didn't want a child of mine born in Phoenix because of the city's primitive state of development at that time. I was repelled by repulsive attitudes toward minority populations, and lax gun customs.

This birth could likely happen here, as Howard's assignment extended to many additional months. I kept occupied, writing and typing Howard's new book, *Office Work and Automation*, and swimming in the on-site pool. He took little notice of my pregnancy, actively supporting me by pressuring the company to allow us to return East. Permission finally granted, we embarked on that lengthy cross-country trip back to White Plains, with my protruding baby belly squeezed behind the steering wheel. I managed to share the driving and went into labor within a few weeks after we arrived home.

Janet was born at the White Plains Hospital. She was a gorgeous newborn with a heart-shaped face and wisps of blond hair. I could hardly believe this beautiful infant was my very own daughter. Hugging her often, I loved our bonding and my treasured new role. Howard arrived at the hospital after work, exhausted, complaining about the tedious Wall Street–White Plains commute. He seemed distracted, barely dragging himself to the nursery to *kvell* with me over our first born or ask how I was feeling after my difficult labor.

I felt alone, like a single mother, the same way I often felt as a wife. Despite my awe of motherhood and feelings of supreme joy, I wept with despair after Howard left. He never shared the exquisiteness of *our* special event. It was only *my* special event, my solitary undertaking.

I named Janet after the movie star Janet Gaynor. She was Mom's favorite, an upcoming starlet whom she probably discovered in the 1931 film *A Star is Born*. Evelyn's face glowed, and her voice trembled, when she spoke about the actress. Movies had been a special joy for Mom, providing a break from her burdensome life. Totally unaware, I had selected a name signifying my still-living stepmother—strictly forbidden in the Jewish tradition, but basically honoring her. Despite our troubled, distant relationship, this choice reflected my deep hidden love for Evelyn.

When I first held the baby in my arms, I was overcome with adoration. Remembering Gloria, a new enchantment came upon me—to name my daughter for her, memorializing my deceased dearest friend. With Howard so remote, I hesitated reopening the subject and decided to stay with our agreed-upon choice. I chose Gloria as Janet's middle name.

When I returned home from the hospital, the essence of family finally entered my life with a visit from Flora, my brother Lester's sister-in-law, accompanied by her four-year-old daughter, Rose. Flora's kindness and generosity, traveling from New Jersey to rejoice in the new baby, moved me deeply. I was friendless in White Plains, having just returned from Arizona, and already feeling lonely. Flora's visit partially filled my need, arriving laden with gifts—a luscious pink satin comforter, a lace-trimmed cranberry velvet bonnet, and other useful newborn items. She nourished my deep need of family, relieving the neglect of a self-absorbed husband.

Howard would phone often from work about problems at the office—personality clashes with his boss or scheduling difficulties—droning on for twenty or thirty minutes. Only occasionally did he ask about my day or how the baby was doing. When I tried interjecting comments, he would quickly interrupt me: "Oh, I'm too busy for that now. You can tell me when I get home." That seldom happened. By evening, he was still wound up about his needs and too fatigued to hear about my joys and challenges. I barely noticed the pain Howard inflicted on me with his dismissals and exaggerated self-involvement. I usually rationalized, *That's just the way he is.* The delight of mothering distracted me, and I thought so little of myself that protesting his disparagements never entered my thoughts.

A small hurricane swept through White Plains as we drove home from the hospital, and all the baby formula they had supplied spilled onto the car floor. At home, after I placed little Janet into her crib, I rushed to the kitchen to prepare a fresh batch to feed my hungry newborn. Challenges can come unexpectedly, even before the new baby settles in.

Janet was a content infant who didn't disturb Howard's routine. We placed her in the master bedroom with the baby equipment. Our bed was moved to the dining room, and a corner area of the living room was designated for eating.

I handled all middle-of-the-night bottle feedings, careful not to wake Howard. He was restless her first night home, fearful he wouldn't hear her cry for a bottle. Afterwards, he slept soundly, assured I could handle her needs.

I gained some confidence from Dr. Benjamin Spock's classic book for new mothers. His opening sentence has stayed with me always: *You know more than you think you do.*

AT HOWARD'S WORK IN NEW YORK CITY, his Ebasco Services supervisor assigned him to improve the computer system for their client, the New York Stock Exchange. Intrigued with stock movements, Howard quickly detected their possibilities for creating a stock-trading model that would make money fast. He designed a personal system in his spare time that became a part-time home business—Probability Fund, Inc. His mathematical and statistical know-how, combined with the advanced programming skills of friend and colleague, Jim Townsend, developed an effective plan. In their newly formed organization, Howard appointed himself President; Jim became Vice-President, and I Secretary/Trader. After I integrated Jim's adjusted calculations into the model, I phoned the trading signals to Reynolds & Company each morning after Janet's early feeding. Her two naps daily allowed me ample time to focus on these responsibilities.

Computer computations brought consistent profits, and friends eagerly bought shares. We generated excitement at cocktail parties by predicting the next day's stock movements. I traveled to the New York City IBM Computing Center to integrate model changes that Jim had developed, all on punched cards back then. I reveled dressing up in business clothes, moving beyond being a housewife and mother.

Howard noticed the commodity market was more volatile than stocks, offering more profit opportunities, trading either up or going short. We switched from stocks to commodities—soy beans, pork bellies, etc. True gambling. We consistently reaped profits, which continued for several years.

Part of me relished partnering with Howard's extraordinary abilities and energy. I also enjoyed that money was more available. After awhile, though, I started questioning so much time spent just acquiring money. I had become more relaxed about my early life spending hang-ups, but the *intensity of just making more* brought new discomfort. I wondered: *Shouldn't extra leisure time pursue ideas that can enrich life's journey?*

WHEN JANET WAS ELEVEN MONTHS OLD, I introduced her to the pleasures of Rye Beach, paralleling my love of the shore from my Chicago childhood. As I placed her at the water's edge, she was delighted being teased by the gentle waves coming forward to tickle her, then receding. She giggled, slapping at the water, responding as to a playful companion. An appreciative crowd, smiling in response, soon encircled my joyful, sun-drenched child, engrossed with rhythms of the ocean.

When I tried sharing these moments with Howard, he was usually too preoccupied to listen. "Howie, let me tell you about the wonderful time I had with the baby at the beach today."

He dismissed me with a wave of his hand, saying, "I haven't got time for small talk. There's some really serious stuff going on at the office I have to discuss with you." His successful work life enabled us to enjoy a leisurely lifestyle, yet he deprived himself of the profound joy of a father–daughter relationship. Janet missed out, too.

At Janet's first birthday, my lonely habit well established, only the two of us celebrated. I placed a cupcake with a solitary candle on her highchair tray. I snapped many pictures of her bright smile, watching my fussing about.

Outdoors, a gloriously bright day suggested more photographs, my glowing one-year-old, in a fluffy little-girl pink dress, matching the day's sunshine. I felt isolated, the only one there to enjoy this luminous sight. Howard showed no interest in celebrating our daughter's first year when he arrived home that evening.

Janet particularly enjoyed my reading to her. I often chose books as much for their prized art work as for the story content.

She continued to grow and thrive, alert to unusual concepts at a young age. During a car trip in her toddler years, Janet noticed the on-coming traffic and asked, "Why are they going back?"

At two years of age, Janet developed her first childhood friendship with slightly older Rickey Hayes. His parents had moved into the down-stairs across-the-hall apartment, and they played together almost daily. His understanding parents allowed him to enjoy dolls, kitchen equip-ment, and other cross-gender toys. Janet similarly played with his trucks, tools, and other boyhood playthings.

Marilyn and I exchanged babysitting regularly and shared many friendly coffee interludes. I was pleased to be invited to her midnight mass one Christmas Eve, attentive to the sacred reenactment. My interest in ecumenical events and people of diversity has always attracted me the way a romantic is drawn to moonlight.

When Janet was ready for nursery school, I discovered an ideal choice in Elmsford, which included children from this interracial neighborhood. I went door-to-door in my housing development. "Have you heard about the cooperative nursery school, enrolling kids from mixed backgrounds? It's only a few miles away, and we could carpool together." No mothers were interested, perhaps regarding these different conditions as substan-dard. I did all the driving; I didn't mind, grateful for an exceptional school that reflected my values. Additional pluses included opportunities for classroom teaching and evening parent-education lectures. Howard babysat with Janet, having no interest in the after-hours program.

WITH JANET READY FOR SUNDAY SCHOOL, I tried enrolling her at the Westchester ECS pre-school in nearby New Rochelle. Although classes were filled, I nevertheless went to the Sunday Services alone while Howard again babysat. Attending without family felt somewhat lonely, but since the members and lectures were ethically and intellectually stimulating, the experience served me well.

I particularly appreciated the Leader, Henry Herman, functioning as a rabbi or minister. He was a well-informed humanist guide, introducing societal issues that we attendees discussed with spirited and knowledgeable opinions. Since I had been drawn to the Society's Movement in other cities, I was now grateful to discover another branch.

We moved to New Jersey in April 1959, when Howard discovered this would greatly improve his Wall Street commute. In searching for an apartment, my foremost priority was a location convenient to Maplewood's Essex ECS. We rented a duplex two-bedroom garden apartment at Springfield's Troy Village, approximately four miles from the Society.

My next priority was finding another good-quality nursery school for Janet. Inquiries suggested the very best around was Playhouse Nursery in West Orange. Directed by Jeannie Ginsburg, an iconic personality in early-childhood education, she invariably guided children gently and expertly toward healthy development. I was determined to enroll Janet in this exemplary school.

When I phoned Jeannie, enrollment was already filled for the September class. I pleaded without success. Despite my disappointment, I became the beneficiary of Jeannie's wisdom. She pointed out, "Even if there were space, there are no other children enrolled from your area. Without a carpool, the commute from Springfield to West Orange would leave you little time for your own needs and personal pursuits. Good parenting involves this important consideration."

What a rare thought. I'd never seriously considered this idea before, except during glimmers of over-preoccupation with Probability Fund. My mother had taken no quality time for herself, never for her own pleasure or enrichment, only fund-raising occasionally for a children's organization. Howard's expectation of me was primarily promoting his own goals. Jeannie's wisdom was a revelation. I later discovered many mothers of children attending Playhouse became community leaders.

I eventually selected a nursery school for Janet that was merely acceptable. I always regretted that I didn't have the very best for her that final year.

When Janet was in kindergarten, I met Gertrude White, who later became my best friend and part of my extended family. Included were her husband Sol and her three daughters, Ina, Loretta, and Susan, who generously shared their family life with me.

We met when they moved to Henshaw Avenue in Springfield and Susan was enrolled in Janet's kindergarten class. As a volunteer classroom mother, I phoned Gertrude to welcome her to the community. For a later class trip, I offered to pick up Susan, welcoming a companion for Janet. After my second such deed, Gertrude gave me a gift of chocolates. I thought, *What a mensch* (a person of character).

Prior to meeting Gertrude, I had driven down Henshaw many times and noticed a large brick one-story ranch house under construction. Its style was in striking contrast to the more modest two-story homes lining the street. I thought, *What foolish people, building such an ambitious house. They'll never get a decent return on their money.* It was Gertrude White's family who was building this seemingly inappropriate house— but for good reason.

The house was designed to be accessible for a disabled person, equipped with oversized doorways and conveniently placed equipment in the kitchen and bathroom. The White's eldest daughter, Ina, used a wheelchair, having sustained a birth injury. She had never walked.

Ina's parents recognized their daughter's bright mind and wanted a solid education for her. In moving from Elizabeth, the Whites searched for a town with a public school system that would mainstream their daughter. Springfield filled this need when the principal of Florence Gaudineer Middle School, Thelma Sandmeier, welcomed the Whites. It was on Henshaw that the Whites had found a lot sufficiently level to accommodate the style of house they needed.

As I came to know Gertrude, I found her to be an extraordinary woman with many admirable qualities—unselfish, unfailingly considerate, and full of generosity. Her lovely blond hair, twinkly eyes, loyalty, and gracious manner were attractive qualities to which most of us were inevitably drawn. These characteristics marked every experience, no matter how trying. In later years, when Howard became threatening at home one evening and I felt it prudent to flee with the children, Gertrude readily accepted us overnight into her home. My thank-you gift brought a typical response: "Betty, the flowers were lovely but there was no need to send them. You know, I'm always here for you."

Gertrude was a zealously committed member of Women's American Organization for Rehabilitation and Training (ORT). She became national president, traveled internationally on its behalf, and built its membership to its largest ever. She pointed out, "With California's early three-hour time difference, I can work till midnight and solicit many new members."

Janet (and later, my daughter Wendy) loved her, too. Appreciative of her endearing ways, they bestowed on her the title "Aunt Gertrude." Their faces always lit up when I told them, "You'll be staying with Aunt Gertrude after school today, as I'll be away for a few hours."

After Ina completed her high school studies with honors, she continued her education at Kean College in Union, New Jersey. At that time, the campus was expanding, under construction, resulting in numerous obstructed paths. Ina needed assistance to maneuver her wheelchair to the various buildings. When ads for help produced no results, Gertrude arranged employment on campus to be available for Ina's 'transportation' needs. Her job at Kean's Child Study Center developed into an important one, resulting into a close relationship with Director Marie Siegel. Dr. Siegel eventually served as the principal speaker at Gertrude's funeral.

JANET STARTED ATTENDING SUNDAY SCHOOL classes at the Essex Ethical Society at age six and continued until graduation. I served as a Sunday School teacher when the staff discovered I had been a member in other Societies and was knowledgeable about its concepts. I taught for five years before joining the main congregation, finally becoming a regular member. Howard rarely accompanied us. Janet spoke little of her Sunday School experience, questioning its necessity, but attended at my insistence. Its progressive lessons, nevertheless, alerted her to societal conditions. One day, criticizing her public school history book, Janet complained, "Mom, it doesn't describe the treatment of American Indians accurately and sensitively."

I always encouraged Janet's awareness of our natural world. For a December holiday home celebration, I created a Winter Solstice children's "Trim-the-Tree" party for bird friends. They made and brought garlands of bird goodies—popcorn, seeds, cranberries, and nuts to trim our outdoor evergreen tree for birds to enjoy during the sparse winter months. Prizes were awarded for the longest and prettiest garlands. After I photographed the decorated tree, surrounded by playful children, festivities concluded with hot chocolate and cookies. This photo became the invitation for Janet's friends the following year. A glistening snowstorm one year provided a particularly beautiful card. Howard never took note of this annual gathering.

WHEN JANET WAS IN SECOND GRADE AT CHISHOLM SCHOOL, Bette Powers, the principal, called me in for a conference. She reported that Janet, though an exceptionally bright child, was performing below expectations, especially in reading. The principal added, "Sometimes home conditions can interfere with children developing their full potential."

Shocked, I said little. Mrs. Powers continued, "I would suggest you and your husband consult with a psychologist, which might prove helpful." She then presented me with a list of professionals.

That evening, when I told Howard about the conference, his response was explosive. Screeching and waving his clenched fists, he barked, "There's nothing wrong with Janet or our home!" His cataclysmic response felt as if he would tear down the walls if he could. I remained silent, though I felt the principal had given me crucial information.

Though Mrs. Power's revelation concerned me deeply, I remained powerless and lacked the initiative to seek professional help without Howard's support. Janet was burdened with problem parents— a mother who, however conscientious, was insecure, lacking assertiveness; and a self-centered father full of denial.

At Chisholm, Janet received enrichment, nevertheless, participating in the Audubon Club, which Mrs. Powers had organized during their lunch hour. She presented new dimensions of learning; bless this inspired educator for her commitment.

Family life with Howard rarely moved smoothly. Whenever there was conflict between his needs and those of our daughter, he screamed, "I never agreed to a 'child-centered' family!" I believe my inability to challenge Howard and respond responsibly to Janet's healthy, growing needs contributed to some setbacks for her. I had to go along with him in order to survive.

I introduced a music box to comfort Janet at bedtime. With the melody, Brahms' *Lullaby*, tinkling in the background, I sang to her, quietly ending with a tender kiss and murmuring, "Sweet dreams." I hoped the serenity of the ritual might soothe Janet's upset that day.

JANET REPORTED A TROUBLING DAILY PATTERN in her Chisholm class. The children recited the "Lord's Prayer" and read five stanzas from the Bible. I was puzzled that she told me, not likely knowing this practice was a violation of the separation of church and state. I was upset and phoned Mrs. Powers to question its legality. In her respectful manner, she said,

"I'll look into it and get back to you."

Within a few days, she called to confirm the practice, explaining, "It's happening in classrooms in all forty-eight states. It's the law of the land." I felt crushed though I later heard the practice was under review by the Supreme Court, challenged by the ACLU. I reluctantly accepted this ritual but hoped it would be changed eventually.

JANET WAS SEVEN YEARS OLD when Wendy was born in 1962, and I planned to bed the new baby in the master bedroom. Janet vehemently insisted her new sister share her room, though I explained she would be awakened by Wendy's middle-of-the-night feedings. Janet pleaded, "Mom, I promise if she wakes me up, I'll go right back to sleep." I complied with her wishes, and the sisters shared the bedroom.

Janet's quiet personality contrasted with Wendy's lively one. Shortly after Wendy's birth, I noticed Janet's reclusive behavior when picking her up after school. Though I greeted her lovingly, she recoiled from me, pulling toward the side door. I didn't recognize that she was reacting to a new child in the family.

In the summer, we swam together almost daily at the on-site pool, where Janet became particularly competent. Our apartment development also abutted a natural deep quarry, whose mysteries she explored.

WHEN JANET BECAME OLD ENOUGH, I enrolled her in ballet classes but was disappointed, finding them too rigid. After I discovered modern dance, a freer dance expression, and brought this art form to the ECS, I became Founder of their Creative Arts workshops. Many other studio arts followed. Enjoying this new challenge, I then firmly told Howard, "I'm not managing Probability Fund any longer." He posed no serious objection, since the trading model wasn't making much money anymore.

In later years, I expanded the school to include humanistic studies. Thus emerged a family school, the Educational Center—and I felt new vistas had opened for me.

When she was nine, Janet received a letter suggesting she could earn money by selling greeting cards. I pointed out greeting cards were also available from UNICEF, with an added advantage: "This unique organization helps children on the other side of the world who are often hungry and sick." Janet's interest was piqued, and she decided to volunteer, supporting UNICEF to benefit other kids.

Supplies of these cards weren't easy to get back then, mail order catalogs not being generally available. They could be obtained only at the United Nations Gift Shop in New York. Ethical Culture member Suzanne Gluck traveled regularly to the UN for supplies. I also discovered a local South Orange meat market proprietor with a social conscience who stocked them. Janet sold these cards after her Sunday School class in the Society's foyer where enthusiastic members lined up to make their purchases.

AT SPRINGFIELD'S GAUDINEER MIDDLE SCHOOL, Janet's class was assigned to write biographies of three civil rights leaders. After choosing two, she had difficulty making a third selection. I suggested, "An eminent civil rights leader, Rabbi Israel Dresner of Temple Sha'arey Sholom, Aunt Gertrude's synagogue, officiates right here in Springfield."

I explained that he was the first rabbi to march with Martin Luther King as a Freedom Rider in Selma, Alabama. After Janet decided to interview him, I suggested she plan her questions in advance.

Meeting in his study, Janet was well- prepared, with one particularly penetrating query: "Why would you as a Jew go down South to object to the practices there?"

This question brought the rabbi's forthright response. "Because I *am* a Jew. I could not remain idle and silent while the rights of peoples were grievously violated. I needed to express my objection to Negroes being treated so disgracefully."

I was proud of Janet's thoughtful question and impressed with the Rabbi's forthright response. She had learned that heroes can exist close to home, not just in some dusty, remote history book.

BECOMING BETTY

MY BIRTHDAY WAS COMING, but I could expect nothing from Howard. Our marriage was unraveling as his career became highly successful. I wasn't certain if Janet and Wendy were aware of my birthday. With Howard infatuated elsewhere, he was not likely to suggest our daughters send me a card, but I felt I couldn't allow the occasion to pass without bringing it to their attention. The integrity of the family must be maintained and was important to me, even if the marriage was in trouble.

On the evening of my birthday, after dinner with my daughters, (Howard was rarely at home for a family meal), I brought out a gooey cake and small, gaily wrapped presents for the children. They were delighted to find out it was my birthday but puzzled at the turn-about celebration. I simply told them I didn't know if they knew of the occasion but thought some marking of it was important.

The following summer, when Janet was away at camp at the time of her birthday, I had arranged with the camp Director to have a cake made for sharing with her bunkmates. That day, I received a letter from Janet with plans for her birthday celebration *at home*, in absentia. She had arranged a treasure hunt within the house for gifts she had hidden in various rooms before she left for camp. Not only were there gifts for Wendy and me but also for our devoted housekeeper, Mary, who she knew would be working that day. The letter contained the clues for finding our presents. Such merriment as we rushed from room to room to discover the surprise packages!

Janet's thoughtfulness warmed me deeply as I contemplated her experiences in making these advance plans. Wendy, Mary, and I, flushed with pleasure and excitement, seemed to affirm: No matter the direction of giving, it is the love and joy that is celebrated.

DURING JANET'S MIDDLE SCHOOL YEARS, we moved to Short Hills, where she continued in public school. Howard noticed her bright mind and started teaching mathematical concepts to his daughter. It was gratifying to see their heads together. Howard was finally paying attention to Janet, companions in teaching and learning, especially when it related to his favorite subject.

On Saturdays when Howard was home from the office, he would announce to Janet and Wendy, "I'm going on errands—getting a haircut and the car washed. Who wants to come along?" They often accompanied him, pleased for his companionship, having rarely seen him during the week.

I would suggest to him, "How about taking them afterwards for a hamburger or to Grunings for a sundae? They would love it." I don't remember if it ever happened.

WHEN JANET GRADUATED FROM SUNDAY SCHOOL in 1968 at age thirteen, she wanted to pay tribute to the Ethical Society. Together with fellow graduate Rosemary Sklar, they planned a gift of trees, requesting I make the selection, for which I chose a stand of birches. To my knowledge, no other graduating students had ever awarded a gift to the Society. Janet's gift ultimately reflected a profound meaning, which she discovered and shared eloquently in a Sunday Service at the Society seven years later.

Howard attended this hallmark experience along with Wendy, our leader John Moore, and a number of members and friends. I was enormously proud as I snapped many photos that Sunday afternoon. Unfortunately, the trees survived only a few years.

Janet also paid tribute to Ward Freeman, a member/teacher whom she commended as contributing significantly to her education—and to his wife, Marie, who provided weekly refreshments for the Sunday School children.

Janet had never before mentioned her warm feelings for the Freemans. I wondered what other thoughts she kept private. I suddenly realized, all during her growing-up years, Janet and I had rarely shared any free-and-easy chatter. She had not revealed any of her ideas or musings. I believe this absence is highly significant, reflecting negatively on the unique mother–daughter relationship. This rich experience is important for healthy maturation, and not too surprisingly, I suffered the same problem with my mother. Though the reasons were very different, the pattern was being repeated.

I was deeply troubled, though previously unaware, that I had contributed to Janet's situation, not protecting her from her father. I hoped, nevertheless, that my daughter had the internal resources to flourish despite both parents letting her down.

WHEN JANET WAS IN HIGH SCHOOL, I became chair of the high school PTA's Interrelations and Diversity Committee. After the Newark riots in the late Sixties, several Essex County communities responded in support. In Millburn, I joined with the efforts of Father Wickens of St. Rose of Lima Church; Reverend Stevens, Pastor of St. Stephens Episcopal Church; and a woman congregant of Wyoming Church. We organized "Target Education," a plan to tutor Newark children after school in their own community. We hoped Millburn teens would serve as volunteers. I offered to drive them to Newark in a "reverse busing" arrangement, and the Millburn Red Cross agreed to return them home.

Janet and her friend, Nancy Lifson, became the only students who volunteered. I was grateful for their participation but disappointed other students didn't join us. In her typical generosity to society, Janet later served also as a candy-striper at a local hospital.

Janet's creativity took a significant spurt about this time. She had been continuing her participation in the ECS Arts Workshops and was now enrolled in Creative Dramatics, taught by the emerging architect, choreographer, and producer Robert Wilson. As he suggested, Janet and other students were about to appear in his major production at the Brooklyn Academy of Music. Unfortunately, we had to withdraw, because the distance and time requirements became too complicated.

Janet also became deeply interested in the residential Peters Valley Craft Center in Layton, New Jersey. It provided an environment for Janet's talents in which she learned to use a potter's wheel, creating several bowls still used in my home. My favorite, a medium-sized vessel, has a glaze applied in varied earth hues, ivory tones merging toward its borders.

Janet also sculpted a log found there, following its natural contours into an intricately shaped stool. It has traveled her path from teenage home to the corner hall of her marital home. When this remarkable stool was still in my post-divorce home, noticed by a visiting high-ranking artist-official from the New Jersey Arts community, he shook his head in admiration, commenting, "Your daughter is mighty creative, and oh, man, does it suggest sexuality!"

Janet doesn't exhibit her notable sculpture prominently, neglecting appropriate recognition. She tends to shy away from acknowledging credit she deserves.

I believe my daughter evolved significantly as an individual through expressing her inherent creativity. This process probably helped heal some family wounds.

My guilt remains that I didn't counter the damage from her father. As I look back, I believe my then-timid personality succumbed to his dominating one, "spacing out" in our triangular relationship. My otherwise compassionate qualities became frozen as an ice floe. Janet was thus deprived of recognition as a creative, imaginative daughter that she had every reason to expect from a caring mother.

Janet and I were home one evening, Wendy already asleep, when Howard returned home late, drunk, demanding Janet join him downstairs. She refused. After a destructive rage resulted in his eviction from our home, a judicial hearing to decide its outcome was scheduled on the day of Janet's high school graduation. With her newly developed determination, she disagreed with my idea to have her court appearance postponed.

"I want to get it over with," she insisted, though it would mar her celebration. She remained resolute in the face of her father's behavior and expressed her own feelings in opposition to mine. Janet's emerging strengths felt as a turning point.

WHEN JANET WAS SEVENTEEN, I started therapy with Matt to save my marriage. After several months of treatment, I changed my goal to rescuing myself and my children.

At this time, Janet found important ways to connect with Wendy, her younger sister. She gave her the book *Hope for the Flowers,* by Trina Paulus, a parable about honoring an authentic life, not sacrificing one's identity to the relentless ambition condoned in our society. I don't know how Janet found this unique volume, nor was I aware of her gift to Wendy at the time. We had never discussed it.

When I first met Trina Paulus at a church peace meeting, I recognized her as the author of that distinctive publication. I became excited when introduced to her, exclaiming, "You wrote *that book*!" As Trina and I became friends, I found her a deeply spiritual woman. As I came to better understand the book's message, I presented it as gifts to many friends, including children.

THE DIVORCE WAS GRANTED WHEN JANET was ready to attend college. Although Howard wouldn't include college expenses as part of the settlement, we made plans for continuing her education in the hope he would come through.

With Janet leaving home, I hoped her zest for learning and ongoing creativity would continue. To her credit, she maintained her core self during those troubled growing-up years, central to her stability and growth. At that time, I wish I could have affirmed her strengths more clearly.

Despite our relationship remaining distant, I would have liked a frank discussion with her, how all this tumult had affected her, encouraging Janet to unburden herself. Perhaps this will happen someday.

Janet was initially tempted to choose Prescott College in Arizona, an innovative institution emphasizing a curriculum based on the wilderness as a frame of reference. This perspective allowed a deeper understanding of traditional subjects, related to concepts of progressive thinkers: Ivan

Illych, Buckminster Fuller, Jean Piaget, and John Dewey, reputed to have influenced this educational approach.

"Mom, it sounds ideal, a great nature program." She nevertheless hesitated. "I wonder about its effectiveness."

Janet was more comfortable with a traditional curriculum and chose Grinnel College. Gratefully, Howard paid Janet's college expenses from the onset and continued until she had completed her graduate education. He could be generous with money, but his inherent compassion was often locked in some forsaken emotional prison.

Janet studied anthropology at Grinnel, participating in some digs. Her awl, from that experience, still functions as my convenient household tool. She eventually met students who had attended Prescott and they confirmed, "That school's for real—they *do* accomplish their goals." Janet transferred to Prescott after completing her freshman year at Grinnel. I admired her guts in switching to an experimental college and hoped that Prescott would provide the quality experience she wanted.

Their activities included a challenging survival course involving three days in isolation. I hadn't fully appreciated Janet's grit and asked, "How did you manage?"

She said with pride, "You know, Mom, how I love reading and writing. The time passed okay." Despite her early-life difficulties, her passion for reading had evolved steadily. Janet was sometimes reading five books simultaneously, feeding her fertile mind. Today, her home library is a literary dream which could occupy a thoughtful person for a lifetime.

Janet wrote glowing letters from Prescott. The students had arranged a sacred ceremony, preparing to roast a goat for supper and expressing gratitude for its sacrificed life. I admired my daughter's open mind and appetite for adventure.

After completing her first year, Janet called me, weeping bitterly, that she would be leaving Prescott, "The place I love most." She added, "I've got to return East. I want to talk to your therapist, Matt." Janet had apparently experienced some emotional upset that could profit from psychotherapy.

I never asked the reasons for abandoning her cherished college, nor did she offer to share them—typical of the gulf between us. Janet couldn't seem to talk about these things, and I felt she would resent my intruding into her private feelings. I was relieved she'd be consulting with a competent therapist for whatever troubled her. My further thoughts: *What a courageous decision Janet is making, abandoning the college she values so highly in favor of another compelling need.* Though Janet and I had never discussed my own psychotherapy, my greatly improved life had probably influenced her decision to see Matt.

In New York City, she started therapy while continuing her college studies at the New School for Social Research. Janet secretly squeezed out payments to Matt from the allowance Howard provided and completed her final two years of undergraduate studies. Her therapy fees were supplemented by my fledgling psychotherapy practice.

Janet implied she didn't let Howard know of her therapy, which he would have opposed. She knew secrecy was vital for maintaining a relationship with her father. Howard abhorred Matt, believing he had persuaded me to divorce him.

Several years later, when Prescott was near bankruptcy, Janet found time to earn money for the college by mowing lawns in Short Hills. One homeowner called me. "You have a remarkable daughter, no nonsense, hard-working." He continued, "It's so unusual for a resident of our upscale Short Hills community to dirty their hands with such strenuous work." A photo illustrating her arduous labors appeared in the local Millburn *Item*.

At age twenty-two, Janet gave her fifteen-year-old sister a holiday card marking the Solstice season featuring the scene "Dawn on Masada," a photo she had taken on her trip to Israel. Included also was the inscription, "The Place Where Men Meet to Seek the Highest is Holy Ground," the motto featured at the New York ECS Meeting Hall podium. Janet had become a member there and possibly wanted to bring

this influence to Wendy. I believe Janet's support was significant in helping her sister in those post-divorce years.

JANET'S FIRST MYTHOLOGY COURSES at the New School opened her understanding of symbols in language and life experiences. She introduced
me to the concepts of the Triple Goddess—Maiden, Mother, Crone—the
latter designation signifying the feminine that evolves into mature wisdom, Cronehood. I proudly wear the necklace she gave me depicting
this wisdom along with my Peace emblem. CRONE, a bumper sticker,
another of Janet's gifts, carries an interpretation in smaller letters, Creative Researcher of New Experiences. In her quiet way, Janet had acknowledged my stretching out to life.

Janet achieved deeper comprehension of her individual life— the reason
she had planted the trees at her Sunday School graduation seven years earlier. This discovery resulted in her asking, "Mom, I'd like permission to do
a Sunday Service at the Ethical Society." She wanted to share the significance of her Sunday School graduation gift and its meaning for her life.

Her presentation in 1975, "Nature, Mythology, and Ethical Culture,"
was an innovative event for both Janet and the Society. To my knowledge, a past graduate had never returned to present a program. Janet
discussed her mythological insight about trees and the larger meaning of
nature. She explained, "A tree symbolizes a very strong and sturdy life
force that is living and growing as a part of nature." From this understanding, she recognized her strengths, contrasted with the frailty she
sometimes endured in her earlier years.

Janet described her wilderness and nature experiences eloquently,
even with religious fervor, quoting profound thinkers: Henry Beston:
"Nature is part of our humanity. . .without that divine mystery, man
ceases to be man," and theologian William Pollard: "Earth is choice, precious and sacred, beyond all comparison or measure."

Janet's further portrayal: "While reading these eloquent words, I was
sitting. . .on a hill on the deserted Baja peninsula overlooking a vast ex-

panse of blue sea, framed by numerous mountain ranges. . . . I became overwhelmed at a sense of awe at the glorious wonders of earth. . . .a truly religious experience." She connected these thoughts to mythological ideas "that as human beings, each of us have a touch of god within ourselves." Janet had linked humanistic concepts in nature to a favorite motto in the religious precepts of the Ethical Culture Movement regarding "holy ground." Janet's conclusion: "I also experienced a spiritual juxtaposition, reading deep philosophical ideas while immersed in the awe and sweep of nature".

I sat at the edge of my seat that Sunday morning, moved by the profundity of her ideas delivered with such clarity. At the end of her presentation, I dissolved in tears on the shoulder of my friend Suzanne Gluck, overwhelmed by the depth and beauty of Janet's service.

Though I had reared a child through significant traumas while impotent to intercede, Janet had transcended her early experiences to evolve into a beautifully sensitive adult.

She also offered a bread-breaking ceremony that Sunday morning. Janet had baked bread the previous day with long-time member Marion Josephson, our "earth-mother." Together, they had immersed their hands in the dough, caressing and molding the batter in Marion's *haimeshe* kitchen. As Janet broke the bread, she paid tribute to Marian, her commitment to bread-baking with "creativity and love, symbolizing our humanity, keeping the connection to our Mother Earth." Janet extended her lecture into the substance of an earth-derived food.

She delivered additional talks at the Essex Society, "The Importance of Ritual for Modern Man," and at other Societies, topics on anthropology.

Her strengths continued unabated as she pursued graduate studies, first at Columbia University, where she earned a master's degree in Education followed by a second, an MSW at Adelphi University. This latter degree was one I had fervently desired but never achieved. My pride in Janet was enormous.

Janet's first job, with the Police Athletic League (PAL) in New York

City, involved tutoring young people in a classroom setting. She settled further into the city, and Howard agreed to pay her rent. I thought, *His consistently paying Janet's expenses demonstrates he's finally behaving as a responsible father, thank goodness.* She had rented a room in the home of a sociology professor. Janet exclaimed, "Mom, what an extraordinary book collection he has. I'll be reading forever." Eventually, Janet found a solo apartment on New York's West Side, with Howard still paying her rent.

Janet's students at PAL were street kids, some of them ex-felons, who were learning reading and writing skills. Their success, and hers, were demonstrated by the unusual quality of their essays and poems. She published them in a community newsletter she showed me during a casual meeting in New York. Janet was exhibiting an increased ability to take credit for her good works.

She also told me of her students' enthusiasm about the books she brought to class. They would excitedly paw through her knapsack to discover what treasures she carried. Their big thrill was the day they found Erich Fromm's *The Art of Loving*, perhaps thinking the subject was sexual. Janet was clearly a gifted teacher, intuiting what topics excited her students.

She had become a woman of integrity through relentless striving. Janet not only overcame the many parental problems she had encountered in early years but was contributing to society's quality of life.

At the New York Society, Janet became good friends with Senior Leader Algernon Black, an elder statesman of the Movement. As he came to know her unusual qualities, he suggested she consider becoming a Leader (clergy) in the Movement, but Janet declined in favor of other goals.

I was thrilled hearing my daughter mentioned on radio station WQXR: "Janet Levin will be the speaker at the New York Society for Ethical Culture this coming Sunday, February 4 [2007]," a paid announcement declared when the station was still commercially operated.

BECOMING WEALTHY
AS THE MARRIAGE DETERIORATES

WHEN WE RETURNED FROM PHOENIX, Howard resumed his consulting job with Ebasco Services in New York City, advising the New York Stock Exchange on electronic trading procedures. After this venture and launching Probability Fund at home, Howard changed jobs again.

He became employed by the Greyhound Leasing Corporation and quickly grasped leasing operations. Howard brilliantly advanced his career and became a bold innovator in the business computer field. He developed a ground-breaking alternative for companies acquiring computers. They usually rented or purchased them from IBM; Howard introduced another choice, *leasing* a computer, a more flexible option. Companies could update to advanced systems more expeditiously in this rapidly changing technology. To jump-start their business, Howard and Jim courageously arranged bank loans to finance their initial purchases. This leasing plan was quickly adopted by many companies. Overnight, we became rich!

Howard's creative mind then conceived an even more advanced option—*non-payout leases*. Companies were able to switch into improved systems without completing payment on their current financial obligation. The rapid tempo of the industry convinced Howard he could always lease relinquished computers to other companies.

His exquisitely conceived idea, somewhat of a gamble, became a new company, Levin-Townsend Computer Corporation. We were beyond rich—*we were wealthy*! They had originally entitled the company Levin and Townsend. I suggested the rhythm of a hyphenated name would sound better.

Howard became president and CEO, personally selecting members for their board of trustees. The company was listed on the New York Stock Exchange and took off. A friend excitedly told me one day, "You know, the stock topped over 70 yesterday!"

These momentous events occurred in 1962, the same year of the birth of our youngest daughter, Wendy. When my best friend, Gertrude White, called our home for a report on the new baby, Mary, our housekeeper, more like family, responded, "Mrs. Levin is a joyful mother to another sweetheart of a daughter!" With money more plentiful, we were able to add several days weekly to Mary's work schedule.

All this wealth and power affected Howard dramatically, revealing a darker side. He became even more domineering and showed less interest in me. He would ramble on about his business dealings and rarely inquire about my activities, becoming testier and more controlling. He became distant as a new father, an alien in our home, which hardly seemed to contain a precious new infant.

Howard remained remote in his relation toward Janet as well. I pleaded with him to pay her more attention, as I enviously saw other fathers dote on their children. In our tense life together, Howard's behavior was never to be questioned; he usually ignored my suggestions.

Soon we had ample resources to purchase a house. I had discovered an architectural gem located on Moraine Place in the luxurious estate section of Short Hills, amid stately mansions and colonials. It appeared at first sight as a modest cottage but gradually exposed its full beauty when approached from beyond the front woods. Its interior treasures included rare teak walls lining the living and dining rooms, flagstone flooring, huge picture windows revealing expansive lush grounds, and a lower-level greenhouse for my gardening passions. This ideal house provided all the beauty I had always longed for.

Since we had planned to build a colonial, Howard regarded this possibility reluctantly. "Let's get this house out of your system." When seeing it, though, he was as smitten as I, and we made plans to buy it.

Despite our shared enthusiasm, I was hesitant committing to a house before we substantially changed the quality of our marriage and family life. I pleaded, "If we don't improve our relationship, I would feel I was living in a velvet-lined prison."

He patted me on the head as if I were a puppy, responding, "Just be a better Betty, and our marriage will be okay."

I felt demeaned but deluded myself into thinking that matters could work out. I was blinded by finally living in the house of my dreams. I now realize how I failed both the children and myself.

We retainedan eminent decorator to furnish the house with the finest appointments. I later added a rock garden, a miniature waterfall, and a gurgling stream to the private front garden of the master suite. Despite my love of gardening, during the eight years I lived there, I never used the basement greenhouse, distracted by marital unrest.

Our vacations consisted of going on cruises. After several such indulgences, I started finding them utterly boring. Many passengers were absorbed with elaborate plans for making and spending money. I started thinking, *If I have to attend one more cruise, I'll scream!* I must admit I did enjoy wearing the elegant formal gowns for these occasions, purchased at Saks Fifth Avenue and Bonwit Teller boutiques.

Howard's company eventually bought a limousine and hired a chauffeur. The purchase of an airplane changed our vacation plans considerably. The crew often flew us down to the Caribbean on winter escapes. At Newark Airport, we were privileged to use a secluded tarmac, available exclusively for those with private planes. The pilots personally loaded our luggage from the limousine and regularly chose Howard's favorite selection for the plane's CD player, Frank Sinatra's "I Did It My Way." We indulged the good life.

Howard finally acknowledged my mother, now widowed, by occasionally inviting her to join our travels to the Caribbean. She conveniently provided babysitting services. Wendy, now almost three years old, playfully wore my bathing cap trimmed with fanciful artificial hair. She enjoyed frolicking in the gentle waters with Grandma Evelyn.

Additional luxuries started becoming a feature of our extravagant life. Howard took pleasure in taking me to Fifth Avenue's Tiffany or Van Cleef & Arpels to purchase ostentatious jewelry. I protested the *uber-*sized diamonds, especially the six-carat earrings. "Howard, they're so huge. I couldn't possibly wear them to the events we attend. They're really only appropriate at places like Las Vegas." I tried to persuade him to exchange them for more reasonably sized ones, but he was determined. It was useless trying to bend his will, and I sighed with resignation as I safely tucked them away in a drawer.

Las Vegas capers did eventually enter our lives. First, we built our art collection. This interest, and their value, eventually became my passport to freedom.

I had been drawn to art from our early marital years when we had only modest income. Back then, I suggested to Howard that we join the art movement for beginning collectors. The Print of the Month Club featured economically priced graphic arts, generally offered for less than a hundred dollars a print. Now, in the 1960s, we bought only the most desirable fine art available. Among our acquisitions were Chagall, Roualt, Nolde, and Valtat. The latter two were purchased at Sotheby's by Ted Schapiro, my art teacher mentor and special friend, on our behalf. I appreciated most of all, though, a small Henry Moore sculpture, *The Family*, which reflected my deepest desires—people caring about one another.

Howard behaved as a distant father, rarely acknowledging his daughters or spending quality time with them. They had become court attendants.

BECOMING BETTY

Our marital relationship continued to deteriorate as Howard's impetuousness and need to control moved into downright hostility. Arguments flared regularly at the breakfast table, as we read in the 1965 *New York Times* about the major violations of civil rights and the Vietnam War horrors. We disagreed strenuously, as Howard expressed no sympathy for the unjust treatment of Blacks in the South and justified the moral excesses of the Asian war.

When we still lived in Springfield, the community had been privileged by a visit from Martin Luther King, Jr. at Jonathan Dayton High School. This event had been arranged by Rabbi Israel Dresner of Temple Sha'arey, who had marched with him in the South.

As King entered the high school auditorium, the audience rose as one in homage to this valiant man. Everyone was on his feet except one. Howard remained seated, glaring at me arrogantly.

In 1968, we launched our Ben Shahn art collection. Late one morning, Howard called me from New York. "You've got to drop everything and get here quickly. I'm at the Kennedy Galleries on Fifty-seventh Street, where they have a magnificent display of Ben Shahns. Come in right away and help me select some choice works for our collection."

I quickly arranged babysitting and joined Howard at the Galleries. The Shahns were indeed outstanding, and among those we selected were a gouache, *East Side Soap Box,* and another major work, *Identity,* that Howard particularly admired. The Biblical inscription on its upper margin seemed to move him:

> *If I am not for myself, who will be for me? But if I*
> *am only for myself, what am I? And if not now, when?*

I was surprised that Howard was attracted to this work. His current life was oblivious of this message. Howard had become a man different from the one I had married.

In 1969 when Ben Shahn died, the New Jersey State Art Museum in Trenton mounted a 1973 retrospective, memorializing this internationally acclaimed artist. When the curator asked to borrow our Shahn collection for the exhibition, I replied, "Of course, I'd be pleased. The walls, though, would be partially stripped without them."

The curator's solution became a unique privilege. "Come to our museum and select any works you wish, to temporarily replace the Shahns."

In this ultimate shopping spree I selected a work by Prestopino, an artist I had always admired who didn't interest Howard.

At the Trenton Museum gala retrospective for Shahn, we attended along with dignitaries who enjoyed the special benefits of being rich, prominent art collectors. We were also present for his black-tie memorial concert by the New York Philharmonic, conducted by Leonard Bernstein. It featured an interlude of Yiddish folk music that Shahn had particularly enjoyed.

Despite this privileged life, it didn't compensate for the daily personal indignities inflicted by Howard.

MEANWHILE, I HAD BECOME FRIENDS with the eminent artist Jacob Landau, who had coached me in planning the course, "Revolution in the Arts" for the Ethical Society's Educational Center. Jacob and his wife had often invited us to special events at their Buckminster Fuller studio in Roosevelt, New Jersey. Howard had usually declined to attend. When the New Jersey State Museum in Trenton honored Jacob with a one-man show, Howard and I were invited to the gala formal cocktail reception.

En route to the festivities in Trenton in his luxurious Mercedes convertible, Howard in black tie and I in a glamorous gown, he suddenly started to verbally attack me about some irrelevant subject. I was considerably shaken. Out of control, Howard pulled into a roadside diner parking lot. He was red with fury, and I had mascara streaks on my tear-stained cheeks. My greatly anticipated evening was ruined, and we returned home without showing up for my friend's celebratory event. I wondered, *Is Howard jealous of my personal relationship with an illustrious artist?*

Howard's relationship with his Executive Board wasn't doing much better. Though he had hand-picked those men, their business interactions became strained, contaminated by his dictatorial ways. More than once, he scheduled board meetings on Sunday summer afternoons at our Short Hills home, with wives mandated to attend. Since most of these men were ardent golfers, the command appearance intruded seriously into their recreational time. I'm certain their wives were equally displeased with these demands. I questioned them. "Howard, you can't treat people so thoughtlessly."

He would rebuff me sharply. "*Yes,* I can. I pay them enough money."

The Las Vegas adventure followed, in which he bought numerous properties—a small casino, the radio station, and a luxurious country club. I was expected to accompany him there, with the children in tow.

During daytime hours, I romped with Janet and Wendy in the hotel swimming pool, my time of greatest contentment. Evenings became something of a chore as I accompanied Howard to the various night clubs and gambling casinos. Admittedly, I did enjoy blackjack as my favorite game of chance and became a competent player, winning modest sums.

I particularly enjoyed visiting cousin Nate, Dorothy's brother, who had settled in Las Vegas for relief of his asthma. When I showed up at Nate's modest bungalow, he had not seen me since my early childhood years in Chicago. He took a long look at me, leaning back in admiration, with a wide, glowing smile. He lovingly clutched my hand, exclaiming, "Sister, you look like a million bucks!"

HOWARD'S BUSINESS DEALINGS also involved antagonistic relations with IBM. I occasionally overheard references to their legal entanglements, lawsuits hurled in both directions. He always overcame these difficulties, apparently stimulated by his David-and-Goliath encounters. Howard seemed to thrive on battles, which probably stimulated his testosterone.

He also started buying shopping centers nationwide, which required frequent travel. Howard handled these chores almost entirely alone, absenting himself often from home. I complained they interfered with building sound father–daughter relationships and suggested he hire additional personnel. He defended his methods, asserting, "No one is as smart as I am for handling these responsibilities." Howard never addressed the parental issue, apparently not a priority in his mind.

When Mother developed stomach cancer, and I was eager to visit with her in Chicago, the dilemma of hiring a housekeeper–baby sitter for the children became a issue. I panicked. In my absence, Howard would be the sole parent responsible for them. I relied solely on phone calls for contact with Mom during this time and protected her, never mentioning my marital difficulties. My one visit with her occurred when we combined it with Howard's trip to Minneapolis when he became financial chair of Hubert Humphrey's vice-presidential candidacy. In an outrageous manipulation, he convinced me to accompany him on his Minneapolis trip. "If you come with me, I'll plan our route through Chicago, where you can visit your mother."

My mom was terminally ill, and he was merely throwing me a bone. Intimidated, though, I grabbed the opportunity.

In other ways, our luxurious lifestyle occasionally seduced me. At home with Howard, a dinner table conversation:

Betty: "I saw two beautiful cocktail handbags today while shopping and can't decide which to buy."

Howard: "Buy both of them!"

It was clear that I needed to eventually address my personal infatuation with our over-the-top lifestyle. My change happened unexpectedly one day after Howard had said to me, "You know, you should finally buy a real full-length mink coat, not just that short, unimpressive fur you toss over your shoulders when we dine out."

Dutifully, I shopped at one of the exclusive Short Hills furriers and became delighted with a beautifully designed informal fur, chic for wintry

-day grocery chores. As I extended my charge card to the salesman, my enchantment suddenly shifted into a new clarity.

No! I must stop this crazy lifestyle. This frivolity means nothing. I simply can't take anything more from Howard. It only buys disrespect.

I abruptly left the shop, leaving the salesman perplexed with my contradictory behavior. This new awareness brought a reality more ready to be anchored to my basic values.

Howard's changed personality, however, remained constant. His aberrations started invading my thoughts, bringing me much distress.

I had visions of his possible fate as mirroring the film, *The Picture of Dorian Gray.* The subject's dissolution was depicted as paint seeping down until the image was no longer recognizable.

I pleaded with Howard to change his behavior, but it was futile.

His lofty position in his own company almost collapsed when the Levin-Townsend Board tried to throw him out. Through clever legal maneuvering, he was able to forestall that crushing action. I sensed doom and pleaded with him, "Howard, if you don't mend your ways, they'll try to evict you again, and perhaps succeed." Discounting me as usual, he dismissed my warning with a wave of his hand and quickly left the room.

The inevitable happened. The board again moved to legally remove Howard, this time covering all angles, including an armed guard at the entrance to the elegant Turtle Bay brownstone offices.

Howard telephoned me from New York, his voice meek and seemingly filled with shame. "Well, they did it. I'm out." He sounded like a schoolboy, caught in a minor transgression.

My emotions were conflicted. I felt empathy for the tragedy of his losing his life-long aspirations, and in such a humiliating way. Another part of me was saddened that he wasn't able to temper his willfulness.

I was also approaching the end of my rope in our marriage. *How can I kick him out, though,* I asked myself, *when he's suffered such a loss?*

Howard's resilience and strength reemerged. The traumatic ejection occurred on a Friday, and by Monday morning he had acquired a new office, a plan for a revitalized skeleton company, and even telephone lines when the city was experiencing a serious shortage. Most important, his loyal, irreplaceable long-time secretary/confident extraordinaire, Celeste, chose to remain as his employee. Howard was back, behaving as if he were invincible. Several months thereafter, Celeste's husband, a warm, sensitive personality, committed suicide.

I was horrified! Her tragedy evoked many thoughts about the road I was traveling with Howard. I wondered, *Should I extricate myself from this ugly morass?* I decided I needed more forbearance, having already hung in there for twenty-four years and two children. I thought, wouldn't it be great to celebrate our twenty-fifth anniversary together? This was not a time for decisive action.

A repetitive disturbing nightmare, however, kept intruding: *I was driving through a toll booth, about to pay the fee. Suddenly, inextricably, I died there.*

These dreams of death made me realize I needed to stop paying the costs of a malfunctioning marriage, which could even contribute to my demise. Perhaps marital counseling could help. Our extravagances and indulgences again entered my conscience as enormous trivialities: *With my social concerns and values, why haven't I found more constructive outlets for using this wealth?*

In one particular argument with Howard, he tried to mollify me, "I'll buy you an Ethical Society," revealing how little he grasped its basic humanist values.

In a generous moment, Howard *did* contribute fifty thousand dollars to the Society to hire a full-time Leader. These funds enabled our retaining John Moore, an accomplished anthropologist, for two years. Both the Society and I appreciated Howard's generosity. Howard lacked even a fragmentary understanding or commitment, however, to the principles of trying to create a more humane world. These ideals had become entirely foreign to him.

MY SECOND DAUGHTER, WENDY

L ET'S PLAN AN ADDITION TO OUR FAMILY," I suggested to Howard in 1960, my eyes twinkling. His eyes matched mine as he broke into a grin and agreed. Our sex life grew, but I failed to become pregnant. We were still living in the Springfield, New Jersey, Troy Village apartments with our daughter Janet, who was then five years old. This was before he became very successful as founder of the Levin-Townsend Computer Corporation.

Just as I had abandoned thoughts of another child, I unexpectedly conceived a second time, delighted to anticipate becoming a mother to two children. Wendy was born just before midnight on May 30, 1962.

She was named for the British actress Wendy Hiller. As with Janet, her name was influenced by my stepmother Evelyn's passion for the movies. The choice of Robin as Wendy's middle name memorialized my deceased birth mother, Rebecca.

At Newark's Beth Israel Hospital, immediately after leaving the delivery room, newborn Wendy and I shared the elevator. She was en route to the nursery, screaming, and I to the maternity ward. The accompanying nurse commented, "This new one doesn't seem to like our world."

I was greatly offended—what a thoughtless remark following the welcoming of a new baby. Wendy's persistent crying was probably her being suddenly ejected from the comfort of a protective womb into an alien environment, expected to breathe on her own.

When she was brought to my room for feedings, resting upright against the nurse's chest, her back to me, I immediately recognized my infant by the shock of thick brown hair along her neck. Wendy then settled peacefully into my arms, sucking blissfully on her bottle.

In our two-bedroom duplex apartment, we placed Wendy in her sister Janet's room, who had urged this arrangement. A bond began, but the seven-year difference in their age was a barrier for the sisters to become actively connected for many years.

At three months of age, Wendy became cross-eyed. A gifted optician rejected surgery in favor of patching the normal eye, and her sight was normal by her first birthday.

Wendy grew into a high-spirited toddler who appreciated good food. First thing in the morning, perched on the top of the stairs, she piped out, "What's for breakfast, French toast or waffles?" Her appetite for life was always a joy.

One day, in her excitement, she slipped and fell down the full flight of stairs. I ran to comfort her, but it wasn't necessary. Wendy responded with her usual resilience. She determinedly picked herself up, with no display of upset or tears, and ran to the dining table to enjoy her favorite first meal of the day.

Wendy was barely four years old when she showed an interest in music. By then we had moved to Short Hills, and we bought her a Steinway upright piano. Wendy was intrigued and repeatedly fingered simple notes. Soon, she had written her first piece of music.

"What will you name it?" I asked.

"Swimming Pool," she blurted, a place she loved.

Our artist friend, Ted Schapiro, noticed Wendy's continuing interest at the keyboard. "Even though she's so young, why don't you consider giving her piano lessons?"

I looked for a teacher who would be sensitive to a precocious child. Miss Halpern, a Bergen County teacher, seemed to have a sound philosophy. "I don't believe in pushing these very talented children to acclaim.

I gently nurture their unusual abilities."

Wendy's weekly lessons and quarterly in-home recitals involved many travel hours. Howard never joining the repeated drive many miles up north annoyed me. In the five years Wendy pursued her talent, he showed no inclination to participate. She never expressed concern about her father's distance.

Her lessons stopped abruptly when Miss Halpern anticipated more than Wendy was ready to express. She believed her student was ready to perform duo recitals with her. At a special program with prominent teachers attending, Wendy had a bad day and flubbed many passages. Though Miss Halpern and I reassured her, she lost interest in piano lessons. I was disappointed that Wendy had dropped her involvement but respected her need to choose her own interests.

At her Hartshorn School kindergarten class in 1967, the teacher planned for the girls to create Easter bonnets of large paper plates, decorated appropriately. With a recording of "Easter Parade" playing in the background, the children strolled in their festive hats, on display for their mothers gathered in the classroom. Wendy stood out among the other children. She was the only one who swaggered, mimicking fashion models, hands angled, confidently displaying her creation. The parents laughed heartily at a strutting five-year-old who loved becoming the center of attention. I was the proud mother of a beautiful, self-assured little daughter.

Later, Wendy told me her class started with the "Lord's Prayer" and readings from the Bible, exactly as Janet had reported seven years earlier at Chisholm School. I don't know how Wendy knew this issue would concern me.

When it happened in Janet's school, this practice was still legal nationwide. Back then, I had objected, but by 1967, the Supreme Court had ruled that public school prayers were unconstitutional. Would I have to confront this issue again?

Howard pushed me to challenge the school's practice, always ready for a battle. I was initially reluctant to support his tendency for dissension. But at a deeper level, I was furious by the school that routinely shredded our Bill of Rights.

At the next parent conference, I asked Miss Parsons, Wendy's teacher, "Do I understand correctly that the start of kindergarten classes each day involves the 'Lord's Prayer' and verses from the Bible?"

"Oh, yes," Miss Parson replied, pleased to acknowledge the ritual. I voiced my objection, citing the Supreme Court decision and emphasizing my personal abhorrence of the practice. The teacher admonished me, "Mrs. Levin, we *must* provide moral instructions for our children."

"I agree, but with appropriate limitations. These teachings are the responsibility only of home and parents." Miss Parsons looked past me, moving on to another subject, apparently dismissing my opinion. Her self-righteous attitude made me angry.

I decided to act, determined to confront this illegal action. In a phone call to Miss Parsons, I said, "You already know I object to the illegal classroom religious procedure. I believe it's only fair to warn you. If you don't agree to stop these practices, I plan to voice my concerns to your school principal." Miss Parsons offered only her silence.

In the few minutes necessary to redial Hartshorn's phone number, Miss Parsons apparently had already decided. The call was answered by the principal's secretary, and when I identified myself, she swiftly responded, "Mrs. Levin, if you are phoning about the prayers in Miss Parson's kindergarten class, they're going to be stopped immediately." I was relieved that speaking up for my values would bring change in Wendy's classroom.

IN HER SECOND GRADE TALENT SHOW, Wendy decided to perform a dance in which she had choreographed simple, saucy movements to the music of Aaron Copeland's Billy the Kid. Wendy rehearsed after school to taped music, practicing her choreography repeatedly during an unseasonably hot spring. The overheated gym had no air conditioning.

"Wendy, dear, don't you think that's enough for one day? The dance has really has come together nicely."

BECOMING BETTY

Perspiration dripping from her forehead, she retorted, "No Mom, I have to try it one more time."

I was not going to block my daughter's ambitions and admired her drive. Wendy chose a black leotard for her costume, punctuated with a red bandanna around her neck and a black leather belt at her waist. Her classmates looked on with delight, impressed with her performance and imaginative get-up.

Wendy also developed an interest in creating visual arts. My favorite, "Autumn Dancers," a dynamic linoleum print, was inspired by the Ethical Society's Creative Arts Workshop. The work was almost destroyed in a brain tumor nightmare I later experienced. Thankfully, both the art and I survived.

WHILE WENDY WAS IN FOURTH GRADE, the District Special School for the Disadvantaged, located in Millburn, was threatened by permanent closure. Louise, a friend from the Ethical Society and a South Mountain Troup Leader for the Girl Scouts, planned a demonstration of protest during lunch hour. When Wendy heard the plans, she wanted to participate, insisting I pick her up from Hartshorn and drive her to the endangered school. After the school was temporarily saved, in gratitude, the students presented a talent show for township students. Wendy befriended a vocalist at the reception; impressed by these children, she encouraged her teacher to invite several students to a Valentine's Day party held at Hartshorn. Wendy's sensitivity to the disadvantaged became apparent in her early years.

As an active member of Hartshorne's PTA in the early Seventies, I volunteered to bring an interesting film for parents to view. The antiwar film, produced by a Canadian Film group, shows children's fascination with department store displays exhibiting soldiers in crisp uniforms manning their various battlefield equipment—machine guns, armored trucks, and other armaments. The scene slowly shifts to reality as the children's imaginations witness wartime scenes of death and destruction.

Parent were furious with me for showing what they considered an "anti-American" film and accused me of being a communist. I realized that, back then, my anti-war perspective differed from those of my contemporaries.

AT HOME, ARGUMENTS AND OTHER UPSETS between Howard and me occurred frequently, aggravated by his drinking. My mother had developed cancer, and I shielded her from our marital problems. Whenever Howard and I had a disagreement, he warned me, "If you don't become a 'better Betty,' I'll tell your mother how badly you're behaving."

One day, he picked up Wendy and me from an errand, driving his luxurious two-door Mercedes-Benz convertible. After we had settled in the car, Wendy on my lap, Howard said, slightly smacking his lips, "Well, I called your mother to tell her that our marriage was in trouble."

Shaken by Howard's admission, I dissolved into spasms of moans and tears. *Such gratuitous cruelty*! As I heaved uncontrollably, I wondered what Wendy was feeling as I trembled beneath her. I didn't confront him about his dreadful act; I believed compassion and logic would lead nowhere.

Wendy and I never discussed the incident—I didn't know what reasonable explanation to offer her. I phoned my mother to reassure her that, despite my marital difficulties, I would protect the children. This vow became far more difficult to keep than I had anticipated.

Wendy continued to witness chaotic conditions at home, and she knew I was struggling to get a divorce. Her anxieties increased when her father was legally evicted from our home for his abusive behavior. This father–daughter separation led to their having weekly visits.

Wendy's behavior then became clingy. For summer plans, she agreed to attend a day camp only, not a sleep-away. This is the age when many children go to camp for a whole month, sometimes an entire summer.

IN MIDDLE SCHOOL, WENDY WAS ASSIGNED a dramatic piano solo in an introduction to a musical performance. She urged me, "Mom, can you convince Dad to attend the program? Please emphasize his arriving on time to hear my opening."

I assured Wendy I would try but mentioned my limited influence on her father. Howard did attend but arrived too late to hear his daughter's star moment.

Everything shifted for Wendy at this time. She longed for her father's attention and approval—especially his love. I ached for her frustrations. He consistently withheld affirming the deepest needs of his youngest daughter.

During one particular visit, Howard waited at the front door while Wendy ran into the bedroom as I sat at the desk. Without comment, she grabbed the adding machine sitting beside me. Equipment in hand, she left the room and joined her father. I considered: I guess Howard needs an adding machine and has recruited his daughter to claim ours. If Wendy's obedience demonstrates her loyalty and love for her father, this priority is clearly worth relinquishing my property.

WENDY WAS ELEVEN YEARS OLD WHEN I WAS GRANTED MY DIVORCE. We downsized to more modest housing. Her reaction was restrained when I told her I had bought a new house on Millburn's Sagamore Road. She tried to look pleased, feigning approval, but her tense face said otherwise. I should have realized all was not well. Looking back now, I know I wasn't sufficiently aware of what these changes would mean for her. She would have to live an ongoing separate arrangement from her father and in a less comfortable lifestyle.

I tried to introduce a lighter mood into our new life together. I arranged a sightseeing trip to Washington, D.C., and was relieved to see her respond enthusiastically. Just the two of us, we shared a pleasurable vacation.

At home, we furnished her new bedroom as a more grown-up sitting room. Our new post-divorce life had diminished to a family of two with Janet away at college.

Wendy continued trying to adjust to the divorce. The next summer, she agreed to a sleep-away but only for two weeks. In traveling to the pick-up location for the camp bus, she slid helplessly to the floor of the car and vomited. I was exasperated at what I regarded as infantile behavior. I thoughtlessly scolded her, not linking her upset to conflicted loyalties about her parents' divorce. Wendy's turmoil extended to her falling out of her bunk in the middle of the night during her camp stay.

I didn't fully sense the agitation she was experiencing. Wendy no doubt felt loyalty and love for me but also devotion to her father. She couldn't take sides—nor should she have had to. She needed *both* a mother and father, faults and all. Wendy found herself in an unspeakable quagmire, impossible to navigate without guidance to sort out her feelings. As a caring mother, I should have opened a discussion with Wendy to unburden herself or find her a therapist. I regret to this day that I didn't do more to relieve her conflicts.

MATT, MY THERAPIST, SUGGESTED DELAYING the divorce until Wendy was older, but I was too impatient—I wanted to shed my miseries. Someday I'll try to discuss, with her, the timing of the divorce until her more mature years. I hope she can be frank and tell me if she felt my needs were not sufficiently sensitive to hers. Most particularly, I hope she can forgive my mistakes. I am more aware of how blind I have been.

Wendy's Sunday visits with her father took place at his Verona Claridge House apartment when she was twelve. She told me they often involved his heavy drinking with a female companion. Wendy had become apprehensive when Howard, somewhat drunk, drove her home through the South Mountain Reservation. She described the challenge of maneuvering Brookside Drive and Cherry Lane. "I had to focus intently and guide him through the turns as we drove along those curvy roads."

I became worried for Wendy's safety but was reluctant to challenge Howard. It would involve another legal battle to confront him about proper visitation conditions. I could pick her up for the return home but didn't want to enter his turf. My somewhat lame solution was to give

Wendy a twenty-dollar bill to take a taxi home. In retrospect, she was too young to make that difficult decision.

Wendy knew I was still consulting with Matt in New York City. She sometimes asked to skip school to go with me. I should have realized she was trying to make me aware of her distress. Matt spoke privately with her before he invited her to play his living room piano.

Somehow, I couldn't grasp the detrimental effect my divorce had on Wendy. Handling Howard's bullying dominated my waking hours and masked its impact on my daughter.

Fortunately, Janet was supporting Wendy during this difficult time. She gave her sister the Trina Paulus book *Hope for the Flowers* and made another connection with a Winter Solstice greeting card featuring a Masada photograph from her trip to Israel. I wasn't aware of Janet's presents back then, but now believe they helped her sister in those difficult post-divorce years.

During Wendy's high school years, she joined the Color Guard, which supported the football team during the games and handled wooden rifles in intricate maneuvers. She soon became head of the group, choreographing their dynamic movements. Those Saturday mornings, Wendy almost danced out the house in her crisp blue tailored uniform, cap perched on her curly, permed hair, prepared to lead her team's cheering.

WHEN WENDY TURNED SEVENTEEN, she asked to celebrate with a dance party at home, complete with a DJ and swirling silver ball to jump-start the festivities. "Mom, you'll join in, too—not just be the adult in charge." I was delighted to be included in her party.

We pushed back the living room furniture, rolled up the rugs, and were off. A dozen teens jammed to the loud, repetitive beat, including me. Noting my dancing, Ed Levine, Wendy's musician friend, asked, "Can we dance together? You know, you'll do your thing and I'll do mine."

We each moved in individual gyrations, paralleling one another, never touching, digging the rhythmic music. A phone call interrupted late into the night, complaining of the raucous noise. We then toned it down and partied on.

Despite this relaxed time, the general tone of my relationship with Wendy continued to reflect my lack of awareness. This became apparent when she started dating Alvin and developed an unusual relationship with his mother.

Wendy visited and even bowled regularly with Alvin's mother, independent of her relationship with him. I now realize preoccupation with my new liberation and professional ambitions distracted me and contributed to our flawed mother–daughter connection.

With graduation coming, Wendy's choice of college became an issue. I noticed she seemed interested in colleges only within commuting distance, suggesting her reluctance to move away from me, often a sign of conflicted feelings. After discussion with Matt and much thought, I gave Wendy an ultimatum. "Come September, after your graduation, you're out of here. I hope you'll choose an appropriate college, but if not, you'll look for a job and your own apartment. In any case, you're not living at home. It's time to move on into the larger world."

Wendy heard me loud and clear. She chose the innovative Hampshire College in Amherst, Massachusetts. Her father agreed to pay the tuition, a welcome development considering he had previously insisted otherwise. It was at Hampshire that she met fellow student David Ackerman, from Albany. Wendy didn't mention this important relationship until years later, typical of our checkered relationship.

WE GREW FURTHER APART DURING HER COLLEGE YEARS. I'm puzzled why I wasn't more involved in the excitement of Wendy attending such a unique institution. Despite my excitement about Hampshire as I perused their engaging literature, my visits there were routine, without much camaraderie between Wendy and me. I didn't discuss her studies, nor did she offer any information.

Long after Wendy left home, I discovered among her papers an essay she had written of a drunken father behaving irresponsibly. I was crest-fallen—another example of her hidden distress withheld from me. We had never discussed the crucial triangle of Wendy's love for her father concurrent with our divorce. I remained oblivious to its effect on her.

Instead of treating her essay as an opportunity, I regarded the revelation as an uninvited entry into Wendy's private life and ignored it. The barrier between us continued.

Only much later did Wendy mention that Howard had pulled her out of college from time to time while she was still involved in her studies. Wendy had never before mentioned these college irregularities to me, knowing I would disapprove. Eventually, she was asked to leave Hampshire because of insufficient progress in her studies.

After Wendy left college, her life became irregular and uncertain. She clerked in a record store in Albany, New York, while she and David lived together for a short time; I visited briefly.

AFTER HOWARD'S EVICTION FROM HIS COMPANY, one of his new ventures was a business in Atlantic City, a small video arcade. He wanted to use Wendy's skills to benefit his new enterprise. Wendy joined Howard in Atlantic City, where she settled in, working regularly for him in the arcade. In her new life with her father, she consistently distanced herself from me, not phoning, returning my calls, or attempting to visit. I felt as utterly defeated as I had been during my marriage.

I admit I contributed to the chasm by my strong disapproval of Atlantic City. In the Sixties, it had become a luxurious gambling and recreational resort, displacing its long-term residents. I frankly detested the whole scene.

I started missing Wendy very much and confided my feelings to friend, Helen Tepper. She suggested I put aside my distaste for Atlantic City, travel down there, and renew the relationship with her. "You'll take the bus—it'll be easy. A friendly lunch together, and the standoff will be broken." Her idea was admirable, and my muddled thinking cleared.

I wrote Wendy the idea, and she phoned, agreeing to the plan. I was buoyant seeing her again after our lengthy separation. I suspect she was anxious, arriving almost thirty minutes late.

The ice melted when we were together. When Wendy told me Howard had assigned her the arcade's overnight shift, I remained silent, squelching my feelings. I was careful not to express disapproval, having learned to not add to Wendy's stress.

I FINALLY FLOURISH

I N THE MIDST OF ALL THIS MARITAL UPSET, at age thirty-five, I salvaged a vital part of myself of which I was barely aware. My latent interests in the arts flowered when I discovered modern dance, whose symbols are more allied to my humanist ideals. This was partly in response to my daughter Janet's need for a more free-dance experience. I initiated this program at the Essex Ethical Culture Society and became Founder and Director of their Creative Arts workshops.

I organized other courses in the arts tht were added steadily—visual arts, music, and creative dramatics. Educators attuned to the deeper needs of students sensitively led these workshops.

Ted Schapiro, friend and art teacher, had said, "Betty, your Creative Arts School is a gem. Would you consider expanding your educational efforts to include humanistic studies? It could become a comprehensive family school." Three years after the Creative Arts Workshops began in 1964, his inspiration gave birth to the Educational Center.

Our humanistic philosophy shaped the curriculum: personal development, family living, community issues, and broad social concerns. Professionals with a high level of expertise taught in an informal atmosphere that encouraged frank discussions and an exchange of views. Ethical Culture member-volunteers provided all the staff services. My personal funds covered the expenses of a well-designed catalog, printed by the White Printing Company, owned by Sol White, Gert White's husband.

Howard had been depositing two hundred dollars weekly into my checking account, but he took no notice of the school and my role there.

Social-change challenges of the 1970s influenced many courses: teenage dilemmas, equal rights, the Feminist Era, non-violence, and balanced nutrition. Since our professional teachers often accepted minimum salaries or contributed their services *pro bono*, student fees remained modest. The school flourished.

I was most proud of "Revolution in the Arts," featuring both lectures and demonstrations of evolving art forms. Its concept was developed by Jacob Landau, a dear friend, prescient artist, and commentator on the human condition. Professional artists explained the evolutionary changes in the current art scene, augmented by semi-professional demonstrations. The South-Orange Maplewood Adult School (SO-M) co-sponsored the course and provided their junior high school theater facility for the performances.

My role in the successful Educational Center was discovered by a *New Jersey Star-Ledger* reporter. In our interview, I described myself as "living with every pore," not admitting my marriage was failing. As the Director, my leadership anchored me. Creative opportunities fed my excitement for living. Matt, my therapist, had observed that the Center kept me "sane" during those tumultuous times. For me, the crowning touch of the interview was the article's headline: "Mankind Is Her Family's Name."

I felt flattered and redeemed.

DURING THIS TIME, A HUGE CREATIVE FORCE entered my life—Thelma Newman. Her energy was channeled into imaginative ideas with a wide glistening smile that captured me. As an educator, brilliant artist, and proponent of Open Classroom, she had received a New Jersey grant to offer an educational enrichment program, for advanced educators, entitled Classroom Renaissance.

Its mission was to demonstrate the power of the creative arts and to bring learning to a more dynamic and profound level. As Director of the Educational Center, I was qualified to participate.

We met on six successive Fridays for six hours, staffed by leading artists representing varied art forms. Fridays were magical days on which I was transported to new levels of understanding. The staff mixed with students socially—no hierarchal separations there. In a friendly lunch with Thelma, she introduced me to the concept of *process*, how learning unfolds gradually, each step building in turn from another, merging into new depths of knowledge. I felt reborn by this unique educational experience, so very different from traditional academics.

Thelma and I became good friends, as I did as well with Marilyn Amdur, the visual arts teacher, and Rosilyn Wilder, who taught creative dramatics. In Roz's class, five students worked together in an improvisational assignment with eight minutes allotted for our project. Our goal: to create a dramatic skit depicting a problem of our contemporary society. Someone in the group needed to assume leadership—select the theme, shape the story, assign roles, and suggest appropriate dialog. Spontaneity would bring emotional honesty.

We chose the emerging hard-drug use by young people and the then-controversial question of reporting illegal behavior to authorities. The skit's scenario: *A mother is shocked to discover drugs in her son's bedroom and is conflicted about exposing his habit.* I was designated the role of mother, and another student was assigned as a family member, with no time to flesh out her role.

In our presentation to the audience, in pantomime, I exhibited shock at discovering the drugs. Mimicking extreme upset, I staggered down an imaginary staircase, troubled about how to handle this part of my son's life. The relative met me at the bottom of the stairs and responded to my distress, spontaneously putting her arms around my shoulders to comfort me.

In reality, I actually experienced her emotional concern and spontaneously burst into tears, which was not part of the script. No one had ever offered me that kind of understanding before, certainly not my husband. Her compassion brought my awareness of how emotionally bankrupt my relationship with Howard had been. This insight eventually helped me confront my disintegrating marriage.

Staff members became friends and taught me new educational concepts. When the program ended, Thelma and I continued to meet, sometimes at her Westfield home. It was exquisitely decorated with crafts befitting a highly talented artist. The staircase banisters, for example, were intricately carved with uniquely designed motifs. Her living daily with these beautiful designs made me wonder if I would ever achieve such beauty in my environment.

Thelma shared her history with me. Her career in the arts had been launched with the creative use of plastics. "How did you learn so much about the subject?"

"School and formal classes are not the only source of knowledge. I searched for the foremost manufacturer of plastics and picked the CEO's brain to acquire pertinent information." As she spoke, I envisioned her donning a lab coat, observing the talented technician at work in his laboratory, posing the crucial questions. She later wrote a renowned book on the topic. It disappeared from my collection while I was away healing from my brain surgery.

Thelma gave me one of her creations: a clear-plastic vertical cylinder, about fourteen inches tall, with gas-like bubbles floating upward in it. Today, it adorns my living room coffee table.

Another gift was an enlarged photograph, by Thelma, of an indigenous woman tending a fire, an infant strapped to her back with homespun fabric. This photo, which had appeared in the over-sized African book, presently graces a room furnished with items depicting African culture.

The larger gift was Thelma generously sharing her friendship and creative knowledge. One particularly enriching conversation concerned use of the human hand. She pointed out its crucial role in creativity. Thelma believed the connection of the hand to the brain powered this ability, which had allowed primitive peoples to evolve so successfully.

In later years, when I attended a three-day writing workshop, I was distraught that my portable typewriter had broken en route. The instructor consoled me by saying, "You'll do even better writing by hand."

IN A QUIET CONVERSATION ONE DAY, Thelma told me of a small lump in her breast as she planned an African trip with her son. "I'll check it out when I return home."

After the trip, her arts colleagues, including Marilyn and Roz, arranged a tribute luncheon for Thelma, honoring her significant contribution to the integration of arts and education. Thelma looked glorious that bright, sunny day, her bountiful red hair flowing in the autumn breeze. She commented to me afterwards with a wry smile, "That celebration felt like a summary that will stay with me always. . ." her voice trailing off. Thelma died of breast cancer some time later. A scholarship fund has been established in her memory at Kean College in New Jersey. Her legacy lives on for me always.

Marilyn and I also continued our friendship after Classroom Renaissance. We enjoyed a particularly stimulating journey of discovery to the Peters Valley art colony in northwest New Jersey, resplendent with crafts.

She visited my home one day with an intoxicated Howard present who made a vulgar comment about our sex life. We were both embarrassed, and she left quickly. I lost contact with her, absorbed with my divorce struggles.

Many years later, I found her living in New York City, now retired from teaching, and we made plans to reunite. She canceled our city reunion with no explanation, promising to phone. I never heard from her, and my Christmas card was returned undelivered, with no forwarding address. A friend and vital creative force had mysteriously disappeared from my life, another casualty of my broken marriage.

Roz and I also became friends after the program ended. She had a unique style, walked with flair, often wearing a colorful flowing scarf or quaint hat. We visited together regularly at her Montclair home, decorated with husband Ben's sculptures. During this time and after his death, Roz and I enjoyed many suppers together, with stimulating conversation about our progressive ideas.

She launched "Autumn Stages," an improvisational creative dramatics workshop, and "Life Drama" programs primarily for senior citizens. Roz' goal was to inspire others to use their creativity to affect the future. She was the only individual I knew who had visited Cuba, long before President Obama re-established relations with the country. I was enormously fond of her and admired her humanism. I have set my compass to align with her ideals.

When Roz became seriously ill, she deliberately stopped taking her medications. Her daughter explained, "Roz felt it was time to accept the end of her life."

After her death, her two daughters held an informal gathering at her apartment. We were invited to rummage through Roz' dresser drawer, where she kept her large collection of colorful scarves, to select one as a memento. I'm not sure the scarf remains, but her vision clearly does.

INSPIRED BY THE CREATIVE DRAMATICS IMPROVISATION in Roz' class, I opened a discussion with Howard about our marriage.

"I'm unhappy about our relationship. I think we should get marriage therapy."

He replied casually, "Yeah, sure," as he quickly left the room.

I found a practitioner in New York City, in a location convenient for Howard. Matthew Besdine had been recommended by good friends Anitta and David Cancell. When I told Howard we had a therapist, he barely remembered the conversation and said, "Oh, I'm not doing anything like *that*!"

I then made a life-changing decision—*to seek therapy alone,* a more responsible decision than when I was Janet's timid mother during her elementary school problem. Back then, I had failed to protect her when she needed it most.

In my initial session with Matt, I curled up into a fetal position whimpering, "Help me save my marriage."

I couldn't imagine being alone. After a lifetime of inhibitions about spending money, and now having it so readily available, why was I unhappy?

At the beginning of my therapy, Matt said little. He allowed me time to unburden myself of all the doubts, slights, hurts, and disrespect I had experienced in twenty-four years of marriage. After several months of sessions, three times weekly, I moved to the couch. There one day, I experienced a powerful fantasy.

I was climbing a challenging mountain, struggling to reach the precipice, feeling compelled to not only reach the top but know what was on the other side.

A commanding thought came upon me—I'll never discover the other side of the mountain without first extricating myself from this destructive marriage.

I knew, as one knows conclusively with one's whole being, I must divorce Howard. I told Matt of my decision then and there. I believe I surprised him with its suddenness and certainty. His response was perfect. "If you want to divorce Howard, I shall support you. If, on the other hand, you change your mind, I shall support that decision, too."

His wise words released me, affirming my independence and self-assurance. I was on my way.

Later, I became more aware of the profound process I had traveled, realizing why I was ready to create a new life. When I read the following passage from Rainer Maria Rilke's *Letters to a Young Poet*, I was struck with its exquisitely accurate description of my interior journey:

> *"the natural growth of your inner life will lead you. . .to insights. . . . Your opinions. . .must come from deep within and*

cannot be. . .hurried. . .bringing forth in the unconscious, be-
yond. . . one's own intelligence, and await with. . .patience the
birth. . .of a new clarity; that alone is living the artist's life: . .
understanding . . .and creating."

I had found my truth, rich beyond inspiration.

My fear of Howard's vicious temper deterred my telling him directly of my divorce plans. He discovered my decision only when served papers by my attorney.

I chose Arnold Mytelka of Clapp and Eisenberg as as my attorney after rejecting two prior candidates. Arnold was known for his strong personality, high intelligence, and sharp insight. I wondered, as I looked down the uncertain divorce road ahead, Could I stay the course, dealing with all the obstacles Howard would throw my way?

As I had anticipated, Howard tried to discourage my divorce action by mobilizing devious maneuvers. He rallied his ingenious bullying skills as heavy armaments for the battle with a startling strategy. After we had arranged temporary alimony and child support payments, Howard concluded that some part of these monies was paying for my therapy. He had always blamed Matt for the divorce decision, believing that he had convinced me to take this action. Howard sent Matt a letter, threatening to sue him if he continued treating me.

The bomb dropped when Matt reported Howard's ominous letter, telling me he would have to terminate our treatment. "I've consulted with several highly experienced therapists who agree I have no choice but to end our relationship. I'm dreadfully sorry."

I was stunned. It took all my strength to keep from bursting into tears. *My trusted friend, my mentor, my guide—how could I manage without him?*

I regained my composure when I heard Matt add, "There is one way we can continue to work together—if you can arrange to pay for treatment out of your own funds."

My spirits perked up momentarily—but then reality set in. I had no money of my own. With thousands of dollars flowing through our bank account all those years, I had never taken anything for myself. The three-thousand-dollar inheritance from my mother's estate had become the down payment for one of my discarded divorce attorneys. But I told myself, Somehow, I'll find a way to pay for my therapy.

I realized I had forgotten about the diamond earrings that languished in my drawer. I had the Steuben glass animal collection, which I sold immediately. I reluctantly parted with the petite snail that Howard and I had purchased to celebrate Janet's birth.

Matt lowered my already-modest fee, but I still needed more money to continue treatment. Providentially, a new resale shop opened in South Orange, specializing in fancy gowns. I had plenty of this "collateral damage" merchandise, which I was ready to discard. Within two weeks, I had resumed therapy with Matt, totally independent of Howard's money.

THE NEXT HEAVY BLOW WAS HOWARD CLAIMING custody of Wendy. The charade of that move was intended to punish me. He was clearly an emotionally distant father.

I was summoned by the custody officer for a hearing regarding each parent's role in Wendy's life. When asked to describe Howard's contribution, I faltered, perhaps influenced by Wendy's deep attachment to her father. I defended Howard, distorting and depicting his parenting in favorable terms.

By my next session with Matt, I had realized my error. "Matt, I goofed up with the custody officer. I described Howard as a conscientious parent, even glowing a bit—"

Matt had already responded with a gentle, forgiving smile. "You're so accustomed to protecting him that you fell into a bad habit. Here's a way to undo the damage. Call the officer for a second session, and explain just that. Hopefully it'll work out okay. Good luck."

In my second session with the custody officer, I presented a more accurate description of Howard's neglect of his children and my foolish habit of protecting him.

I was relieved to be granted sole custody. Since I heard nothing further of Howard's custody plan, I suspect he was plotting other battles.

He repeatedly delayed sending my alimony–child support checks. Coping with Howard's ongoing roadblocks often required my working several times weekly in my attorney's Newark office. This made it impossible to continue as Director of the Educational Center. With no one to assume this responsibility, I was forced to close the school. Unfortunately, I had neglected to train the support staff for leadership.

Matt commented one day, "With all this stress, perhaps you should consider some constructive outlet, such as returning to college."

I loved the idea, still harboring dreams of becoming a master's level social worker. The Rutgers University MSW Program required full-time attendance—impossible. I chose a part-time master's program in Counseling at Seton Hall University. Then I remembered that foolish jewelry in the drawer. Their proceeds covered my tuition nicely.

When I returned to Van Cleef and Arpels to sell the earrings, I was pleasantly surprised by their accommodating manner as they presented me with a handsome check. They explained, "Mrs. Levin, we believe that your having a married a wealthy man. . .it just might happen again." They were unaware Howard was unemployed and practically penniless when I married him.

In 1973, thirty years after earning my B.A., I entered the Seton Hall Masters Program. After this long absence, academic learning became enormously refreshing again. I investigated the teaching quality of the staff and was advised to avoid a particular professor, Dr. O'Malley, reputed to be somewhat rigid. Just my darned luck, the mandated basic courses assigned were under his tutelage.

Yes, indeed, he was not only rigid but his unfortunate attitude went further. Negative comments about women and Jews occurred from time to time. After several repetitions, I challenged him openly in class. Dr. O'Malley sputtered some response, but the spurious comments ceased. I nevertheless enjoyed his unusual intellect and deliberately selected him for subsequent electives.

Some time later, I encountered him in the cafeteria. In a friendly conversation, he said, "You know, Mrs. Levin, it's been refreshing having you in my classes. I've had the most rewarding year of my teaching career in my long tenure here at Seton Hall. Your challenging my unfortunate comments in class last year gave me much to think about."

I felt rewarded to have had a constructive effect on my professor though I had been uncomfortable challenging him.

THE "COUNSELOR AS SOCIAL ACTIVIST" COURSE really fired me up. The instructor's approach granted permission to break counselor boundaries to assert my ideas. The feminist movement and its effect on men particularly interested me. Even as I supported women's issues, I became an advocate for men's groups. This latter idea received no significant attention back then.

HOWARD CONTINUED HIS DRUMBEAT of constant harassment. I decided to visit my brother in Clearwater, Florida, during the children's winter break. February also marked my birthday, an event I took special pleasure celebrating with Lester.

But even in Clearwater, I could find no peace.

THE ART THIEF

DON'T CALL THE POLICE when you get home," Howard said in his call to me in Clearwater in 1973. "The art's gone from the walls, but it's safe. There's no need to be alarmed." He ended simply, as if he explained he had merely put out the garbage.

Howard had moved our art collection to his Levin-Townsend office in New York City. His call was meant to interfere with my vacation. I needed to escape his persistent bullying and ongoing intimidations, deliberately maneuvered to convince me to abandon our divorce. Howard seemed determined to use any measures.

Since art is community property, he must have known his scheme was thievery, pure and simple. He had become a gambler as his financial success grew. I was an enabler. At his request, I had naively given him the many original bill of sale documents from the files I had maintained.

HE ALSO MEANT TO CONTAMINATE my birthday celebration with my brother Lester and his wife Ruth. On the morning of my forty-seventh birthday, Lester cheered me when we had awakened with his warm greeting, "Sis, it's your birthday. We'll do *anything*, go anywhere you *want*."

I was moved by his caring and asked, "Is there an art museum in town?"

"I dunno," Les replied, perplexed. 'We'll hop in the car and drive downtown. I'm sure we'll find something interesting to do," he said.

We were off. Taking a shortcut, Lester drove through a shabby neighborhood. Suddenly, I noticed a sign in a storefront window: CRAFTS.

"Stop here," I shrieked, "I found what I want!"

Puzzled, Les asked, "What's here? I don't see anything unusual."

"I do. Trust me. Let's go in here."

Inside, I found high-caliber crafts, reasonably priced. I had always been enchanted with crafts despite the ongoing controversy over whether crafts were worthy of art status.

Squealing, I moved excitedly from one display to another. I couldn't buy much, since I had little money or suitcase space. I settled on a medium-sized raku pot, place mats of woven twigs, and a quilted pink velvet wall hanging created by the postmaster's wife. Back at my family's home, I showed Ruth my purchases while describing the unexpected location.

After I left Clearwater, my sister-in-law, curious about my experience, decided to visit the shop. She found the location abandoned, with a sign directing interested customers to a new address in downtown Clearwater. Arriving at the more fashionable spot, she introduced herself as a relative of that enthusiastic customer who had made a number of purchases several weeks earlier.

"Oh, we remember her well," declared the owner. "Her visit came at a crucial time for our business. We were considering moving to this location but were conflicted over the considerably higher rent." She added, "What clinched our decision to move was the realization that, if one customer could be so excited about our crafts, there must be others like her. Thus far, it has proved to be a successful move."

I hadn't been previously aware that my enthusiasm affected the behavior of others.

BACK HOME IN NEW JERSEY, I found the walls stripped of our art collection, all missing except for one notable work, Ben Shahn's *East Side Soap Box*. I had hidden it in the attic for safe keeping before leaving for my

Clearwater vacation. It was propped on the floor, and I sensed something untoward could happen if I left it that way. The piece had never been hung, since our large sweep of windows limited wall space for exhibiting art.

At home with Howard and the children, he confronted me, enraged that the Shahn work was missing. He accosted me viciously, thrusting his rigid chin near my face. "Where is it?" he demanded.

I remained calm and silent. He followed me around the house, stalking, screaming his question. Howard trapped me in the corner of the house's upper level. Seventeen-year old Janet and ten-year old Wendy were at my side, as they were getting ready for bedtime. Howard continued spitting out his question, turning beet red with fury, clenching his fists, and then grabbing my hair.

I next heard Janet's question. "Whose hair is this on the floor?"

Howard had torn the hair out of my head in rage about the missing painting.

In all the years of our marriage, he had never before physically attacked me. There was frequent emotional abuse, but never physical. I glossed over the incident, ignoring Howard's violence, focused only on protecting the children.

My daughters and I never discussed the incident. We were emotionally closed, similar to the circumstances of my childhood years. My parents avoided discussing highly emotional events. This pattern prevented my understanding meaningful experiences.

ABOUT THE "TRANSFERED" ART, I CONSULTED with my attorney and we decided to sue Howard for joint ownership of the art collection. The court case was a novel one, unique in the annals of art ownership. Works of art do not bear a deed as do real estate properties. The case rested partly on my knowledge of art and its selection. I testified on my own behalf while an attorney friend testified for Howard. Nan Kaplan, my friend from the Ethical Society, who coincidentally had encountered us at the Kennedy Art Gallery when we had made our Ben Shahn purchase, also testified. The court proceedings unnerved me, and I briefly took up needlepoint to keep myself steady.

In the meantime, Howard belatedly suggested we try marital counseling—but with a clinician of his choice. I agreed. She was a licensed psychologist and held a lofty position in New Jersey's professional hierarchy.

The decisive moment came in our third session. The therapist said to me quietly, "You know, he'll always take care of you."

My reply was swift and sure: "That's not *good enough* for me!" My voice boomed like a cannon shot. Even I was surprised at the spontaneity and confidence of my explosive response.

After my passionate outburst, the psychologist accepted the futility of counseling, that continuing made no sense. As we departed her office after that final session, she said to Howard, "I'll give you some feedback that might prove helpful. . . . You are quite a contemptuous person," she added emphatically. "Here is just one example. Your manner was clearly derogatory as you looked over my credentials on the wall and commented, 'If you displayed your credentials more prominently, you could command higher fees.'" Howard never responded.

SOME TIME LATER, AFTER THE ART OWNERSHIP TRIAL and our marriage counseling had ended, Howard blundered seriously. He returned home at ten p.m., after a late cocktail lounge meeting. He called for Janet to join him downstairs. I heard his slurred speech; he was clearly drunk. She refused, and called out, "I'm watching a TV movie with Mom upstairs in the guest room." He called repeatedly as he stumbled upstairs to the locked door, knocking, and asked that she open it. Janet refused again. He pounded the door with his fists, becoming more violent. I kept looking at Janet, but she was adamant, refusing in her quiet way to respond to his demands.

After a while, the pounding stopped. Howard returned with a hammer and continued the pummeling. I feared for both Janet and me and shouted to my husband, "I'm going to call the police if you don't stop beating on the door."

He continued his relentless pounding until the slender door started to splinter and I called the police. When they arrived at the front door, Howard immediately changed his demeanor. He greeted them with his charming chatter. I joined them and reverted to my timid ways, offering no explanation for my phone call. The police never questioned me. I was embarrassed at the scene, trying to ignore my thumping heart.

I'm surprised they accepted my silence, probably reported it as a simple domestic dispute on the police blotter. Howard's breath reeked of alcohol.

By the next morning, I had regained some confidence and phoned my attorney to report the traumatic events. Arnold immediately sent a cameraman to photograph the splintered door and introduced an emergency court action to have Howard removed from our home. The judge so ordered, and he was given three days to gather his personal belongings. Howard was allowed to enter the home only in the company of a friend who would be responsible for his behavior.

The judge set a date for a hearing about whether Howard's absence from the home should be continued, partly to be determined by interviews with the children. That hearing was set on the day of Janet's high school graduation. Greatly distressed, I told Janet I would request a postponement. She insisted that we keep the court date. "Mom, I want to get it over with. This has dragged on too long."

I was extremely upset; neither the court nor my attorney had told me of the children's crucial role in this weighty matter. I would have liked to prepare them for their session with the judge. They needed to be reassured that their feelings about their relationship with their father were far more important than the difficulties between their parents.

The judge reported that both Janet and Wendy preferred their father not return home. I still feel guilty that I hadn't commiserated with them on that fateful day. That's a huge burden, more than two kids that age should have to bear.

FINALLY, THE DIVORCE

THE DIVORCE WILL NEVER HAPPEN without some kind of trial," said some onlookers of the contentious three-year battle. They were correct; but it was the art trial that became decisive. To my great relief, the judge ruled I was equal owner of the art collection. The financials apparently convinced Howard to settle this aspect of our marital lives, accepting the inevitable. He made an acceptable offer, a modest one considering the many millions he had earned.

Nevertheless, he made one last appeal over remaining issues that included ownership of some miscellaneous possessions, more of sentimental than financial value. Among these items were our theater playbills collection and a handsome Czechoslovakian glass bowl purchased at the New York World's Fair. Also, of great importance to me, was the Tully Filmus oil portrait *Old Jewish Man*.

In almost comic relief, Arnold appealed to Howard's affinity for gambling. He suggested that this final distribution be decided by a chance drawing. Howard agreed. Each item, listed on a scrap of paper, was folded and placed in Arnold's emptied office waste basket.

Even before the lottery, in an amiable conversation, Howard and I agreed to divide the playbills equally. These parting mementos had represented magnificent theater experiences and a comfortable life style, tragically contaminated.

As for the "Old Jewish Man," this treasure presently hangs in the dining room of my second lifetime home on Sagamore Road.

REGARDING THE FINANCIAL SETTLEMENT, the dollar amount was almost equal to my share of the value of the art. But money had never been my motivation. I was fighting for my freedom to create a life with dignity and respect, a second lifetime, honoring my humanist values.

Earlier, Sara and Ruth had believed I wanted a bigger chunk of Howard's money. Sara asked me one day, in a plaintive tone, "Why are you divorcing him?"

"He treats me disrespectfully, like a 'non-person.'"

"Don't talk like that. I don't like that word."

AFTER THE ORDEAL, ARNOLD SAID, "I'll never handle another divorce again in my career."

Both attorneys sighed in relief and with a touch of humor, agreed, "Now that we've succeeded in bringing this to a peaceful conclusion, maybe we could tackle the Israeli–Palestine conflict."

Howard and I signed the divorce papers in the attorney's office. His final blessing as we parted: "You'll fuck up your life."

DESPITE HIS MALEVOLENT FAREWELL, I was happy, happy, happy—like a child with an enchanted gift, anticipating a bright future. I realized I was now fully in charge, eager for my journey, solely responsible. Friends asked, "Do you plan a party to celebrate your victory?"

"Absolutely not. My dream of marriage and family has been shattered." I murmured further, "There is remorse beneath the joy of having won a hard-fought battle. I'm determined to learn from my mistakes and create a meaningful life."

DISPOSING OF THE MARITAL HOME
AND BUYING A SECOND CHANCE

SOLD MY SHORT HILLS HOUSE IN 1975, when I was forty-nine years old, always knowing that losing that gem would be the price of my freedom. Isn't much of life a trade-off? I had also been prepared to relinquish the art collection, except for two cherished works. I mourned losing *The Family*, our small Henry Moore bronze that had rested on the leather-trimmed living room desk. I was finally able to make peace that I no longer had possession. Its theme of togetherness had always remained elusive in our marriage. Luxuries mean little when the quality of life is in shambles. I felt satisfied that Shahn's *East Side Orator* was safely in my care, its labor message speaking of my basic values.

Selling the marital home meant disposing of an almost thirty-year accumulation of stuff. The inevitable garage sale was handled by loyal friends Helen Tepper and Suzanne Gluck, who volunteered to be salespeople for the tedious day.

SADLY, MARY, MY LOYAL HOUSEKEEPER of twenty years, was not present. She suffered a severe bout of rheumatism at this crucial time. Rarely ever missing a day's work, she became ill toward the end, suffering with the sad closure of that brilliantly designed home. Deeply stressed, she had borne witness to the rise of our luxurious marital life and its subsequent collapse.

Mary and I shared a similar early life, raised by a stepmother after the deaths of our mothers. We had bonded, becoming like family, both finding relief from feeling like orphans. Evelyn had said to Mary with mock seriousness, before departing after a visit, "You'll take good care of my daughter."

In the past, I had reminded Mary, "How lucky I was finding you at a B. Altman's white sale—rummaging among the towels—and a neighbor promised to find me household help. I remember how coming into our family brought you some relief—recovering from that tragic killing of your only son." Mary looked at me quietly, nodding in appreciation. Our final parting brought many hugs with tears.

We remained in touch regularly by phone after Mary returned to North Carolina. I always remembered her Halloween birthday with a card and check. Mary returned briefly for Janet's wedding.

AT THE END OF THE GARAGE SALE, a violent thunder storm erupted, washing away the garbage bags down the Moraine Place slope into the bowels of lower Short Hills, stuffed with all the rejects. At first, I was annoyed. Then some neighborhood boys had torn open the bags and mockingly dressed up in the women's dresses. They clowned and danced like buffoons in the downpour, a comedy *fantastique*. I chuckled at the garbage floating down the hill, flagrant detritus. What an appropriate ending to a lengthy flawed marriage!

I required a new home, a passable one. My financial future was uncertain with a just-launched private psychotherapy practice and modest alimony. I felt a strong need to nest, a house to call my own. My preference was Maplewood, an interracial community and location of the Essex Ethical Society. I chose Millburn so as to not disrupt Wendy's schooling.

A simple house married to the land would do, set attractively into the geological contours of the property, like the house I had just lost. Having three or four bedrooms was a goal, with a room for each daughter. My heart was also set on an additional room for my brothers when they visited, including an extra bathroom.

Frustration and reality continued as a daily experience in my search. One day my friend Mary Slavitt recommended I see a house on Sagamore Road, "very dark and gloomy, only two bedrooms, one bath, but you should see it nevertheless." By then, I was desperate, with my Short Hills house already sold and my departure imminent.

I went to see this likely disappointment. Entering via the patio, I was immediately impressed. What a setting! Surrounded by lush shrubs, encased like a protective womb, with a small, well-planted green rise looming beyond, a sense of peace engulfed me. My mood changed, though, when I walked into the dark-paneled adjoining family room.

Heavily brocaded gold drapes covered three walls above dark red carpeting. A huge semi-circular sofa seemed to squeeze the very air out of the room. No windows were apparent. Most depressing.

The situation improved when I entered the kitchen, and my heart surged. I smiled in recognition as I viewed the dining table in the middle of the room, suggesting sociable meals, just like the Chicago Winthrop Avenue kitchen. That apartment of my young teen years had introduced me to the first bedroom of my own, bringing a new start after my depressed childhood. Its salient feature, the adjoining outdoor balcony facing the sun, with two concrete planters, invited spring flowers to bloom.

The kitchen stirred crucial memories—maybe a two-bedroom house would work after all. *Could a new beginning be possible?* I couldn't let go of that thought.

I had also seen a suitable ranch at an affordable price, containing the extra bedrooms and bathrooms I wanted. I became conflicted and consulted with my brother Lester on the phone. He later chuckled, recounting that call, until almost the end of his days. He mimicked my emotions: "Despite her indecision, she heaved constant sighs whenever she referred to the house with *that kitchen*," demonstrating my emotions by breathing noisily and deeply, with successive heaves and dips.

I finally knew what I must do. From premature rejection to steely determination: *I must have that house.*

Janet would have to sleep on a daybed in the family room, though, hardly an acceptable arrangement. I couldn't slight her needs; I would have to rethink this heart's desire.

Everything changed with Janet's call home from college, though distressed, revealing her new plans and emerging maturity. "I'm coming East to see your therapist, Matt, and continue college in New York City. Don't count on me being a kid at home anymore. I'm an adult now."

When I told her about the house I wanted to buy with only two bedrooms, Janet reassured me, "Mom, if it's what you really want, go for it. Don't let me stand in your way." I was relieved. *Yes, Wendy and I could manage nicely in this small house.*

Then frustration set in. After repeated offers to Mr. Lerro, the owner, I received no response. I had heard another prospective client had a similar experience and finally abandoned pursuing the purchase.

I had noticed that the house and grounds featured numerous ceramic figures. Inquiries revealed that Mr. Lerro had built this house for his wife, an enthusiastic ceramicist, who had subsequently died. These many figures were his last lingering memories of their time together. The reason for selling the house was his mother's move to Florida, beckoning him to join her. Apparently, the house was for sale, but *not quite.* He felt great reluctance saying a final farewell to his dear departed wife. The house had been on the market almost six months by then.

I would have to respond sensitively to Mr. Lerro's conflict if he were to relinquish this house. I told the realtor, "I want to speak with the owner privately."

She resisted my idea. "That's highly unusual."

"This is a highly unusual situation," I insisted, having learned determination from my former husband.

Mr. Lerro and I met in the kitchen. He graciously suggested, "May I offer you a glass of my homemade wine?"

"I'll drink with you only if you sell me the house." Using my newly achieved counseling skills, I expressed reassurance. "I love this house almost as much as you do. You can visit any time you wish."

He seemed to be warming toward me; it was time to discuss the financials. Remembering past offers he had ignored, I braced myself and asked, "How much money will it take to buy this house?"

"How much are you willing to offer?"

I brazenly named a figure slightly below the asking price. He took out paper and pencil, and made some laborious calculations, lips silently mouthing numbers, looking troubled.

"After I pay the six percent realtor fee, my share will be considerably less than I expected." In a surprisingly soft tone, he then added, "If you love this house so much, you can have it."

I was ecstatic. We drank his wine together, the deal sealed with a handshake. As an afterthought I asked: "Can you throw in the refrigerator?"

"Oh, you need one?"

I nodded. After he agreed, he said he wanted the living room carpeting. I would have given him the walls if he wished. My joy was total.

As I look back, I understood why Mary Slavitt had regarded this house as "dark and gloomy." I believe she had initially entered through the dimly-lit garage and basement. Her poor impression was fortified by the depressing family room, very different from my bright entrance via the patio and familiar kitchen with sweeping Chicago memories. Today, my home is like a greenhouse, with plants flourishing at almost every window.

On the day of the house closing, Mr. Lerro dressed formally in a handsome white suit, complete with vest and white spats on his shoes, as if attending a wedding. My heart felt remorse for him but my happiness overshadowed all.

A NEW PROBLEM CAME UP regarding the continuity of leaving the Short Hills house and taking possession of my new one, which necessitated a layover of two days. This so-called difficulty was actually a bonanza. I now anticipated two full days of erotic laying over with a lover.

During this interlude of relocating, I had met Ben, a married, sex-starved, handsome man just "rarin' to go!" We eagerly planned to "lay-over" during that leisurely time as I arranged for Wendy, age eleven, to stay overnight at a friend's home.

As he came on to me, my slumbering libido awakened to new possibilities. This was a bonus of divorce I had never anticipated—a virile suitor courting me.

It was an incredible awakening for me. In that stress-filled time of trying to divorce Howard, three laborious years, I was not only deprived of sex but my natural desires lay quiescent, as though dead inside. The sexual chemistry exploded between my paramour and me, especially when he brought a suitcase of sex toys for our pleasure. It was a total surprise and delight. From this erotic "divorce dividend" emerged the new sexual Betty.

We met in motels as opportunity and appetite suggested. In a serious discussion with Ben, I asked how he felt about violating his marriage vows. He explained, "My wife can't expect me to live like a monk." I was grateful to benefit from his erotic needs.

Our promising plans were waylaid, however, when the same violent rainstorms that arrived after my garage sale also flooded the basement of his marital home. His wife insisted he spend those two days pumping out the water and cleaning up the mess.

Our exciting plans had vanished. My disappointment was tempered by focusing on the engrossing books I had brought to the motel room. I wouldn't be defeated.

This frustration activated some deeper thinking. Surely, this lifestyle was not the goal of my three-year divorce struggle. A satisfying sex life was important but too limited in my ultimate life's journey. I deserved more, much more—*a companion sharing similar values in an endearing relationship where we could grow old and wise together.*

I ended the relationship as gently as I could. "Ben, you're a fine man who has reawakened my sexuality, for which I'm grateful. I'm just not able to continue with a married man." We parted amiably.

It was time to settle into my new home and develop my psychotherapy practice.

SETTLING INTO MY NEW HOME

FTER MOVING INTO MY NEW HOUSE, despite recent successes, vestiges of insecurities plagued me. On the first day of preparing to make it a home, I misplaced the shopping bag containing crucial papers—divorce, house title, bank book with monetary settlement—*Where did I put it*? I felt terrified. Was I living out a harbinger of failure? With much effort, I tried to remember but drew a blank, confirming the curse Howard inflicted on my future: "You'll fuck it up." Does he always know more than I do? I anesthetized myself by wiping down the kitchen counter tops and mopping the floor. After several hours I finally remembered—I had tucked the bag safely in a corner of the master bedroom closet.

In the kitchen, the stove oven door wouldn't stay closed, impaired by a broken hinge and missing spring. At the closing, the inspector had warned me, "Plan to buy a new stove soon."

Janet, home for summer college break, created a clever paper-clip device that kept the oven door closed. When that solution later failed, she came up with a new device—a simple pencil stub placed carefully did the job again, for a while at least. It was time to get experienced help, and I phoned Maytag for repairs. When they heard how old the stove was, they dismissed my inquiry. "Forget it, lady, we stopped making those parts years ago."

Hearing of my oven problem, my friend, Anitta Cancell said, "My neighbor's a good handyman. Here's his phone number." Anitta was a constant friend who telephoned me first thing each morning during my divorce proceedings. She told me later she wanted assurance I had safely survived the previous night.

After finding the rusty spring and hinge buried in the oven cavern, the handyman said, "Ask the folks at Maytag's if they have similar parts, like for a dishwasher. I'll reshape them to fit the oven."

I visited the Route 22 warehouse with the rusty parts in hand. The counterman, looking puzzled, departed to the rear storage area. Next I heard, "How many of these do you want, lady?" He had the precise parts needed for the oven door. My handyman completed the repairs but wouldn't accept payment for his good work. I made a contribution to his church, realizing altruistic people did indeed inhabit my world. I hoped I could also become resuscitated into working order, a new Betty. If only Howard had been so easy to fix.

I discovered that my property included land with an extraordinary planting. The postage-stamp rear lawn ended in a rise, planted with a massive display of azaleas, about thirty, cascading down the slope. During Mother's Day week of blooming appeared a multi-colored tapestry of purples, reds, whites, and pinks, intermixed with evergreen shrubs— strikingly beautiful. Another gift was my property adjoined the South Mountain Reservation, a backyard of more than two thousand acres. I marveled—how did I get so lucky?

The azalea display deserved to be shared. Each year when blooms peak, I host an open house, usually a wine-and-cheese fund raiser to benefit the Ethical Society.

A small pond sits at the rear of my property, most likely a catch-basin for underground water. One workman suggested that possibly, Native Americans had settled here in centuries past. "They always search out good water sources. Don't be surprised if some arrowheads show up eventually."

What a privilege, possibly connected to our country's ancestors.

Janet brought me watercress seeds one day when she realized the property's flowing water invited their growth. Many friends, including my gardener, have enjoyed this healthy, organic crop. When Janet attended my celebration of forty years in private practice, she picked some watercress to enjoy at home, the fruits of her early gift when I had first settled here.

During the early years in my home, I added fish and tadpoles to the pond, a natural paradise. Its perimeter invited flowers where I planted ajuga and impatiens. I tried to complement the naturalness of the setting, avoiding a manicured appearance. I also discovered a few isolated wild flowers among the woody plants, trillium and jack-in-the-pulpit. A stand of hemlocks lined the left rear property.

The front property features a high-rising stone wall with azaleas and velvety pachysandra overlooking the driveway. Japanese maple trees punctuate the slope. Additional pachysandra carpets the far left beyond the driveway, where I added forsythia shrubs. These latter hardy plants allow a winter bonus. Often, cuttings in late January or February brought into the house bring forced-blooms, a brilliant yellow overture to spring. Settled on my living room coffee table, they are a welcome sight on a gloomy winter day.

A scattering of white dogwood trees had delighted Evelyn during her infrequent visits. They disappeared as she did, cherished but not forgotten. A huge tulip tree anchors the bottom of my lengthy driveway hill where my *Be About Peace* sign, with complementary American flags, sits proudly among the summer hostas. Other greenery emerges in the spring where woodland creatures—chipmunks, squirrels, and wild turkeys scamper freely.

Another bonus: In later years, a Millburn Avenue bookstore, now out of business, gave me their decorative wooden storefront wishing well. My later boyfriend, Tom, hefted it to the rear of my property, a rustic addition to the home's patio entrance.

I had created a growing, nurturing environment, successfully continuing my teenage Winthrop Avenue urn-planting efforts. I had achieved a true *second lifetime.*

Now, forty years later, major changes but still great joy. Some perennial plantings have disappeared but other charming additions claim their turn. The wishing well, discarded by the contractors during my brain surgery, has been replaced by a small antique library staircase, shipped from Cambria, California, by my cousin Paul. With his *goldene* hands, he constructed an elaborate structure that assured its undamaged arrival to my home. Varied house plants decorate the successive steps during the summer season. I consider Paul a cherished brother. Rarely has a man so endeared himself to me.

BEYOND THE IMMEDIATE AREA, I encountered Vaux Hall, New Jersey, an interracial neighborhood, just a few miles from my new home. Driving by one day, I witnessed a funeral in progress, reminding me of the special people of my Chicago past—African-Americans Aurelia, one of my cherished mothers during childhood, and Roscoe, an appreciated employee of my dad's shop. As the memories swirled, I wrote a poem that connects these cherished individuals from my early years with this respected new experience.

> *The hearse sits quietly*
> *at the curb.*
> *The small church rises slightly*
> *above neat, drab houses.*
> *People flow soundlessly from*
> *dusty paths and jagged walks.*
> *A bow-legged woman*
> *waddles sadly,*
> *dark hands clasping a*
> *familiar book.*
> *A man, head erect,*

wears a neat beard that
frames pained eyes.
Lingering behind,
an elder of forgotten years
decorates his grief with
white gloves and flowered lapel.

Around the corner
the car caravan huddles
to start its wail.

Now living in a middle-class neighborhood in contrast to my former upscale lifestyle with Howard, I appreciate that my world continues to expand.

After settling into my new home, Cousin Dorothy visited from California and noticed the Ben Shahn gauche *East Side Orator* on the wall. The Yiddish comments particularly attracted her.

"Sister, do you know what that man is saying?"

"Not exactly."

"Would you like me to translate his words?"

I marveled at her knowledge of Yiddish. "Of course."

Dorothy's translation: *Nature has given everyone an appetite, but the bosses have stolen the key.*

Impressed with Shahn's poetic observation, I asked, "Dorothy, please write the translation on the back of the work of art." We rejoiced in the message Shahn had portrayed in his painting. I knew he had given the labor unions a dynamic voice but I hadn't known the precise words.

About a year later, the curator of the Jewish Museum phoned me.

"Ms. Levin, we are planning a special exhibition of works of art that private collectors have pledged to donate to our museum. May we include your Shahn's *East Side Soap Box* among them?"

What a development, I thought. With the past nasty ownership struggle, it felt *beshert* (meant to be); some celestial movement had entered my sphere.

"I feel honored to be included among the benefactors. Frankly, given my financial circumstances, I couldn't agree to that arrangement." Then on a whim, I added, "Since you value the work so highly, would your museum be interested in purchasing it?"

After a brief hesitation, he replied, "I'll certainly discuss this possibility with my board. Give me some time, and I'll get back to you."

Within a few weeks, the call from the curator exceeded my greatest expectations. "Yes, we would like to purchase the work of art and are prepared to offer you $40,000."

I agreed instantly, but with a special requirement. "I'm pleased to accept your offer, but with a special request. Someone very important to me, my cousin Dorothy Yuditsky, translated the Yiddish comments and wrote them on the back of the painting. I would ask that the translation be credited to her when the work is exhibited."

"I must caution you that a gauche is not shown frequently because of its fragility."

I felt triumphant. I had no need to explore possible higher offers from private galleries. This past ugly affair had shifted into a peaceful course. *East Side Orator* was now settled in its proper home, its wise Yiddish comments translated by Dorothy, my surrogate mother of peasant lineage.

May everyone rest in peace.

LAUNCHING MY CAREER

A S I SETTLED INTO MY NEW HOME with the divorce and sexual adventure behind me, it was time to seriously develop my profession as a psychotherapist.

I looked back to my earlier months, when I had just started my Our House internship as part of the requirement for completing my M.A. degree at Seton Hall University. Simultaneously, I had been completing my dissertation as well.

"Just go upstairs and rap with the kids," said my Our House supervisor as I started my first day in training as a psychotherapy intern in 1974. This South Orange, New Jersey, setting was a drop-in center for rebellious teenagers, established by Harvey Samos, a philanthropist with a social conscience.

In a way, I was a rebel too, insisting on an internship instead of a "practicum" (practice counseling with fellow students). I called this latter method "Mickey Mouse stuff." I felt triumphant achieving a true clinical experience by fighting the system. What a realistic way to learn doing therapy—-right on the job, guided by professionals who knew the ropes. I had the advantage of two supervisors from diverse perspectives, a psychiatric social worker, John Boyne, and a clinical psychologist from Argentina, Dr. Isaac Tylim. Another psychologist, Dr. Edwin Bokert, conducted group meetings for the staff of professionals together with the custodial and clerical folks, free of any hierarchal structures. Each was valued for their individual ideas.

When I entered the upstairs living room at Our House, I found about twenty teens creating a cacophony, teeming and screaming. *With all this bedlam, how can I rap with them? They don't even know I entered the room.* Some perched on the sofa's back edge; others seemed to be hanging from light fixtures. Overwhelmed, I took an empty seat at the end of the sofa. A young girl of about fifteen joined me, and I initiated a conversation.

"My name is Betty," I said, extending my hand. "What's yours?"

Her curt reply, with chin on chest, was, "Sally"

"So, Sally, what brings you to Our House?"

"Home sucks."

"How's that?"

"My folks are always on me for my messy room and poor grades."

"Yeah, parents do seem to have their own agenda." Then I switched subject. "How's school?"

"Awful—tests, tests, tests. What do they think we are, pieces of machinery?" Her despair seemed to increase. "Those multiple choice ones—they never seem to include the ideas I have. Don't they know I have opinions of my own—why don't they just ask me?"

"Yes, schools have their own agendas, too."

The other teens who had joined us nodded in agreement. Our rapping had begun, and they started to trust me.

As for one-on-one counseling sessions, Our House kids wouldn't accept this style from the professionals. Isaac's innovative solution: with the teens' permission, we would request their parents join groups, at no cost, to learn about raising troubled teenagers.

Essentially, we taught parents to become "assistant therapists" to their children. This approach was so effective that I planned to use the perspective in my private practice.

Fees became an emotional issue, even with no cost. Our staff hotly debated the subject, including me, who objected to professional services without some small financial contribution, that families needed to acknowledge the intrinsic value of therapy. Those opposed pointed out clients' limited finances. After our energetic debate, we voted to charge five dollars per session. One parent protested vehemently, "Five dollars! That's an outrage!"

I appreciated the important clinical skills my internship taught me: to become a more carefully attuned listener; understand the greater depth of some dilemmas; be aware of the problems many teens face in growing up, living in that "in-between" world of no longer being children but, inside, fearing demands of adulthood. Teens were often grappling with their serious conflicts between parental standards contrasted with peer expectations, the latter sometimes highly irresponsible.

By some idiosyncratic timing, in April 1975 I completed my internship at the same time of my divorce and the purchase of my new home.

The internship evaluation had pleased me as John commended my eagerness to learn. My university advisor also encouraged me with his heartening recommendation: "With your unusual abilities, I suggest you stay on to earn your Ph.D."

I responded, "Yes, I'm eager for more education, but with a different emphasis. I want to study at an analytic institute where the focus is more on the complexities of our emotional lives."

With this completion of my M.A. in Counseling, my future studies were clearly in sight. Meanwhile, though, I needed a paying job, and I asked John for a position as a professional.

He responded, "Betty, we'd love to have you on staff, but the money is just not there."

Since I loved the work and kids, I continued as a volunteer. This was doable. As an intern, with no pay, I had been squeezing by okay with just alimony and child support. I felt I could manage.

After only a few months, to my delight, funds unexpectedly became available—I had "arrived," my first paying job as a psychotherapist! Fervor became a daily high. My first fifty-two dollar paycheck thrilled me;

I wanted to frame it. I resisted the temptation, because I needed the money badly.

I'll never forget the day a client said, "I don't like a clinic and can afford a decent fee. Can I see you privately?"

My supervisors approved, and other Our House clients followed—rare that a recent intern would move so quickly to a private practice. The clinic patient who had earlier complained of the five-dollar fee there also switched to my private practice. She became willing to pay the higher cost as she saw her son's life improve. I was exuberant.

When my private practice first started, while on daily errands, I would meet neighbors and friends who commented, "I hear you're a therapist now."

I replied enthusiastically, "Yes, I'm proud of my new profession. My office is in my own home, in a separate wing with a private entrance, right on the reservation."

Soon the phone would start ringing with referrals from street encounters. I made a point of dressing tidily when leaving my house for grocery shopping.

Fees are always a delicate issue, especially as a newcomer. For my private practice in1975, I usually asked thirty-five dollars per session but also used a sliding scale, settling on "a fee we can both live with." I believe that psychotherapy is a gift of such merit that financial circumstances shouldn't be a barrier to treatment.

At that time, insurance companies were not yet involved in mental health coverage. When they entered this lucrative area, their presence often became intrusive, influencing the diagnosis and dictating the number of sessions. My colleagues complained bitterly over these patterns. I also heard about the extraordinary time demands discussing payment rejections, often based on company's administrative errors. I therefore resisted joining insurance panels, which has allowed my independence in maintaining a "health-based" model. This allows the process to include possibilities for an individual's maturation into a full life.

I knew many people wouldn't enter therapy without insurance coverage. Until recently, I resisted becoming an insurance provider but have now modified my position, accepting patients with insurance coverage for those who are highly motivated.

My attitude is also inclusive. I sometimes provide young people therapy *pro bono* when I casually meet individuals with special qualities. They may be merely a clerk whom I notice as unusually perceptive and conscientious. After identifying myself as a therapist, I invite them to come to my office to discuss their life goals.

MY PART-TIME ANALYTIC TRAINING started in the autumn of 1975 at the American Institute for Psychotherapy and Psychoanalysis (AIPP) in New York City, suggested by my analyst, Matt. Though he had been first president and founder, together with eminent Theodore Reich of the National Psychological Association for Psychoanalysis (NPIP), he recommended I bypass it. "I've severed my association with NPIP. I believe their approach has become too rigid."

After becoming an advanced student at AIPP, I was greatly flattered when their Community Guidance Clinic (CGC) offered me a job as a staff psychotherapist. Despite their enticing offer, I declined, not wanting to commute to New York City. I also eagerly anticipated the challenge of growing my own private practice. In retrospect, I was a bit rash to forgo the stability of an established clinic and face the uncertainties of independent work. Fortunately, my private practice continued well. I felt truly successful when the CGC later asked me to become their New Jersey referral therapist. Though I never received any referrals, their recognition confirmed my professionalism.

NEW CLIENTS WOULD COME UNEXPECTEDLY, occasionally from a colleague's family or acquaintance, often referred by satisfied clients. A Rabbi friend referred a member of his congregation. From the outset, I believe recognition of my humanist ideals, inherent as Director of the

Ethical Society's Educational Center, influenced referrals. As a community member with respected values who had become a professional, my practice increased nicely.

It grew idiosyncratically, my professional life moving ahead in confluence with my life as a single woman, each supporting the other. I developed ideas for workshops springing from my leading singles groups at the Morristown Unitarian Fellowship and personal experiences as well.

I presented workshops at various suburban colleges and even a Barnes and Noble bookstore, topics on "Self-Identity" and "A Socially-Enriched Life." The Women's Movement also inspired my volunteering my service as head of the Essex County NOW "Hot Line" and several Advisory Councils of social agencies. I also presented on Radio Station WSMU and later on television. It was heartening to know others were keen about these changes, that I was not alone in my enthusiasm.

Stretching further, concerned about the opposite sex during this vast social upheaval, I offered "Men's Liberation" workshops. My efforts went nowhere, since most men ignored their emotional needs back then. I did join an informal support group for Jewish gay men who were rejected by their synagogues. It was particularly gratifying to observe children they adopted benefiting from solid nurturing.

Requests for supervision came from various professionals—MSWs in private practice, counselors in training, and even from a social agency therapist, who wanted to augment her free supervision.

A particularly challenging supervisory experience troubled me. A trainee had arranged her own "agency" internship, an anti-abortion facility, not a bone fide social agency. I carefully researched her questionable setting, to avoid my liberal leanings distorting the professional dilemma.

Finally prepared to confront the intern, my anxiety increased and with hesitation, I said, "Joyce, I'm afraid I have some disappointing news for you." I took a deep breath. "Your ambition for becoming a professional counselor is admirable." I continued slowly, "However, there's serious difficulty with the setting you've chosen for your training."

Joyce looked at me questioningly. "What's the problem? The people there are good folks, friendly and competent."

I conceded her statement. "I respect your regard for them—that's not the dilemma. It concerns the agency's *mission.*"

She replied aggressively, "I don't understand—what's the big deal?"

"You've chosen a setting with a pre-set agenda. This violates all social service standards. Simply stated, these standards uphold a process in which clients must be allowed to freely express their own ideas in making life decisions."

Joyce became angry with me. "I don't like your attitude."

I believe she was responding to our different values. I maintained my professionalism and said, "You're clearly an intelligent candidate. I suggest you not confuse training goals with your personal interests. I'm certain you can find another agency that will accept you for training. Please look further for your own benefit."

She left, very upset with me, but within two weeks, she phoned in a friendly tone to say she had found another setting. I wished her well, but she didn't resume our supervisory relationship. I suspect our different perspectives upset her.

What I found most disturbing about the experience with Joyce: She had revealed she had prior approval from the "higher-ups" for the anti-abortion setting for her internship. Though greatly troubled, I never pursued the point further.

IN LATER YEARS, AT A SPIRITUALITY CONFERENCe at Princeton University, I recognized Dr. Edward Bokert from Our House days. With joy, I exclaimed, "I know *you!*"

His face lit up as he recognized me. "Yes, I know *you,* too!"

This re-acquaintance moved to a personal relationship. We started socializing in refreshing new ways, including weekly meditation gatherings he conducted in his Maplewood home. He and his wife Karen became members of the Essex ECS, which brought us closer. My relationship with Karen has taken on special qualities as she's become a board member and I'm a student in the chair yoga class she teaches there.

I FIRST STARTED WRITING PROFESSIONALLY in 1988, beginning with my interest in peace activities. The film *Changing the Silence,* regarding the ongoing nuclear threat, showed teenagers angry with their parents for not discussing the issue. I showed it widely in the community, then to a professional group social work meeting. It was later selected for their professional conference and chosen to be published in their official proceedings in *Roots and New Frontiers in Social Group Work* (Haworth Press, 1988; see appendix). The essay captured the excitement of social workers functioning as activists, describing the spontaneous social action aftermath. Thereafter, my peace activities expanded considerably, and by 2014, I had declared myself a Peace Educator.

During my membership in the American Academy of Psychotherapists (AAP) in the early 1980s, I met Dr. Edward Tick, editor of our journal, *The Art and Science of Psychotherapy.* We became friendly, particularly since we shared similar liberal ideas about the practice of psychotherapy and the need for social activism in the larger community. When he planned an edition on "What We Believe and Live For," he declared, "I want you in before I am out," as he anticipated becoming involved elsewhere. I wrote a first description of my philosophy of practicing psychotherapy, entitled *Quiet Miracles,* which appeared in that special edition in 1992 (see appendix). He later founded the organization, Soldier's Heart, where he brings healing of PTSD to veterans of American wars, which he terms "soul murder."

Another significant AAP connection was befriending colleague Alexander Jasnow. We shared a keen interest in art and I was captivated with the book he was writing, *Freud and Cezanne: Psychotherapy as Modern Art.* I felt greatly flattered when he proposed, "Betty, I've been asked by a journal editor to select a therapist to write a review of my book for its publication. Would you be willing to undertake the project?"

I was exhilarated—the arts and psychotherapy, two of my great interests!

I gave it my all, immersed in Al's material, taking copious notes. Al reviewed the evolution of art and suggested a similar journey for therapists. My review appeared in *Pilgrimage: Reflections on the Human Journey* (see appendix).

I later obtained an adjunct teaching position at East Orange, New Jersey's Upsala College in the late 1970s. Their Morning at Upsala Program helped women complete their unfinished educational goal. Several students became my psychotherapy clients, a bonus. The fulfillment of my new life continued to amaze me; my previous suspicion that there was more out there was becoming a reality, but my stimulating experiences went far beyond anything I had ever imagined.

As a professional counselor, I felt quite satisfied. Part of me, nevertheless, still identified with social workers. My early goal had been to become part of that profession and obtain my MSW (Master's in Social Work).

My Chicago roots included Hull House, of Jane Addams Hull fame. I was impressed with her history of starting the late nineteenth-century settlement house movement in Chicago, the first in North America. Immigrants who settled and established themselves in America continued to draw my attention.

The movement also reflected my parents' struggles. Witnessing their experience through Hull's vision, I'm certain this influenced my high school experience of volunteering at a neighborhood settlement house.

Social work appeared more comprehensive compared to individual counseling. Cultural and societal conditions seemed more dynamic factors in affecting people's lives. I was also affected by John Elliot's accomplishments, an early leader in the Ethical Culture Movement, who founded the Hudson Guild Settlement House in New York City.

Without an MSW degree, I was excluded from the social work profession. When returning to graduate school, I was not able to attend full time, necessary for an MSW program.

I regularly attended many New Jersey Association of Social Workers events, and an empathetic association president pointed out I could qualify for a newly established category, "associate member." I gratefully joined and became a volunteer member of a stellar committee, Social Workers as Psychotherapists.

Edythe Gutman, our admired committee chair, supervised our popular annual conference, which featured highly competent speakers. This successful conference produced large sums for the NASW treasury, later invested for hiring lobbyists to achieve licensure for social workers as Medicare providers. Through a quirk in legislative rules, licensed counselors (LPCs) were not similarly qualified to serve as Medicare providers, although our academic training was similar. I nevertheless worked on social workers' behalf to gain the profession this Medicare-reimbursement benefit.

Our speaker one year was a highly regarded therapist, Sophie Freud, niece of the founder of the psychoanalytic movement. When I picked her up at Newark Airport in her travels from Massachusetts, of course, we discussed her famous Uncle Sigmund.

I was pleased to be selected as presenter one year and conducted a workshop, "Healing a Patient Through Intensive Dream Analysis." My material was based on meticulous dream records of my client, a deeply troubled but highly creative young woman adjusting to a broken romance, geographic relocation, and a family history of suicidal tendencies. Treatment consisted of twice-weekly sessions over a period of about four years. She terminated therapy successfully with marriage, a new home, and a career in the creative arts. I felt affirmed by the therapy process my client and I had patiently navigated during those difficult years. One conference attendee commented afterwards: "Either she is an extraordinary patient or you are an unusually competent therapist."

The more I worked with clients, the more I became impressed with the power and effectiveness of individual psychotherapy. My ideals about social work became less important as I supported individuals with their unique problems and courageous life journeys. My shift was also influenced by my own dramatic life changes through psychotherapy. In time, I became solidly grounded as a psychotherapist and psychoanalyst.

GOING BEYOND MY PSYCHOTHERAPEUTIC PROFESSION, my interest in Peace Education grew. I had been influenced by individuals I have had the good fortune to encounter—Naomi Drew and her extensive peace writings, my friendship with Lou Kousins and the Peace Site Movement, World Citizen's Lynn Elling who influenced the expansion of my peace activities, and the Ethical Culture/UN's Culture of Peace. My peace work is yet to flower, but with this memoir put to bed, I plan to invest more time in this vital endeavor.

When I first launched my private practice in 1975, I had encountered the New Jersey Association of Women Therapists (NJAWT). Colleagues Sheila Dancz and Renee Jacobs had organized the association for budding and seasoned therapists, providing professional development and fellowship. We met monthly in private homes where experienced therapists addressed the challenges of private practice and related clinical issues.

After several years, the founders apparently burned out and decided to put out a call for therapists with fresh energy or consider dissolution. I was barely established in my new profession, but passionate about my work and offered my help if the founders would provide a liaison. Sheila Dancz joined me, and we worked together with a committee for solidly establishing NJAWT.

To grow beyond the forty therapists, we required governance procedures. We wrote a mission statement, by-laws, compiled a membership directory, and elected officers. My good friend Anita Roberts, though not a member, volunteered to type the first directory and administrative materials, in loyalty to our friendship.

We have energized and now, forty years later, have expanded to 110 members. We meet at a local church with three general meetings annually, peer supervision groups, conversation hours, and movie and book groups, as well as an ongoing newsletter. When we conducted a contest for naming our newsletter, *The Third Ear* was chosen, submitted by Sheila Dancz (now Dr. Dancz.)

Several years ago, all past presidents were honored, myself included.

The citation is one I treasure: "As a founder and past president, she is honored for her wisdom and contributions to the creativity and development of the Association, and also her pioneer role for the greater recognition of the field of psychotherapy."

I had been privileged to belong to a fine peer supervision group of seven therapists for almost twenty years. It disbanded about five years ago, when several members retired. I am now part of a new peer group of four members that has been meeting my professional needs.

My practice continued to thrive, having achieved twenty-eight patient hours weekly at its peak. It has now slowed as I approach my ninetieth birthday with other commitments.

My forty years of psychotherapy practice and elder years have become material for lectures on "The Wisdom of Aging."

My "Aging" interest stems from my own longevity but also evolved from earlier years and the tacit encouragement of my first analyst, Matthew Besdine. He always alerted me to current gerontology conferences. I particularly admired Dr. Robert Butler, who pioneered "Aging" as a field of study. He opened my understanding of the aging process, offering potential for enriching one's entire life.

Aging wisdom also came from poet Stanley Kunitz, whom I met at a Geraldine Dodge Poetry Festival: "As an individual ages, the body will deteriorate. What remains, however, is *one's creativity and spirit*." This latter phrase was pronounced pounding the air with clenched fist up-right. Kunitz has been the only poet to publish a volume of poetry after the age of ninety.

When I was sixty-five years old, on the evening before I attended my first gerontology conference, I had the following dream.

> *My body is bent over, leaning on a walking stick, similar to a Margaret Mead stance, but with bright, beady alert eyes. Two women who observed me have this conversation:*
>
> *"Is that Betty Levin?" One woman asks the other.*
>
> *"Yes."*
>
> *"And she's still around?"*
>
> *"Yes, she's still around. . . ."*
>
> *"And still practicing as a psychoanalyst at ninety-two?"*
>
> *"Yes, still practicing as a psychoanalyst."*
>
> *"Who would go to a ninety-two-year-old psychoanalyst?"*
>
> *"Seventy-two-year-olds who are sick of EST!*
>
> *I awakened howling with laughter.*

When I told Matt the dream, his response troubled me—the only time in our long, respectful, productive relationship he had revealed vulnerability. In a tone bordering on haughtiness, he said, "Imagine, dreaming you'd be the oldest living psychoanalyst."

I was surprised to hear his cynical comment instead one of affirmation. How unexpected, from this wise elderly gentleman, who had brilliantly shepherded me through the most egregious bullying that Howard could muster. Matt suffered trauma in concert with mine during the divorce upsets. Howard had reported him to the IRS for possible tax evasion related to his accepting my possessions as therapy payments.

After a time, I dismissed my hurt. *After all, he's only human, not a god.* He has sensitive areas as we all do. I couldn't bring myself to openly criticize or challenge this parent figure. Matt was then a vigorous eighty-year old with a generous shock of white hair.

My reluctance to confront Matt brought an insight that has benefited my own practice. Many patients have problems with honest, respectful challenges, possibly a reflection of their self-esteem issues.

After a few sessions with a new patient, I routinely ask them for feedback about our relationship, both positive and negative.

"What do you think about our work together? About me as a therapist? As a person? Is there anything you don't like?" They soon learn it's invaluable to be forthright about our relationship, even citing areas for criticism. It enhances our work, offering true integrity. Possible disagreements can open a refreshing area for discussion.

In other situations, a familiar dialog that often emerges: After a client demonstrates an admirable quality that I affirm, their response invariably brings a traditional "thank you." I always respond, "No need to express thanks. Commend yourself—you're the one who's achieved this quality. I'm merely observing and acknowledging it."

MY PSYCHOTHERAPY PRACTICE CONTINUES to be greatly satisfying as I enjoy good health, full of piss and vinegar. Despite my advanced age, I have no plans to retire. In the meantime, since everyone has potential for growing and learning until the end of their days, I plan to continue this path, encouraging my clients to do so also.

I trust I shall continue this pattern—paralleling the process with my clients. Challenged by their dilemmas, I welcome the opportunity to probe my own internal resources. I hope this wellspring continues to offer guideposts for my clients, to navigate their dark night of the soul to new ports of hope.

MY MAIDEN TRIP

AFTER MY LIBERATING DIVORCE, my choice for a first solo vacation was to feed my music-loving appetite at the Tanglewood concerts in the Berkshires. I planned to stay at an unfamiliar facility, Chanterwood, a bungalow colony on a lake in South Lee, Massachusetts. I eagerly drove the five hours to downtown Lee and turned "left off the main road into the woods," as the driving directions specified.

With the left turn, my high mood changed suddenly to anxiety as the dirt road became a single wooded lane through a desolate forest. The interminable drive made me apprehensive, sweaty hands clutching the steering wheel intensely as I rounded each blind curve. *What if I meet another car? No place to turn back.* The one-mile distance was never mentioned in the directions. *What did I get myself into? Why didn't I get some advice about a conventional place to stay?* I scolded myself.

With my goal of bunking on my own in the Berkshires, I had consulted the *New York Times* "Rooms & Inns" Vacation Section and seen the intriguing Chanterwood ad. I didn't know the exact location of South Lee but figured it couldn't be too far from Tanglewood and Jacob's Pillow, the performing dance center, another great interest of mine. Having just purchased a bright yellow Volkswagen Dasher, I felt confident. *I'll manage to find them both.*

With arrival at Chanterwood, my misgivings dissolved. I gasped at the panoramic view. It appeared like a summer Shangri La, a utopia I didn't know existed on Earth. This secluded paradise included simple charming cabins dotting a hillside, overlooking a clear, tranquil lake with a single float. There wasn't much of a beach, hardly a disappointment, considering the other pluses. The rustic bungalow dining hall of this woodland camp was served by talented musician waiters. We were privileged to watch them practice and perform their classical music during off hours. A large bulletin board in the main building listed Berkshire community activities including the town's movie offerings and schedule.

WHEN MY DEAR FRIEND DVO MARGENAU heard I was heading to the Berkshires, her summer country home locale, she had insisted, "You'll stay with me. I'll make you comfortable and show you around." Her strong personality was tempered by generous good–heartedness and creative impulses. Dvo had long-time connections with artists and studios in the area which made her invitation particularly inviting. Since I was just recovering from an acute dependency on Howard, I needed strong willpower to resist her kind offer.

"Thank you, Dvo, but I want to be on my own," I had told her, thinking, *I'm not going to become that overly agreeable Betty again.*

I didn't want to offend my loyal friend. She had rescued me when I needed an alternative dance class for my daughter, Janet, who had left a prestigious New Jersey Royal Ballet School. After I had later witnessed Dvo's sensitive teaching of Janet's modern dance class at the local "Y", I had timidly asked, "Would you teach your class at a place called the Ethical Culture Society?"

I was delighted she agreed to the gig and also knew of the Movement. She and Ernie had been married by an Ethical Culture Leader! Dvo's modern dance course sparked other courses in the arts and helped me launch a Creative Arts School at the Society. Most important, under Dvo's tutelage, Janet was guided into discovering her lithe body and its artistic expressions.

During my Berkshire vacation, I visited Dvo's historic rustic country home in West Stockbridge and enjoyed Tanglewood concerts as well. With limited funds, she volunteered as an usher, where we met during intermission to discuss the merits of the performances. Dvo introduced me to her colleagues, music lovers all.

Some days, we tramped through the charming streets of Stockbridge, visiting interesting shops but mostly just looking. Dvo had exquisite taste in design and served as a discriminating guide to her favorite haunts.

I remember a past excursion to Bucks County, Pennsylvania, where we window-shopped. Her trained eye noticed an intricate, Mexican-style gate leaning against a rotting barn. She pointed out, "Betty, that would make a fine headboard in your bedroom. It's too attractive to pass up."

I expressed doubt, not recognizing its potential. "It's rusty and heavy—is it really practical?"

She reassured me she could repaint it and would be able to lift it into her car. To this day, I enjoy this picturesque piece and warm memories of our friendship.

At Dvo's West Stockbridge home, we dined on her delicious home cooking with husband, Ernie. He had installed the kitchen cabinets with the discarded ones from our Short Hills house when we remodeled. Much of Dvo's house was decorated with many creative finds her discerning eyes had discovered.

Outdoors was a striking seven-foot bronze figure created by Ernie, an accomplished sculptor. His work depicted a farmer hoeing, which expressed his respect for the earth. I had the pleasure of owning several of his smaller works, the bronze *Reclining Woman* for which Dvo posed. I donated a replica to the Ethical Society, on display in the Meeting Room. Another became a therapy payment to my analyst Matt. A third, a plaster-of-Paris version, I gifted to my household cleaning man. He was thrilled I had succumbed to a generous moment, wanting to spread the pleasure of owning an original work of art.

One day, Ernie gave me a sculpture of two loving figures, sitting back to back, that he had created as a wedding gift for a special couple. In his typical gentle manner, he softly commented as he presented his gift,

"Betty, perhaps someday the togetherness of this piece will become part of your life, too." Still another sculpture he gave me is a small, sad female figure, head sunk in her two hands, a mood more typical of my recent marital past. I treasure them all, particularly the friendship I enjoyed with both Ernie and Dvo.

Despite Ernie's misshapen body, almost bent in half from an extreme arthritic condition, his *goldene* hands and soulful artistic sense have never deterred his creative accomplishments.

ONE OF DVO'S GREAT GIFTS as a teacher was opening students' imagination to create dance improvisations. For the younger children, she suggested, "Imagine you're a pussy cat just awakening from a nap."

With teenagers, the final class before high school graduation and college journeys: "Improvise your farewell to one another."

For our adult classes, Dvo's suggested improvisations were equally engaging: In the LP she brought to class one day, Dvo surprised us with a selection of wild tempos and strong drum beats. Most of us responded with frenzy—breathlessly thrusting and lunging with carefree abandon around and across the expansive room. After we paused to wipe our sweaty faces, Dvo identified the selection we had enjoyed—the sex orgy in Carl Orff's *Carmina Burana*. That exciting work, an introduction for me, is still one of my favorites.

Dvo shared some personal dance experiences. She had withdrawn from the Helen Tamiris Modern Dance troupe's performance in Moscow because of her pregnancy. She subsequently gave birth to her only child. Dvo's love of children was immense, expressed in her intermittent, though conscientious care of her granddaughter, born out of wedlock.

Dvo's death ended a vital chapter of my life. She succumbed to a severe abdominal problem, this "sister" and dear friend who had launched my leadership in creative arts at the Ethical Society. Her memorial service was held at her West Stockbridge home. I attended with Tom, my significant other, with her granddaughter present. Even following her early abdominal surgery, Dvo had managed to plan an intimate dinner in West Stockbridge for the four of us.

After her passing, Ernie developed a heart condition. Without his loving partner of so many years, he suffered a heart attack and died.

I still feel the loss of dear, wise Dvo. I retain many of the LP musical warm-up recordings from the Society's modern dance classes. Her advice: "Even when your muscles ache, don't succumb entirely to their discomfort. Try some simple poses to remain supple."

I can still imagine Dvo practicing postures at her kitchen sink while washing dishes.

THE BERKSHIRES WERE ONLY PART of my maiden voyage. My heart was also set on Provincetown, Massachusetts, the picturesque Cape Cod locale, where I joined my art teacher, Theodore Schapiro. He was a proud gentleman, in his seventies, head held high on a stately, gaunt body.

I first met him when I was desperately seeking a common interest to share with Howard, to enrich and possibly save our marriage. Howard and I shared an enthusiastic interest in art, a subject first becoming offered in the suburbs back then.

Ted taught an art appreciation course, sponsored by the New York University Extension Division, held in Teaneck, New Jersey. It was a bit of a drive for me but an easy New York commute for Howard.

"Howie dear, what do you think of our enrolling in an art course together?" He agreed, but only with mild enthusiasm.

On the evening of the first class, a driving rain storm developed, so violent that, several times en route, I was tempted to return home. *What am I doing driving on this frightful night way up to Bergen County on some whim that my marriage can be salvaged?*

Some unseen force drove me onward to discover this extraordinary course and gentleman of profound talent. Howard showed up for that first session but not too many thereafter.

Mr. Schapiro's explanation of the deeper meaning of art, its sweeping importance encompassing culture, history, sociology and psychology shook me to my bones. I could hardly keep leaping from my seat, as I experienced an "ego orgasm" stimulated by his soul-stirring lessons. I recall one of Ted's notable comments: "An artist, typically with keen, deep understanding, possesses an antenna that reflects and sometimes anticipates the conditions of society by his creative output. Picasso's *Guernica* is an example of this concept."

Inspired and impassioned by Ted's teachings, I responded to a contentious issue regarding conceptual art, expressed by a lay person in the *New Jersey Music and Arts Magazine.* I wrote my response, which appeared in the November 1974 issue. The editor later told me my letter was considered controversial by their editorial staff but that they had decided to publish it anyway (see appendix). Another issue that evoked my passion was the censoring scandal regarding the Mapplethorpe affair, the indictment of the museum's director for exhibiting Mapplethorpe's art, which was considered pornographic. I'm not certain I shared my essay with others but I felt good expressing free speech. I had been taught that, in totalitarian countries, it is the artists and writers who are muzzled first. I think both Ted and Matt would have been proud of me. (see appendix).

Ted encouraged my deeper interest in art that furthered a warm friendship with this father figure. His vision moved me to expand the Ethical Society's Creative Arts School to include humanistic studies, renamed "Educational Center." Ted also became a consultant for our personal art collection, bidding on works being auctioned at Sotheby's. He told us one day, "There's a fine Nolde watercolor being offered which I think we can get for a little over four thousand dollars, a good buy." *Dampfshiffen* thus became a modest addition to our growing collection.

TED SCHAPIRO AND HIS WIFE FANNY vacationed each summer in modest rooms in Provincetown and suggested he could arrange a similar one for me. I jumped at the idea, my second stop.

Ted was a genial host, introducing me to his artist friends and favorite haunts. We dined at selected eating spots known for good food and value.

We played together in the ocean, Ted's lean body bounding over the waves with ease. Acquainting me with the changing tides, he consulted the tables each morning before setting our swimming schedule to enjoy calm seas together.

I finally had the opportunity to romp with an attentive father, enjoying the benefit that every daughter needs—a sound father–daughter companionship that lays the foundation for a satisfying relationship in her adult years.

Indeed, what a father was Ted Schapiro! His daughter, Miriam, became a renowned artist, encouraged by him from an early age. He said, "Yes, women can become accomplished artists. Mary Cassatt was not the only one."

Miriam achieved much recognition, first elevating women's domestic sewing skills into an art form, then expanding her talents into highly colorful, flamboyant collages. Her art has been shown at many well-known New York galleries. Miriam also became an accomplished lecturer, in demand at many prestigious universities.

My friendship with Ted and Fanny continued in New York City where I visited with them regularly on East Avenue C. Miriam occasionally joined us; Howard never did.

We eventually purchased a few of her works and she gave some to us as gifts. One of her major works, a colorful vibrant collage, *Celebrating Women's Lives,* hangs in my psychotherapy office. Miriam also gave me her personally designed address book decorated with her colorful collages. I use it daily there, too.

During one of my visits with Fanny and Ted, prior to my divorce, he looked at me wistfully and said,

"If only I were thirty years younger!" I was surprised, even a bit enchanted, that this brilliant man could harbor such feelings.

When Ted and Fanny started having serious health problems, they discouraged my visits. Miriam phoned telling of her heavy responsibilities in trying to place them together in the same senior facility. Their very different medical conditions thwarted that goal.

When Ted died, Miriam called to describe her father's memorial service amongst his cronies in East Village. I was crushed, not having been told of his seriously deteriorating condition and impending death. I had never bid my final farewell to Ted and lost the opportunity to pay tribute to a beloved friend.

IN 2013, I ATTENDED A RETROSPECTIVE for Miriam Schapiro in the Chelsea neighborhood of New York City. I was gratified to be included on the invitation list—I hadn't been forgotten. The event was entitled "Trailblazer," curated by two Rutgers University art professors. With much pleasure and surprise, I viewed Miriam's early works, many of which I had never seen.

I was acutely disappointed when Miriam did not attend; I was told she was ill with a serious cognitive condition. The scholars who had organized the show believed it important to highlight Miriam's contribution and stature in the history of art.

I was also told that her only child, Peter, was also seriously ill. I was deeply saddened with this desolate news, that my dear friend Ted's family was suffering ultimate decline. I had arrived at Miriam's show, prepared for a celebration and renewal of our friendship, but instead was engulfed with grief. Squelching my tears, I discarded the flowers I had brought to honor her. Life's mysteries move on inexorably.

I had returned home from my maiden trip, my coveted friendships reconnected and cemented, marked with deep affection and mutual respect, till 'death do us part.' I vowed I would return to Chanterwood one day with a special man.

WHEN I WAS CONTEMPLATING MY DIVORCE, I had asked myself, if I divorce Howard, what will I find on the other side of the mountain? With the shape of my new life now developing form and meaning, I had found the answer:

There's absolutely nothing on the other side of the mountain other than what you create for yourself, being willing to engage the struggle that promises nothing, to find meaning within the process itself.

MY SOCIAL LIFE AS A SINGLE WOMAN

NOW A FORTY-NINE-YEAR-OLD single woman, developing a social life became a priority for me, especially with a male companion who offered a future. After becoming fatigued by the same crowd at the Morristown Friday night groups, I stretched my wings and joined a New York singles theater group which offered a reasonably priced package. It seemed perfect: a cocktail interlude on a Saturday night prior to a theater performance and time to socialize after the show. I signed up but couldn't attend the cocktail party because of babysitting complications. For the promising evening, I chose a demure black dress, rejecting the one with a low bosom, complemented with simple jewelry and black pumps.

I arrived just on time for the play, not meeting anyone prior to the performance. When it ended without an intermission, I had made no connections. I spoke to my seat mates— "Hello, my name is Betty, one of the singles group—" to the right of me, left, front, and those seated in back. The response was uniformly negative; everyone was puzzled about my inquiry. Still alone, embarrassed by my brash initiative, there was no singles group in sight. Had I been I taken? Was this a scam?

Leaving the theater frustrated and disgusted, I found myself at 11 eleven p.m., alone on a Saturday night, my young daughter safe at home. Stopped at a traffic light, I gripped the steering wheel furiously. *I'm not going home! I'm going to find something interesting to do in the Big*

Apple.

Flipping through my playbill, I saw an ad for the Algonquin Hotel. Aha! Through the years, I had heard of many interesting cultural activities there, especially the Round Table, conducted by luminaries of the literary world. *That's where I'm going*—just a left turn, and I was there.

Feeling insecure about parking, I feigned confidence as I ordered the valet, "Just take the car!" I noticed later that a public garage sat right across the street.

As I entered the Algonquin, a charming British-style sitting room welcomed me. Just beyond was a luxurious dining room, tables set with heavy cloths, brass candlesticks, and a buffet table laden with main courses. I noticed burnished roast chicken with juicy stuffing, succulent roast beef floating in *au jus* gravy, crown of lamb still sizzling. I approached the *maitre d'*. "Supper for one, please."

"Do you have a reservation, *madame?*" he inquired stiffly.

"Oh," I started to stammer, "You need one?"

"*Oui, madame,*" he replied politely. "This is Saturday night, you know."

"But I'm just one. Certainly you can find *one* place."

"*Mais non,*" he insisted. His French accent elevated the event in importance. I wasn't going to be easily dissuaded from saving that disastrous evening. "Maybe you can set up a small table behind your *maitre d'* stand?"

He looked at me incredulously, as if thinking, *Who do you think you are, visiting royalty?*

He signaled a porter, though, and in a moment, a small table, a heavy linen cloth, and even a candlestick appeared for my pleasure, set up just as I had suggested.

And what a magnificent supper I enjoyed— the most succulent chicken I had ever tasted, accompanied with golden roast potatoes and green beans flecked with toasted almonds. My waiter recommended a white wine, a Jermann pinot grigio, to accompany my feast. Luscious pastries decorated the groaning board. All my choices were served with aplomb, as if I were indeed visiting royalty.

Sitting alone, enjoying my sumptuous supper, I engaged in a favorite pastime—people watching. The loving couples in intimate conversation evoked my jealousy, and how the women were dressed in designer clothing—*el-e-gante!* I inhaled the experience and vowed, "I shall return someday and with a desirable male escort."

My very first Saturday night venture as a single woman became a hallmark for my new life: *When encountering disappointment, reach for other creative possibilities.*

IN LOOKING FOR ELIGIBLE MEN in my personal life, I attended varied social and educational events, occasionally inviting other women to join me. Sometimes I hit resistance:

"That's the night I wash my hair."

"I'm not in the mood."

I decided to not be discouraged by the inhibitions of others. I never feared going alone to explore possibilities and seize what life had to offer.

I was a bit unbelieving and enthralled that I had fled the velvet-lined prison of my marriage for this enlightening journey. My intuition had told me there was more out there, but my most expansive dreams had never anticipated such a bountiful existence.

That fateful day on Matt's analytic couch, wondering about my post-divorce future of and what was on the other side of the mountain, had truly taught me about what *you create for yourself.*

THE CLOSEST I COULD GET TO ACADEMIA, a long-held dream, were a few workshops, based on my experiences as a single woman, offered at colleges in Montclair, Caldwell, and Bloomfield.

I was particularly pleased to be hired as an adjunct instructor for an inventive program, "Mornings at Upsala," presented at the in East Orange, New Jersey college. Its mission was to offer a fresh opportunity for women who had not completed their college education or had entirely bypassed it. I felt privileged to participate, guiding mature students toward bright new futures.

"Psychology of Women" and "Interpersonal Relations" were among the courses I taught, the latter a special interest of mine, considering my childhood and marital inadequacies. Martin Buber's *I and Thou* jumped out at me as a rich source to explore.

As a legend and modern prophet, he probed this profound concept. Buber teased out the intimacies implied in the I–Thou relationship, avoiding the superficial I–it.

Functioning as an 'it' had usually characterized my childhood experiences. Through therapy, I had become a more fully functioning person but an intimate relationship still remained in my future.

I quoted Buber's ideas,

> *The basic word I–you can be spoken only with one's whole being. The concentration and fusion into a whole being can never be accomplished without me. I require a You to become; becoming I, I say You. All actual life is encounter.*
>
> *I–You establishes the world of relation. . .the purpose of relation is the relation itself. . .touching the You. For as soon as we touch a You, we are touched by a breath of eternal life.*

I was rewarded when a student commented at the conclusion of the course, "Thank you for making these profound ideas more understandable."

Now, in 2016, I believe people can become overly infatuated with sophisticated technology and ground-breaking robotics. Easily neglected in personal relationships are the powerful concepts described by Buber. The excitement of the high-tech life can too easily sacrifice the value of "I" and "Thou" within interpersonal relations. Balance between these conditions can more likely bring life satisfactions to a deeper level.

As a middle-aged single woman, I enjoyed contributing to the education of my students. Memories of past teachers I appreciated, the fine education they had provided, flooded me. There were debts I owed, and felt I regret for never having expressed gratitude.

I recalled when my daughters encountered fine teachers, this aphorism awakened me: *A teacher is like infinity. You never know where her influence stops.*

I often had this expression executed in calligraphy and framed as a gift of appreciation to these teachers.

I was thrilled to learn one day that my fourth-grade teacher from Chicago's Hayt Elementary School, Helen Haas, was still alive, now ninety-two years old, and residing in my old neighborhood on Chicago's Granville Avenue. I exclaimed to a friend, "My goodness! How I loved her!"

In a cauldron of emotion, I composed a letter to Miss Haas:

Your devotion as a teacher approached that of a caring mother. I don't expect that you remember me, but I remember you well. You transported me to a world of wonder and learning that remains with me still.

The body of my letter also included details of my educational life, past marriage, and beloved daughters, as well as career aspirations.

In Miss Haas' response, she described her simple life and pleasure in being remembered. She expressed appreciation for one particular circumstance—having lived long enough to receive recognition from a former student for her life's work.

My passion for education became more concrete when I discovered an old Seth Thomas school clock in a dusty shop of collectibles. I recognized it immediately as a memento of my early learning days. It remains as a valued treasure in my kitchen today.

WITH NEWFOUND LIBERATION, beyond ongoing educational, career, and cultural activities, my singles life continues a spiritual path. At my religious home, the Ethical Culture Society (ECS), I have pursued my peace interests, family education, and the Social Action Committee.

My cultural life has included performances of the American Ballet Theater, symphony concerts at NJ-PAC and New York's Avery Fisher Hall, and various museum visits. A particular favorite has been the Folk Arts Museum, which exhibits artistic expressions of the early common man. The New York Botanical Garden is a particular love of mine. When I'm too old to walk, I trust some caring person will push my wheelchair among those glorious plantings.

FOR MY PROFESSIONAL DEVELOPMENT, I have attended many outstanding workshops in far-distant locales, including Mexico and Europe. The American Medical Education's program brought me to France, Austria, and Italy. In Vienna, my delight in visiting Freud's apartment and office was offset by my frustration with other participants who wouldn't join me to visit the Mauthausen Concentration Camp. I reluctantly bypassed the opportunity but felt particular regrets when I later learned that my Ethical Culture friend Norman Gershman had visited several concentration camps in his European travels, saying the sacred Kaddish (Jewish memorial prayer) at each location. Troubled by this past Holocaust, I noted the white-gloved doormen at our fine Viennese hotel and wondered about their roles during the Nazi era.

I PHONED THE GREEN PEACE HEADQUARTERS one day. "I'm an American visiting your country who admires your courageous activities. Could you arrange that I meet one of your participants to acquaint me with more of your good work?"

In my encounter with a nicely attired young man in a quiet cafe, one of my questions involved his family. He explained, "Oh, they think I'm peculiar. My brother lives a conventional life, making money. I choose to pursue my ideals."

After commending him, I offered some financial aid. He refused, saying, "Contribute to your Green Peace in the U. S. They need your support more than we do here."

MAINTAINING MY PHYSICAL HEALTH, I have enjoyed occasional folk dancing and swimming three times weekly at the local "Y". I later added the non-martial Tai Chi Chih, continuing for four years with advanced instructor, Dan Penchiak, at the Union (New Jersey) Hospital. The third syllable, "Chih", signifies a particularly sensitive interpretation of this Eastern-derived skill. When the hospital closed and I was unable to find similar quality classes, I pursued chair yoga. Currently, at age ninety, I attend classes twice weekly, both at the ECS and also at the one sponsored by the Millburn Township, as well as Healthy Bones. Sally Fullman, leader of the latter program, brought a Tai Chi Chih instructor one day. I have reconnected with Dan, will renew this skill and anticipate continued well being.

In viewing TV, I focus almost entirely on the Public Broadcasting Station (PBS), which formerly offered my favorite commentator, Bill Moyers, when he was still so engaged. He discussed vital social issues not usually carried by everyday media. Moyers reminds me of early TV's glorious journalistic days—Edward R. Morrow and Walter Cronkite. My gratitude extends to the network as well for introducing me to Joseph Campbell and *The Power of Myth*. My classical music passions are fulfilled mostly by radio station WQXR, with early-morning host Jeff Spurgeon, delivered almost constantly through my two Bose radios, located at both ends of my small home.

IN THE MIDST OF ALL THESE RICH ACTIVITIES, I continued participating energetically at the ECS. When I discovered the true origins of Mother's Day, that mothers had contributed actively in society dating back to the Civil War and continued improving society's quality of life well beyond that era, I phoned the *Star-Ledger,* and they published a photo of members who were so participating.

Newcomers to our Society are introduced to our creed: We try to create a more humane world. Additionally, we "bring out the best in others, thus in ourselves." Our brochure is usually provided, which mentions the historic organizations we help launch: Planned Parenthood, First Free kindergarten, the NAACP, Visiting Nurses, ACLU, and National Ethical Services at the UN.

NOW IN 2016, THE TUMULTUOUS international scene has found some refuge in New Jersey. Nine Syrian legal immigrant families with twenty-five children are settled in our state—only thirteen miles away, in Elizabeth! These refugees have survived the present ethnic cleansing inflicted on their native country, another kind of Holocaust. Sponsored by the International Rescue Committee, they have many needs, supplied in part by Work Mom, a Millburn–Short Hills volunteer organization. Huda Shanawani, a forty-year resident of Short Hills, serves as president of SAC, promoting understanding of the Syrian-American community.

Members with dual Arabic–English skills provide tutoring for the children at the Elizabeth Public Library. Millburn's Maya Bloom, of Beads for Peace, enriches the women with instruction in knitting and crocheting, while my grandson, Spencer, has offered to provide music lessons for the children on five different instruments.

Our opportunity to offer some assistance to these refugees is rewarding. This was rarely available to victims persecuted during the World War II Holocaust. The tragic ethnic cleansing currently occurring in Syria is comparable to the deadly conditions under the Nazis. The Righteous Gentiles come to mind who volunteered help to those persecuted back then, at the clear risk of their own lives. My capacity to help, which I hope to expand, involves no such danger. For the present, my ECS Social Action Committee collects supplies for their needs.

SIMULTANEOUSLY, OUR COUNTRY is currently preparing for the 2016 Presidential election. I am actively supporting Senator Bernie Sanders, the liberal Democratic-Socialist from Vermont. His concern for the egregious 1 percent–99 percent income gulf in our population, part of the powerful billionaire domination of the United States and its effect on the policies of the Republic-dominated Congress, represents the courage of a valiant statesman. His wisdom and independence in voting against the Iraq War demonstrate a prescience we desperately need in these troubling times, as our democratic values continue to erode.

As President of the United States, I believe he would uphold the best of what our country represents, the values established by our Founding Fathers. As a citizen of the wealthiest country on Earth, he is concerned that many children go hungry, veterans sleep on the street, and senior citizens can't afford their prescription drugs.

To support Bernie's campaign, I have contributed financially, made some phone calls, and placed lawn signs on my property.

MY PERSONAL LIFE CONTINUES RICHLY. Hardly a week passes without an event that declares: "Life offers meaningful experiences; grab hold and enjoy!

I am so grateful.

MY SEX LIFE AS A SINGLE WOMAN

AFTER THE AFFAIR WITH BEN ENDED and I began focusing on my new home, career, and otherwise enriching my life, my sexual desires returned.

In New York City, while walking from the Port Authority Bus Terminal to my analyst's office, I passed the shoddy Ninth Avenue theaters with their pornographic films, some illustrated on the marquees. My curiosity was aroused. One afternoon, I decided it was time to see what it was all about. I ventured into the theater, choosing a seat in its mid-section. After I had watched the lascivious film, I departed, primarily with "been there, done that" satisfaction. As I walked down the long aisle toward the exit doors, the men noticed a woman in their midst. My presence was heralded with verbal hooting, whistling, and lip-smacking leering.

Once outside the theater, I realized I had forgotten my hat, which I had left on a seat beside me. Bracing myself, I wondered, Dare I subject myself again to that ridicule by returning for it? *Yes!* I told myself. I liked that hat and I meant to reclaim it. With a "sticks and stones will break my bones, but names will never hurt me" attitude, I went back into the theater, head held high, and concluded my mission. Yes, the men shouted their enthusiasm again, probably thinking I had returned because I relished their boyish outbursts. I concluded: Let them enjoy their fun.

I decided to take the plunge at Su Casa, reputed to be a lover's delight, a free-wheeling locale for overnight sexual adventure.

"Be certain to use condoms," was the compelling message in the time of the emerging AIDS epidemic.

When registering for that popular setting, I noticed an attractive man of color also inquiring about the facility. My legs went limp with desire. Could I have sexual intercourse with a man from a different culture? Shaken, I reconsidered whether I should attend such a place. After further thought, I cheered myself on: *Betty, go for it. There will also be attractive White men there. And if a likable Black man appeared, your broad-minded attitude would bypass any possible barriers.*

I connected with a good-looking, well-built White man who had brought his own tent to the grounds for intimacy. We spent an erotic night together, and I invited him to continue an overnight at my home. It went nowhere, though, as his dull personality failed to match his powerful body.

Long Island's Fire Island featured weekend companionship, though not necessarily for sex, with ads listed in the *New York Times*. I attended several weekends during two successive summers and was frankly disappointed when sexual encounters failed to happen.

Another summer experience occurred at a New Jersey Unitarian–Universalist weekend seashore locale, furnished with comfortable, oversized bungalows—good discussion groups, especially around current social issues, splashing in the waves, decent meals, and bedding down at night with a mate for those mutually attracted. It was a pleasant escapade, but only that; my companion and I both agreed further involvement didn't seem promising.

During one of my adventures, I met an attractive suitor living in the East Village who invited me overnight to his apartment. The next morning, I found my new bright yellow Volkswagen Dasher, parked on the street, smashed by a hit-and-run. I concluded this life of meandering sexually, with men not solid enough to build a future, was not for me.

I visited Eve's Garden in New York City to purchase personal sexual toys for masturbation. I buried myself reading Nancy Friday's *My Secret Garden.*

When my libido continued to beckon, the sex toys did their job. I answered ads from men who expressed interest in becoming both a "friend and lover." I also found formerly overlooked *Pleasures,* by Lonnie Barbach, on my crowded bookshelf. At least some of my needs could be satisfied until I connected with a promising man.

About two years ago, I responded to an ad I considered very hopeful. The man described himself as a retired social worker; his past profession suggested we would have similar interests and values. I didn't notice he was seeking only "companionship" as I composed a letter describing my vibrant activities. A connection of meaning seemed a good possibility.

The timing complications made me anxious. The suitor's reply could arrive while I planned to be away on an important five-day trip. I could lose this desirable man to another eager woman.

I was very hopeful when I saw an unfamiliar personal letter in my mailbox. Yes, it was a response to my letter. It was all for naught, however, as our priorities didn't match. Convenience was his primary emphasis, location of services relative to his apartment—supermarket, laundry, post office. When I inquired about his life-enriching activities, he was totally silent. In a discussion about family, he seemed to boast, "None!" adding, "I have a brother I hope to never hear from again."

If I ever discover a cultured suitor who is socially aware, excited about life, and holds promise for the future, I shall eagerly explore the possibility of a serious relationship.

Hopefully, he will also have a libido to match mine.

FAREWELL TO HOWARD

Dear Howard,

It's been sixty-eight years since we married, and forty-one since our divorce, when I launched my Second Lifetime. This latter experience has been exhilarating for me; I'm not sure what it's been for you.

In many ways, I'm grateful to you. You inspired me to leave my single life, which was moving toward becoming stagnant. Your energy and joy of living were infectious; I loved them! What amazing determination you possessed—it impressed me tremendously. I later discovered that, unfortunately, this quality trampled too often on others. Most important, our blessings— two daughters and three grandchildren—are of immeasurable value. These unalloyed gifts remain as sacred dividends that transcend any measurement we know. Your dreadful final illness was cruel, one you didn't deserve. Upon your passing, I wrote the following eulogy as both a tribute and a forgiveness. I didn't have an opportunity to deliver it when you died. I hope you feel it does you justice.

As Howard Levin's former wife for twenty-seven years, I shared over half his adult life with him. How do you remember such a man and do justice to memorializing him—his brilliance, creativity, ambition, exuberance about life?

He was highly ambitious and loved to write. His visionary Office Work and Automation, *published over fifty years ago, was translated into three languages, among the first of its kind in the new world of office technology. Howard was founder of the computer-leasing field and his own company bearing his name.*

But a person can be too ambitious. He had everything that could make a man content and at peace. He had two fine daughters who loved him; yes, and a wife, too. Sometimes the gold we have cupped in our two hands is the gold we have most trouble seeing.

He was a man imprisoned. His heart, many times generous in material goods, lacked an ongoing tenderness, locked behind bars that blocked expression.

Though we had been separated for many years, I felt I still knew the man—the man I married, the core man who could show warmth. This he clearly demonstrated when playing with his two granddaughters, Stephanie and Samantha. I believe if more of his deep self could have been released from its binding prison, his heart would have said to his daughters:

"Janet and Wendy, I have always been proud to have two such lovely daughters as you. If only I could have shown more of my soft self to you, how much richer and more complete my life could have been."

In this religious service which speaks of forgiveness—the generous human heart must both give and accept.

I'm writing this letter to say I forgive you. Howard dear, Rest in Peace.

As always,
Betty

Howard S. Levin died July 28, 1989, at age sixty-five, of amyotrophic lateral sclerosis (Lou Gehrig Disease).

A SIGNIFICANT RELATIONSHIP WITH TOM

LET'S STAY YOUNG TOGETHER," Tom's anniversary card murmured to me. I loved the idea and we shared a twenty-two-year relationship with many romantic moments and exuberant vacations.

I met Tom when he attended a Saturday evening party at the Essex Ethical Culture Society in 1979. He was gaunt and in pain, leaning on his cane and the podium in the main room. As we chatted amiably, I noted his fine vocabulary, articulated in a resonant, masculine voice, which minimized his physical impairment in my eyes. Tom mentioned he was separated from his wife after a long marriage. I said I'd been divorced for several years.

When suppertime arrived, I realized Tom couldn't easily handle both a cane and a buffet meal. After I brought us food and shared dining with light conversation, I felt cozy with him and even some attraction.

We parted quickly, without mentioning any continuation of our chance connection. Tom had explained he had come at the suggestion of Society member, Suzanne Gluck. I later discovered she had invited him to the event at the behest of her friend Eileen, Tom's wife. I heard she had implored Suzanne, "Help get him out of his apartment. He's terribly depressed, maybe even suicidal."

Wanting to know Tom better, I called Suzanne the following Tuesday for his phone number. His enthusiastic response to my call warmed me. "I was going to get your number, too. You beat me to it."

Tom asked for a Friday night date. Though pleased, I had to decline.

"I have a prior commitment—facilitating a singles group gathering at a local church."

"Can I come too and be your date?"

"Of course, it'll be a pleasure."

At the church gathering, discussion among the dozen attendees flowed smoothly. Tom listened attentively, remaining quiet. He later commented, "What an impressive job you did—to meet with a group of total strangers and encourage them to interact so easily. I was mighty surprised."

We dated almost weekly thereafter—movies, light suppers at a local diner, or a simple meal at my home. I discovered he was a pharmacist with a small business in a nearby suburban town, Roselle, where he lived in an apartment. Tom filled in his background. Many disappointments seemed to mark the events of his life despite his fine attributes.

His profession was a compromise, since he had been blocked from his goal of becoming a physician. In the post-World War II discharge interview, having served as an interpreter in France, he told the Army vocational counselor his professional aspirations—to become a doctor. The counselor ridiculed him. "Jews don't become doctors!"

This suggested that Tom didn't always assert his best interests, especially since it's obvious the medical profession includes many intelligent Jews.

His wife, Eileen, known as an outstanding educator, had ended their marriage of many years by leaving him abruptly. She'd put the house on the market after Bonnie, the youngest of their three daughters left home.

Tom said he wasn't aware of any significant marital problems, but mentioned Eileen was unhappy with his modest pharmacy, which served only local residents. Her goal was to have him become a successful businessman with a chain of stores. In Tom's one free evening, she insisted that he join her in playing bridge, a game that didn't interest him.

BECOMING BETTY

IN TOM'S EARLIEST YEARS, when in kindergarten, his teacher had asked, "Is anyone here able to read?"

Tom had proudly raised his hand. When the teacher handed him a book, he'd turned it around, easily reading the words upside down. The teacher became flustered by Ted's unusual habit and insisted that he read conventionally. After their tussle about the proper position for reading a book, the teacher bolted from the classroom and reported Ted to the principal. He was humiliated instead of earning recognition for his precocious feat. His unique ability flowed from many years of his mother reading aloud to him, sitting across from him on the floor. He had learned to follow the words, reading them upside down.

Tom was second youngest of five sons, who were often competitive with one another, but he was usually cast in the least desirable position. His devotion to his mother was expressed matter-of-factly—when the kitchen floor needed scrubbing, Tom cleaned. His *haimeshe* qualities attracted me even more—how different he was from Howard. My parents would have loved him.

IN TOM'S JEWISH TRADITION, he became affiliated with a just-emerging conservative Springfield, New Jersey, synagogue, which brought out his leadership qualities. Since there was little money for hiring a rabbi or renting a building, Tom became one of its founders and performed the Friday night services at a neighboring church that donated its basement space. Many years later, the synagogue celebrated its landmark anniversary, now housed in an impressive glass-and-brick structure with many creative touches. Tom's early founding role was never acknowledged.

After Tom's separation from his wife, he had an accident. He fell from a tall circus bicycle. Hip replacement surgery left him in pain and an uneven stance, one leg shorter than the other. This was his physical and emotional condition when we met at the Ethical Society gathering.

I saw Tom as a gifted man who had experienced bum raps in life but was somewhat passive. As we became better acquainted, my attraction increased. He possessed an extraordinary intellect, and an acute appetite for good books. He was unusually articulate. His ability with words enabled him to successfully complete, in ink, the Sunday New York Times crossword puzzle. Tom's tender qualities endeared me even more. I was falling in love with him.

As Tom awakened my libido; casual necking on the sofa after a date left me wanting more. I took the initiative, suggesting, "Would you like to stay the night?"

He slumped over visibly, looking miserably indecisive, but finally gathered his strength to firmly declare, "Yes, I would."

Despite his infirmity, Tom made love through the night.

The Thanksgiving holiday was approaching, and to my delight, Ted suggested we spend the weekend together in a Pocono Mountain resort hotel. I heartily agreed. We shared pleasant days, strolling the crisp woods, still punctuated with lingering color, chatting amiably, and dining well.

After we made love that first weekend night, I felt fulfilled. Standing at the window, gazing at the glistening moon, I was quietly joined by Tom who asked me solemnly, "Would you mind if I had sex with my wife again?"

I was stunned. I wish I could have responded appropriately. My annoyance only brought questions to my mind. *How could he spoil our weekend with such a question and revelation? If his intent was to resume sexual relations with his wife, why would he reveal this to me? And ask my permission, to boot? What is it with this man?*

I never protested, much less challenging him with a probing question, *Are you still emotionally attached to her?*

Even if he had answered affirmatively, I'm not certain I would have ended the relationship. Though deeply hurt, I was too invested in my budding love affair to abandon it. I continued the weekend as though not affected by Tom's stupid question.

Was I being stupid, too? I rationalized, Well, it couldn't be so bad. He is so gifted, with other fine qualities. Maybe it could yet work out. Anyhow, she had abandoned him, so his fantasies couldn't be realistic. No relationship is ever perfect.

Now, years later, I wish I'd had opened a discussion with Tom about this incident.

Most important, Tom had a kind heart. The love of his mother, now deceased, channeled generously into our relationship. He was unusually considerate of my needs, gentle in almost every way, and would surprise me with a bunch of daises for no particular reason.

"I saw these flowers begging for you, then a second bunch. I couldn't ignore them, so I bought you both."

Tom thanked Howard in absentia for "being such a bastard," freeing me to become available for him. His wit could lighten many situations.

WE HAD ARRANGED A PLAN to share our lives. Tom and I continued living in our respective housing, he in his Roselle Park apartment and I in my Millburn home. We joined together twice weekly at my house, all day on Wednesdays, and again on weekends. After our "weekend marriage," Tom returned to his apartment and work on Monday morning.

In an amiable financial arrangement, we each paid our own expenses. I was comfortable with this plan, since my psychotherapy practice was flourishing and Tom was burdened with financial obligations to his second daughter, Caroline, who was having problems. He mentioned that his wife, Eileen, had phoned to ask for money for her, and that he traveled upstate on occasion to visit Caroline. My attitude changed when I heard his taking his daughter to dinner included his wife, who lived nearby. I questioned Tom, "Are you still attached to your wife?"

He tried reassuring me. "Our relationship is of no consequence."

I wondered if he was aware of his deeper feelings.

At my home, he made repairs and did chores with promptness and skill. He set up a worktable in the basement, arranging his tools, always at the ready. Like my stepmother Evelyn, he possessed *goldene* hands.

His favorite TV program was PBS's *Nature*. Looking back, I regret I didn't share more of these presentations with him. Now, I've come to appreciate these offerings much more, seeing them through Tom's eyes.

While attending a folk dancing session alone at the MetroWest Jewish Community Center, an aggressive woman accosted me, arms crossed stridently across her body: "How dare you—dating my husband!"

I assumed she was Eileen. With dignity, I turned away, not responding. I didn't burden Ted by telling him. Several years later, Tom mentioned that Eileen had decided it was time they were divorced, to which he readily agreed. I realized his wife probably made all the major family decisions. I wondered in which areas he expressed his own personality.

TOM WAS EXTRAORDINARILY KNOWLEDGEABLE about Shakespeare, quoting his works frequently. For Ted's birthday, I presented him with a fine collection of Shakespearean plays, illustrated with exquisite drawings. He never suggested our pursuing his interest for shared pleasure.

He rarely recommended activities or ideas to explore, always willing to go along with my preferences. We had a smooth relationship with no disagreements, but at the same time, it became flat, lacking freshness and stimulation. It started wearing thin. We attended numerous Broadway plays, a particular passion of mine, and other Manhattan cultural activities, always of my choosing. I made all the arrangements, including ordering the tickets.

THE GREATEST PLEASURE OF OUR RELATIONSHIP was our summers at Chanterwood, the bungalow colony in South Lee, Massachusetts. This was the haven I had discovered during my post-divorce maiden trip. It became our most favorite vacation spot, where Tom and I occupied the same picturesque bungalow for thirteen summers, until the facility closed. Our routine at the Berkshire retreat included a brisk pre-breakfast swim in the crystal-clear lake immediately upon awakening. My most beloved photo of Tom shows him emerging from the lake, smiling broadly with a twinkle in his eyes, his capacity for pleasure apparent.

We regularly attended the Tanglewood Boston Symphony concerts, where we also visited with my dear friends Dvo and Ernie at their West Stockbridge home. Jacob's Pillow became another cultural arena to which I introduced Tom. He dutifully accompanied me to art galleries and gift shops as I pursued my appetite for the creative arts. Tom's tag-along comment: "You've certainly earned a black belt in shopping."

We vacationed at several intriguing Elderhostel offerings. One North Dakota community college program explored the impact of geography on Native-American culture. The gifted teacher, Kent Smith, had arranged a lecture by the Chief of the Pine Ridge Indian Reservation. This enrichment motivated me to write Kent a fan letter when the course ended. Tom remained uncommunicative throughout the experience.

Another notable Elderhostel course at the Albany Medical College featured lectures on "Healing and Culture." Mid-week, the visiting Chinese doctor surprised me by asking, "Would you be willing to present to the attendees your philosophy of practicing psychotherapy?"

"Of course. I'm flattered. But why me?"

"The nature of your questions suggests you have special insights to offer."

I was very nervous but thrilled to present my ideas, culled from many years of thought and study. Tom never commented on this unusual recognition.

I combed Elderhostel summer offerings for other interesting choices. Ted always went along with my ideas, never checking out programs that might satisfy his interests. After I selected the "Albert Einstein Cape Cod Institute" for the "Aging Well" course, I received an unusual laudatory comment. At its conclusion, the young wife of the instructor, Professor Levinson, singled me out, saying, "You're the model for how I would like to age." Almost sixty years old then, I felt validated. Ted never acknowledged the moment. These educational trips, meant for sharing, left me lonely. I wondered, How far does his noncommital manner extend? Where's his energy? I was becoming disillusioned about Tom.

We both loved beaches and swimming. During a beach vacation in 1987, Tom showed some interest in small sail boats. I suggested, "Tom, for a small fee, you could ask the lifeguard for an introduction to sailing." This began his intense love affair with sailing. He eventually purchased his own small craft, awakening early on weekend mornings to enjoy a solo sail. He often chose local waters that included swimming facilities where I could later join him for my interests.

Between vacations, our usual New Jersey summertime Wednesdays included beach swimming at Sandy Hook State Park. Our day on the beach invariably concluded with a fish dinner at a local restaurant.

One day we impetuously chose a luxury restaurant that required dinner jackets for gentlemen, which Tom lacked that day. The waiter led him to a large closet with assorted garments. The handsome one Tom chose fit him perfectly. Playfully, I suggested he make an offer to the management for purchasing it. *Voila!* We arrived home after an exhilarating beach day, an exceptional dining experience, and a fine clothing addition to Tom's wardrobe. This easy purchase was particularly satisfying, since he detested the drag of shopping.

Unfortunately, those happier experiences were often isolated ones. Even they were marked with Tom's passivity and silences. His laid-back personality could temper even fun times.

Having dated for over ten years, our Wednesday beach days droned on week after week throughout the long summers. The habit started becoming laborious, a dreaded chore. I found myself lamenting, *Oh, another draggy day at the shore with Tom, no stimulating conversation about our mutual interests. . .where is this going?* After a time, I suggested we eliminate the Wednesday get-togethers, confining our relationship to just weekends. Tom agreed without protest or comment. As usual, he acquiesced to my ideas.

Intermittently, we took other trips that I initiated, many to Southern California to visit my cousins Dorothy and Mathilda. We also traveled to Hawaii on New Year's Day, 1981, for Charles Campbell's festive induction into the State Senate. Since deceased, he had been married to my cousin Naomi back then.

After several trips together, Tom mentioned a phone call from his ex-wife Eileen. She had commented on our many travels, which hadn't been part of their marriage. He'd become defensive. "Well, we have two incomes to work with." One of Tom's daughters had probably reported our activities to her mother.

On one of my solo California trips, I bought colorful trousers for Tom, a striking all-over pastel print of multi-colored squares. His delight was expressed in naming them his "Hollywood" pants.

EILEEN REMAINED AN ISSUE IN OUR LIFE TOGETHER. Family gatherings became particularly awkward. Whenever Tom wanted to attend an event where she would be present, he schooled me in advance for appropriate behavior, apparently dictated by his ex through the intercession of his daughters.

"We must keep to just one side of the room, opposite where she's socializing, so as not upset her."

I felt demeaned, subservient to her whims in this charade. The coalition, operating behind the scenes, undermined my relationship with Tom. A *mensch* would have protested such connivances.

I later discovered that Tom's professional pharmacy association offered attractive excursions, including cruises. I was furious that he had never suggested we participate in those enticing activities, depending instead only on the opportunities I offered. I was feeling burdened with his dependency, the weight of keeping our relationship alive.

THE MAJOR PASSION of my post-divorce life beyond my psychotherapy practice had involved my membership and spiritual commitment to the

ECS. Tom accompanied me to the Sunday morning Services and apparently enjoyed the stimulating programs and individuals. Though I had never mentioned his possible membership, he took the initiative one day and announced he had decided to join. His decision added new zest to our relationship, at least for awhile.

As an active member, Tom first became Newsletter Editor. He was a superb word-smith and successfully shepherded our monthly publication for several years. He also decided to become an Associate Leader for Special Services, namely, officiating at wedding ceremonies for couples wanting to integrate humanistic ideals into their nuptials. For couples with different religions and backgrounds, they composed nuptials of common ground. Tom's role as a marital clergyman brought considerable income to the Society; he glowed with his new responsibilities.

In 1995, Tom was chosen as recipient of our annual Honorable Member Award Dinner for his distinctive services to the Society. The large attendance included his three daughters, my entire family, and appreciative members who celebrated Tom with many tributes. I beamed, pleased that he was finally receiving the accolades he deserved.

We participated together in the Human Faith Project, an innovative program conducted by its founder, Society member and psychiatrist Dr. Calvin Chatlos. Its principles emphasize the power of constructive human relationships through genuine *faith in people,* without exception, no matter the barriers. To experience the strength of these ideas, Calvin challenged all attendees to commit themselves to a special project: to develop a sound relationship with a person with whom they felt presently distant and which they felt *impossible to accomplish.*

Tom selected Bonnie, his youngest daughter, for his project, the only one who had become a mother, with three sons. He had not spoken to her for ten years or had any contact with his grandchildren. She would phone Tom at my home, leaving poignant messages: "Daddy, please call. I love you."

Tom never responded and was unable to identify the barrier between them. I encouraged him to return these calls but he would offer the lame excuse, "I don't know her phone number."

Following his Human Faith commitment to re-open his relationship with Bonnie, Tom experienced a severe anxiety attack about his decision. He frantically phoned Calvin. "It's impossible. I can't go through with it!"

"Ted, take time for reconsideration. Your daughter and grandsons are important to your life."

Tom calmed himself sufficiently to eventually find the faith to undertake his project. The steadiness of the process enabled him to maintain faith despite fears, and to move toward a genuinely caring relationship with Bonnie.

In their new warm experience, Tom encouraged her to marry her beloved companion, Paul, with whom she had been living for several years. Ted was thrilled to officiate at his daughter's wedding. After several years, Paul died tragically in an automobile accident, without a will. As his widow, Bonnie was protected financially.

Our personal relationship didn't flower. Strangely, Tom never invited me to his daughter's wedding. Our uneventful relationship moved from tedium to outright boredom. He entered psychotherapeutic treatment twice, but nothing improved. Tom expressed love for me, but I felt unable to make an unwavering commitment to him.

I HOPED OUR RELATIONSHIP WOULD IMPROVE when Tom found a New Jersey property. It was on an attractive lake, and for sale at reasonable cost and distance from our living area. If I sold my Millburn house and added the funds to Ted's resources, we could purchase this new home together, joining our futures. I became very excited as Tom made plans for us to meet with the owner to view the property and discuss financial arrangements.

I eagerly awaited the day for this climactic moment, ready to drive with Tom to see the property. Everything collapsed, though, and we never went. Vaguely, Tom explained, "Well, the owner didn't call to confirm the appointment."

Tom made no effort to contact him further, apparently unaware this could have been a crucial development in our relationship. The arrangements I had anticipated with hope never occurred for lack of a simple phone call. Tom's passive behavior doomed the arrangements and, in my mind, the relationship as well. I was crushed, remembering how he had lost the lease on his pharmacy business because he had neglected the details. I then realized conclusively our relationship would never fulfill its potential.

I knew I wouldn't receive that symbolic ring from Tom so I bought one for myself. Ted Lowy, a noted South Orange craftsman whom I admired, was retiring and reduced his prices considerably. I hadn't before been able to afford his work. *Now I could and should.*

The petite, solid-gold ring, with an elegantly curved setting, set with a lustrous black pearl, became a celebratory moment. I wear it on my left pinkie finger for special occasions.

I was very fond of Tom and wanted a friendship with him but not a romantic one. It was 2001, twenty-two years since our journey together began, a lifetime for many others.

When I told him my decision, his reaction was instantaneous. He swiftly removed my house key from his ring, returning it to me without comment. His rapid response made me wonder if he had harbored a similar idea—but I was the one taking the initiative. I had felt a bit guilty about my decision, which we never discussed. His quick return of my key relieved me.

Tom sank into old patterns, resigning his important positions from the Ethical Society. *There he goes again,* I mused sadly. *Despite impressive talents, he's again withdrawing from life.*

We didn't speak often after that. With his business gone, Tom continued working as a pharmacist for the New Jersey Prison System and, later, part-time at various locations. Bonnie found him a comfortable apartment in a

Berkeley Heights complex, where decorator friend Anita Roberts and I advised him on furnishings. I gave Tom a colorfully decorated Mexican tray to cheer his new surroundings.

Within several years, he became ill with Parkinson's disease. Requiring more care, he moved to a senior facility where his oldest daughter, Emily, visited him lovingly and often. When I came to see him, Tom acknowledged me with a meek smile. "Yes," he said. "I had two marriages."

In later years, he deteriorated further. When I phoned Tom with birthday wishes, I'm not sure he knew who I was. Soon afterwards, he moved to a nursing home.

My visit there became our final one together. Tom was sleeping, and I briefly checked his closet, recognizing his "Hollywood" pants still among his clothing. I selected a random book off his shelf to read to him when he awakened. When he did, I greeted him with, "Hi, Tom" but he never noticed me. I realized the end was near and left quickly, taking the book with me.

I LATER DISCOVERED THE BOOK was a journal I had gifted Tom, a year after we met, entitled *The Nothing Book*. I noted my inscription, dated December 24, 1980: *To Tom, for all your wonderful and inspired "nothings." Love, Betty.*

He often brought this journal and other books on our trips, to occupy him while I attended workshops.

Within the journal, Tom had recorded notes of our travels together, mostly brief airline schedules, including restaurant meals and opportunities for swimming. Many entries concluded: "And so to bed."

Hidden between banal reports, however, were perceptive observations regarding lectures he attended with me. His comments affirmed my appreciation of his keen ability to recognize quality and substance:

The book "Other World" by Paul Davies particularly evoked knowledgeable comments—parallel universes, black holes, quan-

tum theory, Schoeldinger's Cat. Heady stuff but written clearly. Will share w/B. She is already aware.

He had never discussed these expansive ideas with me although he knew I was intrigued by the new physics. What a lost opportunity for a meaningful discussion.

He had attended a week of lectures with me at the Cape Cod Institute, presented by a therapist I deeply admired, James Bugenthal. Ted wrote several pages of comments daily in his journal:

Day 1. Def. Existential Humanism—Basic Issue of life is life itself. Potential within...Jim Bugenthal a gifted teacher. . .gifted talk.

Tues. J.B. extraordinary Human Being. You can feel the warmth and empathy. Discussion Spirited and free.

Thurs. I read a short story by Ciardi, "Cadillac full of Diamonds," at J.B's request. Very emotional session,

Fri., Last day—very emotional Prof. B. Got a lot from the whole week, mostly—must be myself—more authentic—Had a great week—off tomorrow morning early—Goodbye to the Cape. Hello to N.J.

I was dismayed we had never discussed the special impact Bugenthal had on Tom. *Existential humanism, basic issue of life—a concept I love probing. How much richer our shared experience could have been. Yet he never verbalized the emotions Bugenthal's daily lectures had evoked for him.*

How did I miss the importance of this shared experience? Didn't I detect some welling of feelings coming from him? Did I let him down by not asking his reaction? Again, another missed opportunity.

At the same time, Tom had some responsibility to take the initiative. I was already carrying the lion's share of the relationship. He was too often functioning as my prince consort. Sadness enveloped me. His journal entries illuminated the relationship's final skewer to the coffin.

TED DIED IN NOVEMBER 2010, an unfulfilled chapter for each of us. His funeral service was conducted by his younger and last remaining brother, a successful psychologist, accomplished ballroom dancer, and ordained rabbi. At my request, Ted's eldest daughter, Emily, retrieved the Mexican tray, which now rests in my psychotherapy office. She later asked me about the unusual Shakespeare book I had given Ted many years earlier. To my knowledge, it was never found. I have visited bookstores trying to replace it, without success.

The true sadness were the roadblocks that thwarted this unusually talented man from fulfilling his extraordinary potential. I shall bequeath his incomplete journal to his oldest daughter Emily, who was his most constant companion during his final illness.

I noted with some satisfaction that two of his grandsons attended his funeral. The Stars and Stripes from his coffin, folded by the U.S. Army Honor Guard, was presented to second daughter, Caroline, as a final farewell. Heartbroken, she sobbed constantly as both Eileen and I looked on.

Tom's photo with his twinkling smile, emerging from the lake at Chanterwood, will remain with me always.

A NEW EXPERIENCE

MY CURIOSITY LED ME TO VISIT THE GUNNISTON nude beach at Sandy Hook, New Jersey. Although Tom and I swam almost every summer Wednesday at the main Sandy Hook public beach, we never discussed the nude facility just a stone's throw north. I had heard of it but hadn't mentioned the possibility for exploration. How could I resent Tom being "closed up" when I exhibited identical restraint on this topic?

Now that our relationship was over and I was in my mid-seventies, I felt it was finally time to explore riskier possibilities. I arrived at the nude beach fully clothed, a bit anxious, but with a bag to hold my clothing should I decide to disrobe.

Yes, people were really all nude, quietly engrossed in chatting, snacking, reading, playing volleyball. In that serene landscape, no one was behaving obnoxiously; men weren't aggressively lusting at women or acting in otherwise egregious ways. What's all this fuss, I wondered, about nude beaches?

I noted the bodies in all their nudity—some women were ample above, some men below. An entire range of size was represented, women from pendulous to swollen buds, men ranging the size spectrum from succulent sausage to a diminished penny whistle. The Great Master provided the basic equipment, while Mother Nature enriched the scene with varieties of shape, size, and color.

Everyone was so casual and proper that I relaxed enough to want to join the crowd—to not be unfashionably overdressed by remaining in my Oscar De La Renta sun dress. I finally disrobed in the rest room and joined the neighborhood, wondering how my equipment would measure up to that of the crowd. I apparently achieved the norm; no one reacted. Relaxed, I applied suntan lotion to the crucial places.

To lounge in my beach chair, I picked a book with lofty literary standards, not a pornographic one. Everything was so normal, quite boring. I decided to depart but was pleased I had taken the risk—though I harbored no curiosity to ever return.

What's all this fuss about nude beaches?

GLORIA'S DAUGHTER, CORINNE

I HAD BEEN DETERMINED TO STAY CONNECTED to Corinne and her family, husband Bruce and sons, Jonathan and Daniel. I suspected she felt similarly. During my annual California visits to my brother Lester, she always invited me as a house guest. Today, Corinne and I continue as friends, phoning one another regularly with family news.

As Jonathan grew up, he shared with me his electronic skills in creating personal television tributes to his mother. He's now employed in developing sophisticated electronic ideas for Disney.

I attended his bar mitzvah as well as his wedding in 2011, when I was eighty-five years old. It was a great pleasure celebrating his marriage since I had missed those of his mother and grandmother. Daniel served as best man for his brother, whose bride, Michelle, is a gifted educator and musician. Jonathan and Michelle chose an unusual location for their honeymoon, Iceland, consistent with their adventurous spirit. In recent times, Michelle had visited me in my New Jersey home, driving from Philadelphia after attending a convention there. While dining at a fine restaurant, I asked, referring to her visit, "To what do I owe this great pleasure?"

With a broad smile, she replied, "Well, you're family."

Gloria would be gratified to know that she has given life to a fine daughter, raised warmly and sensitively by Grandma Eva and Corinne's devoted father. She remained a devoted daughter during her father's final illness, visiting him regularly at his senior facility.

In chatting together, sitting in her cozy family room on the flowered upholstered sofa, I occasionally shared memories of her mother, more for my benefit than hers. She seldom asked any questions about Gloria; the subject may be too painful. On one occasion, Corinne exploded passionately, expressing remorse of not having known her. "The vacuum is more than I can ever explain. . .that's just the way it is," she said, closing the discussion. She knows that I'm available if she ever desires to know more.

How longingly I wished for *anyone* to provide details of my birth mother. Perhaps the continuity of Corinne's caring grandmother and loving father, followed by a devoted husband and sons, has filled the void I have suffered.

I have enjoyed an occasional phone call with Daniel, who is physically impaired. I was the person he called when his special college friend died while his parents were out of town. Daniel maintains a positive attitude despite the many hurdles he often faces.

Corinne has become a competent homemaker, hostess to many large family events with her skilled home-made cooking. During one of my recent visits, I presented to Corinne the copy of Whitman's *Leaves of Grass* her mother had given me over seventy years before in Chicago. when our first separation occurred.

Even when death intrudes, rivulets run, perhaps without end.

COUSIN PAUL IS MY BIG BROTHER

A STRANGER PHONED ME IN 2004. "I'm your cousin Paul. I'm going to be in the East in about two weeks, traveling from California. I'd appreciate being a guest in your home for a couple of days. Is that okay?"

Is this a joke? I asked myself. *How presumptuous! I don't really know him. Who does he think he is? Out of the blue, expecting a place to bunk.* I then considered further, *He does say he's my cousin, though, and family is very important to me. I'll just stall until I can check it out.* I replied coolly, "Paul, I'll let you know if I can arrange it. Give me a couple of days—and your phone number, too."

I called Shirley Morris, our family historian, and asked, "Who's this Paul from California? He wants to stay at my home."

"Sis, I don't know much about him. His father is Irving Young, the oldest son of Tante Surrel, and Paul's her grandson. We've had little contact with that part of the family through the years. All I know is that I hired him and his friends to move my piano, which they did efficiently."

I was conflicted. *Yet he is family. Maybe I'll take a chance. I can always call the police if he tries any hanky-panky.*

When Paul arrived at my home, he said, "I brought you something I believe you'll like," as he showed me a video of our first encounter, which he had taped at cousin Dorothy's California apartment. I then remembered meeting him there briefly when Dorothy was recovering from a stroke. By now she had died. .

What a gift, bringing me memories of my cherished surrogate mother! I was overcome and almost threw my arms around him in appreciation. Paul had connected our common roots, and given the everyday term "cousin" new meaning. *Wow, this man has compassion—just like Tante Surrel.*

Paul later offered, "Let me tell you how I know Dorothy. When I became eighteen years old and went out on my own, I lived near her Encino apartment, and later also, when I served in the air force. She often invited me for supper." He added, with misty eyes, "We sure developed a warm relationship."

I found that Paul looked hauntingly like his grandmother Surrel, in his late fifties, tall, handsome, well-built, with a few excess pounds. His resemblance to Surrel captured my heart, another devoted mother who had cared for me when I was orphaned.

He described his present circumstances. "The town where I live, Cambria, is about 250 miles north of Los Angeles. I'm lucky to operate my own business there, in the extra bedroom of my rented house. Computer technology has enabled me to work effectively with the amusement industry, offering printed catalogs and sophisticated methodologies."

We figured out how we're cousins. His dad was Surrel's eldest son, while Rebecca, my birth mother, was Surrel's youngest sister. Their wide age difference made it unlikely they had known one another. Paul and I, the next generation, similarly hadn't been aware of each other's existence.

Paul's mother died young, and his father became disoriented from an injury working in Moishes' stables. This required that Paul and his three sisters be raised in foster homes, all different ones. In California, Paul's sisters were scattered, and he lived with seven different families. Only occasionally did he see his sisters. His father's love for his children encouraged his strenuous efforts to keep the children with him, but that rarely happened.

"Gee, Betty. I watched while he tried again and again to get decent work and an apartment to bring us all together. Things just never worked out for him." Paul looked very sad; during our later trip to the cemetery, his compassion for his father was demonstrated on his hands and knees, tending his father's grave,

Another dimension of Paul's compassion: He had adopted two teenagers, not legally, but "under his wing."

His continuing selfless deeds affirm my faith in human goodness. I have inherited a relative who brings enviable qualities to our family tree and sets a standard to emulate.

Paul credits much of his sound foundation to Mary, his most caring and longest foster placement mother. She had extended herself unselfishly, traveling with him and other foster boys twice across the country by car and train. She introduced them to our country's national treasures, Yosemite and Mount Rushmore.

Paul's other poignant memories of Mary relate to his earliest years. She insisted he complete his homework immediately after school before joining other kids for play. Paul described his protests, accompanied with bitter tears, wailing, "The homework's too hard. . . ."

Mary had resisted Paul's bid for pity, remaining firm. "I know it's difficult, but you can do it."

She raised Paul to become strong and know the satisfaction of accomplishment, which has carried him admirably into his adult life.

He had a major falling out with Mary when he was a young teen after misjudging an act of hers. He thought she had deliberately delayed sending a letter he had written to his father, who subsequently died before it was delivered. Taking charge of his young life, Paul angrily rejected Mary by requesting his removal from her home to live with a different foster mother.

Much later, he discovered the incident was an innocent error, that he had judged her wrongly. In deep remorse, Paul drove across the country to her Eastern United States home and humbly apologized. My admiration for Paul soared, knowing his capacity to acknowledge a mistake and offer forgiveness.

He has assembled a framed tribute to Mary that hangs prominently on the wall of his home, featuring numerous photos of their life together. Other important family pictures have been added to weave common threads.

Though not the oldest sibling, Paul has become the respected patriarch of his family of two sisters, Lena and Rose. A third, older sister, Caroyle, had died recently by her own hand. As a teenager, her misdeeds resulted in bringing the family into foster care. She had married at age twelve and been picked up in Mexico by the police, which had alerted them to the neglect of her siblings. When Caroyle died, Paul drove to Los Angeles, in a sensitive act, to personally reveal the tragedy to his youngest sister, Rose who is a special needs person.

After Paul ended his brief, childless marriage, he began living with Pam Eurich, a loving, intelligent, sparkling woman who works as sales manager for his business.

Despite Paul's limited formal education, I find him intelligent and knowledgeable. He's mostly self-taught, hadn't finish high school, but explains, "I've always associated with very smart people and have learned from them."

When I asked him how he became such a wiz on the computer, he replied, "I read a couple of books and picked some brains."

When Paul visited me in New Jersey, he urged me to get a computer and took me to Costco for the purchase. He set it up, including programming a Skype connection. His caring ways continue. Paul responds to my long-distance phone calls when I'm in distress with computer problems. If his heavy workload prevents his immediate attention, he asks Pam to take over, and she's always ready.

By March 2012, Paul had managed to arrange several reunions with me in New Jersey. I have reciprocated by traveling to Cambria annually, extending my California birthday visits with my brother Lester. I also consider Paul another big brother, whom I have grown to both admire and adore.

In 2013, I urged Paul and Pam to visit me in my New Jersey home for several weeks. We enjoyed family-style togetherness around the kitchen table, eating and gabbing, with Pam kindly taking on many cooking chores.

Paul is well-informed about most tools, undertaking home repairs with great skill. When we visited the Home Depot Super Store for supplies, he scrutinized the varied materials as a college professor might review a scholarly research paper before making a defining decision.

During this trip, Paul told me of the Cambria Rotary International Peace Garden monument, on which he had contributed to have my name inscribed. He gently criticized himself by adding, "Oh, I shouldn't have told you now. I really wanted to surprise you during your February visit." His advance notice enabled my planning a Peace workshop presentation for the Cambria high school students. It received a fine reception and invitation for the following year.

Just prior to one of my Cambria visits, Pam sold a handsome contract for which Paul presented her with an oversized bouquet of flowers. I had noted their many cozy interactions and boldly asked, "Do you plan to marry one day?" They both just smiled without comment. Whatever future they contemplate together, they seem to have developed a comfortable intellectual and emotional relationship.

THE THING I LIKE MOST ABOUT PAUL is his attentive caring. When he found a fifty-year old letter I had written to Dorothy when my daughter Janet was four months old, enclosing a photo proudly holding my infant, Paul didn't simply return these mementos to me. He first enlarged and mounted the photo on canvas, framed the family treasure, and presented this heirloom to me when I visited. It's now exhibited in my kitchen with other coveted family memories. My sending these treasures to Dorothy confirmed I regard her as a cherished mother. Paul's generosity of spirit identifies him as a caring brother.

In a similarly attentive spirit, Paul designed an astonishing birthday card on his computer, illustrated with colorful butterflies. When not resting on my dresser, it travels to his bedroom in Cambria, which he relinquishes for my comfort when I visit. We are clearly connected as loving family. During these visits, he also lends me his heavy athletic suits for sleeping to fend off those cold Cambria nights.

DURING ONE TRIP, I PLANNED TO RETURN to Los Angeles by train but Paul suggested an alternative. "How about canceling your train reservation? I'll drive you down to the city and finally introduce you to my sister Rose."

This sounded great, meeting another member of this recently discovered family. I welcomed getting acquainted and seeing her living arrangements. As a special-needs person, Rose has the services of an aide and social worker. She proudly showed me her compact one-bedroom apartment, furnished with a small kitchen, TV, and additional rear exit. Rose asked Paul for a computer, which he, of course, provided and which she uses with little difficulty.

When I had first traveled to California, I resented the steep state sales tax. Now I appreciate that it helps provide a safe, comfortable, and dignified quality of life for Rose and others like her. In our somewhat indifferent, take-care-of-myself society, this sensitive approach warms my heart. A well-informed government can also support humane values.

Kindness flows from both Paul and Pam. I recall my charming rose-colored caftan meant as a gift for her. She suggested I give it to Rose, whose color matched her name. Paul takes time from his pressured schedule to visit and explain our complex world to his sister. When she became confused about the distance between New Jersey and California, he patiently showed her a United States map on his i-Pad, pointing out the extensive distance I had traveled to visit them both.

Reciprocating, Rose presented Paul with an afghan she had knitted for him. Many hugs were exchanged. He later asked Rose, "Where do you want to go for lunch?

"I-Hop," she replied gleefully.

"Of course. It's your favorite eatery. I know how disappointed you were last time we ran out of time and missed eating there. We'll manage it now." Paul ended with a broad smile.

I was captivated by this truly caring family that Paul has created and nurtured. His commitment has inspired me, at birthday and holiday time, to keep in contact with Rose.

ANOTHER VALUED TIME WITH PAUL was driving together to visit cousin Shirley Morris, who then lived in Tarzana, only one block from Dorothy's former residence in Encino. I mentioned to Paul, "I'd love to see Dorothy's apartment complex. I visited there during many California trips. Can we stop there for a quick look-see?"

He readily agreed. "I'd like that, too."

When entering her former apartment lobby, and on the extended walk to her rear apartment, I was overcome with the surging memories, my tears welling up.

Paul noticed that the tropical tree fronting her apartment had grown to cover it completely—*yes*, we seemed to agree, *Nature moves on its own timetable*. How satisfying that Paul and I, each having known Dorothy under different circumstances, could now share our memories together—and loss as well.

Paul and I also planned a cemetery stop to visit the graves of Dorothy, Surrel, and his father. At Surrel's memorial, I was surprised by my detached reaction, my former loving feelings missing. Apparently, her "giving me away" built a barrier that still obstructs her goodness at a deep level. I'm frankly shocked, even ashamed, by my missing indebtedness, which I don't fully understand. This contrasted with Paul, on his knees, energetically scrubbing the metal inscription on his father's grave, as if kneeling in tribute. His beautiful sensibilities will remain with me always.

While driving on our Los Angeles journey, Paul mentioned we were just a few blocks from the Pacific Lodge Boys Home, where he had been placed when he was seventeen years old. His teenage mischievousness had left authorities no other choice for a placement. Paul had boldly refused to be transferred to still another foster home.

This Boys Home experience sounded important, and I suggested, "Paul, let's just drive by so I can take a picture." He reluctantly agreed as time was short. When we arrived, Paul encountered a strolling staff member and asked about past personnel. Within a few moments, we were heading to the main office, where the supervisor spoke of the changes since Paul's departure some forty years earlier. He now seemed genuinely pleased we had taken the time to recapture his past.

As we drove on, he reminisced about reunions with his early pals: "At one particular gathering, we discussed which residents had become the most successful in their adult lives. Everyone seemed to agree it was Deva, who was the standout, owning a thriving business with many employees and heavy responsibilities."

Casually, Paul pointed out, "Deva interrupted with a very different perspective. She declined the honor, insisting, 'Paul's really the most successful. He has a solely owned company with no personnel complications. It's located in his home, eliminating the headaches of commuting, and he lives year-round in Cambria—a desirable vacation town which people spend big bucks to visit, including me. In my opinion, his success story surpasses all the others.'"

I listened carefully as Paul modestly shared this memory. For me, his true successes are his compassion and thoughtful deeds, the best in being human. I marvel at my good fortune that Paul is both family and friend.

SEEKING MY MOTHER'S
FORGIVENESS AND MY OWN

AUNT BETTY, WHILE I'M HERE, I must take the time to share something very sad with you." When my nephew Roy visited me here in the East, he had insisted we must settle down for a serious talk. Taking a deep breath, he said, "You already know your mother's infant son died when she was escaping from Russia and the Czar's soldiers. Well, I discovered even more tragic information—your mother had accidentally suffocated him. She had held him too close to her bosom when they were in hiding. It was a hideous time."

I was numbed by the news. It seeped into my consciousness only gradually—that Mother had killed her own infant son. She had been dead more than twenty years when Roy revealed this shocking news to me.

The devastating circumstances of her loss struck me powerfully, particularly since I realized how profoundly it had damaged our relationship. She needed to raise me in exaggerated ways, even desperately, to assure nothing disastrous could ever happen to me. I experienced her intense caring as suffocation and callously rejected her most of the time.

I realized anew the pain I had inflicted on my mother. My guilt was immense. In anguish, I blamed myself: *Yes, it's easy to judge others without knowing their suffering.*

I asked myself, *How can I make amends?* With mother in her grave, it was much too late to ask her forgiveness. My need for remission became all-consuming.

I have enjoyed a gratifying life despite some hardships. My mother's caring contributed significantly to my comfortable circumstances. I became resolved to somehow redeem her efforts and find solace for myself.

THE WISE WORDS OF THE EMINENT PSYCHOLOGIST Abraham Maslow came to mind. As an innovator in Third Force Psychology, his profound message: *If you can imagine your finiteness, you can imagine your god-likeness and dare to become the person you imagine in your most perfect moment.*

His idea brought me comfort, eventually offering direction.

There had been moments when I expressed genuine caring for mother, but I could have done better. I had always honored her birthday and my parent's anniversary. One year, I arranged a purchase with my brothers—a matching vase and candle holder set as a gift. To my child's eyes, this grouping seemed perfect to please Mother.

Shamefully, though, I had almost never helped with household chores —washing the dirty dishes accumulating in the sink or using the dust cloth. That expression of love carries more weight than a celebratory gift. I lived as an indulged child.

Maslow's words suggested that trying to emulate Mother's goodness could approach a meaningful path. She was thoughtful and kind to everyone who entered her life. Despite our modest finances, she gently acknowledged a neighbor's child from a large family who came with a note asking for money.

Mom encouraged my response to the sidewalk organ-grinder's playful monkey, expecting a penny or two. She would thrust the money in my hand. "Here, Sister, give the penny to the monkey." He would doff his hat in appreciation.

She guided me to become open-hearted, aware of those needing support. Her passionate interest was the Hillman L. Jacobsen Day-Night Nursery, which cared for young children, some of them orphans. At an organization meeting, she gave me two quarters and, knowing my timidity, softly encouraged me to walk up the long aisle to the podium. "Sister, be sure to tell them your name when you give them the money."

I sensed the organization's important mission by mother's unprecedented act: She took me out of school on visiting days to view the hapless children.

At Interweave, a Spiritual Learning Center in Summit, New Jersey, where I discussed my dilemma, my instructor asked, "What do you think your mother's response would be to your problem?"

Uncertain, I replied, "The answer might appear in my dreams."

I later realized that I didn't have to await my dreams for resolution. I believe she would have confidence I could find a road for forgiveness and meaning. *Isn't that what good mothering is about?* I trust she believed her conscientious nurturing, though flawed, could eventually bring me a peaceful course.

I VISIT MY MOTHER TWICE ANNUALLY—on the *yahrtzeit* (anniversary) of her death, July 4, and her birthday, December 1. By the glow of the Jewish memorial candle, I share with her the gratitude and loving messages I withheld during her days on Earth.

Among wishes for my mother are those for peace—including ultimate freedom from her suffering—and know that she gave the very best she could. Beyond that best, her unusual nurturing was influenced my emulating her father, whom she adored. This would have pleased her very much. Mother often told me,

"My father filled the role of the wise man of our shtetyl. Villagers would tramp the path to our cottage seeking his advice."

It seems to me my current work as a psychotherapist is not too different from that of her father.

Struck by the tragedy that marked my mother's life, I finally became aware of her heavy burdens. I imagined a letter my mother might have written to Freud, asking advice about her burdensome life.

MY SHETL MOTHER WRITES TO PROFESSOR FREUD

Dear Professor,

I hear they say you're a smart man. I have a problem, with no one to ask. So I ask you.

I know a bissel *(a little) about smart men. My father in the* shtetl *(Jewish village) reads the Torah and other good books. Men from many villages came to talk, read, and talk some more. Sometimes my father would let me listen when the men did the talking.*

Rifka, my sister-in-law, whose butcher's son knows writing, is writing this letter for me. I married a nice man when I came to America. He had two boys and a little girl his wife left him when she died. I don't know what to do about the kinder *(children). They have long faces. The boys fight and the girl is too quiet. Mein* man *(my husband) works hard, is a* shtarke *(strong) man, but he only works, eats, and sleeps.*

I heard from my brother Hymie's son, who likes learning, that you say what goes on with the kinder *in the family can be important for their whole lives. Is that* emmes *(true)?*

I'm a good cook, clean, and do the laundry, the house sparkles. Before I light the candles on Friday night, I wash the floors and cover them with newspapers to start the Shabbes *(Jewish holy day) right. That doesn't stop the boys from fighting. I see love in their eyes, but they hit and kick so much. It's the little girl that gives me a sore heart most of all.*

The tante *that was raising her didn't want to give her back when* mein *man married me, but I could understand. Mein* man insisted, and I know what it means to lose a loved one. When the czar's soldiers came with their big boots and bayonets, I lost my mother, husband, and baby son. I was lucky to escape with Hymie and Rifka and their kinder. But I don't want to talk about those bad times.

I helped take care of their kinder for seven years in Rumania while we waited to come to America. Rifka says she doesn't know how she could have managed without me. I always wanted a family to call my own.

Now that I have a family, I'm not sure I know how to be a good mother. The little girl is so sad, pale, eats like a bird. She gets sick a lot with colds and earaches. I give her rock candy with warm milk; rub her chest with Mentholatum, wrap her in warm flannel. But she sleeps bad and wakes with bad dreams. I'm up many nights while mein man snores.

The tante takes the girl many weekends. The little girl's face lights up. I keep quiet. When mein man married me, he said he wanted most of all a mother for the kinder. I don't know where I fit.

I hope you can help me. I hear they say people lie down to tell you their troubles. I hope my sitting up won't change your answer.

Now, a touchy subject. I have little money. Mein man gives me for the table; I take nothing for myself. You wouldn't want me to take from the kinders' mouth to give you, would you?

I hear they eat well in your country. I make a fine gefilte fish and pickle my own herring. Everyone wants my recipes. Rifka's butcher's son would be glad to write them out for your wife. I know you men like meat, but my fish is better than my meat. Smart men should have the best.

Maybe you're too busy to write. But please try.

Yours respectfully

My letter flowed from better understanding of my mother's troubled life. With new appreciation, my goals have centered on more conscious attention to relations with all peoples—understanding, patience, and compassion—reflecting the goodness I was blessed to learn from my stepmother Evelyn.

Beyond discovering my mother's caring, my profession as a psychotherapist has brought me great fulfillment. I'm also fortunate to have discovered the depth of the Ethical Culture Movement within our American society. My participation brings meaning, whether in family, community, or our larger global co-existence. This has contributed to my having become more conscientious as a humanist and Peace Educator. I humbly walk this path for ultimate forgiveness and tribute to Evelyn, my devoted stepmother.

MY NEPHEW ROY

I WAS THINKING SERIOUSLY about my end-of-life plans and wondered to whom I should confide my concerns. Which family member would be the sturdy rock from whom comfort and perhaps some guidance could flow for my daughters if they felt uneasy about our relationship after I'm gone. I felt Roy, Lester's son, was the person to whom I could speak frankly. He had matured well into his adult years despite some early-life setbacks. With his insights from life experiences and therapy, he could be a pillar of strength for my family in troubled times. Though Roy and I had had limited personal contacts through the years, my understanding of his development and growth, enlivened by our personal experiences together, convinced me that he was the individual on whom to rely.

I phoned him during the New Year 2016 weekend and explained my deep need. "Roy, dear, you're my family. Can I rely on your help after I'm gone?" He listened patiently, compassionately, wisely. I felt I had chosen well and believe Roy could truly be helpful if my daughters requested his insights.

ROY WAS BORN IN CALIFORNIA when I was thirty years old. I was delighted to become an aunt to a nephew who showed promise of flourishing well into maturity.

Since I lived on the East Coast, though, I rarely saw Roy and wasn't directly involved in his life. Phone calls with his parents, Ruth and Les, kept me informed about his growing-up years. Our few personal contacts were mainly brief, during family reunions and my occasional Los Angeles trips to visit cousins Dorothy and Betty.

I sensed Roy's early childhood had been somewhat overshadowed by his older sister, Susan, who was born with Down syndrome. I suspect this imbalance brought him some struggles. During infrequent visits, I noted Roy was often on the sidelines of family life. I avoided bringing up the subject of his childhood, not wanting to offer advice about child rearing. After hearing the latest problems with Susan, I wish I had at least ventured a leading question to the family: "How's *Roy* doing in the midst of all these difficulties?"

I now regret I didn't make an effort to single him out for special attention or excursions.

In our phone calls, Ruth and Les spoke compulsively of Susan's developmental challenges. As loving parents, I believe they provided Roy with decent nurturing but may have innocently overlooked his deeper needs. Even well-intentioned, devoted parents are not always aware of this effect on their other children.

Roy learned nevertheless to cope remarkably well. He once said that, by the age of two, he had decided that the best way to manage was to be a good boy. I retorted, "Roy, this probably came to you naturally. I'm sure you didn't have to delve deeply for that fine quality." I also wondered, Did he overdo being admirable, sacrificing assertiveness to avoid ruffling feathers?

I reminded Roy of his worries during his teenage years. He presumed that his Aunt Flora and Uncle Harry had financial difficulties with their hardware store, which troubled him. Roy expressed determination to find a way to lessen their problems. His compassionate concern for their situation, as he perceived it, was the idealistic dream of a young man, already demonstrating his finer qualities. I was surprised that Roy's teenage generosity could be so unrealistic, even a bit arrogant, thinking he could improve their finances.

I was surprised to learn that, in a social studies assignment in elementary school, Roy expressed some appreciation for me. When students were asked to name their three favorite personalities, he responded "Theodore Roosevelt, my cousin Mathilda and Aunt Betty."

When Roy had his bar mitzvah, I traveled from New Jersey with Howard. For this landmark event, Ruth had designed a five-foot cardboard clock. She proudly paid tribute to her son, along with family and friends, advancing the hands of the clock to the decisive *13*, marking Roy's passage to manhood in the Jewish tradition.

The celebratory lunch was modest, constrained by Lester's job difficulties. When my mother heard there would be no sweet to accompany the ice cream dessert, she baked cookies for an added treat.

This kindness reminds me of her cookie jar, which Roy liked very much. It was a yellow ceramic likeness of a plump chef with a perky hat, affectionately called "Johnnie." It was prominently displayed on a kitchen shelf in my mother's Chicago apartment. She kept it filled with her home-made cookies. Children could always rely on dipping their hands inside to enjoy a delight. Roy mentioned he'd like to have this cookie jar some day, because it brought back many loving memories of his grandmother. I remember the chip on the edge she had repaired with red nail polish. This glaring imperfection didn't detract from its warm connection. After my mother died, I packed the cookie jar and carried it onto the airplane as I returned home from the funeral. I later gave it to Roy, a memento of those days of our close family ties.

ROY GREW TO MORE THAN SIX FEET TALL, a kind and gentle man. In his junior year of high school, when Lester accepted employment in Clearwater, Florida, Roy temporarily accompanied the family, returning to California for his senior year and staying with family friends. I wondered if he needed some separation from his parents.

During his college years at Pomona and the University of California-

Irvine, he earned a Bachelor of Arts in Social Ecology. He traveled to Sweden, interested in a woman student from that country, and pursued some college studies there. I was kept informed about his experiences primarily through his parents.

When the woman married another suitor, Roy moved on. He took a job developing special high school programs in Sweden, some presented in their native language. He later studied in the School of International Development Studies at England's University of East Anglia. He was eager to expand his knowledge of third-world countries, including Turkey, Iran, Pakistan, India, and Nepal, where he had previously visited. I'm chagrined I never discussed his worldly adventures with him. I was told of my nephew's pursuits but was too distracted by my own life to focus on his international experiences.

He casually revealed that he had survived by his ingenuity, resorting to earning money in low-level jobs—as a subway ticket seller, home assistant for seniors, and parking lot attendant. Roy's resolve reminded me of his Uncle Leonard, who had also lived by his wits when he hitchhiked across the country.

I DECIDED TO VISIT ROY when he returned to the States and settled in Seattle. He proudly emphasized his adopted city's forward-thinking policies when Tom and I visited him there. Roy took us to a socially-aware community program site for which Seattle is noted— mass-transportation for citizens, organized to respect sensible environmental standards. He told us about his ten-year involvement with the Seattle Men's Council, a monthly gathering for sharing life experiences and newfound wisdom. Roy's concerns with water conservation resulted in his mounting a cautionary note in his apartment bathroom, generally familiar to the younger generation but perhaps a revelation to the elder population:

> If it's yellow
> let it mellow;

If it's brown
flush it down.

By the end of my visit, I felt satisfied that I had spent quality time with my cherished nephew.

Roy was passionately involved with the environmental movement. He was arrested while protesting the destruction of old-growth forest in Washington State. In Roy's first encounter with Stephanie, Janet's twelve-year-old daughter, she heard of his principled involvement around this incident. Stephanie squealed with delight, "Oh, you're a tree hugger!" She dashed across the room to embrace him. Roy also possessed much wit. At Les' seventieth birthday honoring party, Roy said, "Living with dad was like a stroll in the park—Jurassic Park."

ROY AND SUSIE'S JEWISH WEDDING IN 2005 was a major reunion attended by most of my family—Janet and her children, Samantha and Spencer; Wendy, as well. The couple's nuptials embraced sound environmental practices. I remember many phone calls with Roy. "We're continuing our search for just the right setting for our wedding, close enough to the city but a place respecting environmental needs." They finally located an unspoiled ranch, a lovely venue near Gig Harbor, Washington.

Roy married an extraordinary woman. Susie is not only a skilled knitter and artist but also an independent individual who is serious about her religious ideals. She quietly shared with me that she was raised without specific spiritual leanings and searched for a belief system to embrace. After exploring possibilities, Susie chose to become Jewish. She met Roy at a Hanukkah celebration.

I admired Susie's striking bridal gown—simple, charming white linen, purchased at a thrift shop. Her trim figure showed off its elegance as if couture-designed. Consistent with their theme, their matching rings had also been recycled, early-era silver spoon handles, skillfully shaped for their fingers. Violin music for the nuptials was provided by my grandson,

Spencer.

I felt great respect for this remarkable couple, realizing that the organic vegetarian wedding dinner was appropriate for their substantial values being honored. They went to great lengths to affirm their beliefs at this landmark event. As Roy and Susie said: "We've achieved our goal of minimizing our footprints on our precious earth." With such remarkable cousins as family, I hope my children and grandchildren will develop and maintain a close relationship with them in future years.

When Roy came east with Susie, they visited my home for several day, as well as that of his cherished Aunt Flora, Uncle Harry, and cousins. It was on that occasion that he told me the tragic news of Evelyn having been responsible for the accidental death of her infant son. Roy learned this sad information from his mother, to whom Evelyn had confided in the absence of a close relationship with me.

The couple now live in Tucson, Arizona, where Roy serves as Membership Services Coordinator of the Arizona Historical Society.

SUSIE HAS ALSO ESTABLISHED a notable role for herself. Despite some health issues, she actively markets her fiber art. In a phone call, she said, "A customer bought the knitted gloves right off my hands. They also bought the remaining four pairs I had just finished." She has joined a studio, Art Awakenings, where she paints in oils and acrylics.

Several years ago, I commissioned Susie to knit a warm wool cardigan sweater for me. She created an original design, with stitches based on Celtic themes. She characterized the intricate motif as "symbolizing your life" and provided an illustrated sketch. A note interpreted their specific meanings:

> *Love, that you give and receive; your appreciation of Nature;*
> *trophies to symbolize accomplishments; vines to show new things*
> *blooming about you; braided cables—remind me of* challah *and*
> *your Jewish upbringing; two hearts represent your two daughters;*

triple intertwined cables on each sleeve, one for the three siblings in your family, you, Lester, and Leonard; the other represents your three parents, your father, your birth mother, and your step-mother.

Susie helped care for her sister-in-law, Susan, in California, in her final days before she succumbed to Alzheimer's. On the first anniversary of her death, for the return to the cemetery, Susie painted colorful designs on the traditional remembrance stones for family and friends to leave at the grave site in Susan's memory. I have much admiration for Susie's boundless creativity.

ROY TRAVELED TO SOUTHERN CALIFORNIA three or four times each year to visit his parents and keep tabs on their well being. I respect Roy's loving nature, expressed in his devoted concerns. During his father's final illness, Roy was a steadying force, caring for both parents. He conscientiously attended to my needs as well.

On my final, sad California visit, I had contracted a severe throat infection, and Roy drove me to urgent care facilities several times for medication. After Les died, Roy and Ruth arranged a Celebration of Lester's Life gathering for family and friends. Susie also honored her fond relationship with her father-in-law, creating a conceptual painting of what happens after one dies. Her celestial vision of "hereafter" clearly identifies Les as "that sphere with the glasses." Susie commented, "I imagine these little spheres as souls of the recently passed, drifting into light."

Roy and I maintain an endearing friendship through phone calls and letters. He never fails to send me a birthday card, always whimsical and witty, with a loving message. My brother Lester has given me a fine nephew. Roy possesses solid values that demonstrate how to live life courageously by overcoming all the difficult circumstances that have come his way.

We can speak openly to one another about my blind spots and shortcomings. When we were both visiting California, I asked him to drive me to the airport for my return east. I tenaciously focused on a particular flight I wanted to take. Since it was not convenient for his schedule, I pressed him. "Roy, I've got to return promptly to New Jersey for my busy therapy practice and other commitments. Please get me to the airport for this earlier flight."

He reluctantly conceded to my pleas. As it turned out, my flight was delayed on the tarmac for three hours and eventually canceled. I returned on the later flight that Roy had suggested. Many weeks later, referring to that incident, Roy gently commented in his wry way, "Well, it seemed celestial forces had their own ideas." His tactful criticism helped me become aware of my too-strong demands. Few others have taken that liberty with me. I appreciate his honesty.

Roy has responded to a new challenge. With his father gone and he the only remaining offspring, he felt it even more imperative to see his ninety-six-year-old mother more regularly to maintain their devoted relationship. He also oversees her complicated financial affairs. Roy conscientiously shepherded his mother's move to Tucson and personally accompanied her flight from California. His grateful mother is now nicely settled in a Tucson independent living facility for seniors.

At times, I sense that Roy is burdened by his responsibilities. He deserves better. I wish he could bring more playfulness into his life. I value my relationship with my nephew and hope my need for his input after my death will not become a hardship for him. Roy has developed true character. I celebrate the joy of having such a wise nephew.

MY DAUGHTER JANET, PART II

A HUGE CALAMITY OCCURRED IN JANET'S LIFE when she was twenty-five. She phoned me early one Sunday evening from New York City. "Mom, I've been raped," she said calmly.

I gasped and thought, *This is some nightmare. I'm not hearing right.* I backed up from the wall phone, groping for a kitchen chair to steady myself. "Are you serious? Did I hear right?" I was trembling but tried to calm myself. Janet didn't usually exaggerate.

"Yes, Mom, you heard me right. I was bringing groceries to Dad's office kitchen when this guy attacked me in the hallway." Howard's company was located in a luxurious Turtle Bay converted brownstone. I was in shock, wanting information and wondering how I could comfort her.

Questions poured from my mouth: "Are you beaten up? What can I do to help? Where are you *now*?" I asked.

"I'm calling from the police station," she explained coolly. "They examined me and injected some stuff in my bottom to prevent infection. I'll be OK."

I pictured her being handled gruffly by all these anonymous people. I wanted to cry out, *What a horror!* Instead, I said, "Jan, I'm coming to the city right away. Where can I meet you?"

"No, Mom, thanks anyhow. There's no time. I have a babysitting job in a couple of hours." She added, "I can't let them down. The family has an important event."

Bursting with frustration, I asked myself, *How can she be so calm and rational after such an assault?* "Jan, stop this craziness! After such a devastating experience, don't be so heroic! I'll fill in for you in the babysitting job."

I was hysterical. How could she carry out responsibilities with young children after being so violently abused? As I calmed myself, I asked, *Where does she get this determination?* Then I tried reasoning with her. "Jan, I'll give you the babysitting money. Give up this nonsense after the ordeal you've just experienced." I wasn't sure where I'd get extra funds, but I would find a way.

No amount of persuasion would change Janet's mind. Other thoughts emerged after this upsetting conversation. I was struck with the raw emotion of my concern, in contrast to Janet's detachment as if it had happened to another woman. I was also surprised to discover she was babysitting beyond her regular job while studying advanced college courses.

Another realization: Janet was sharing her life, a striking change and welcome development, though it didn't bring me comfort. I washed dishes compulsively that evening to pass the time and picked up my needlepoint to calm myself for sleeping that night.

I phoned Janet regularly, but, as usual, she wouldn't discuss her situation and discouraged our getting together. Distraught, I asked Matt, with whom I was still in therapy, "How's Janet doing about handling that dreadful experience?"

He reassured me, "She'll be alright," without supplying any details. Frustrated, I reluctantly accepted the confidential boundaries of their therapeutic relationship. I felt severed from Janet, ineffective in protecting my daughter.

Janet and I continued our parallel lives for several decades. Her ongoing maturity resulted in marrying a successful podiatrist, Dr. Martin Rudolph. She demonstrated a rare connection to me when she declared, "I'd like my wedding to take place in your home," which thrilled me enormously. The number of guests, however, forced us to abandon her idea.

JANET AND MARTY WERE VERY EAGER to become parents and had three children. They both proved to be conscientious and creative nurturers. At their first daughter Stephanie's early-age birthday party, she and Marty entertained the children with a *Sesame Street* skit they had written. For take-home presents, Janet had collected interestingly shaped glass jars and filled them with colored sand.

With the birth of each successive child after Stephanie, she relied on me to babysit at their Long Island home to care for the at-home child. Occasionally, I cared for both daughters at my home while Janet and Marty enjoyed a weekend vacation. All three children, Stephanie, Samantha, and Spencer, attended the Long Island (Garden City) ECS Sunday School and today, live as humanists, fourth-generation Ethical Culturists.

For Thanksgiving Day family gatherings, Janet and Marty have usually hosted the event at their home each year. This tradition started when they were living together, before their marriage. In that first year, to our great amusement, their dog devoured the frozen turkey, left on the kitchen countertop to defrost. They located another one at the last minute, smaller than the original choice, but heartily enjoyed the dinner together nevertheless.

A change for celebrating Thanksgiving came in 2014. As ostensible head of the family, with good health and abundant energy despite my elder years, I felt it was time I host the holiday event. To my great pleasure, the much-increased family attended—Janet and Marty and two of their children, Stephanie and Spencer, who brought a girlfriend, as well as Wendy and her husband David, including his aunt Judith, with whom I had developed a close relationship. I had finally brought some family togetherness to my home, of deep meaning to me. I wondered why it had taken me so long to make it happen.

MORE INFORMATION ABOUT JANET'S RAPE didn't come my way until twenty-five years after the event—when a Letter to the Editor that Janet wrote was published in the *New York Times* on August 4, 2005. After expressing compassion about a rape perpetrated on a Pakastani doctor, Janet revealed her past experience and how she had come to understand the violence she had endured:

> *As a rape survivor. . .I remember the sense of shame. . .the sense of being damaged. . .the police told me not to tell anyone . . .here is what I learned. . .rape will hurt anyone it touches and will corrupt any society that condones it, ignores it or victimizes the survivor. . .it is not about sex: it is about power, perpetrated by "little boys" who have no concept of true power. As Gandhi and the Rev. Dr. Martin Luther King, Jr. have taught us, true power comes from inside ourselves. It cannot be taken from us externally.*

I was breathless. What an incredible daughter I have! Janet's inner resources had transcended a traumatic experience with great wisdom. I concluded, *Janet is a singular individual. Her depth seems boundless.*

The parallels of the flawed mother–daughter relationship between me and my mother, and my daughter and me, are striking, though for vastly different reasons. I rejected my mother's need for closeness, repelled by and not understanding her overbearing treatment of me. As the person responsible for this distance, I'm not entirely surprised these qualities also dramatically color my relationship with Janet. I simply had no experience of mother–daughter closeness.

Janet's aloofness still leaves a huge vacuum, but, fortunately, it doesn't significantly mar my life. Mine is separate and full, including many energetic and spiritual activities. Janet continues her own admirable achievements. This is appropriate, as we raise children to be separate from us, mature and fulfilled. Remembering Janet's past teenage gift: "There are two lasting gifts we can give our children—roots and wings," is a mantra I hold within. This wisdom I struggle to honor. I falter mostly when I feel vulnerable and lonely, missing family life. I avoid pushing ongoing contact with Janet. Perhaps one day a shift will occur that allows us to be closer. I hope this happens before time runs out.

Today, Janet has become a fascinating and brilliant mature woman, a world traveler, highly creative and philosophic as a photographer and writer. She has been in a solid, loving marriage for over thirty years and, with her devoted husband, Marty, has raised three talented children. Their eldest daughter, Stephanie, is a successful non-profit attorney, functioning similar to a social worker, working with under-served clients in New York City; their second daughter, Samantha, is in medical school with the goal of treating populations of other cultures, and is soon to be married to her college beau; and their son, Spencer, a musician, offers instruction to students on five instruments, some to adults, simultaneously composing ensemble music.

Janet again presented a Sunday morning Essex Ethical Culture service in 2015 as a "homecoming,"—"The Spiritual Life of an Ethical Humanist." Additionally, she has recently written and published, *One Gods: A Mystic Pagan Looks at the Bible.*

In March 2016, an unprecedented event occurred at the Essex ECS when three generations of Ethical Culturists appeared at the podium to present a Sunday morning Service. For a religion only 140 years old, this is an unusual occurrence.

My granddaughter Stephanie presented a program on her legal activities: defending under-served New York City clients living in neglected housing. Her work has been reported in the *New York Times*. Janet, a Sunday School graduate of the Essex Society, introduced her; I had the privilege of presiding for the event.

I have a keen appreciation of Janet's extraordinary qualities and am left with this sense: If I were to incidentally encounter her on life's path, it would be a privilege if she considered me worthy of being a good friend.

MY DAUGHTER WENDY, PART II

WENDY SOMEHOW LEFT THE EMPLOY of her father in Atlantic City and returned to Albany, finding both a new job and boyfriend. I wondered what had transpired that enabled her to renew a life of her own.

At that time, President Clinton had inaugurated a program in which employers were financially rewarded for hiring the *underemployed*. Wendy found a clerical position with a major corporation in their Albany, New York, office. She told me her father had ridiculed her employment, that "only a U. S. President's decree enabled her to get a decent job." Nevertheless, Wendy was satisfied with her new opportunity. I shared the joy of her independent work life—a steady job with a solid company.

Tim then became the new man in Wendy's life. She met him in a bar, and his occupation seemed vague. In the early 1990s, she moved in with him in his father's house, but they occupied separate bedrooms. Wendy explained the constrained arrangement: "They're a Catholic family and frown on unmarrieds living together."

In Wendy's clerking job, she applied for a more advanced position, monitoring and managing procedures in several of their outlying offices. Her new promotion brought an additional bonus—work assignments in locations near Millburn. Wendy came home regularly and stayed overnight in her former bedroom. We had a warm relationship again. Together, she as my guest, we vacationed at Canyon Ranch, a health spa in the Berkshires, where we enjoyed our companionship together.

Wendy thrived in her new advanced position. She used her creative abilities to significantly improve her company's procedures, all on her personal time. Executives in the Memphis corporate offices soon noticed her contributions. They decided her talents belonged in their central headquarters and offered her a promotion to join them there, with a substantial salary increase. Wendy expressed serious reservations, even distaste. "Mom, I don't want to live in Memphis."

"Just tell them no!" Despite her refusal, these alert executives recognized an outstanding employee and wouldn't be dissuaded. "Come on down, look the situation over—we'll help you buy a house of your own, and give you other perks, too!"

By this time, she and Tim were living together, independent of his father. Wendy raised new objections. "Well, I have a steady boyfriend. He'd have to relocate and find employment."

"OK, we'll fly him down for two weeks at company's expense for a job search." The dialog continued, and they made offers she couldn't refuse.

Wendy finally accepted the new job and moved with Tim to Memphis. The company paid all expenses.

I don't know if Tim ever got a job in Memphis or even had one in Albany. When Wendy visited me in New Jersey, only occasionally with Tim, he was usually sipping beer, a camouflaged can clutched constantly in his hand.

They invited me to visit Memphis and stay in their modest home. Wendy was a conscientious housekeeper and Tim a skilled handyman. They extended themselves, arranging everything for my comfort. I visited the Civil Rights Museum alone as they showed no interest.

AFTER SEVERAL YEARS IN MEMPHIS, Wendy received an unexpected phone call from David Ackerman, her Hampshire College boyfriend of twenty years earlier. He still lived in Albany, had been married and divorced twice, and had three children—Alain, an adult, and two younger children, Celina and Robert.

David wanted to rekindle the relationship. Wendy's indifferent response: "I have a good job, a nice home, and I've been living with a guy for many years—he takes good care of the house, and we're settled in nicely." Her message seemed to be, *Go away, don't bother me.*

David, however, was persistent. "Look, I know you travel a lot for your job. How about meeting me in Chicago for a weekend—I have a wonderful father there with whom we could stay—and we'll see if there's anything still between us."

Wendy finally agreed and after a momentous weekend together, she returned to Memphis, engaged to be married to David. They superstitiously set the date of 07/07/07 for their wedding, some eight months into the future. I was pleased she was finally settling into a stable relationship with a future.

Wendy ended her twenty years with Tim and discovered he hadn't been paying the mortgage. Resilient as usual, she had to declare bankruptcy to resolve her financial affairs. Encouraged by this promising second chance with David, Wendy handled these complicated tasks with grace.

Several months later, David was in a serious automobile accident. His SUV flipped off the road and landed into a putrid pond. Miraculously, three motorists witnessed the accident, stopped their car, and saved David's life by pulling him out of the water. In addition to his physical injuries, his body was infected with a toxic fungus from the pond. He was treated at the Albany Medical Center and placed in a coma to promote healing.

Wendy responded heroically. She commuted from Memphis to Albany every weekend to be with David. Slowly, he mended, and they were able to marry on July 7, supported by an eleven-thousand-dollar gift from me for wedding expenses. I *kvelled* seeing Wendy dressed in her off-the-shoulder floor-length white wedding gown, decorated with black-flecked highlights. With a radiant smile, she posed for the traditional photos. My joy matched hers.

Wendy was happy to become part of a Jewish community. Under the *chupah* in David's family synagogue, with the Cantor officiating, Wendy and David could barely keep their hands off one another during the ceremony. David's younger son, Robert, happily sauntered down the aisle. Celina, his daughter, glistened as the flower girl.

Janet played a prominent role in Wendy's wedding, serving as maid-of-honor. Stephanie and Samantha were bridesmaids, and Spencer performed on the violin for the wedding ceremony and reception.

My friend, Helen Tepper, and special neighbors Evie and Behram Bharucha, joined me in celebrating the marriage. Lester and Ruth, and their son and daughter-in-law Roy and Susie, flew in from the western United States, as did Samantha's boyfriend, Lucas. I snapped many photos and compiled a mini-wedding album.

The couple withdrew for a lengthy period after the ceremony, allowing time for David to recoup his energy. I'm glad Wendy heard the congratulatory messages, particularly David's father praising her as "a miracle" in David's life. Introduced to the guests was one of the men who had pulled David from the wreckage of the automobile accident.

Their honeymoon plans included New England destinations, stopping at Hampshire College en route home. David wrote me a letter their wedding night, 7/7/7:

Dear Momma Betty,

How can I begin to thank you for raising this lovely little girl into my blushing bride. She could never have done it without you!! You have not lost a daughter, but you do have a few more family now—and three grandchildren, too.

Decorating the note were playful cartoons of hearts and a portrait of David saying "Thank you." He affectionately named me "Mini-

Mom."

Prior to their marriage, Wendy had negotiated a new employment contract with her company. Their agreement established her daily work site in Albany plus traveling once monthly to the Memphis corporate offices.

After an agreeable interlude and some pleasant weekend trips to my home, Wendy was confronted with a new challenge. The company exploited her readiness to travel and directed her to numerous troubleshooting trips at western sites. I was puzzled that Wendy cooperated so readily with this intrusive development.

Her immense creativity seemed to have found its destiny—channeled into the corporate world, just like the best part of her father.

In June 2013, I went to Albany to attend the annual Assembly of the American Ethical Union, the national organization of the Ethical Culture Societies. David and I met for lunch; Wendy was absent traveling. The car accident had left him unable to work, and he was receiving Social Security disability payments.

My spirits heartened on Sunday, Father's Day. Wendy had returned and we enjoyed a family brunch together with all three generations—David's mother, Carol, and the two younger children.

After a leisurely visit, the family joined together to contribute to a project for David, a flea market opportunity with a four p.m. deadline. He planned a booth to sell his collection of drawings, books, comics, and baseball cards. We had to first stop at home to gather lumber and other materials to build the booth.

Rushing home, the family scattered throughout the jumbled backyard, organizing the needed supplies. They loaded them on the top of two cars, which they drove to the site for assembly. The family worked in harmony.

At the flea market—more a chic boutique—the family again organized itself. They helped David complete the construction, making the deadline. A responsive family had paid a Father's Day tribute to David—

loving deeds trumped a store-bought gift.

I was enormously pleased that Wendy had married into a caring family. In her growing-up years, during my marriage, Howard rarely showed responsiveness to individual needs. He seemed to be living in his own cocoon, not often reaching out to his children. By the time of Wendy's marriage, Howard had died. Had he still lived, I believe he would have gladly attended.

I WAS ENTICED BUT CONFLICTED when David invited me for their 2013 Thanksgiving Day gathering. My dilemma centered on my relationship with Janet; my acceptance wouldn't be fair to my daughter, who annually hosted the event.

Her invitation that season, though, was guarded. "Mom, Thanksgiving won't be much this year, with so few of us around. If you want our usual gathering, I'll be glad to arrange it."

I said, "I'll let you know."

Visiting Janet's home included satisfactions of family, particularly witnessing the free-and-easy mother–daughter relationship between Janet and Stephanie.

It was time to rethink the holiday arrangements. I still enjoyed good health and abundant energy despite my elder years. As the ostensible head of the family, I would greatly enjoy hosting Thanksgiving Day at my home. Hopefully, both daughters and their families could all attend to celebrate together.

I wrote a letter to both families with what should have been a warm invitation. But I contaminated an otherwise gracious message by including an open airing of a grievance with Wendy. My complaint to her: Wendy had made no contact with me for many months. And I then offered a stinging comparison: *Your pattern follows a strong similarity to your father's—buried in his career, sacrificing loving family needs. And the price we all paid for his egregious behavior.*

These are very private and delicate issues, raised only under special circumstances. An open letter was totally inappropriate, terribly poor judgment on my part. It spoiled the invitation that hoped for good family relations. My letter put me to shame.

I was not surprised that Janet was undecided about a future Thanksgiving at my home and replied honestly. She rightfully admonished me for including a negative message with my plan. Wendy remained silent. My oldest granddaughter, Stephanie, phoned me, expressing displeasure that I had openly criticized Wendy in my letter. I appreciated that she could be forthright with me.

I apologized to Wendy and my family for poor judgment. Yet I fervently hoped that some fresh perspective and healing could happen by the 2014 Thanksgiving. For the 2013 holiday, I remained alone.

Wendy forgave me and invited me for twin celebrations in June. Her stepson, Robert, was graduating from middle school, and stepdaughter Celina from high school. My family life was enriched by Wendy's marriage, just as David had predicted in his honeymoon note to me.

Among the gifts I acquired was Aunt Judith. She lives in New York City and attended the June party. I always append the affectionate "aunt" to her name. We have since bonded and have continued our friendship. She represents an important link to Wendy and her family.

I admire Aunt Judith, an energetic, progressive, *hamishe*-looking woman in her seventies, committed to many social causes. Her graying hair falls in a long braid down her home-made caftans, which swirl casually about her sturdy, medium-height body.

We share common interests. Aunt Judith and I went to the September 2014 Climate Change demonstration in the city, where we sang with the Raging Grannies. She keeps me up-to-date about Mumia Abu Jamal's near-fatal health condition in a Philadelphia prison, and her support of his cause. She had a brief marriage but no children of her own, and is an aunt to eight children and great-aunt to eleven. Aunt Judith shows particular interest in Wendy and asks about her often. Her generous, loving ways remind me of a contemporary Tante Surrel.

The family did finally agree to celebrate 2014 Thanksgiving at my home—Wendy and David, Aunt Judith, Janet, Marty, Stephanie, and Spencer, who brought his girlfriend. Samantha attends medical school in the western United States and reserved her trip east for December, when she celebrated her engagement to fiancé Lucas.

I managed the dinner well but with the help of Aunt Judith. She not only prepared some side dishes but washed all the dishes afterward. We speak frequently on the phone and shared a city theater experience in 2015 to celebrate her May birthday. Wendy has the benefit of an idealistic, dynamic aunt on whom to rely.

Wendy lives the wisdom of Janet's poster I quoted earlier about giving our children roots and wings. I believe it has also become Wendy's guidepost, which I need to accept. *Therapist, heal thyself.*

Wendy now has a new job. Her employer of thirty years demanded she move to Memphis permanently or be terminated by year's end. Wendy rejected the ultimatum and her present employment includes more reasonable working conditions. Her home and marriage have a fresh opportunity to become more relaxed and stable, especially since they have purchased their own house in Albany.

Wendy and David, along with mother-in-law Carol, hosted the first night Passover Seder in April 2015, to which I was invited. The spirited Passover service included twenty family members, but Aunt Judith who had had surgery for a shoulder problem, didn't attend. I paid tribute to her at dinner and passed around a get-well card for messages. I had brought a gift for Celina and Robert, a copy each of *Hope for the Flowers*, continuing a family tradition started by Janet. Carol cooked all the food.

On Saturday, David rested from the major preparations of the week. I felt close to Wendy as we shared the entire day together shopping. We searched for quality stationery to make invitations for my forthcoming party, a celebration of forty years in private practice as a psychotherapist. Wendy agreed to design the invitation on her computer, and the initial proof looked mighty attractive. She bought me a pair of earrings I had admired during our shopping. I was grateful for Wendy's skilled efforts and our time together.

WENDY'S MOTHER-IN-LAW, CAROL, turned eighty on July 4, 2015, with a celebratory party in Albany for family and friends. Families traveled from California, Vermont, Connecticut, and Buffalo, and I came from New Jersey. I had a glorious time, though almost everyone was a stranger to me. They were invariably warm and friendly. With my new open ways, I initiated conversation. "My name is Betty. I'm Wendy's mother. What's yours?" I then whipped out the family tree, sketched by Aunt Judith, who's related to most of these folks, and playfully asked, "Tell me, where do you fit on this chart?" An immediate connection was created.

There were many African Americans at the party—never had I been to a group social event as diverse. Some were interracial couples, all good friends with Carol through their many political and social activist interests. I remember when it was impossible to invite my African American friends to my own wedding.

I loved the mosaic of other cultures—folks who brought platters of food, providing variety to the catered dishes and traditional barbecued hamburgers and hot dogs. Children of all ages, and several dogs, scampered about inside and around the mammoth white tent mounted on the backyard lawn. A tire swing provided children with extra diversion.

It was at this gathering that I first heard of Bernie Sanders. The Vermont relative was wearing a T-shirt calling attention to Sanders' senatorial position. I listened with interest as he enumerated the lengthy liberal convictions of Sanders' many years in office as an admired congressman and senator. I noted I must pay closer attention to a Presidential candidate who advocates policies that uphold the best of our democracy.

Music rang out also. A small rhythm band composed of Carol's friends played rock music, augmented by an electronic system. Aunt Judith and I swayed to the melodies, dressed in our flowing caftans as we danced together, wiggling our fannies, grinning impishly. The warm gathering made me realize how starved I am for family life.

Except for Gertrude White's family, it's been many years since I've enjoyed such festivities. In an earlier time, I remember annual family reunions with my brothers and their children. I deeply miss those reunions. The even older generation, the Rosenstein Family Club of my birth mother's family, hearkens back eighty years to my childhood, which had felt gushy good. These gatherings were complemented on occasional Sundays with the Karel349

s, Evelyn's family, and the Goodmans, Dad's family.

I have the privilege of sharing current reunions with the Gertrude White family. They celebrate important holidays—Thanksgiving, Channukah, Passover, Rosh Hashanah—as time schedules of a far-flung family permit. Some travel long distances—from Chicago, Massachusetts, and even overseas, as one foreign service cousin is able to arrange his leaves. I am invariably invited via Ina White as the relatives are becoming *mishpocha* (clan). Initially, I was the outsider looking on, but changes are happening as this inclusive, loving family extends its generosity and inherent warmth to me. Among the folks of these reunions is a diversity reflecting our changing contemporary society—a grandmother to an African American child and a lesbian mother of twins.

My own marriage rarely emphasized family gatherings. Recently, Stephanie, now an adult, and her mother have given priority to visiting Howard's Aunt Ruth in Chicago, who survives to age 110. A tradition of family togetherness would be an invaluable legacy, transcending fractures that misunderstandings can bring.

WENDY HAS DEMONSTRATED much intelligence, strength and resilience throughout her life. It warms my heart to see the possibility for family reunions in this and next generations, as each individual enjoys one another's uniqueness, with peace and forgiveness. These core qualities, within the foundation of family, even with dissension, can eventually embrace the true contentment we all seek in life.

MY BIRTHDAY ILLNESS

THE POUNDING ON MY FRONT DOOR AWAKENED ME. I was in trouble, having been unconsciousness, deep in a seizure. My mind cleared enough to shout, "Call the police!"

Susan, a psychotherapy patient, had been ringing the bell for her scheduled appointment. When her repeated attempts received no response and she noticed the piled-up newspapers and mail, she'd become alarmed and banged on the door.

It was February 2009; immediately prior to this incident, I had been alone in my home, planning to soak an ailing foot. I had lowered myself into the bathtub, but before I could fill it with water, I suddenly succumbed to a seizure that included this nightmare:

> *I am in a senior citizen facility, lying chest down on a table, with a pulley moving overhead whose metal hooks have grabbed the flesh of my back. I feel I have been abducted. Hearing an occasional airplane overhead, I think I've been taken to a small town. A phone jangles intermittently. Suddenly, I'm back home. Lying in the middle of the bathroom floor is* Autumn Dancers, *the linoleum print Wendy created. Upset, I caution myself, "Be careful to not trample it." Oversized colorless succulents surround the area. The hot, steamy atmosphere makes it difficult to breathe. I call my older daughter, Janet, to rescue me.*

At that point I was awakened from my nightmare.. When I heard several men approaching my bathroom, I remembered I was naked. "You can't come in here!" I shouted. They assured me there was a woman rescuer among them. She wrapped me in my terry robe, hanging on the bathroom door. I noticed with relief that *Autumn Dancers* was safely on the wall where it belonged.

I felt comforted the unreal experience was ending. The Millburn first aid squad, and the police and fire departments, had arrived. They mentioned the day—Tuesday, February 24, my eighty-third birthday. I'd been in the tub five days. The rescuers couldn't have chosen a more fortuitous time.

I was confused, but the emergency staff steadied me. "Would you like to be checked out at the hospital?" one asked.

I agreed but first found the strength to gather my favorite books, writing paper, and pens from my bedroom to accompany me on the stretcher. I noticed some new clothing strewn on the bed, which I had purchased the previous Friday, five days before. Then we were off to St. Barnabas.

Both daughters were notified and joined me at the hospital. My bizarre seizure was diagnosed as a brain tumor. Surgery was essential.

During the operation, I experienced another nightmare. *I physically fiught with the attendants, insisting the anesthesia mask wasn't giving me enough oxygen. I tore it off my face and tried to escape. As I struggle, the attendants hold me down.*

When I awoke from surgery, my mood had shifted to a tranquil, even playful one. On the wall of my hospital room was a striking Chagall print. Alongside, another art work had a cottage nestled in a seaside scene with lush woods in the foreground. I mused, *Oh, they must have run out of rooms and placed me in a private home.*

My room adjoined administrative offices, and I heard muted conversation. I thought, *My hosts are having a cocktail party.* This lightheartedness continued even before anyone told me my tumor was benign. Reaching for pen and paper with unsteady hands, I felt peaceful and printed a mantra which I repeated often throughout my healing: *I am so grateful.*

Another pleasant interlude was my roommate's daughter-in-law sharing her *hamantashen* (holiday pastry) with me during this time of Purim.

My good humor continued as Janet made genuine efforts to bring me necessities, traveling by train from Long Island, picking up my car in Millburn, and driving to the hospital. Wendy asked that she be phoned as early as seven a.m. to keep her up to date on my condition. I envied the attention of my roommate's family, though her son was one of the in-house physicians.

Despite missing my daughters, I continued my good mood.

I was transferred to another hospital room and, after gathering my books and other personal items, heard my roommate whine, "She's been here only a few days and has more stuff than I do." Half amused, I thought to myself, *Did she think I've been commuting to the Short Hills mall for shopping?*

WHEN FRIENDS COMMENTED on my new up-beat tone, I explained, "When the surgeon removed the brain tumor, he also took out the cobwebs."

In my new room, a ceiling pipe emitted annoying, tinkling, repetitious sounds. Irritated, I thought, *I bet it'll be tough to get a handyman to fix it quickly.* My mood suddenly shifted to playfulness and the musical rhythm became amusing. *The beat's kinda pleasant, like a Philip Glass interlude.*

At times, I felt utter rapture. I'd awaken in the middle of the night, freshly aware of my amazing survival from the seizure and tumor. I'd sob with boundless joy and then fall into a peaceful slumber.

I told my daughters to sell the house. Set high on a small mountain, I didn't think I could manage its uneven terrain after my surgery.

At my bedside one day, a doctor inquired about my mood. My instant response: "Ebullient!"

"Of course," he countered matter-of-factly, "you missed the bullet."

I was annoyed he was dismissing my good mood. "Oh, no, it's not that simple," I said. "Despite my illness, I'm incredibly optimistic, hopeful about my future life and what it may bring."

I had already achieved far more than Howard's prediction of "fucking up" my life—a successful psychotherapy practice, a significant role in my Ethical Culture community, and a pleasant tenure in a modest but comfortable home.

My hospital aides, primarily from the Caribbean and Africa, attended me with care and efficiency. Their distinctive voice patterns were often difficult to understand. I thought, *I must take the initiative to assure effective communication.* I adopted two strategies. First, I always inquired of the person tending me, "Could you please tell me your name?" I believe this attention honors their personhood and encourages their cooperation. Secondly, I introduced a mantra, stated with deliberation— "Please speak slowly and loudly." My plan worked splendidly.

On another occasion, when I expressed anxiety about my partly shaved head ever becoming full again, one aide assured me, "In Africa, when an infant is one year of age, we shave its head entirely, with good results."

I appreciated the advice but had no need to adopt their custom. Eventually my hair returned, even with a bonus: some gentle waves appeared where there'd been none before. This was a bonus, considering my severe Buster Brown haircut in childhood, relieved only by occasional expensive hair perms.

Some aides were so extraordinarily helpful that I kept a record of their names. If my healing continued and finances permitted, I planned to celebrate with a party for them afterward. My intent was to honor them, including their children, for contributions to my recovery.

I fantasized that the hospital human relations executive who had befriended me would arrange such a gathering. It would include African drumming, Babatunde Olatunji style. As Baba's student at Omega Institute in Rhinebeck, New York, I had been deeply inspired by his workshops, having absorbed his cultural ideas, never to be forgotten. My experience: *I had entered a unique universe, tasting new folkways, language, and ways of being that reflected the gentleness and spiritual wis-*

dom of the African culture. Kindness was everywhere, help and support the norm. Drums were regarded as gems of nature, standing on hollowed tree trunks, polished with pride. They were covered lovingly with goat or antelope skin, respected as living objects. Baba's message: "Give children drums, not guns. Then their true selves will emerge."

I wanted to return the gift my aides had given me. Unfortunately, my plan never materialized but my gratitude remains always.

My good spirits also contributed to the well-being of two of my hospital roommates. Eunice, a former British citizen, had lived in England during World War II. During those times, Londoners endured the blitz, the intensive Nazi night bombings causing massive destruction and loss of life. Many children were relocated to the safety of the countryside. As a teenager, comfortable in the States, I was not aware of personal hardships of those in England. In the hospital room, I listened carefully to Eunice's story.

These children, called "Blitz babies," included her sister. She was fed poorly during her country stay and died of malnutrition after the war. She was only forty-eight years old. What Eunice omitted were her own wartime deprivations. At our mealtimes, I had wondered about her gross habit of gulping her food.

During one of my joyous middle-of-the-night awakenings, I heard her gasp and choke violently. I rang the emergency bell for the aides who responded promptly, and exclaimed, "I think my roommate is in trouble." As they closed the privacy curtain with a sharp swish, I sensed the situation was serious. They tended her and ultimately saved her life.

Eunice had never mentioned she, too, had been a Blitz baby, had only five teeth in her mouth and couldn't chew her food properly. That night, she had regurgitated the residue, almost choking to death.

I realized with sadness the war's impact on her family. Military authorities call Eunice's situation "collateral damage." Yet they continue to wage wars, apparently immune to the pain inflicted. I felt outraged by my roommate's wartime experience—why isn't there more concern for the personal suffering that wars bring? I was thrust into witnessing its tragic, indiscriminate harming of an innocent. I'm certain that her trauma contributed to my later becoming a Peace Educator.

Another healing episode, while I was in rehab, happened with roommate Rosa. When she was first brought to my room, chaos entered as well. For almost thirty minutes, behind the privacy curtain, I heard several staff members trying to calm her as she churned in bed, struggling and gasping.

She boldly declared to the weary staff, "I'm calling a taxi and getting the heck out of here."

I wondered the cause of her disturbing behavior, annoying all of us. After they'd quieted her, she again caused another upset at eleven p.m., awakening me from a deep sleep. *How did I get stuck with this ornery gal?* I wondered.

The next morning, both of us refreshed, we became acquainted, and I discovered the cause of Rosa's distress.

"I apologize for the upset I caused last night."

"You must have had your reasons."

"Yes. Most people don't realize I have an advanced case of macular degeneration, and I'm almost totally blind," she said. "I rely on my books on tape for comfort and meaning. They're back in my apartment. Without them, my life doesn't seem worth living, and I panic easily."

"Oh, I'm sorry. I didn't realize. . . ."

She mentioned that her rehab stay was due to knee replacement surgery. I thought, *I have the comfort of my books here in rehab, always my companions, including my favorite,* At Seventy, *by May Sarton.* I asked Rosa, "Since I have my favorite book here in our room, would you like me to tell you something about her and perhaps read some passages to you?"

She said, "Let's hear more." I then gave her my impression of May Sarton's background. *She had aged gracefully despite living a solitary life. I was always taken with her vivid descriptions of the sweeping ocean*

and sky, with its ever-changing, wind-swept colors, as well as her garden-
ing and flower arranging. At the same time, I always reflected— could I
ever achieve as satisfying a life?

When invitations for college readings of her books and poetry were
sparse, Sarton always found meaningful activities to fill her days. I often
immersed myself in her works as a devout religionist finds succor in the
Bible.

Can you imagine what the New York Times *wrote about her when*
she died? Her obituary reported she had never published a best seller,
but her publications could be found in almost every town library in the
United States. I must admit I was envious of Sarton and wondered if
my writing could ever make a contribution.

After my long exposition, I asked Rosa, "Is this a good time to share
some passages with you?"

"Let's try it," she said.

A daily reading became part of our usual routine. We relished the
cozy experience, and as our friendship grew, Rosa offered a suggestion
that helped solidify it. "When one of us needs an aide, perhaps we can
both ring the bell. Then we'll more likely get their prompt attention."
This strategy worked well.

It seems that peace and good will can be practiced in most circumstances. Our relationship started with annoyance and shifted to companionship, then friendship. This rewarding change continued after Rosa
preceded me in returning home from rehab. I phoned her. "How's your
homecoming doing?"

"Oh, Betty, I'm so happy back with my reading machine," she said.
"Now I also can take a daily walk in the park across the street."

My rehab also involved questioning by a team of healers. A psychiatrist, social worker, and nurse checked my mental capacities with
banal questions: "What's the name of this hospital? What day of the
week is it? Who's president of the United States?"

The next day, the team social worker returned to my bedside to share a memory. She said, "I used to be head of that team, during the George H. Bush's presidency, asking the questions." She explained further, "When I got to the question of who's president, I couldn't bear to ask." We both smiled at one another, understanding our shared feelings.

I attribute my remarkable recovery partly to the continuing support of my religious/spiritual community, the Essex Ethical Culture Society. Members Karen and Ed Bokert visited me in the hospital almost immediately, marveling, "To think you were in that tub for five days without food or water!" Dr. Edmund Bokert had been one of my supervisors during my counseling internship thirty-four years earlier.

Get-well notes arrived regularly, as did occasional floral arrangements. The president of our Society, Terri Suess, employed full-time, managed to visit on four separate occasions.

"Terri, it's so cold here today," I complained to her during a visit. Quickly, she removed her soft blue jacket and gently helped me place my arms through the sleeves as I sat in bed. When I returned home, fully recovered, I had the jacket cleaned for its return to Terri. She refused, with a chuckle. "Just keep it as a souvenir!" I still associate it with fond connections to a compassionate, generous community member, as it has become a regular part of my wardrobe.

Early one Sunday morning, I awakened with a thought: *I must have that special book.*

Too Soon to Say Good-Bye, by humorist Art Buchwald, tells of his serious illness, which required dialysis. He refused treatment and was placed in hospice. He recounted his pleasures as friends and luminaries entertained him with copious visits, accompanied with gifts, delicacies, and uproarious memories.

This book was languishing on my living room bookshelf. How could I get it to the hospital? *Who could I phone at the ungodly hour of seven a.m. to bring it to me? There's only one person who would graciously respond to this outrageous request, our clergy leader, Boe Meyerson.*

I phoned, waking her from a sound sleep. After apologizing profusely, I asked, "Boe, there's a book I must have. Can you pick it up and bring it to me at the hospital?"

I explained which neighbor had my house key and where to find the book. I hoped retrieving the book wouldn't delay her presiding for the Sunday Morning Service at Ethical. She carried out the request with warmth and grace, delivering the coveted book to me the next day. I read and reread it. I chuckled, remembering the recurring dream Buchwald reports during his hospice stay:

> *I am at Dulles airport and have a reservation to go to heaven . . .Heaven is the last gate. . .I didn't realize how many people were on the same flight. . .open seating on the plane. . .you have to sit three across. . .(even en route there).*
>
> *He asks, "Am I entitled to frequent flyer mileage?". . ."you won't need any, because you're not coming back. . . .Because of inclement weather, today's flight to heaven (was) canceled. . .come back tomorrow, and we'll put you on standby."*

I concluded there's not much more comforting than having a community for support. Yes, for me now, it's too soon to say goodbye.

I recently discovered musings I had written in November 2010, following my illness and subsequent recovery. I referred to them as "a vacation."

> *A strange but wondrous vacation has come to visit me. It's like a stranger now lives with me, bringing unprecedented energy for life, amazing contentment, a certain feeling of wisdom, a resilience to deal with disappointments and setbacks. I don't truly own these circumstances and the vacation will end. For now, though, I'm content beyond reason.*

In 2014, engrossed in writing my memoir, I attended a workshop, "Memoir and Mindfulness, Writing and Understanding the Essential

Self," organized by Lorraine Ash, a New Jersey journalist and author. It was held at Pine Wind Zen Center Jizo-An Monastery in Shamong, New Jersey. There I first met two distinctive personalities—Lorraine, who introduced and discussed excerpts from notable memoirs, and Seijaku Roshi, a Zen teacher, who spoke on mindfulness.

Lorraine's selections were so compelling that I later purchased several of the books she highlighted. I resonated mostly to *A Book of Secrets* by Deepak Chopra. This author encompasses values I appreciate.

Roshi's presentation also impressed me. Several days later, I realized that I had the privilege of having the acquaintance of an Eastern sage, right here in New Jersey. I sensed he would be approachable—what an opportunity—to discuss my unusual medical experience with a man of unique wisdom.

I phoned Roshi and related my erratic operating table incident of six years earlier that I hadn't resolved. The doctors to whom I had mentioned the experience never gave it much attention.

To Roshi, I described the entire breadth of the 2009 events—the five-day seizure, the nightmares, the operating table battle, and my ebullience afterwards. I ventured further: "I felt Buddha-like. Do you think I had a near-death experience?"

"Most certainly," he said. "It would account for the unusual series of events." I felt affirmed.

"I didn't feel near death," I added. "I had little fear until the operating table incident. There I fought like a tiger."

"Yes," he said. "You seemed to be struggling for your very life, appropriately so." I felt affirmed.

Regarding "affirmations"— they came into my life only gradually, greatly delayed. As a motherless child, feeling abandoned and insecure, I didn't receive any consistent individual acknowledgment until the older years. These validations—marked by fighting for my divorce, becoming a contributing Ethical Culture member, achieving a reputation as a notable psychotherapist, and being loved by Tom—didn't arrive for almost half a century.

Shifting to Roshi's accomplishments, I said, "Roshi, you are too modest. I didn't see the book you wrote during my stay at the monastery. I wanted to buy it."

"I'll send you one as a gift," he said. I reciprocated and sent him *The Coming Interspiritual Age*, by Kurt Johnson. I received his book, *Kokoro—The Heart Within*, accompanied by a gracious letter in which I immersed myself. He also confirmed my request of his willingness to speak at the Essex ECS.

Unfortunately, Roshi will not be speaking this season in our series on varied religious beliefs. Another Buddhist teacher who practices locally is more connected to the Society. I trust we shall be able to invite Roshi to address us at another time.

This entire experience has brought a particular poem by e.e. cummings to mind, quoted here in part:

> *(i who have died am alive again today,*
> *And this is the sun's birthday; this is the birth*
> *day of life and love and wings; and of the gay*
> *great happening illimitably earth)*
>
> *how should tasting touching hearing seeing*
> *breathing, any—lifted from the no*
> *of all nothing—human merely being*
> *doubt unimaginable You?*
>
> *(now the ears of my ears awake and*
> *now the eyes of my eyes are opened)*

Knowing I still have much to contemplate and digest, I'm certain of only one thing—my mantra: I am so grateful.

BECOMING A PEACE EDUCATOR

MANKIND IS HER FAMILY'S NAME," declared the headline of an article in the *Star Ledger* by the reporter interviewing me in 1971 when I was forty-five years old. She wrote it after she had interviewed me as Founder and Director of the Essex Ethical Culture Society's (ECS) Educational Center. The reporter detected my expressions of humanist qualities, reverence for the kinship that inhabits our precious earth, for life itself. These ideas have come to underlie my commitment to the ideals of peace, trying to create a more humane world for all peoples.

My journey from childhood to age forty-five was marked with profound childhood losses but balanced with loving family who possessed unusual compassion. Their openness and intelligence brought me to Chicago's Ethical Culture Society (ECS) when I was only eleven years old and eventually to a new level of understanding.

In time, I came to believe that, if indeed there is a God, he/she/it has bestowed immense treasures—celestial Nature, highlighted with majestic mountains, generous bodies of water, exquisite landscapes, an infinite variety flowing from this miracle of Creation. Albert Einstein termed his "God" belief as "the awe and mystery of Life." I believe similarly.

Through some hallowed process, we humans have been gifted this sacred place, to create an Eden of our choosing. I believe we owe allegiance for this gift, to maintain a peace befitting the generosity of the bequest. To slaughter humans and their environs in defense of some man-made, conflicted belief system seems massively ungrateful, truly barbaric. We the people of the United States are doubly blessed, living in this democratic society, patriotic and proud of our guaranteed liberties.

My path to understanding our country's patriotism from a humanistic perspective started when I was thirteen years old. In 1939, when I was in eighth grade, Hayt Elementary School was celebrating May Day in the school yard. With the raising of our Stars and Stripes in the bright sunshine, I thought I knew what love of country truly meant.

A favorite teacher, Florence Reed, commented to me, "This glorious patriotic display helps you understand why men would be willing to *lay down their lives for their country.*"

Her remark made me think, I love my country and feel genuine pride as an American. Yet she triggered uncertainties that troubled me. I realized, men do volunteer to die for their country as a patriotic act. I questioned, Is this the only form of patriotism to express love of country and honor its glory?

As I grew up, I thought more deeply about my country's role in the world's orbit. My patriotism accepted the necessity of World War II, when my brothers served as soldiers. I also contributed to the war effort—worked in a war plant, sold War Bonds, and even became War Bond Queen in junior college.

The dropping of the atomic bomb on Hiroshima and Nagasaki horrified me. Slaughtering innocent women and children shifted my sensibilities. I questioned, *How could President Truman commit our country to such a loathsome act?* For me, the acts of warfare had been elevated to the most horrendous levels of destruction. My peace ideals were clearly roused.

After I married and had children, I educated my two daughters about the larger world with its diverse, rich cultures. We visited the New York World's Fair Pepsi-Cola exhibit of "Wide, Wide World" repeatedly. I encouraged my girls to collect money for UNICEF at Halloween as part of their contribution to the needs of the world.

"Hey, who has the heaviest box of coins?" My daughters would playfully compete. Their interests were a seismic difference from those of my childhood. Mischief-making was the custom marking Halloween back then—soaping storefronts and ringing doorbells in large apartment buildings. Our triumph was hearing the echoes of bells responding to our pranks.

By the time of the Vietnam War, its misguidedness marked by atrocities, I was staunchly opposed. My good friends were demonstrating in Washington, where I was eager to join them. My husband felt differently, and my timidity kept me from opposing him. I seethed alone at home, mute, banging pots in frustration instead of joining the protests. My fury about the war was expressed in this poem:

> *My country 'tis of thee,'*
> *Sweet land you crapped up.*
>
> *Where is the land that*
> *earns honor and respect,*
> *to these noble ends you stand*
> *blind and deaf.*
>
> *Mother Country, you are a mother f—.*

In the peace of my writing room, I could find my voice.

Peace Education was introduced to me at age forty-nine by the brilliant Naomi Drew and was a turning point after my 1975 divorce. Her approach was an outlet for my troubled feelings of patriotism, which felt erroneous when they condoned death and destruction. Naomi founded the organization "Partners in Peacemaking" and wrote a children's peace curriculum for New Jersey public schools.

She invited me to join her board of directors, where we supported her ground-breaking book, *Learning the Skills of Peacemaking*. When we celebrated its publication at signing parties, teeming crowds of parents with children showed up at bookstores to honor Naomi. She also wrote other children's peace education books for which she was acclaimed.

I deeply admire Naomi's vision and determination. To my grade school teacher, Florence Reed, I am also grateful for questioning the deadly cost of our usually accepted patriotism, which has stayed with me to this day.

SEVERAL YEARS LATER, I MET A SENIOR CITIZEN also affected by the ongoing threat of our nation's deadly warfare. Lou Kousin, an erudite member of New Jersey Sane in Montclair (now New Jersey Peace Action in Bloomfield) was passionate about his convictions. His simple appearance—tall and lanky, thin wisps of hair accompanying a quiet, gentlemanly manner—didn't suggest his hidden energies. When working for goals of peace, he performed as a bold executive.

Lou committed his retirement years to establishing "Peace Sites," an antonym to military sites, a new mindset to influence constructive efforts for peace in homes, schools, government establishments, businesses, houses of worship, wherever people gathered. Efforts toward resolving conflicts amiably could be initiated locally, nationally, even internationally—anywhere in the larger arena of human endeavors. Lou had been nominated for a Pulitzer Prize in journalism and used his writing skills to compose and type his own letters that promoted peace.

His zealousness influenced me in supporting our Essex ECS to become a Peace Site, the first ever, possibly in the world. On October 4, 1981, dedicated by Father Dan Berrigan as keynote speaker, the ceremony took place on the Society's expansive front porch. Almost one hundred people clustered down the stairs and onto Maplewood's Prospect Street, traffic rerouted for this special occasion. Established in memory of a beloved deceased past lay leader, Gabe Williamson, his portrait painted in oils by an ECS member, Janice Guidicelli, it was presented to Vera, his widow as part of the ceremony.

"Why Peace Sites?" Lou's advocacy in honor of newborn first grandchild, Leah, was published in a 1982 *New York Times* op-ed article (see Appendix). I deeply admired this father figure.

More Peace Sites followed. Lou concluded in his *Times* article:

> *We are trying to apply in principle what the late Gen. Omar N. Bradley declared on his retirement: "The central problem of our time is how to employ human intelligence for the salvation of mankind."*

I gathered Lou's writings into a Peace Site scrapbook to archive his work, the cover designed by ECS member Anita Roberts with her *goldene* hands. I plan to follow up his 1986 Peace Site Vatican inquiry to Pope John Paul II, considering the extraordinary role Pope Francis now fulfills in that sacred mission. Another goal—outreach to the United Nations and its "Culture of Peace" Program, a follow-up to Lou's letter to the Secretary-General in 1991.

The Peace Site concept took hold; before long, hundreds were established throughout the country and then internationally. I became a loyal friend and occasional companion to Lou in his lonely office. A highlight of his day (and mine) was his excited phone call to me, "Betty, we have another new Peace Site!"

He affectionately called me his "Peace Emissary" as we lunched together at a local Cranford restaurant while he explained his new strategies. Lou sometimes prepared a simple meal for me at his home. I treasured this relationship with my hero.

In 2010, more deeply involved in Peace commitments, I arranged a re-dedication of the ECS's Peace Site for which Lynn Elling, Founder of World Citizens in Minneapolis, was the keynote speaker. Before Lou Kousin died, he had chosen Lynn as his successor for leading the Peace

Site Movement. As a weekend guest in my home, Lynn's passion for peace was ever present, quoting Mahatma Gandhi frequently: "If we are to ever have peace in this world, we must start with the children." Lynn fervently urged me to take leadership and introduce peace ideas into my Millburn–Short Hills community. "Betty, you *must* take the initiative to promote peace, just as I've done in Minneapolis. You can do it!"

Sometimes I felt this optimism was unreal, even a bit pushy.

A new Superintendent of Schools, Dr. John Crisfield, inaugurated his tenure by heralding the need for character development in our students. This presented me an opportunity, particularly since a teenager from his departing school district had just been acclaimed for her efforts in developing "Pennies for Peace." When Dr. Crisfield heard of my commitments, he asked, "What elementary school did your daughter attend?"

He quickly arranged for my first Peace Workshop at Short Hills' Hartshorn School.

In Amy Blake's second-grade class, I read Wangari's *Trees of Peace* to the children, in which an issue of conflict is peacefully resolved. Their crayon drawings contained spontaneously printed comments on their works:

"They used words instead of fists."

"This story reminds me of Rosa Parks. These people changed the world."

Their reactions affirmed Mahatma Gandhi's visionary words and Lynn Elling's drumbeat of encouragement.

Other books also help educate young children to become aware of their basic goodness, which is fundamental for peaceful living. I chose *All That You Are* and *Somewhere Today, A Book of Peace* for the pre-K grade at the Jewish MetroWest Community Center in West Orange, New Jersey.

For teenagers, I was offered the opportunity to do a Peace Workshop for the Monmouth County, New Jersey, organization the Center for

World Religions and Ethical Thought. In their meetings, young people representing eight different faiths share their belief systems and visit one another's houses of worship. The students become the teachers, explaining the fundamental essence of their religions to each other. They also render needed services to varied community groups. To extend these ideas to world concerns, they have been invited to the United Nations to learn about the international "Culture of Peace" possibilities.

My teenage workshop in Cambria, California, came about through my cousin Paul. When he visited me in New Jersey, he said, "There's a Peace Garden monument in downtown Cambria, and your name's inscribed on it."

Surprised, I snapped to attention. "How'd that happen?"

"Well, I arranged it. I know how eager you are about peace. When my Rotary International organization came up with this project, I contributed five hundred bucks to list your name there."

I was delighted that Paul had picked up on my enthusiasm, and thanked him for his generosity. I asked a million questions: "What kind of school system do you have in Cambria? Can I arrange to do a peace workshop when I vacation there next February? Who's the school superintendent? Can you get me his phone number?"

Paul laughed and assured me, "Our schools are the best in the state."

I focused on the high school, as many of their teens were members of Interact, an activist school organization for improving conditions in the larger society. They comprise about one-third of the student body (compared to 10–15 percent in most communities) and had contributed to food banks and the homeless, and most recently, purchased an ambulance for an African country.

Steve Spisak, a Rotary member and high school Interact sponsor, arranged a peace workshop for the school. When he could only get a nine a.m. slot on a Saturday, he cautioned me, "Not a great time. Don't expect much of a turnout."

I answered, "No matter. For three or thirty, I'll do my thing."

Fifteen lively teens, both boys and girls, welcomed me. I felt like a homecoming queen as I arrived at the bank where Paul had arranged the meeting. Alison Brunschwiler, an eager student, agreed to serve as scribe for the workshop and continue as my Peace Emissary. Now a new generation, she took on the title given me thirty-five years earlier by Lou Kousin.

The students asked many questions.

"How did you become involved in the peace movement?" I gave them a brief summary of my history, sharing interesting incidents and photographs from newspaper publicity. I cited personalities who had inspired me, like Mahatma Gandhi, and repeated his wise words about children.

I commended the group for their activism in improving the lives of under-served people and their shared working together as they supported the best in one another.

I incorporated African drumming that combined the natural rhythms of the body with spiritual ideas. The vitality of the kids erupted as we drummed together on the table tops.

When I think about my involvements at their age, I don't recall translating my larger world interests into activism. Though my mind had been broadened by a high school course in international relations and by exploring the subject of sociology, my larger concerns were mostly self-serving. My main thoughts were to pursue good grades, excel in sports, and figure out how to become attractive. My role as a true activist didn't happen until after my divorce.

I believe the primary strength of the workshop was opening their consciousness around peace as a way of being. Here also, I mentioned the United Nations emphasis on the "Culture of Peace," that a session with those officials might be arranged for students traveling to the East Coast.

Alison later commented to me, "The numbers that showed up—and the conference table. It was much friendlier than a classroom. The kids seemed to like the chummy circle where everyone was in full view. They appreciated the bibliography, too."

I had been especially pleased when one of the students spoke out to say, "I'm just in awe of your passion, considering your age."

Their reaction reinforced my often-quoted adage: *Aging well can be the climax to a life well-lived, wise and full.*

WHEN LYNN HAD BEEN A GUEST in my home for the re-dedication of the ECS Peace Site, he spoke of his many activities for World Citizen's Peace Sites in numerous elementary, middle school, and high schools. He also emphasized his leadership as Co-founder of the Nobel Peace Prize Festival in Minneapolis.

For the many school Peace Sites, Lynn's imaginative vision for their classrooms included creating a photo replica of Planet Earth traveling in space, reminding children of our planetary peace journey. In an "Open Letter to the Entire Human Family," Lynn has conceived of these sites as our launching pads here on Spaceship Mother Earth.

Earth is whirling through space with no one in control save this generation of children–space travelers who share the responsibility of creating a safety net of Peace. Our human journey travels at eighteen and a half miles per second in our orbit around the sun. The 189 passenger compartments (Nation/States) do whatever they wish, waging war on their neighbors, spending over 1 trillion dollars annually on the arms race, polluting the ecosystem. There is no effective bridge or control center on our spaceship either (see Appendix for full text of peace plan).

With a photo of Earth traveling in space displayed in each classroom, teachers are encouraged to weave a "Global International Peace component" into every subject, grades K-12. This Earth–space photo also appears on my Peace Educator professional card.

Lynn's Peace Site efforts have extended to the governor's mansion in St. Paul, the Mall of America, the Carter Center in Atlanta, Georgia, the Concordia International Language Village, numerous churches, schools and private homes.

Many students from the Peace Site schools attend the annual Nobel Peace Prize Festival at Augsburg College, dressed in the ethnic clothing of their families' origin. The Peace Prize laureates of previous years are traditionally invited, and many attend. If unable, they usually provide a video that speaks of their work for peace. Many students honor the laureates with concerts and art works of peace. In preparation, the students study the lives of the laureates, tracing their personal journeys to become prize-winning citizens of peace.

A DVD of the Augsburg's ceremony that I showed at my eighty-fifth birthday peace celebration in 2011 showed Geir Lundestad, representing the Norwegian Nobel Institute as director, declare with a chuckle, "This has been more fun than my experience in Oslo." Those laureates honored have been former president Jimmy Carter, Wangari Maathai, author of *Trees of Peace*, President Barak Obama. and Doctors Without Borders.

I RECENTLY RECONNECTED WITH THE CAMBRIA FOLKS and discovered both the middle and elementary schools also have special programs serving those in need. In elementary school, the children call themselves "peace ambassadors." I plan to learn more about their good works before I return to Cambria.

I phoned Alison where she is continuing her education at the University of California, Davis. She is excited about her college experience and has joined a cooperative housing living arrangement. Harmony becomes apparent in these students from diverse backgrounds. Alison particularly appreciates the community values inherent in the living arrangements and its connection with her environmental interests. She says, "The natural relationship between peace issues and environmental concerns becomes easier to understand."

I feel privileged to witness the blooming of a young woman who is moved by many socially relevant ideas.

Back in 1984, a professional conference at Stone Mountain, Georgia, sponsored by the American Academy of Psychotherapists (AAP) unexpectedly galvanized my peace interests.

A presentation by Ruth Cohn, a dignified, articulate woman raised in Germany and trained as a therapist in Switzerland, sparked a broader awareness beyond psychotherapy skills. She asked, "How can you bright professionals be so indifferent to international concerns? With the world so awry, and you individuals free and comfortable in this democratic country—well-educated, able to think independently and speak out— why are you not more involved in societal affairs, in your individual lives or as an organization?"

I admired the rousing message flowing from her broader world perspective. Silence followed her presentation. Participants never discussed her message, not after her speech or the cocktail party or lavish dinner afterward. I was frustrated by my colleagues' seeming indifference and approached an associate. "What did you think of her presentation?"

He said, "Oh, she's out of line. We didn't come here to hear the world's problems!"

Disappointed, I contemplated some of my colleagues' reasons for attending—a bit of camaraderie, an opportunity to boast about or increase their therapy practices and perhaps pick up some clinical pointers. My colleague's unspoken message: "Who wants to hear of society's problems when I'm on something of a vacation, written off partially as a professional expense?"

I was also guilty of this attitude. Truthfully, we were all too satisfied with our lives to acknowledge trouble brewing out there. Yet I couldn't shake off Ruth's wise message as I left the conference to continue my vacation in the Smoky Mountains with Tom. It was late June, and after a few days of exploration, I got an idea. "Tom, wouldn't it be delightful to spend the Fourth of July in small town U.S.A, here in the South, sharing an old-fashioned holiday?"

After we consulted our AAA map, we selected Wytheville, Virginia. The town green was already gearing up for the July 4 festivities. A band was playing spirited marches amid laughing families with children in tow, punctuated with balloons, hot dog stands, games, souvenirs, and other regalia marking the occasion. Tom and I strolled among the happy crowd for about an hour, joining the fun, swaying to the upbeat rhythms.

Our pleasure was interrupted when we encountered a raucous teenager. He was shrieking at two women tending a booth with petitions protesting nuclear bombs. He exclaimed, "Nuke the commies!" His fists were clenched as the women tried to calm the boy. He looked all-American, with blond hair and handsome features, resembling a young Robert Redford. After repeatedly shouting his venom, he finally left.

I spoke to the women about their anti-nuke petitions and later, the troubled teen. "Is there an organized effort in town? How much support do you get?"

One woman, a local librarian, explained she and her friend were tabling as private citizens. "We believe the threat is for real. We're very upset about nuclear weapons and their potential for destroying civilization as we know it." About the teenager, she said, "I know nothing about him."

Driving home, the incident haunted me. I attended my weekly poetry workshop, conducted by Bette Distler in her West Orange, New Jersey, home. She noticed I was preoccupied and asked, "Betty, you're unusually quiet today. What's up?"

I told her about the kid in Wytheville. She suggested, "Try to put the experience into a poem. That's what the art form is about."

I struggled to find the style and rhythm that voiced my concerns. With Bette's guidance, I wrote the following poem:

July 4, 1984, *Celebration, Wytheville, Virginia*

bingo! clownin'
buyin' a chance
town green heavin'
to the children's dance.

frolickin' kinfolk
baby smiles
boisterous birthday
country style.

bingo! clownin'
buyin' a chance
town green heavin'
to the children's dance.

and the boy
and the boy
by a booth
anti-nuke

and the boy
and the boy
by a booth
anti-nuke

and the boy
and the boy
was for tellin'
his truth.

"nuke the commies
nuke 'em first
blast 'em good
star-war burst.

nuke the commies

BECOMING BETTY

launch the bomb—"
sing song
childhood gone

And the
boy
and the
boy
launch
    the
        bomb

and
    the
      boy
and
    the
      boy
child
hood
    g
      o
        n
          e.

bingo! clownin'
buyin' a chance
town green heavin'
to the children's dance.

Having poured my guts into its creation, I felt appeased for a time. I shared the poem with friends and the experience that propelled it. A peace activist friend said she would share it at subsequent July 4 celebrations. Perhaps my deep feelings were affecting others as well.

Two colleagues, a psychotherapist and psychiatrist from New York's National Institute for the Psychotherapies, which had become a Peace Site, later invited me to view a provocative film, *Changing the Silence*. Created in 1984 by students at Northfield Mount Herman School in Gill, Massachusetts, it involved the ongoing nuclear threat. Teenagers expressed anger at their parents' failure to discuss this fateful danger under which they all live. They also criticized government leaders who pay insufficient attention to this menace.

"How could authorities believe hiding under our desks would protect us?"

Impressed by this younger, prescient generation, in contrast to the Wytheville teen, I felt impelled to show this film to fellow citizens and conduct discussions. Houses of worship, community centers, and libraries seemed likely settings, wherever I could get invitations. Robert Jay Lifton's description of "psychic numbing," emphasizing this silence, motivated me further.

An AAP colleague, Harry Rockberger, agreed to initially co-facilitate the groups with me.

I needed a test run before adopting this plan, and the Essex ECS did a try-out as a Sunday morning service. About eighty people participated in discussing the film, filling every room in our Victorian meeting house. Their concerned responses encouraged me to commit many weekends to the program,which I spearheaded for several years.

Viewers' comments were sobering. Most expressed incredulity. "How could our government leaders mislead citizens about the massive danger of nuclear armaments?"

Participants expressed formerly unspoken fears. One family, both high-level professionals, openly admitted their plans for themselves and their adult children "to all die together" if they had sufficient warning of a nuclear bomb attack. I felt chilled by their doomsday plans, but I understood their train of thought. Perhaps more folks might awaken from their apathy.

I also presented this workshop at a professional social work conference, later published in their official proceedings.

WHEN LOU DIED IN 1996, his newspaper obituary reported that Peace Sites International had established more than four thousand sites worldwide. His loss was a sad time for me and for the peace movement as well.

There was a significant lull in the movement after Lou's death until the year 2000, when Madelyn Hoffman became Executive Director of New Jersey Peace Action. I anxiously contacted her about current Peace Site effort, which was reactivated in 2014. She reassured me that Judith Arnold (then a volunteer, who later became president) was conscientiously pursuing past sites for possible reinstatement.

Judith reported there are about forty Peace Sites in New Jersey, including homes, schools, churches of many denominations, art schools, and a few business organizations. Three to four are added annually, but she's eager to reinstate sites that have become inactive. I'm glad that Lou's ideals continue to be pursued by these committed women. My discussions with Judith lead me to believe their Peace Site project is seriously understaffed. I have since suggested she connect with the leadership of Lynn's World Citizen organization to learn about their successful approaches.

IN 2008 AT DREW UNIVERSITY, after leaving a lecture by Dr. Virginia Heschel, I noticed a lone student standing at a table in the corner of the adjoining vestibule with a peace sign. I stopped to inquire, and Marnie Valdivia explained her activity. Their peace organization was a modest university group of only twelve students, but her personal story developed into a much broader one.

She would be graduating in June with a degree in Religious Studies, was a Critical Language Scholar in the Arabic language, and planned to leave for Egypt immediately after college, where stirrings of democratic activity interested her. I asked her how she became involved in worldwide issues. She explained, "My parents are my role model. They each come from a different class and culture, yet they've forged a beautiful marriage from which I have learned."

After Marnie completed her overseas missions during Egypt's Arab Spring and attended an environmental conference in Israel, she returned to the United States to complete her graduate studies in Applied Geography at George Washington University.

Her current job helps develop creative solutions for the world's more complex problems. Marnie creates intricate geographic maps that serve to protect tribal populations' legal claims to their lands. The documentation safeguards their human rights from grasping industrial interests and warlords who have committed massive violations in the past. This empowers the community to control its shared resources and educates them about their democratic rights to own their land. Without these safeguards, a corrupt government and aggressive industrial interests can disrupt and exploit the land, particularly in areas of mining and deforestation.

Marnie remains an ardent advocate for sensible environmental and human rights, which she'll share in a future program at the ECS. I'm grateful to have befriended a young woman, through a chance meeting, committed to creating a more humane world.

IN 2009, AFTER I SURVIVED two major illnesses, I returned to the ECS's Sunday Programs and wondered how I would experience my spiritual home again. My peace interests were re-energized by Anne Creder, UN Liaison to the Global Alliance for Ministries for the Department of Peace (currently coordinating sponsors for a new Congressional Bill, HR 1111, Department of Peace Builders) whose presentation quoted a passage from our United States Constitution: "*assure domestic tranquility*". . .written into our founding document—language affirming peace itself! I had only heard that our early statesmen, both George Washington and Thomas Jefferson, had encouraged establishing a Department of Peace to counter the Department of War.

What a true homecoming. Thomas Jefferson's early essay, discovered by Anne, is quoted here in part:

> *Peace is our passion. The happiness of mankind is best promised by the useful pursuits of peace. If nations go to war for every degree of injury, there never will be peace on earth. Peace and justice should be the polar stars of the American societies.*

This document confirms that our Founding Fathers had peace on their minds.

After two medical crises, what further motivation did I need to continue pursuit of my peace activities?

In 2010, I was torn between my peace and professional interests. My conflict was the dual scheduling of an important psychotherapy conference planned in Santa Fe, New Mexico, during the August 4 anniversary of the United States dropping the atomic bombs on Hiroshima and Nagasaki. I usually attend these anniversary observances in New Jersey, sponsored by New Jersey Peace Action. I decided to forgo this current event with the *Hibakusha* (survivors of the atomic bombings), though I always recall their horror stories with heavy heart:

> *We who have been exposed to the poisons of nuclear contamination are "marked" as people who should avoid marriage and procreation for fear of extending the poisons to future generations. We have become like lepers, separated, sometimes reviled, by our fellow citizens.*
>
> *Nevertheless, some of us do marry and have children, but always with fear—will they have all their limbs or extraneous ones?*

Hearing these stigmatized people describe their suffering has always provoked a sharp sense of the cruelties we inflict on victims of warfare, its savagery of blood, guts, and limbs.

At the Santa Fe town square on the August 4 anniversary, directly across the street from my hotel, a large demonstration with colorful banners was featured. Heartened by this cross-country peace connection, I joined the participants between professional workshops.

I introduced myself to the master of ceremonies as a compatriot in the peace movement from the East. Handing me the mike, he said, "Here, share your message with the crowd."

In my brief speech, I commended them for their peace efforts and spirit. I was thrilled to join their efforts and realized Lou Kousin's assertion was on the mark—"Peace can be advocated anywhere."

IN A 2014 SUNDAY SERVICE at the ECS, along with Vice-President Zia Durrani, I explained John Horgan's "The End of War." Since then, I've been privileged to participate in a discussion at the United Nations about their Culture of Peace. The Essex ECS has launched a family education program with the goal of raising children to become global citizens. Amy Blake chairs the Curriculum Committee, and I serve on the Planning Committee.

In 2014, I declared myself a Peace Educator, adding to my profession as a psychotherapist.

Though I'm eighty-eight years old, I'm not retiring—I'm adding another keen interest of mine. Today, I continue to offer "Imagine Peace" workshops for children and adults, free of charge, just as I did for my adult workshops, "Changing the Silence," many years ago.

Becoming a Peace Educator in my elder years is a guidepost to define the culmination of my human journey. I plant seeds of gratitude for the true value of peace. These activities will potentially benefit my children, grandchildren, and perhaps the seven generations designated by our Native Americans. I feel this commitment as an imperative. When my days eventually draw to a close, I hope to die at peace, my optimism intact.

When some people notice my prominent peace necklace, created by ECS member Joan Mendelson, they comment, "I *like* your necklace." I then identify myself as a Peace Educator and whip out my peace cards. I encourage them to suggest that their churches and synagogues and town libraries offer my "Imagine Peace" workshop. This message hasn't yet brought many gigs. I'm optimistic and wait patiently.

Just this year, February 2016, I contacted Lynn Elling's World Citizen's organization in Minneapolis and received a blow, the news of his death at age ninety-four. I feel remorse for allowing our important relationship to have been neglected. Within a day of this sadness, however, I was uplifted with reports from the ongoing World Citizen leadership, charging ahead with plans to maintain his extraordinary legacy. I believe, somewhere in the cosmos, Lynn is smiling.

Kathy Millington, Executive Director of World Citizen, has written a tribute to Lynn Elling with a vow to "pursue a just and peaceful world" which was the core of Lynn's "driving dream." Specific plans can be followed on their website: www.peacesites.org. She has affirmed that she would gladly make herself available to New Jersey Peace Action, to advise on approaches to reinstate former Peace Sites. Perhaps we can form a trilogy to work for Peace—World Citizen, New Jersey Peace Action, and the Essex ECS.

Dr. Edward Tick and I met as colleagues during our membership in AAP some thirty years ago. We became friends and allies—seemingly the only members interested in larger societal concerns beyond our professional work. This deeply compassionate humanist, broadly educated with knowledge of mythology and poetry, has committed himself to healing U. S. war combatants from the Vietnam hostilities and other wars as well. In Ed's role as Founder and Executive Director of Soldier's Heart, his insights cut through distortions of war: PTSD, which he terms "soul murder," and the warrior archetype. His latest publication, *Warrior's Return—Restoring the Soul After War*, describes these ideas.

Ed's intense interest in Vietnam Vets and their damaged spirits has gripped me, particularly when he showed past films at the ECS. In their return to Vietnam, it was wrenching to view the men, sobbing and screeching at the memory of their killing encounters. I admire Ed's commitment to alleviate warfare suffering. Just recently, he said, "The Vietnamese have no PTSD in their country, though they incurred three million casualties, including women and children. They bear no grudge against Americans. When U. S. servicemen return to Vietnam to ask forgiveness, the people respond, 'You've done nothing requiring an apology. You were noble warriors serving your country. It's the military leaders and politicians who committed the grievous acts.'"

At the Sunday Program, Ed initiated the healing process.

Two men, each strangers to the Society and his approach, emerged from the experience with new hope: apparently determined to continue healing at a Soldier's Heart Retreat—perhaps even accompany Ed on his sixteenth trip back to Vietnam. One man had avoided Vietnam service by escaping to Canada, and, some forty years later, has remained ridden with guilt. After hearing new insights and possibilities, he said with confidence, "Now my life can begin again."

Another, an outstandingly decorated Muslim in the Marines at the time of 9/11, was jailed by his authorities, treated cruelly in prison, and court-martialed, his innocence not accepted. In attending at the ECS, he had been looking for a community with understanding, where he feels he can trust and become comfortable.

My peace efforts are a tribute to my parents, Evelyn and Barnett, as well as cousins Dorothy and Mathilda. My parents' steadfast ongoing labors led to accomplishments by their children they would have never dared imagine. My peace work strives to honor and express deep appreciation for their efforts, despite their personal hardships, always for us children. I also credit my cousins, never having had their own children; they nurtured and inspired me with their brand of spunk. If only they all could have lived to know of the Peace Garden with my name inscribed there.

My work as a Peace Educator also counters my many marital years of strife. Despite having enough money to buy anything I could ever want, this abundance taught me an invaluable lesson. The true values of life carry no price tag. We humans can reach this precipice mostly through committed efforts of empathy, understanding, and forgiveness, resulting in a peace that can enrich one's entire tenure on Earth.

Forgiveness, a unique quality from which everyone can profit, significantly contributes to the complexities of human relations, taps into our spiritual being. We are all flawed—only gods are perfect. A moral compass that accepts our errors and forgives ourselves can bring great satisfaction. This can become an ultimate peace.

MY FAMILY TAPESTRY

A S I LOOK BACK, the need for loving and cherished families is central to my story. After the death of my birth mother at my early age, my growing-up experience was complicated yet extraordinary. My family of mothers, and my father as well, contributed invaluable roles. They raised me with unflinching devotion, depth of character, and generosity of spirit. All gave the best they could with what they knew.

All the families withheld the truth of my earliest years, as secrets were the norm of the day. Deprived, I longed for in-depth information about my birth mother, to know about her as a person. Her actual existence was mostly passed over, and she became something of a phantom. Only my name, "Sister," remains as a sign of her love.

I was nevertheless enriched by those responsible for me. Evelyn, my stepmother, brought me her essence, despite her being emotionally handicapped by guilt for her infant's accidental death. I wish I had known her truth earlier, when I could have appreciated her abundant love. The eventual revelation makes her overbearing behavior more understandable. I abhor that I rejected her, and my deep regrets still remain. Mathilda—our connection through Evelyn's endearing family, has inspired me with her compassion. Tante Surrel's loyal, strong peasant roots provided a sturdy base. Cousins Dorothy and Betty—how fortunate they loved their Aunt Bea, my birth mother, so much they graced me with their rich nurturing and heritage. Aurelia, our African American household help, extended her cozy mothering to me when Evelyn was too busy working in Dad's shop.

In writing memories of my father, I have come to know him in a surprisingly new glory. I rejected him while he lived. Only now, tragically belated, have I come to appreciate his unremitting labors, deep sacrifice, and wisdom, insisting his children be reunited in one home. His bequeathing me two brothers has constructively shaped my feelings toward men, even my ability to marry a man like Howard with all I gained there. Despite our sharp marital difficulties, the gift of two daughters and three grandchildren has brought me heartfelt, undying pleasure. When occasional misunderstandings intervene, the glory unquestionably endures.

My childhood anger has been basically laid to rest. Omissions nevertheless did bring some resentment, contributing to insecurity. Today, I occasionally struggle with feeling weak, fragile, flawed.

My early upsets, mostly cushioned and comforted by a myriad of caring mothers, caused a rending, then a mending, not perfect but sufficient. What imperfections remain do not irreparably mar the tapestry of my life. Although there are sections somewhat awry, the cloth is mostly whole, sturdy, and woven with highlights of color.

One basic fragmentation, however, remains. I have never achieved a solid, unbroken family life with warmth and consistency. Starting with childhood, continuing into marriage and my elder years, this pattern has persisted. I still long for experiences of intimacy—but no one achieves everything on life's journey. At times, I feel the global family encompasses my world.

All things considered, I am quite fortunate. Who hasn't experienced some imperfections? By some good fortune, I have escaped crushing upheavals in my ninety years. My divorce trauma only served to strengthen me. My brain surgery exposed a fresh ebullience, a new zest for life.

There is much wisdom in our family. Howard, my former husband and father of our children, used his creative mind for impressive accom-

plishments. His brilliance, unfortunately, lacked the emotional component that brings the most vital of human experience—*compassion*. Understanding this essential quality can become an invaluable legacy for
our family.

Upon their father's death, I wrote a eulogy for him, citing his great
gifts, suggesting his shortcomings. Our children are fortunate to have
inherited an invaluable legacy from both families, marked with great con-
trasts. They will have much opportunity to sort, sift, and choose the
paths of integrity that speak to them for their personal journeys. My
blessings accompany their contemplation and choices.

As my life approaches its final chapter, the conclusion of Mary
Oliver's poem "When Death Comes" speaks to me:

> *When it's over, I want to say: all my life*
> *I was a bride married to amazement.*
> *I was the bridegroom, taking the world into my arms.*
> *When it's over I don't want to wonder*
> *If I have made of my life something particular, and real.*
> *I don't want to find myself sighing and frightened,*
> *Or full of argument.*
> *I don't want to end up simply having visited this world.*

About immortality: I believe it best expressed by trying to emulate,
here on Earth, the goodness of our deceased loved ones.

Essentially, I have been enriched with a life of substance and meaning.
My belief in, and commitment to, families, humanism, Peace Education,
and Ethical Culture's Family Education Program has provided a wealth
that surpasses any measures I know.

Again, always, I am so grateful.

AFTERWORD

"When I came to understand that there are mythic patterns in all our lives, I know that all of us, often unbeknownst to ourselves, are engaged in a drama of soul which we were told was reserved for gods, heroes and saints."

—Deena Metzger, *Miracle at Canyon de Chelly*

APPENDIX

1. *At home with myasthenia gravis, unable to speak,*
Betty's note to home health aide

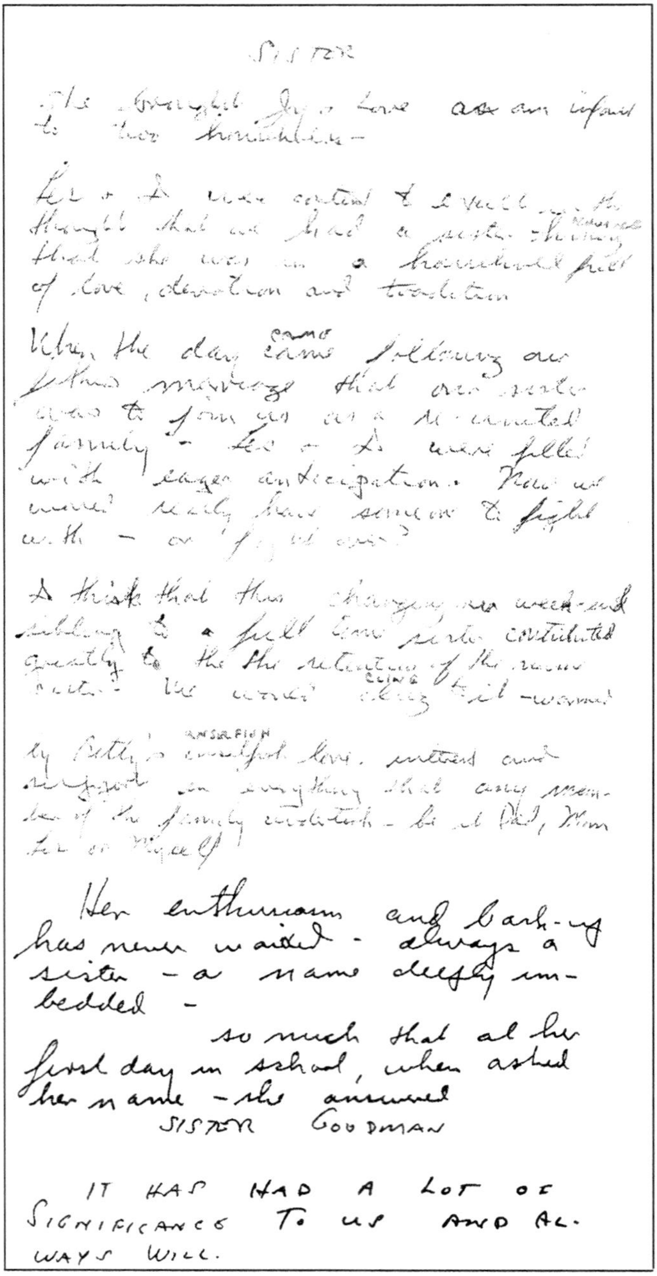

SISTER

She brought joy & love as an infant to two [illegible] –

Lee & I were content & excited with the thought that we had a sister knowing that she was in a household full of love, devotion and tradition

When the day came following our fathers marriage that our sister was to join us as a re-united family – Lee & I were filled with eager anticipation. Now we would really have someone to fight with – or fight over?

I think that this changing our week-end sibling to a full time sister contributed greatly to the the retention of the name Sister. We would cling to it – warmed

by Betty's unselfish love, interest and support in everything that any member of the family undertook – be it Dad, Mom Lee or Myself

Her enthusiasm and back-up has never waivered – always a sister – a name deeply imbedded –

so much that at her first day in school, when asked her name – she answered

SISTER GOODMAN

IT HAS HAD A LOT OF SIGNIFICANCE TO US AND ALWAYS WILL.

2. *Leonard's undated letter anticipating "Sister" coming to live with the family when Father married Stepmother Evelyn.*

```
                    Big Brother

    Long years
    galloped away
    burying
    our early days of
    laughter
    high school pranks
    your MIkado costume
    frightened me
    then I giggled
    you brought fun
    to the house


                ENVY
    hiding the
    you the big brother
    me the coddled little one
    each seething with jealousy
    like logs shooting sparks
    on the fire


    Remember, you drove me
    five hours to college
    hardly a word passed our lips


    I married, moved away
    sparse visits
    letters mostly money things
    like my share of cemetery upkeep bills
    for Mom and Dad


    Now I want
    to pay my full share of upkeep bills
    and other debts
    before the earth gets
    cold.

                                Betty Levin
                                "Sister"
```

3. Abbreviated poem to my brother Leonard after his death.

What is America to me
A name, a map, or a flag I see
A certain word, democracy
What is America to me

The house I live in
A plot of earth, a street
The grocer and the butcher
And the people that I meet

The children in the playground
The faces that I see
All races and religions
That's America to me

The place I work in
The worker at my side
The little town, the city
Where my people lived and died

The howdy and the handshake
The air of feeling free
And the right to speak my mind out
That's America to me

The things I see about me
The big things and the small
The little corner newsstand
And the house a mile tall

The wedding and the churchyard
The laughter and the tears
The dream that's been growing
For a hundred and fifty years

The town I live in
The street, the house, the room
The pavement of the city
Or the garden all in bloom

The church the school the clubhouse
The millions lights I see
But especially the people
That's America to me

4. *"The House I Live In," words sung by Frank Sinatra in his early, inspired days of democratic ideals. Lyrics by Abel Meeropol (as "Lewis Allan").*

5. *"Identity," by Ben Shahn, from art collection of Betty and Howard Levin.
The inscription reads: "If I am not for myself, who will be for me?
But if I am only for myself, what am I? And if not now, when?"*

E. BETTY LEVIN

Excerpts – "Changing the Silence: Communicating About the Nuclear Threat"

SUMMARY - Most people are numbed about the nuclear danger. At the Symposium nuclear workshop, participants transformed their numbing into action. The social group work profession is challenged to face the nuclear threat and bring its unique skills and cherished tradition of social action to this work as a "call to life."

CONCLUSION –The nuclear threat is the ultimate mental health problem. Most individuals, including mental health professionals, igmore this issue. They resort to psychic numbing and reduce themselves to helplessness around this danger. The despair/empowerment workshops help participants lift their numbing and open the possibility for constructive action.

In the Symposium workshop, participants experienced an unusual release of creative energies that were channeled into immediate and concrete action. This experience clearly demonstrates the potency of the despair/empowerment concept and the small group process. It also suggests that the social group work profession is ready to address the nuclear threat. This is particularly appropriate as a profession concerned with the value of human life.

This work presents a challenge to social group work to discover its mission. The profession embraces a long tradition of social action with organizational ability and skills to bring to bear on this ominous threat. Lifton urges individuals to go beyond their imagination as a "call to life.";

6. *Excerpts on "Changing the Silence," about the nuclear threat, published in Roots & New Frontiers.*

WHAT WE BELIEVE AND LIVE FOR

E. Betty Levin   **Quiet Miracles**

I have been practicing psychotherapy for ᴏᴠᴇʀ 3 decades and my Ethical Culture religion as a life-long journey. My religious belief in the worth of all peoples is given dynamic expression in my work as a therapist and social activist. Living close to nature near a 2,000 acre preserve, I observe its flow and rhythm as well as its ambiguities, trying to glean valid meanings for my own life. I have 2 daughters and 3 grandchildren.

I believe in the sanctity of every person, that each is a treasure, a unique work of art with her or his own inherent abilities, potential, and founts of creativity. I have faith that people can make a difference in their own lives. As a therapist, my role is to help patients discover and mobilize their capacities and inner wisdom to make that difference. I believe that ordinary people have extraordinary possibilities.

I use a health and growth model, one positively oriented to what is nutritiously alive in patients. Some see themselves largely through prisms of negative qualities such as ineptness or hateful anger, dismissing their fine capacities. I try to help patients achieve a more balanced view of themselves and their lives, testing reality as we go. The strengthened observing ego fortifies the patient to grapple more effectively with the shadow part of the self that can haunt and impede the satisfying life.

In therapy as a journey of discovery, I navigate with patients between the Scylla of their complacency and Charybdis of their anxiety, either one presenting serious obstacles of the therapeutic work. My role is to steer a course that prods complacency and calms anxiety so that the work can progress. For this journey I try to build a sound foundation of trust that helps patients find the courage to engage the struggle. This allows teachable moments to emerge. I fill various roles—as teacher, parent, partner, healer, mentor, privileged participant, clinical philosopher. Sometimes I am a warrior, fighting for patients' health when they insist on holding tenaciously to destructive patterns. Sometimes I am a midwife present at a birth.

My theoretical foundation is psychodynamically based but always illuminated by humanistic, ego psychology, cognitive, feminist, Jungian, and body/mind ideas. I treat anxiety as an ally, as one of many symptoms that can provide clues to discovering the patient's underlying conflicts. Body ills

QUIET MIRACLES   37

7. *"Quiet Miracles" Betty's philosophy of practicing psychotherapy, published in the AAP Journal, "The Art & Science of Psychotherapy."*

often are seen as metaphors, expressing feelings somatically as a substitute for handling them appropriately in the emotional/cognitive life. In making therapeutic interpretations, I seek the language of poetry, words that marry the image to the emotion. I utilize the transference phenomenon that can dramatically promote the work or, if knowingly neglected, can backfire with detrimental results. My own countertransference is to know and analyze.

I remain a student always, trying to stretch my understanding of the human condition as gleaned from literature, religion, nature, Eastern thought, the arts, and philosophy. Even then, as Shakespeare states through Hamlet: "There are more things in heaven and earth, Horatio, than are dreamt of in your philosophy."

Life happens in a relationship and whatever the patient's presenting problem, most often the underlying difficulties center on the relationship life. Most people have "heart trouble," problems with spouse, lovers, parents, children. The therapeutic relationship evolves as a "laboratory" in which there is rich opportunity for the patient to achieve understanding of why tender feelings can be accompanied by pain, jealousy, and anger. Patients discover that the learning occurring in the relationship with the therapist can remarkably enrich the relationship life beyond the consulting room.

I help patients learn that change is a constant component of life, not to fear it but see it as an opportunity, that reasonable risks can be taken to improve one's life, that there is never any growth without some pain. And when painful change is imposed from outside such as losses, illness, and death, there can be the possibility of acceptance, finding a measure of peace and occasionally, transcendence.

Acceptance and compassion lead to an understanding heart, which is the strongest heart of all—its capacity for caring is infinite. As patients learn, I learn as well, affirming what is best in being human, and bringing renewed appreciation of a profession that allows me to bear witness to quiet miracles.

117 Sagamore Road
Millburn, NJ 07041

The Meaning of Art—
A Letter to New Jersey Music & Arts Magazine
(Concerning a letter Mr. Angelini wrote to the publication.)

That Mr. Angelini is outraged about conceptual art interpreted by masochistic maiming, human excrement, etc. is indeed understandable. Such displays assault the sensitive and the sensibilities. Where is beauty? Where is creativity? Where is vision?

But as one probes deeper beneath these outrageous acts, other meanings emerge. Art reflects the human condition; it affirms the life of man. The artist as historian and social critic uses his media to reveal his unique perceptions of the human condition. The caveman artist, for example, affirmed his life by depicting animals of his environment who were the basic source of his sustenance and survival. Artists of the Renaissance elevated man to the center of the universe in a new unity of strength and growth. Thus, when societal conditions spurred the growth of the human spirit, the artist conveyed this optimism on the canvas.

The spirit of affirmation ended with the giants—Van Gogh, Renoir, and Picasso. Thereafter, with the failure of science and politics to fulfill their promise of world peace and order, abject pessimism set in. The Dada art movement commented eloquently on this failure. This movement, in turn, fathered subsequent art developments reflecting further deterioration in our social order.

Today the prevailing conditions of our world are characterized by anxiety, alienation, dehumanization, and violence. It is so painful to consider that it is not surprising that most of us refuse to look at these conditions. But the artist, with his acute vision, himself a victim of the violence of society, either consciously or unconsciously communicates

---

8. A conceptual art controversy evokes a letter by Betty as Director
of the ECS Educational Center, published in the
New Jersey Music and Arts Magazine, November 1974.

through his art what he feels about our world. Is it any wonder that his efforts produce such revulsion in us all? If his art does violence to our sensibilities, it is because society itself does, too. In just the last thirty days, our newspapers have reported the outrages of Watergate, CIA intervention in the "destabilization" of the Chilean government, Waldheim's warning of worldwide starvation and "helplessness" and aerosol pollution of our ozone in the atmosphere. Our world is in crisis, and our art, which reflects our condition, is in similar crisis. The failure to stop this headlong plunge toward Armageddon has culminated in the vulgarities of much of the conceptual art movement.

The original questions: "Where is beauty? Where is creativity? Where is vision?" may be demonstrated in the effect such profane art can have on us. It may serve as shock effect to raise thinking and feeling people to new levels of awareness and perhaps some constructive action. It is already producing some dialogue, a thoughtful letter from Mr. Angelini and subsequent further comments. Perhaps people will invoke their creative conscience to move in their own unique ways toward that which is life-giving and life-affirming. Though the odds are formidable, the will of man does make a difference.

If man chooses to affirm that which is uniquely human, so, too, will our art. In the meantime, art uses a negative message to demonstrate that much of our society negates life. Ultimately, conceptual art will have served its purpose of beauty, creativity and vision if it impels us to mobilize ourselves and our institutions to be more responsive to human needs.

Betty Levin
Director, Education Center, Ethical
Culture Society
Maplewood, New Jersey

Art and the Human Experience

The recent indictment of the director of the highly regarded Contemporary Art Center in Cincinnati for the exhibition of the Mapplethorpe photographs would strike one as Theater of the Absurd if it were not so ominous. It reflects profound misunderstanding of the art experience and inevitably the human experience as well. This unprecedented incident parallels our now seriously damaged National Endowment on the Arts, which is restricting the subject matter of creative artists receiving grants. These acts go beyond censorship. The art experience comes from the deepest longings of the human spirit. To circumscribe the artist in this way is tantamount to establishing rules for breathing fresh air.

It is to the credit of the Cincinnati jury, comprised of citizens uneducated in the arts, that the director of the art center was found not guilty. But we are still faced with the spectacle of the National Endowment shackling the creative artist around ideas of "decency, obscenity, pornography" and the like. Joseph Papp has refused three-quarters of a million dollars in grants rather than be constrained by these rules. People may argue that it is only fair that those who won't play by the rules don't get the money. But it is the ignorance and fear of the art and human experience that strikes at the heart of the matter. Note that, in totalitarian countries, it is the artists and writers who are first muzzled.

Art, simply stated, is an affirmation of life. It defines our lives and speaks to our deepest needs, strivings, and pain. To interpret a work of art merely by its surface content is to depict Michelangelo's Sistine Chapel as a colorful ceiling in a nice building. Art is multidimensional with layers of meaning. If one meaning appears unpleasant, ugly, even

*9. Another art controversy, regarding so-called pornography
(the infamous Mapplethorpe affair) gets a response
from Betty, though it may not have*

violent, isn't that a true reflection of our society? Art illuminates our lives, both the beautiful and horrific. The creative artist, antenna and conduit of societal conditions, feels and reports that which escapes the lay person. The artist's work forces us to face certain truths that may be hard to look at. But only by facing these truths can we begin to understand our lives and society. If through our understanding we are influenced to take action for change, then even the distasteful and ugly become an affirmation of life.

Of course, we may choose not to expose ourselves to art that is dismaying—that is our free choice. But to stymie creative artists in their vision is an abortion of their humaneness and, inevitably, ours as well.

I send silent thanks to the Cincinnati jury for their affirmation of our humanity. Ordinary people are truly capable of extraordinary acts.

—*E. Betty Levin*

Freud and Cezanne: Psychotherapy as Modern Art

By Alexander Jasnow

(New Jersey: Ablex Publishing Co., 1993)

Reviewed by E. Betty Levin

How the modern self evolved in the present century through the process of creativity, expanded conscious-ness and transformation is the subject of this imaginative book. The author, an accomplished artist and psychotherapist, views this development through the twin prisms of modern art and psychotherapy. Seen also through the dynamic interaction of the individual and the culture, each creating and recreating the other, further stirs this hearty philosophic stew. The work ultimately poses the question: as we approach the coming millennium, what will be the impact of this evolution on psychotherapy and perhaps on humankind itself? To this daring journey, Dr. Jasnow brings a fresh integration with penetrating ideas for the reader to ponder.

Creativity inherently involves transformation and transcendence. Jasnow defines creativity as break(ing) through existing patterns of perception, thought and behavior, shattering forms of ideas . . . to create new hitherto non-existent wholes;" transcendence as "go(ing) beyond boundaries of limitations, psychological as well as spiritual."

The author develops these ideas by highlighting the contributions of Freud and Cezanne in the watershed period of 100 years ago. Though Freud's publication of 32

his seminal "Interpretation of Dreams" in 1900 and Cezanne's death in Aix-en-Provence in 1906 caused scarcely a ripple, their works altered irrevocably our 20th century thinking. Their impact still reverberates as we encounter the coming millennium. Cezanne's unique interpretation of Impressionism, a re-visioning of the human condition, forever changed art; Freud's psychoanalytic concepts burst open a profound self-awareness in human experience. The creativity of these two giants ushered in the modern consciousness and the modern self.

In the art experience, for example, artists push the boundaries of current trends to achieve transformation to a new art. The author describes how Picasso, stirred by insights from Cezanne's works, incorporated artistic ideas from one culture, i.e., African masks, to achieve a new form in Western culture, his famous "Les Demoiselles D'Avignon." And so Cubism was born. A totally new form was created through transformation and transcendence.

In psychotherapy, the process goes beyond healing to offer possibilities for self-transformation. Individuals draw on their creative capacities to transcend familiar known selves by probing their psychological inner space. They move with growing consciousness toward a newly-created self.

An example of healing and transformation: a patient comes for treatment with frequent panic attacks, almost no sense of herself, a "boat with no sail or rudder, adrift at sea", as she describes. She functions emotionally as a child, looking to her husband and other "authority"

10. *"Freud & Cezanne: Psychotherapy as Modern Art." Book Review by E. Betty Levin published in* Pilgrimage: Reflections on the Human Journey.

figures to guide and direct her. In fact, all people who cross her path, from neighbors to the carpenter hired by her husband to do house-repairs, become authority figures in her mind. Her massive dependencies numb her awareness of her fundamental capacities as a survivor and latent creative abilities to take charge of her life. After I encourage her to take small initiatives, larger and stronger steps follow. Constructive risk-taking emboldens her further. Over time, the panic attacks "heal" and a more solid self-image emerges. With an expanded consciousness, she subsequently transforms herself into an enthusiastic professional possessing much competency. Concurrently, she develops a more satisfying relationship with her husband, more egalitarian, with mutual respect and closeness.

Art and psychotherapy both emphasize individuality and creativity. Jasnow illuminates these parallels: in previous centuries, artists served mainly monarchs, churches and other patrons but in the modern self, individuality is paramount. This is also true in the psychotherapy. Art and psychotherapy are both rooted in liberalist, humanistic ideology, holding faith in the individual's potential "to discover meaning and achieve trans-formation from within the self." Stunningly, in both the artistic endeavor and in psychotherapy, artist and patient become nothing less than the artists of their own lives.

The author asserts that transformation and transcendence are also driven by forces beyond the creative process, namely, by the individual's awareness of mortality. The knowledge that we shall all die serves as a dynamic force to achieve the transcendent experience. Jasnow credits both Otto Rank, who places transcendence at the confluence of religion, art and psychology, and Ernest Becker who states: "The idea of death, the fear of it, haunts the human animal like nothing else, it is the mainspring of human activity."[1]

This consciousness drives the individual to find meaning in this turbulent world. Jasnow declares: "We.. . achieve a sense of coherence and meaning in our lives or else die in despair."

The author contemplates the impact of the creative process on both the practice of psychotherapy and on humankind in the postmodern world. He cautions that the inexorably creative drive that heralds new ideas contains destructive qualities as well. Artists function at the leading edge of culture, disassembling the old and reassembling into the new. Unchecked creativity can bring destruction — witness how humans have transformed Mother Earth into an environment with ominous overtones. We have all observed how the creative genius of science, in the absence of moral integrity, has placed humanity under a black cloud of potential nuclear annihilation. Jasnow states: "Modernism assumes that humans can impose meaning on the world . . . postmodernism raises troubling questions regarding the very nature and existence of meaning in a universe indifferent to humanity."

He suggests that art and the creative process will continue on a dynamic path, though tempered by tradition and other forces, expressing itself in unexpected and implausible forms. The next century

33

may well be dominated by a new cosmology, reflecting a new cultural synthesis and a new vision of humanity.

Jasnow sees the universe in a perpetual state of transformation, unstable, with no hope of achieving a constant harmony. Individuals seeking coherence will need to develop an inner balance in the manner of "acrobats" or "jugglers." He challenges that humanity's task shall be to "establish human meaning that gives names to that which is unnamed and perhaps, unnameable." A perplexing question we might ask: with the coming of the new century with expanded consciousness, what are the possibilities for a new transformation that can transcend destructive forces?

A hopeful path is suggested by the writings of Robert Jay Lifton. He invokes the concept of the "protean self" based on the Greek god Proteus who was able to change shape in response to crisis. Lifton presents examples of individuals who embrace the protean self by holding firm to one's ethical core and commitments, all the while remaining resilient in the face of society's breathtaking historical change. He points to Vaclav Havel as the most dramatic exemplar of public proteanism — from an absurdist playwright to his country's leading dissident and political prisoner, to becoming the first postcommunist president of Czechoslovakia; then with the breakup of the country, its retired elder at age 56, and later, the first president of the new Czech Republic. Lifton sees the individual protean self becoming a "bridge between the modern and the postmodern, a source of continuity that (even) takes in radical discontinuity."[2]

34

Returning to his theme of the common cultural roots of psychotherapy and modern art, Jasnow creates a new synthesis, "psychotherapy art," as a future model of psychotherapy. He singles out leaderless group therapy as a modality for continued self-transformation and pays tribute to his peer group experience which contributes significantly to his own growth. This genre has extended to include lay people as well, in a proliferation of self-help and support programs.

This view of the future of psychotherapy seems to me to be a narrow perspective. I believe a true transformational model, hewing more closely to the process the author develops so diligently in his book, should be more far-reaching. Some models might include Third-Wave Psychology as expressed by Abraham Maslow in "The Farther Reaches of Human Nature" suggesting possibilities for a higher and more holistic consciousness: transpersonal psychology integrating mind/body/spirit; and other models synthesizing Western psychology with Eastern spiritual traditions.

Some see aspects of these models as part of "soul psychology" which connect with Freud's original concept of the psyche. According to Bruno Bettleheim, in the German culture knowledge divides into two important divisions: the natural sciences (Naturwissenschaften) and "science of the spirit" (Geisteswissenschaften). Freud regarded psyche as soul and placed it clearly in the science of the spirit. In a serious mistranslation of his work, this concept was categorized as a natural science and renamed "ego."[3]

This difference is profound, opposed in content and method. In psychotherapy reflecting Freud's concept of psyche/soul, individuals are regarded in their deepest nature, in the full range of being human. This concept allows for exploration of a person's capacity for imagination, passion and reverence as well as the darker chaotic side, with opportunity for neutralizing and sublimating destructive tendencies into constructive paths. On the other hand, the natural science construct represents a mechanistic, medical model seeking adjustment and "cure" This rational model of therapy has flourished in modern psychotherapy, a sharp departure from its original roots and meaning. It clearly has value but generally underplays understanding the deeper aspects of being human.

According to David Elkins, Carl Jung in *Modern Man in Search of a Soul* made spirituality the center of his therapeutic work, stating that of all his patients over the age of 35, not one was healed who did not develop a spiritual orientation to life. Whether theoreticians ascribe the identical meaning to expressions of "soul," "spirit," and "spirituality" is less important than the awareness that the larger and deeper meanings of being human go beyond what Western psychology usually addresses. In pursuing a strictly "spiritual" model of psychotherapy, however, some theoreticians caution of the danger of this approach with those individuals not solidly grounded with a healthy self-structure.

With the onslaught of managed care driven by the corporate profit motive, two sharply delineated modes of therapy may develop — one for clients requiring crisis work and the other, a transformative, holistic model for those individuals exploring growth, depth and transformation. As a practicing psychotherapist for over 20 years, I have integrated both models, helping people with their life crises, helping them build a solid ego structure and helping them explore the larger meanings of their lives.

The question arises: how will people pay for transformative therapy in an age of managed care? In my own practice, the motivation of both client and therapist are primary. My clients, in almost all cases these past years, have paid for their psychotherapy out-of-pocket. I have cooperated by keeping my fees at a moderate level. For the motivated clients eager to understand themselves and become the artists of their own lives, financial considerations are generally not allowed to deprive them of this seminal work.

This stimulating book reconnects with my personal ideas of almost 30 years ago when I delivered my maiden lecture on quality of life, "Art as a Way of Life." After immersing myself in Jasnow's ideas, I am newly energized by my potential for transformation in life and work. To approach the millennium in the elder years, rich with life experience, on the cusp of cronehood, offers possibilities to savor. In "cronehood," I refer to Barbara Walker's definition of a crone as a "woman of age, wisdom and power."[4]

The impact of this book's dynamic ideas is somewhat reduced by repetitive material and excessive wordiness. Tighter editing would have better served this important work. Nevertheless, thoughtful

35

and introspective individuals will discover sagacious ideas to consider in their own lives. Some will accept the challenge: to mobilize one's personal creative process for achieving transformation and meaning in the postmodern world.

Footnotes

[1]Becker, Ernest, *Denial of Death* (New York: Macmillan 1973.)
[2]Lifton, Robert J., *The Protein Self: Human Resilience in the Age of Fragmentation*,(New York: Harper Collins, 1993).
[3]Bettleheim, Bruno, *Freud and Man's Soul*, (New York: Alfred Knopf 1983).
[4]Walker, Barbara, *The Crone*, (New York: Harper & Row,1985).

Jasnow's book can be ordered direct from Ablex Publishing Co., (201) 767-8455 ($19.95ppd).

Our thanks to Betty Levin for this insightful review of this thought-provoking book. She hopes to say more in a future article about her experiences "on the cusp of cronehood." 117 Sagamore Rd., Millburn, NJ 07041. Let me suggest that along with this book one should take the opportunity to encounter the works of Cezanne first-hand—museums or good quality reproductions—a marvelous experience!

One stormy night when my nephew Roger was about twenty months old I wrapped him in a blanket and carried him down to the beach in the rainy darkness. Out there, just at the edge of where-we-couldn't-see, big waves were thundering in, dimly seen white shapes that boomed and shouted and threw great handfuls of froth at us. Together we laughed for pure joy—he a baby meeting for the first time the wild tumult of Oceanus, I with the salt of half a lifetime of sea love in me. But I think we felt the same spine-tingling response to the vast, roaring ocean and the wild night around us.

Rachel Carson

I never get lost because I don't know where I'm going.
Zen master Ikkya

The Ethical Culture
Society of Essex
County

516 Prospect Street,
Maplewood, New Jersey 07040
www.EssexEthical.org
973-763-1905

11. ECS brochure, distributed to newcomers to the society.

MORE THAN FLOWERS

Women to discuss Mother's Day origins

By PATTY EVERETT

Mother's Day isn't what it used to be.

Nowadays, it's a spot on the calendar that dutiful husbands and children mustn't forget—a day in which the individual and personal role a mother brings to her house and family is duly celebrated. It's a boon to purveyors of chocolate, perfume, baubles and flowers. But there were times when the holiday was a boon to the nation at large.

The true origins of Mother's Day—initiated by organizers who believed that motherhood was a political force to be mobilized on behalf of the entire community—will be celebrated at 11 a.m. Sunday by the Ethical Culture Society of Essex County.

The humanistic religious and educational fellowship, based in Maplewood, will return to the broader moral origins of the day when it presents a panel billed as "Morally-committed Moms."

The women—Patty Bender of Plainfield; Susan Teshu of Cambridge, Mass., a former president of Elizabeth; Alice Robinson-Gilman of Maplewood; Anita Roberts of East Orange, and Sue Willis of South Orange—are all mothers and members of the society.

"These five panelists . . . celebrating Mother's Day in its original form, true to it origins, will be speaking about their moral commitments and activities," said moderator Betty Levin of Millburn. "They have expanded the nurturance of motherhood to the larger world concerns."

ETHICAL CULTURE SOCIETY

From left, Anita Roberts, Alice Robinson-Gilman, Sue Willis, Betty Levin and Patty Bender talk about their involvement in the upcoming Mother's Day panel discussion

Photo by Samir J-Deen

moved by moral concerns that extended beyond the home, said Levin, membership chairwoman for the society and a past president.

"In about 1858, Anna Reeves Jarvis, a community activist, organized mothers' work days in West Virginia to improve sanitation facilities in Appalachia. Then she and her friends and compatriots went on to care for wounded soldiers on both sides in the Civil War," Levin said.

In short, they saw their roles as mothers extending beyond the home to the community at large.

> 'Politicians and businessmen opposed to 19th-century women's reforms proposed a more personal way of celebrating the holiday—individually celebrating mothers.'
>
> — **Betty Levin,**
> Millburn

Then, around 1872, Julia Ward Howe, author of "The Battle Hymn of the Republic," proposed a Mother's Day for Peace, Levin said. "I understand this was observed in most Northeastern cities for about 30 years.

"And then, politicians and businessmen opposed to 19th-century women's reforms, proposed a more personal way of celebrating the holiday—individually celebrating mothers," she continued.

In fact, around the same time, "Florists' Review," a publication for the florist trade, heralded the proposal as an idea that could be exploited for economic gain.

12. *ECS members discuss Mother's Day origins. Left to right: Anita Roberts-Gilman, Patty Bender, Sue Willis, Betty Levin.*

Syrian American Council

CURRENT CHAPTERS

We have 15 nationwide chapters and we are constantly growing, please contact us to find the chapter nearest to you or to start your own chapter.

Hackensack, NJ

Los Angeles, CA

San Diego, CA

Dallas, TX

Charleston, WV

Charlotte, NC

San Francisco, CA

Memphis, TN

Miami, FL

Washington DC

Houston, TX

Chicago, IL

Indianapolis, IN

Orlando, FL

Philadelphia, PA

Telephone 202-429-2409 • info@sac-usa.com • www.sac-usa.com
1875 I Eye Street NW Suite 500, Washington DC 20006

13. SAC, the NJ Chapter of Syrian-American Council
promoting understanding of the two communities.

JANET RUDOLPH

ONE GODS: The Mystic Pagan's Guide to the Bible is a shamanic exploration of the Bible's great journeys, struggles, quests, heroes, and heroines. Cross-cultural, spiritual forensics reveal ancient teachings, providing inspiration and concrete tools for readers to add a touch of magic to and deepen their own spiritual journeys.

516-569-4750

Jandelion@gmail.com

http://onegods.com/

14. *Handout for my daughter Janet's book*
One Gods: Mystic Pagan's Guide to the Bible

E. BETTY LEVIN

Babatunde Olatunji, Drummer, 76, Dies; Brought Power of African Music to U.S.

By JON PARELES

Babatunde Olatunji, the Nigerian drummer, bandleader and teacher who was a tireless ambassador for African music and culture in the United States, died on Sunday in Salinas, Calif. He was 76 and lived at the Esalen Institute in Big Sur, Calif.

The cause was complications of advanced diabetes, said his daughter Modupe Olantunji Anuku.

Mr. Olatunji's 1959 album, "Drums of Passion," was the first album of African drumming recorded in stereo in an American studio, and it introduced a generation to the power and intricacy of African music. While field recordings of African drumming had been available, "Drums of Passion" reached a mass public with its vivid sound and exotic song titles like "Primitive Fire."

Mr. Olatunji was born and reared in Ajido, a fishing and trading village pervaded by Yoruba culture, and he made it his lifework to bring village memories to audiences everywhere. His band of drummers, singers and dancers evoked both the village's music and its masquerades, with outsize figures dancing in elaborate raffia costumes. His credo was: "Rhythm is the soul of life. The whole universe revolves in rhythm. Everything and every human action revolves in rhythm."

In 1950 Mr. Olatunji received a scholarship to attend Morehouse College in Atlanta. He was planning to become a diplomat. He studied public administration at New York University, where he formed an African-style ensemble that eventually turned into his full-time occupation.

The group performed at concerts and at civil rights rallies led by the Rev. Dr. Martin Luther King Jr. After the group appeared with an orchestra at Radio City Music Hall, Mr. Olatunji was signed to Columbia Records. Mr. Olatunji secured foundation grants to tour schools. Among the students who were impressed by his performances — dressed in African robes and playing hand-hewn goat-hide drums — was Mickey Hart, who would go on to join the Grateful Dead and later recharge Mr. Olatun-

Babatunde Olatunji leading his group Drums of Passion in New York.

ji's career.

"Drums of Passion" made Mr. Olatunji the most visible African musician in the United States. Bob Dylan cited him alongside King and Willie Mays in "I Shall Be Free" in 1963.

"Drums of Passion" was hugely influential among musicians, helping to spark a wave of African-jazz fusions in the early 1960's. "Jin-Go-Lo-Ba," from "Drums of Passion," was remade as "Jingo" to become the first single by Santana in 1969. Mr. Olatunji mixed African music and jazz on his albums for Columbia in the 1960's. He was a featured performer at the African Pavilion of the 1964 New York World's Fair. With support from John Coltrane, he established the Olatunji Center for African Culture in Harlem, which offered music and dance lessons to children until 1988.

After his Columbia contract ended in 1965, Mr. Olatunji continued to perform, record and teach. Mr. Hart invited him to open for the Grateful Dead's New Year's Eve show in Oakland, Calif., in 1985, introducing his music to a new audience. Mr. Hart also persuaded his label, Rykodisc, to rerelease two independently recorded 1980's albums by Mr. Olatunji: "Drums of Passion: The

Beat" (1986), which included guest appearances by the guitarist Carlos Santana, and "Drums of Passion: The Invocation" (1988), featuring Yoruba chants. Mr. Olatunji recorded and toured during the 1990's as a member of Mr. Hart's worldbeat supergroup, Planet Drum, and made an instructional videotape, "African Drumming," released in 1996. He moved to Washington and then to Big Sur, where he became an artist in residence at Esalen.

Mr. Olatunji also continued to lead his own group, Drums of Passion, which included students and family members: his daughter Modupe and his seven grandchildren.

He is also survived by his wife, Amy Bush Olatunji, from whom he is separated; two sons, Omotola Olatunji, of Brooklyn, and Niyi Esubiyi, of Belle Meade, N.J.; another daughter, Folasade Olatunji Olusekun of Boston; and a brother, Dr. Akinsola Akiwowo, of Alexandria, Va.

Mr. Olatunji's most recent album, "Love Drum Talk" (Chesky) was released in 1997 and was nominated for a Grammy Award. Columbia reissued an expanded version of the original "Drums of Passion" last year, and Mr. Olatunji completed a new album earlier this year.

15. *Babatunde Olajundi had an international musician's spiritual influence on Betty; his obituary appeared in the* New YorkTimes *on April 9, 2003.*

Why Peace Sites?

By LOUIS KOUSIN

IN THE winter of my life, my main concern has been how to keep my feet warm. But shortly after retiring in mid-1980, I realized that there were larger issues than my feet.

This was made apparent by an increasing dread of a nuclear war. The awareness was sharpened by the birth of my first grandchild, a little bundle of joy named Leah (for my mother).

What assurance did Leah, along with millions of other children, have about growing up in a threatening world?

Sometimes, the mix of concern and anxiety can trigger a corrective response. The problem was: How can one deal with such an awesome problem in a creative, positive way?

It occurred to me that military sites dot the landscape, not only in our own country, but also in a considerable part of the world. It then occurred to me that a natural antonym for military sites could be peace sites.

Where and how could such sites be established?

The most obvious places are, of course, in existing institutions in every town, city and part of our country. In brief, where you pray, where you play, where you study, where you work and where you live.

These institutions are places where people gather in peaceful pursuits. So why not try to dedicate them as permanent peace sites, places where

Louis Kousin, peace-site coordinator for New Jersey SANE, lives in Cranford.

education for peace, programs and plans for peace, such as the nuclear-freeze campaigns, can be initiated, reinforced and expanded?

The kernel of the idea led me to the state headquarters of New Jersey SANE in Montclair for a conference with Dorothy Eldridge, the director of SANE here for more than 30 years. Her reaction led to a meeting with the organization's state committee and its unanimous approval in mid-1981.

Using New Jersey as a pilot test project, we undertook to seek a goal of 20 peace sites. These would be followed, if successful, by a plan for similar goals of 20 such sites in other states. In all, a national goal of 1,000 peace sites.

With the aid and cooperation of a very small staff, the process and then a philosophy of the peace-site conception began to emerge.

The original proposal and descriptive material were sent to prospective community institutions in New Jersey, and dedication of the first peace site took place with a brief ceremony in October 1981. By the end of the year, there will be at least 12 such sites in the state.

The process involved personal meetings with key leaders and social-action committees, board meetings and final approval by administrative bodies, a deliberate but productive procedure.

As of now, there are eight specific peace sites, including Ethical Culture Societies in Maplewood-South Orange and Teaneck, the Roman Catholic Church of Our Lady of Sorrows in Jersey City, a professional building in Livingston, a Unitarian Church in Wayne, a storefront peace center in

Highland Park, a synagogue in Union County and a Y.W.C.A. in Montclair.

At least four more sites, including a university and another Unitarian Church, are positive prospects by the end of the year.

An encouraging portion of this project has been the enlistment of support from national religious and community-center agencies. These include the Y.W.C.A., the Union of American Hebrew Congregations and the World Federalists.

Other groups cooperating include the Peace Office of the American Friends Service Committee, the Unitarian Universalists, the United Presbyterian Church, the United Church of Christ, the Roman Catholic Diocese of Newark, Archbishop Thomas Gumbleton of the Detroit Diocese and president of Pax-Christi U.S.A., the American Ethical Union and National SANE.

A national campaign will require the enlistment of peace emissaries in each state. To date, we have enlisted them in California, Pennsylvania and New Jersey.

To balance our efforts here, preliminary inquiries are being made in England, West and East Germany and the Netherlands. Proposals to be addressed to foundations for the support of a national peace-site staff are under way.

In essence, we are trying to apply in principle what the late Gen. Omar N. Bradley declared on his retirement:

"The central problem of our time is how to employ human intelligence for the salvation of mankind."

It begins to look like the peace-site idea is one whose time has come. And my feet are much warmer from marching.

16. *Lou Kousin's op-ed article originating the idea of Peace Sites, in the* New York Times, *1982.*

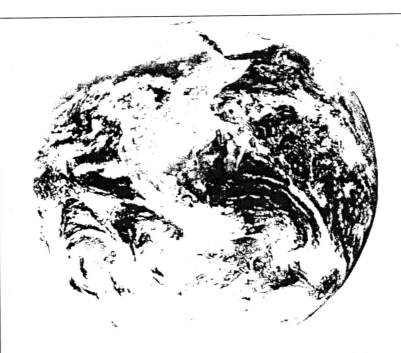

United Nations Day – October 24th, 2001

An Open Letter to the Entire Human Family

Dear Human Family :

This is our Home. Regardless of our many differences in Race, Religion, Color, Creed and Nationality, we are traveling together on this beautiful Spaceship Mother Earth as Passengers. The experts tell us :

1. We are traveling 18½ miles per second in our orbit around the sun.
2. The 189 passenger compartments (Nation / States) do whatever they wish as far as :
   a.) Waging war on their neighbors – they are currently spending over 1 trillion dollars per year on the Arms Race.
   b.) Some support terrorism and even encourage their schools to teach and promote hatred toward their neighbors.
   c.) Polluting the Ecosystem
   d.) Human Rights, Economic Justice, Child Labor, Population Stabilization and Other Human Values.
   e.) Non-Renewable Energy Sources
3. There is no effective "Bridge" or Control Center on our Spaceship. The United Nations should be given that responsibility. However,
   a.) The present charter does not permit them to play this role.
   b.) There is no World Law with Justice.
   c.) They are woefully under funded. For example, the U.S. contributed approximately $10 per person to the United Nations in the last budget. This is in contrast to the $1,000 approximately per capita to the U.S. military budget per year.

17. *"Letter to the Human Family," an innovative concept of the Earth as a space ship with no central control, authored by Lynn Elling, Founder of World Citizen in Minneapolis, Minnesota.*

BECOMING BETTY

4. There are many, many organized religions in our world. Considering just a few, this is the current picture: 32% - Christian, 21% - Islam, 14% - Hindu, 5% - Buddhism, 28% - other smaller religions or none at all
5. The current population is approximately 6.2 billion and growing at the net rate of 1.4% per year. 1 out of 5 go to bed undernourished each night.
6. Our current oil and gas reserves are projected to last, at present rates of consumption, 35 years.

I'm no expert, but as an 80 year old, here are a few of my "credentials" to address these questions and provide my personal views.
- Navy Officer WWII, and exposure to warfare at Tarawa and Guadalcanal
- With success in business, able to travel extensively including Hiroshima, Japan.
- Past President of MN branches of United Nations Assoc., and World Federalist Association.
- Chairman and Founder of World Citizen, Inc.
- Director of the International Peace Site Program
- Co-Chair of 5 Annual Nobel Peace Prize Festivals at Augsburg College.

September 11th, 2001 marked the beginning of a new chapter for the Human Family. I believe, and I am confident, that we can build that Peaceful, Healthy, Non-Violent World we dream about. These are my suggested steps :
1. Concerning the war on terrorism, build on the coalition to deeply involve the United Nations and the World Court. With Kofi Annan and the U.N. as winners of the current Nobel Peace Prize - this should help.
2. As a first step, have a U.N. plane above Afghanistan, 24 hours a day, broadcasting their message by radio in Pashtu and Dari – with local music. Ask for help !
3. Support programs like the International Peace Sites, with over 750 in the world – including their "Planet in Every Classroom" Program.
4. Support and promote the Annual Nobel Peace Prize Festival at Augsburg College. March 10, 2002 marks the 7th Nobel Festival involving some 700 to 1,000 students mainly from Peace Site Schools and/or Youth Groups. CNN plans to cover this event and make it available to some 25,000 schools around the world. This simply means that each of those schools could, in fact, participate in a way in the Festival and "Adopt a Laureate" like the other schools do.
5. Promote and support Peace / Non-Violent Education in every school and youth group throughout the world.

In reference to the "Planet in Every Classroom", these are the essential benefits: Everyday, the teacher and the students are reminded that we are all part of this one big wonderful human family, traveling together on Spaceship Mother Earth. It also reminds the teacher to weave in a Global / International / Peace component into every subject in every grade, K-12. We have many testimonials from teachers and students verifying that this simple symbol of our Home does truly promote Peace and Non-Violence at every level.

This is my personal plea to the Human Family and hope that you will feel free to respond in any way - pro or con. We really do need to work together if we are ever going to have that Peaceful, Healthy World we dream about.

IN PEACE!
Sincerely yours,

Lynn Elling

World Citizen, Inc.
2145 Ford Parkway, Suite 300, Saint Paul, MN 55116 U.S.A.
Phone: 651-695-2587 or 1-800-486-7664 Fax: 651-695-0254
e-mail: ellin017@tc.umn.edu / Home Page: http://www.peacesites.org

Celebrating 58 Years of Peace Making

New Jersey Peace Action

FALL PEACE GATHERING 2015

"Why I Went To Prison For a Nuclear-Free World"

Saturday, November 14, 2015
Bloomfield High School
Bloomfield, New Jersey

18. *New Jersey Peace Action Program,* Autumn 2015, *featuring Sister Megan Rice, "Why I Went to Prison for a Nuclear-Free World."*

Culture *of* Peace

Everything that is needed to build a culture of peace already exists in each one of us. As stated in the United Nations definition, a Culture of Peace is a set of values, attitudes, modes of behavior and ways of life that reject violence and prevent conflicts by tackling their root causes to solve problems through dialogue and negotiation among individuals, groups and nations.

19. *Culture of Peace, an activity at the United Nations with which the ECS is connected.*

CPSIA information can be obtained
at www.ICGtesting.com
Printed in the USA
FFOW02n2107010516
23702FF